The Historical Austen

The Historical Austen

William H. Galperin

PENN

University of Pennsylvania Press
Philadelphia

#50205732

RCV

10   9   8   7   6   5   4   3   2   1

Published by
University of Pennsylvania Press
Philadelphia, Pennsylvania 19104-4011

Library of Congress Cataloging-in-Publication Data
Galperin, William H.
   The historical Austen / William H. Galperin.
      p.   cm.
   Includes bibliographical references and index.
   ISBN 0-8122-3687-4 (acid-free paper)
   1. Austen, Jane, 1775–1817—Criticism and interpretation—History.   2. Literature and history—
Great Britain—History—19th century.   3. Women and literature—England—History—19th century.
4. Austen, Jane, 1775–1817—Knowledge—History.   I. Title.

PR4037 .G35 2002
823'.7—dc21

                                                                        2002074031

For my aunt, Rae Fixel,
reader par excellence

Contents

Introduction

The title of this book is both ironic and embarrassingly earnest. For while I am committed to reading Jane Austen in light of what might be termed her historicity, I pursue this reading as a corrective to "the historical Austen" that currently abounds in literary scholarship.[1] It is surely no accident that well in advance of the "new historicism," whose conclusions with respect to other writers are surprisingly consistent with our received sense of Austen as a writer indelibly marked by imperatives of class and context, the historical way with Austen has almost always been to stress the conservative, largely regulatory work of her fictions, over and against any other prospects they may entertain. As a corrective to interpretations of Austen that work better when we forget that she was a minister's daughter who wrote prayers, such historical readings— whether by Mary Poovey or by Marilyn Butler—carry considerable weight and force. However, in the very way that these readings remain anchored in certain hard facts from which Austen's writing is in many ways inseparable they are also limited to these facts and to the conclusions on which their modes of contextualization weigh.

There is no question that we must be mindful of the imperatives of gender that made Austen responsive to the claims and virtues of propriety. Nor can we overlook in any way the anti-Jacobin feeling, which became more and more of a consensus during the wars with France that were a counterpoint to Austen's remarkable, if somewhat misunderstood, insularity. At the same time, in making Austen's oeuvre a social or political text permeable to elements or influences from which it can no longer beg severance, historical readings invariably make Austen's writings answerable to a given context instead of appreciating the degree to which the novels are just as much a context *in themselves* where matters of history, ranging from the literary to the social to the very reality on which the narratives dilate, work to complicated, if often antithetical, ends.

The study that follows, then, is the result of an historicizing process that I have undertaken rather broadly.[2] In addition to literary history, from Austen's relationship to the contemporaneous romantic movement, to more immediate issues such as the rise of the novel and of women's writing generally, my investigations extend to several other areas, including social history, the history of aesthetics and, in what turns out to be a point of coalescence, reception history. These investigations tend to make more sense in conjunction rather than as discrete modes of inquiry. I find it useful, for example, to think about the rise of the novel in conjunction with social history, in particular the evolving *and devolving* status of gentrywomen in Austen's time, in the same way that the history of Austen's reception is best understood by recourse to aesthetic theory, in particular the aesthetic of the picturesque. This is equally the case with the question of romanticism, which turns out, somewhat surprisingly, to be inseparable from considerations of women's writing of the period, notably the fictions of Frances Burney.

The most important misrecognition regarding the historical Austen remains the tendency to regard her achievement as largely inevitable rather than informed by an understanding of what she was about as a novelist and, just as crucially, a chronicler of the everyday. Although Austen had at her disposal an array of manifestos urging writers to produce texts that would encourage readers to live within their means, chiefly by adherence to the probable as against the marvelous (or the merely possible), she is assumed by most critics to have entered the probabilistic camp with only the most fundamental or class-bound sense of its implications. Critics and cultural historians are hardly benighted in maintaining that Austen's decisions were responsive by and large to the imperatives of her class and gender. But where criticism continues to run into trouble—and I am speaking primarily of historically based criticism—is in the assumption that Austen's practice was necessarily coextensive with the purposes of social regulation. It may seem perfectly reasonable for a critic such as Raymond Williams to stress Austen's particular "way of seeing," where an "eye" that is generally "quick, accurate, and monetary" is apparently also blind to "money of other kinds, from the trading houses, from the colonial plantations," promoting a limited, and (for Williams's part) undemocratic, ideal of "social improvement."[3] But it is equally typical of this kind of recovery to assume that Austen's representational technique could only work in one register and to a single purpose. I say this because although Williams attempts to fold Austen's limited viewpoint into a still larger entity that he describes as a "lightly distanced management of event and description and character" (116), it is almost axiomatic that for Austen's earliest readers and contemporaries light management was tantamount to no management at all, particularly if we follow Williams in regarding management as a type of manipulation.

We need only look, in fact, to the most sustained work of literary criticism on Austen in her lifetime, Walter Scott's review of *Emma* in the *Quarterly Review*, to witness the unease that Scott—quite revealingly—feels with respect to

Austen's tendency to complicate her management of things with the things she should be managing.[4] Scott concurs with posterity in heralding the rise of realistic practice generally, and its function in "presenting to the reader, instead of the splendid scenes of an imaginary world, a correct and striking representation of that which is daily taking place around him" (63). But he is also troubled by Austen's divergence from this initiative. Noting approvingly that Austen's plots—the "narrative of all her novels" (64)—are invariably the same in tracking the progress of a heroine who "is turned wise by precept, example, and experience" (64), Scott is less enthusiastic about the abundance of "minute detail" in *Emma* from which "the faults of the author arise" (67–68). Nor is Scott unclear why the characters of Miss Bates and Mr. Woodhouse, whose representation in *Emma* (and whose "prosing" in particular) stand for minutiae generally, are so much a problem. Initially dismissing these characters as being as "tiresome" in literature as they are in life, Scott can barely conceal the anxiety they produce in militating against what Christopher Prendergast has recently termed the "order of mimesis."[5] These characters succeed in trying the overall "plan" of the novel, which seeks to "comprehend" them, not simply by inducing a tedium but by interrupting the strictly naturalizing work that "detail" should perform in such a text. "[T]he turn of this author's novels," submits Scott,

bears the same relation to that of the sentimental or romantic cast, that cornfields and cottages and meadows bear to the highly adorned grounds of a show mansion, or the rugged sublimities of a mountain landscape. It is neither so captivating as the one, nor so grand as the other, but it affords to those who frequent it a pleasure nearly allied with the experience of their own social habits; and what is of some importance, the youthful wanderer may return from his promenade to the ordinary business of life, without any chance of having his head turned by the recollection of the scene through which he has been wandering. (68)

I will have occasion in Chapter 2 to expatiate on this passage and on Scott's review in general.

In the meantime both the praise and blame in Scott's account work jointly to identify certain details in Austen's fiction as having a similar effect on her ideally complacent reader, as those larger elements that can apparently "turn" the reader from a validating and unproblematic representation of "his" social life and world. But there is a problem with this formulation. While it is easy to see how something extravagant might complicate the familiarizing work of a "class of fictions" that Scott, in anticipation of Ian Watt, describes as having "arisen almost in our own times" over "the former rules of the novel" (59), it is more difficult to conceive how minutiae that create only boredom can be as threatening or as deleterious as Scott contends. In one sense Scott is simply observing that the regulatory function of the novel will be compromised by any elements that fail to hold the reader's attention. Yet if this is the case, the wrenching or turning in which detail (in the analogy of the "promenade") is apparently instrumental, suggests that Scott's boredom in encountering a character like Miss Bates is anything but, and that detail of the kind he deems a liability in *Emma*, anything but prosaic. It is more that "minute detail" is troubling in Austen's writing because such details are consistent with "the ordinary business of life" without also being merely ordinary. Turning, or better still *returning*, what is familiar and probable in social life to a potential and demonstrable otherness, such details are a problem for Scott, and for the new "class of fictions" he supports, in their *inability* to uphold any firm distinction between the probable and the possible.

I will be exploring, of course, how possibility operates in Austen's fictions and how it worked specifically for many of her contemporaries. For the purposes of introduction I want only to observe that Austen's historicizable achievement can be reckoned, following Scott, as an amalgam of the naturalizing and regulatory function that Roland Barthes describes as a reality effect (*l'effet de réel*)[6] and a more oppositional marshaling of the everyday in what one early commentator described as an "irresistible *vraisemblance*" (*Atlas*, 30 Jan. 1833, 40). The notion of a representation capable of overcoming artificiality or contrivance would seem to accord with Williams's sense of the managed and manipulative nature of Austen's world. But what the notion points to, particularly in this formulation, is a circuit of response that has at some point measured Austen's achievement with a *"vraisemblance"* that *is resistible*. While hardly alien to the protocols of reading in our century, where the rise of metafiction and the return of fabulation have followed the critique of realism in sanctioning Barthes's description of the realistic text as "sickening" (Prendergast, 12), such resistance in Austen is far from an anachronistic discovery. Indeed the very notion of an irresistible *vraisemblance*, with its intimations of excess or uncontainability, reveals the degree to which a realistic text on the order of what Scott idealizes in his discussion of *Emma* was capable of provoking a similar—and similarly grounded—suspicion at its inception. Barthes is later sickened by "the mimetic text not because it troubles an order in which everything is in its proper place"—as it is in Scott's "promenade"—"but, on the contrary, because it *confirms* that order" (Prendergast, 12). And this is cognate to the *Atlas*'s appreciation of Austen's achievement, where we are invited to parse a resistible *vraisemblance*, such as Barthes might conceive, and a representation whose irresistibility resides in something other than a reality effect fashioned solely for the purposes of consensus. Far from bearing on the manipulative aspects of Austen's writing, the irresistibility of her representations is lodged (however paradoxically) in the *resistant* or uncanny character of a reality whose proclivity to difference and to otherness is no less a response to something close at hand and altogether familiar.

There are many reasons that Austen would be available to such a reading, ranging from the unsettled nature of realistic practice at the time that she was allegedly bringing the novel to some kind of stability, to the humorless tracts and directives that envisioned such stability as essential to the disciplining of Austen's readership.[7] Another, and quite fundamental, explanation involves the temporal gap, or *durée,* between the first three novels' conception and their moment of publication. In this interval of approximately fifteen years, during which *Sense and Sensibility, Pride and Prejudice,* and *Northanger Abbey* were all revisited and substantially revised, Austen achieved a perspective on her milieu, and on the way she had represented it, that was also indissoluble from the transience of certain initiatives and prospects, whose prestige would be linked increasingly to their anteriority.

Austen alludes to this aspect of her writings fairly directly in the prefatory advertisement to *Northanger Abbey,* where she notes the "considerable changes" in "places, manners, books, and opinions" in the years separating the novel's conception from what would in fact be its posthumous publication. Ostensibly an apology for the novel's satire, whose apparent object, the gothic novel, was no longer an enthusiasm or an especially timely target, the "changes" referred to in the advertisement bear equally on certain prospects to which other aspects of this novel are answerable. Chief among these possibilities, as we shall see, are the practices and proclivities by which the heroine, Catherine Morland, resists her disposability to a narrative where growth and capitulation are synonymous. Such "changes" are also an issue in both *Sense and Sensibility* and *Pride and Prejudice,* whose transformations in form hearken in two directions simultaneously: toward the rise of the novel as a regulatory instrument, where free indirect discourse plays a central role; and toward a past and a milieu, in which the relative indeterminacy of form, or in this case epistolary form, works in consort with certain social practices in fashioning an horizon of possibility whose disappointment or mutability is no less an instrument of authentication and hope.

The slippage between a reality thickened by retrospection and a formal achievement that, however innovative, was in many ways a form of forgetting, characterizes the peculiar difficulty of Austen's first three novels. However, it has equal bearing on the last three novels as well, which were written in rapid succession following the publication of *Sense and Sensibility* in 1811 and *Pride and Prejudice* in 1813. *Mansfield Park, Emma,* and *Persuasion* all lack the specifically temporalized dimension where developments in form are complicated by a pervasive anteriority, which is hewed to and marshaled with sustained appreciation. Yet the latter novels are equally affected by certain prospects, whose "authentically temporal destiny" (to borrow Paul de Man's phrase)[8] was suffi-ciently clear to Austen to make the past—and the particular milieu in which change and suffrage had only recently seemed imminent—an object of increas-ingly nostalgic appreciation.

Such nostalgia hearkens in a direction quite different from the conser-vatism normally associated with Austen or with her contemporary Walter Scott. For its possibilistic dimension, however displaced or in arrears, bears a vexed and vexing relationship to the regime of the probable, whose instruments in turn were directed on behalf of what William Godwin grimly termed "things as they are." Not the least of these instruments was the new style of the novel itself, whose regulatory bent, as Scott recognized and approved, involved a number of formal innovations that, if nicely served by Austen's achievement, were at crosspurposes nonetheless with the particular perspective or retrospection in which composition and revision were simultaneously instrumental. Thus while it is customary to regard Austen's accomplishment in largely formal terms, with attention generally to her deployment of free indirect discourse, the last three novels are also readable to an effect that complicates that technique, particularly as a regulatory instrument. In fact it is not too much to say that, following the reading practices that the later novels encourage invariably at the expense of an incompetent or perplexed narrator, Austen's historical role as realism's most im-portant progenitor has been grossly exaggerated. If free indirect discourse re-mained an achievement in which Austen presumably took pride and pleasure, it was also, in its necessary filiation with a probabilistic agenda, a perpetual prob-lem that would not abate at least until, as Anne Elliot puts it, "existence or . . . hope [was] gone."

Contrary to Scott's opinions, then, Austen's novels were significant in the minds of many of her contemporaries not because they produced better or more entertaining instruction but because they were at odds with the represen-tational desiderata of Austen's particular time and station. Even as readers were able to read the novels in the manner of Scott, many found themselves at liberty to do otherwise, which invariably involved reading for detail rather than for the "narrative of her novels." This practice of reading is perfectly coextensive with the social vision in the fictions themselves, where a structure of dominance, however flexible or open, is no more than a bounding line for practices that, for want of a better term, are unaccountable—though by no means ideologically neutral. On the contrary the particular version of bourgeois hegemony that criticism, and historically based criticism especially, has been responsive to in Austen's texts was as much a force in Austen's work as it remains a backdrop for other representational practices and ways of reading them to which her novels are concurrently available and for which the practices of at least some of her characters, including Frank Churchill, Jane Bennet, and even the reviled Crawfords, are a correlative.

My basis in advancing these claims, as I have suggested, remains historical. But it is historical in a way that takes seriously Michel de Certeau's claim that "over time, and in the density of its own time, each *episteme* is made up of the heterogeneous" (*Heterologies*, 173). Thus the historical Austen is recoverable, but through a composite of histories, from the social to the aesthetic to the conceptual to the geopolitical. In addition to being specific to the two decades over which Austen's perspective on her milieu was forged, the equally important point about these histories is that their very heterogeneity is the answerable method to a representational initiative from which the difference or "density" accruable to a world "over time" was largely inseparable. I begin with a history that is social, focusing on the waning status of women in the relatively privileged class into which Austen was born, and its bearing in turn on a novelistic or again realistic practice where such facts are permitted to speak for themselves. I proceed from there to histories that are more strictly literary or conceptual, where Austen's practice as a writer is weighed not only in conjunction with the achievement of her (mostly) male contemporaries to whom the tag "romantic" has been assigned but in conjunction as well with her female contemporaries, notably Frances Burney, whose demonstrable conservatism jibes uncomfortably with the canonical break that women's writing ideally represents for Austen. Supporting this recovery of Austen as oppositional, which involves a reconception of romanticism (and of much period writing in general) as possibilistic rather than revolutionary, are additional histories that are, broadly speaking, cultural. I explore, for example, the aesthetic discourses that Austen had at her disposal, which she managed alternately to satisfy and to contest, and the response of her contemporaries to her writing, on whose experience or practice of reading Austen any claim for the yield of her work must ultimately rest.

Chapter 1 traces the connection between Austen's concern over the status of women and the peculiar silence or metairony, by which she managed to unmoor the representation of women from certain vehicles of ideology, notably plot. Focusing on the case of Austen's married yet childless aunt, who was arrested and later tried for allegedly stealing a card of lace that she could have easily afforded, I note the parallels between the elliptical silence surrounding this particular event in Austen's letters and the equally indeterminate, if readable, silence in her narratives, which is typically viewed as a management strategy. Eschewing the narrative forms, both progressive and conservative, by which the press accounts of Jane Leigh Perrot's trial, not to mention Perrot's own self-exculpatory narrative, were shaped, Austen's silence accords with the silence or unstable irony of her fiction (as I construe it) in attending to the largely restitutive aspects of her aunt's kleptomania, all of which point to "something" that had been taken from her.

With its antecedents in the indeterminacy of the epistolary novel and that genre's lack (as Ian Watt notes) of a metalanguage capable of exerting full control over either speech or written correspondence,[9] Austen's silence is more than a residual element in narratives that, for all intents and purposes, spell an end to epistolary form. Indeed the silence that takes precedence over narrative authority in Austen serves a purpose analogous to that lavished on her aunt in protecting both her representations and their readers from the various ideologies, notably domestic ideology, to which narrative and plot were routinely assimilable. Here and elsewhere in Austen, silence becomes a way of directing attention to the density or heterogeneity of the real, which in the example of Perrot's theft produced a situation where the imperatives of class and gender were sufficiently contradictory to warrant not just that Perrot stole the lace (which she adamantly denied) but that she stole it under a motivation that can be traced in complex yet revealing ways to both her powerlessness and childlessness. In contrast to recent modes of historical criticism, where such an anecdote is marshaled by way of narrowing or stabilizing a given text or oeuvre, "The Trial of Jane Leigh Perrot" serves an altogether different purpose here. More than just a different account of domesticity, the anecdote proceeds, with Jane Austen's silent treatment, to a different sense of both history and the history of the novel, where, as an historian of the present, Austen may be credited with having retrieved the real from the closure of realism so-called.

Chapter 2 is devoted in part to the aesthetic discourses available to Austen at the moment that she was developing as a writer, from which she derived a remarkably firm sense of the uses and the abuses of a representational practice that we, again, call realistic. Central among these discourses were theories of the picturesque, whose advocates urged the use of certain naturalizing techniques to mask the extent of a person's landholdings, making them continuous with general nature. Richard Payne Knight, for example, notes the parallels between this order of naturalization and the order of mimesis in narratives of probability, which are ideally wedded to a principle of normativity based similarly on a partial version of life. That Austen was entirely familiar with these theories, as she was with similar theories of the novel, is well documented. But what has been generally ignored is the degree of her unease regarding them, which she registers in many places, including such memorable, if cryptic, episodes as Harriet Smith's encounter with the gypsies in *Emma*. This unease was especially evident to Austen's immediate readers, many of whom were struck by the novels' heightened attention to detail in contrast to their probabilistic and naturalizing tendencies. It is these readers, professional and lay, on whom the second chapter focuses. It matters a great deal that a conservative writer such as Maria Edgeworth found *Emma* unreadable in having "no story in it except that . . . *smooth, thin water-gruel* is according to Emma's father's opinion a very good thing & it is very difficult to make a cook understand what you mean by smooth thin water gruel."[10]

Finally, in the third chapter devoted strictly to historicization, I turn to another problem in literary history for which there has yet to appear a satisfying account. I am referring once again to Austen's relationship to British romantic writing. Although it has been customary to conclude, with Jerome McGann, that Austen's novels simply prove that not every notable literary production in the romantic period need be romantic,[11] Austen was arguably the first to disagree. Her appeal—or her narrator's appeal in *Northanger Abbey*—for a new or different canon wages virtually the same argument on behalf of women's writing that Wordsworth and Coleridge made in announcing *their* break and that of their moment from what Charles Lamb disparagingly termed the "past century." In doing this Austen is not necessarily reifying an ideology of the new. Her purpose, on the contrary, is to remove her achievement, as well as an achievement that might be called romantic, from the kind of legitimacy or monumentality that an appeal of this kind invariably promotes. In addition to the obvious contradiction in the narrator's polemic, which repudiates all previous claims to modernity or difference, the appeal in *Northanger Abbey* opens onto an even more specific aporia in literary criticism and historiography. For the countercanon that Austen's narrator proposes in place of Pope, Prior, and the *Spectator*, a canon represented chiefly by the works of Frances Burney, is a good deal more proximate to the tradition to be supplanted than the writings of other contemporaries, men and women, which are mentioned not at all. Part of the problem involves the actual narrator of *Northanger Abbey*, who more than any other narrator in Austen recalls the authoritative and intrusive narrator in Fielding and whose claims, although nominally feminist, are a reminder of the invariable complementarity of a certain order of women's culture—specifically domesticity—to a more conventional order of authority. But the real issue, or again the problem, turns out to be the regime of probability to which domestic fiction is clearly susceptible and to which the possibilistic horizons in both *Northanger Abbey* and romanticism are opposed.

Although Austen's writings are never more than sparing in considering, much less in appreciating, a contemporaneous literary counterculture, she marshals her narrator's antipathy to these movements, especially the gothic, to surprisingly antithetical ends. Thus even as critics have been right in identifying the narrator's digression in *Northanger Abbey* as a foundational moment in feminist literary criticism, they allow the anachronistic appeal of this claim to becloud the fact that the "new" as such, particularly as described in the manifesto, was better and more immediately served by writers *other* than Burney, and by a solidarity apart from one entirely gender based. Focusing on two novels by Burney, her early and influential *Evelina* (whose preface urges an adherence to "sober Probability") and her last novel, *The Wanderer* (whose title alludes to a fairly standard romantic topos), I show that Burney exposes—only to foreclose on—the kinds of possibilities to which Austen's writing is consistently open.

The remaining five chapters are taken up directly with Austen's novels, and with the extraordinarily high degree of awareness, regarding both their "real" and the modes of representing it, that their revision "over time" provided. While plainly mindful of the significance and importance of free indirect discourse in the developing genre of the novel, Austen recognized by the time of her first novels' publication that this mode was also an especially sinister instrument of coercion. I begin with Austen's first two published novels, *Sense and Sensibility* and *Pride and Prejudice*, which were heavily revised for over a decade and, in the case of at least one (and perhaps both), underwent a transformation analogous to the genre of the novel itself in their respective metamorphoses from epistolary form. Without disputing the formal and stylistic advance that the movement to free indirect discourse constituted in this instance, I show—with an assist from *Lady Susan*, the only mature epistolary narrative of Austen's currently extant—that for Austen, unlike Scott, the rise of the novel was not without its costs. Most important among these was the "new" novel's complicity with certain social formations to which the actions of more marginal characters, for example, Jane Bennet, are opposed. While Austen may have succeeded in becoming for a time the subtly coercive writer that literary historians and critics regularly construe, the epistolary legacy suggests that this was not always the case. Beginning with the earliest published novels, the achievement of authority we associate with Austen's realism was an ongoing problem that her continued, and continually vexed, practice of free indirect discourse has also obscured.

The discussion of *Northanger Abbey* that follows in Chapter 5 begins by redressing certain misconceptions about this novel, often regarded as the most rudimentary of Austen's works because it was the first actually sold for publication. Unappreciated in most considerations of this text that hold it (and to a lesser extent *Sense and Sensibility*) as fledgling exercises in deference to *Pride and Prejudice*, is the possibility that *Northanger Abbey* may well have been the first novel that Austen also deemed salable or in appropriate form. We know that an early version of *Pride and Prejudice* was offered to a publisher in 1797 by

Austen's father, only to be rejected. Nevertheless the extent and degree of the subsequent revisions to that text, as I speculate in Chapter 4, indicate that Austen may have ultimately concurred with the publisher's decision and that Reverend Austen's earlier intercession (in which he pointedly likened his daughter's effort to Burney's epistolary *Evelina*) was an initiative with which the author had merely gone along. At all events *Northanger Abbey*'s most striking innovation— its biased and opinionated narrator—marks an important departure from the manipulative operations of the first two published novels in making reading and reading for plot two different practices. Where reading for plot involves an alignment with the narrator in his/her endorsement of patriarchy and its attendant ideology of domesticity, reading per se—over and against the narrator's counterexample—consists with a level of attention where the imperatives of plot are exposed and diminished.

A similar treatment of narrative authority, with more historical resonance, occurs in *Mansfield Park*, where the alignment of the narrator and the heroine, Fanny Price, as readers have long recognized, remains something of a liability. This deficiency, I argue, is very much to Austen's purpose in projecting certain social and political developments, and the role of domestic fiction in serving them, from which there is increasingly no turning back. To the degree that Fanny Price remains a rather odious icon of domesticity, it is in light of specific changes, from the rise of the professional classes to England's impending constitution as both an imperial power and a military nation, in which both women and their fiction were being conscripted. Attending to the tracts and books that Austen was reading in the interval that she was composing *Mansfield Park*, from accounts of the Napoleonic Wars to conduct manuals on the duties of women, I argue that the transformations in English culture and society that these readings variously portend find issue in a novel that is more properly an exercise in the *future* of fictional representation rather than a work whose apparent filiations speak unambiguously to Austen's conservatism. If Austen's narrator is incompetent or biased in a manner that recalls the narrator of *Northanger Abbey*, this bias does more than expose the uses and abuses of free indirect discourse. For in the narrator's unequivocal sympathy with a heroine, who is notably antipathetic to nearly everything else in the world of this novel, the real, or what *has been* the real in Austen's works thus far, is discredited in consequence of being moribund rather than as a negative way from which readers might be dissuaded. The result, in other words, of what I term "Jane Austen's future shock," the treatment of character in *Mansfield Park*, including the character of the narrator, is a reflexive apparatus, whose efficacy consists in an oppositional, and largely *nostalgic*, refusal to speak its name.

These elements, not surprisingly, are also evident in *Emma*, the novel that virtually all readers regard as Austen's masterpiece. In contrast to the previous novel, where both narrative authority and incompetence are used to demonstrate what, in Austen's projection, is largely a fait accompli, *Emma* marshals these elements in anatomizing not just the "decline of the novel" but the related (if still privileged) anteriority of a culture and a milieu in which change or otherness had previously been close at hand. Here, as in *Mansfield Park*, there is little question regarding the value system to which the narrator subscribes, in the same way that there are continued questions regarding the narrator's competence, specifically her knowledge and understanding. The difference is that where narrative incompetence works previously to define the novel as a usable institution for an England that is becoming dystopic, the narrator's failure in *Emma* to know all that is going on in the interval during which the narrative takes place, hearkens in a more utopian direction.

Not only does the narrator's ignorance of the ongoing courtship of Frank Churchill and Jane Fairfax owe a great deal to the epistolary legacy of the novel in general, specifically the technique of writing to the moment on which only a minimum of retrospection and understanding may be exerted. Such ignorance remains, in conjunction with this legacy, a provocation to reread *Emma*. Beyond simply ferreting details to which the narrator has been inattentive, this mode of (re)reading has the broader and uncontainable effect of rendering everything that has been disclosed in an initial reading of *Emma* seeable as if for the first time. Where an initial reading of *Emma* may likely be a reading for plot, and aligned thereby with the pedagogical trajectory that tracks and celebrates Emma's development under Knightley's tutelage, a rereading of *Emma*, in which the reader will resemble Miss Bates in actually "see[ing] what is before" her, is likely to recall readers to all that has been lost in a development where the prerogative of trying to make a difference must be relinquished. Effectively contrasting two kinds of resistance—the more overt or strategic kind represented by Emma's early efforts at matchmaking, from which her eventual complicity with the social order is already inferable, and a more tactical or covert resistance, which directs us to possibilities that are always close at hand—*Emma* charts a development, at once local and historical, where substantive change is increasingly unreadable and out of bounds. Dependent instead on a way of reading where oppositionality and some prospect are perforce linked, the possibilistic arc of the Frank-Jane narrative not only eludes the particular control that the narrator, in imitation of Knightley, contrives unsuccessfully to exert. It also fails in its *indeterminacy* to provide any basis for change apart from the reading practices it encourages, whose resistance is alternately empowered and impoverished by a nostalgia in search of an object.

The final chapter takes up *Persuasion* and the unfinished *Sanditon*, focusing primarily on the retrenchment of Austen's last completed narrative, where the sympathetic treatment of the increasingly benighted heroine provides a temporary reprieve from the problems posed by realistic practice generally. Concentrating on the body and the modes of resistance it performs in allowing the initially defaced Anne Elliot to exit the heteronormative economy and the social order aligned with it, Anne's eventual interpellation, where her beauty and desirability are restored under the triangulated gaze of two men, merely proves the proximity rather than the equivalency of biological and social imperatives. That Anne is reintegrated into a structure of romance and into the middle-class or domestic ideology with which romance is explicitly connected certainly underscores the potency of a new social hegemony, where prowess and achievement are increasingly valued over mere entitlement. But *Persuasion* makes it clear that merely to account for the power and prestige of an emergent professional class—which transpired under the weight of developments and disappointments both public and private—is a far cry from endorsing it and its divisions of both labor and gender.

This position is seconded in *Sanditon*, where the seemingly dystopic community of mostly hypochondriacal individuals is transformed willy-nilly into a utopia of sorts. No longer participating in the susceptibility that reigns supreme in the world of *Persuasion*, the body in *Sanditon* is again a site of resistance: a locus of such intense preoccupation that it literally provides cover from ideology of all kinds. Austen did not live to complete her final—and most politically challenging—work. Nevertheless her development to this remarkably irrealistic end has important implications. Not only does *Sanditon* resuscitate the possibilistic horizons on which Austen's project has been fixated with varying degrees of hope. It reminds us by utter hyperbole that the development of the novel in its seemingly imperturbable progress to realism represents a foreshortening of both literary history and the literary *in* history.

PART I

Historicizing Austen

History, Silence, and
"The Trial of Jane Leigh Perrot"

To speak of an entity called "the historical Austen" is to enter a field of speculation whose unsettled disposition is a consequence, paradoxically, of all that *is* known about Jane Austen and her family, and about the milieu in which the novelist lived and of which she wrote. We know that Jane Austen was the youngest daughter (and next-to-last child) in a large and literary gentry family whose politics were fairly consistent with the ideology of their class and its church. We know too that the Austens' Tory position was further consolidated by the wars with France, waged for the virtual duration of Jane's career as a writer, in which two Austen brothers were active participants.[1]

In recent decades more complex modes of recovery involving issues of class, gender, nationhood, empire—and their multiple intersections—have created a more complicated Austen whose many valences appear to resist any final coordination. Distributing Austen across an ideological spectrum bounded by a fierce anti-Jacobinism (pursuant to class and family interests) and a more progressive, if not always transparent, feminism, historical interpretations range from those that regard Austen's writing as a conservative, largely disciplinary apparatus to more nuanced approaches that steer a middle course between ideological extremities that, in any case, remain a bounding line.[2] Among these last are readings that look more broadly and dialectically at the conservative *topoi* of Austen's fiction and the more radical or disquieting implications that can be drawn from her writings, as well as readings that regard Austen's class, with its investment in patriarchal ideology, as a legitimate bar to anything beyond a moderate or conservative feminism. Deborah Kaplan's recent study of Austen's involvement in the woman's culture of her time typifies this latter type of inquiry in emphasizing the cultural duality inherent in Austen's work.[3] Not merely a divided loyalty to class and gender respectively, this duality was endemic to domestic ideology itself, which imagined and promoted women's culture as a smaller, restricted circle circumscribed by class and patriarchy. Thus the space made available to women like Austen was, as Kaplan describes it, ceded by a hegemony that ultimately thrived in permitting women such as Jane Austen a room of their own.

It must be emphasized that the historical Austen is, in nearly all of the above instances, a figure whose writings speak both to and within a moment whose recoverability remains a guide to what Austen meant when she wrote and not what she may have unknowingly accomplished. When Sandra Gilbert and Susan Gubar argue that Austen's writings dramatize the plight of the educated woman in the early nineteenth century whose options were severely restricted, they presume a consciously, if precariously, held feminism on the writer's part. The same is true of Claudia Johnson, whose investigation of Austen in the company of other women writers, many of them Burkean and conservative, uncovers a subversive current in Austen's fiction that is apparently less a matter of modern-day wish fulfillment than a recoverable agency in women's writing.[4]

Other historical commentaries are less convinced of any direct correspondence between Austen's words and her deeds. Approaches inspired variously by the disciplinary focus of Michel Foucault draw a sharp distinction between the ideological work of Austen's texts and her more politically conscious aims. For Nancy Armstrong, the most Foucauldian of Austen's historically minded readers, it was the novelist's achievement, however intentional, to have formulated a standard of polite writing and, with it, a new linguistic community composed of the "newly empowered groups who read novels."[5] This gesture, in which "the novel supplants the conduct book as that writing which declares an alternative . . . standard" (158), allowed an "elite minority of country gentlefolk quite removed from the centers of power" to figure a new hegemony "that was neither gentry nor nobility as the eighteenth century knew them, yet one that was clearly a leisure class and thus a paradoxical configuration that can only be called a middle-class aristocracy" (158–60). Armstrong insists that Austen "understood as well as anyone could the power of fiction to constitute things, truth and reality" (159). Still, the double movement of this assertion, which emphasizes the regulatory work by and for an order not always fathomable to the writer, necessarily subordinates historical agency—what Austen willfully accomplished in her time—to the agency of historical hindsight.[6]

Something similar obtains for Gary Kelly, who argues that Austen " 'predicted' the identity and the literary culture of the gentrified professional classes who came to dominate society and culture in Britain and elsewhere during the nineteenth century."[7] Like Armstrong, Kelly distinguishes Austen's proleptic function from her more immediate (and less determinate) work as an historical agent. And like Armstrong, he allows the agency of historiography, of what happened in retrospect, a much greater role in assessing Austen's achievement:

More important, however, [Austen] conceals or rather transforms the basis of her art in the rhetorical structure—the formal elements and their ordering and relationship—of the "trash of circulating libraries." In doing so, she concealed the partial, relative character of her own fiction if not from her contemporaries then from successive generations of readers who saw themselves in her version of the novel as moral art and therefore concluded that her novels were and are normal, natural, and normative—in a word, classic literature. (19–20)

In alluding to the "partial, relative character" of Austen's novels, and their tendency to naturalize an arbitrary, ideologically directed version of the real, Kelly is speaking of realistic practice of which Austen's writing is routinely deemed the first, fully realized, instance of codification. Kelly hedges a bit in implying that the naturalizing work of Austen's fictional method may not have fooled her contemporaries and presumably the author herself. But he is characteristically adamant in claiming that Austen's realistic imagination, beyond any explicit intention on her part, was influential in a way that only time would confirm.

Realism and Omniscience

This is hardly the occasion to enter into a full discussion of realism, especially regarding Austen's role as a prototype for the likes of Eliot, Dickens, and others. Nevertheless if we are to speak in any credible way about the historical Austen, we must weigh Austen's contribution to realism against the fact that such practice was by no means stable at the moment that Austen is believed to have ushered it into full being. Nor, for that matter, was realism a practice that Austen could have initiated or participated in at this stage in total ignorance of its potential problems.[8]

There is evidence that Austen knew very well the naturalizing and partializing tendencies of a *kind* of art, or an aesthetic, that claimed a fidelity to the real and to "nature." The picturesque, which figures prominently, and largely satirically, throughout her fiction, was more than simply an aesthetic fad to which, as a comedienne of manners, Austen would have attended. It was an aesthetic where the "natural" was restricted to a number of representational possibilities, none of which was comprehensive or faithful necessarily to what was "out there." To theorists of the picturesque, as I detail in the next chapter, it was fine, indeed imperative, to conceive the natural as rough, ungoverned, and variegated so long as the scene was not also ugly or dull or fraught with any untoward surprises. In addition the particular animus of picturesque theory to the landscape improvements of such English "gardeners" as Lancelot "Capability"

Brown and Humphry Repton (a debate that figures prominently in *Mansfield Park*) was unabashedly ideological in equating a certain kind of landscape gardening—one that was especially self-conscious in exposing the imprint of the human upon nature[9]—with the leveling initiatives in France and at home. In a remarkable reconfiguration of political affiliations and identities, proponents of the picturesque were disposed to league wealthy individuals, who frequently initiated such improvements, with the "revolutionary" masses in an effort to reclaim a middle (and higher moral) ground for the social order, at once conservative and middle class, in whose interests they were writing.[10]

Setting aside for the moment the question of what Austen may have finally accomplished as a fiction writer, one thing is clear: she had at her disposal an aesthetic that, in addition to exposing the partializing tendencies of an art that carried on in the name of nature or totality, was unambiguous in serving specific class and political initiatives concurrently mystified through a discourse of naturalization. Hence if Austen were either the Tory apologist, or even the more Whiggish proponent of a middle-class aristocracy, that the newer historicisms claim with special reference to her practice as a realist, it was likely that she could have been these only with a much greater understanding of what she was doing than most readings generally acknowledge.

Allowing this much is not to say that Austen knew everything about the ideological work of her writings. It is merely to remember, in conjunction with what Austen *did know*, that realism is one of the last things that can be understood adequately through her particular practice as a writer. Far from a standardized mode of narration, realism—or for our purposes classic realism—was very palpably a narrative practice in what Jean-François Lyotard, discussing the premonitions of postmodernism at about this same juncture, has called "the nascent state." And like Kantian aesthetics, which, in Lyotard's seemingly ahistorical contention, more correctly anticipate postmodernism than the aesthetics of high modernism, realism in Austen is marked similarly by a recalcitrance even as it was instrumental in the solidification of an artistic practice that may have become more politically unconscious.[11]

Such claims for Austen's perspicuity depend equally on the wisdom of hindsight. Yet there is a real difference between this *kind* of history, which attaches Austen to a moment whose peculiar overdetermination in social as well as literary history provided greater scope, particularly for women, and the history that contains or otherwise limits Austen in terms of the genre of "classic literature" she helped formulate and of what transpired in British culture and society in her aftermath. And since the "rise of the novel" as we ordinarily construe it is by and large a retrospection from the culminating example of Austen in the early nineteenth century, the implications of Austen's historicity as a writer—as distinct now from the literary history she was in-strumental in helping others write—are considerable.[12] Although there were other writers, notably Frances Burney, on whose works Austen undoubtedly modeled her third-person narratives, the realistic practice that she is widely be-lieved to have perfected, with its particular deployment of free indirect style, is less an advancement upon an earlier type of omniscient narration—specifically Fielding's—than a practice that consists equally with aspects of the epistolary mode in which as many as a third of Austen's major fictions may have been con-ceived. We need only look to *Lady Susan,* the one mature epistolary narrative of Austen's still remaining, to witness this particular and paradoxical development. In ending as it does—with an abrupt and disingenuous turn to Fieldingesque omniscience and moral authority—Austen's novella explicitly rejects this latter (and earlier) mode of narration as a damping down of the largely indetermi-nate text that precedes it. Chapter 4 examines *Lady Susan* in greater detail. But the point to be stressed is that regardless of whether Lady Susan may be deemed a good character, or whether Austen can be said to have endorsed that charac-ter's subversions and manipulations, the task of moralizing about her devolves upon a narrator whose belated appearance is also a declension from the plea-sure and instability of the preceding text.[13]

To argue, then, as Ian Watt has, that the great improvement of the omni-scient style for Austen (and for others) was that it filled the indeterminate silence that had previously existed between individual points of view in the redaction and dissemination of letters by fictive hands is to simplify matters. For, among other things, there remains a real question whether Austen aban-doned or could have abandoned that silence, and the indeterminacy that at-tends it, in transforming either *Sense and Sensibility* or *Pride and Prejudice* into third-person narratives. It is arguable, and demonstrable, that in apparently giv-ing voice to the "unwritten" text that had previously been pressed in the service of verisimilitude, Austen was doing more (and doing less) than simply render-ing that text in language.[14]

There is no doubt that by the time of her novels' publication Austen was very much committed to deploying a written "metalanguage" in conjunc-tion with the "object language" that was increasingly spoken now as opposed to written in letters. Nor is there any doubt that her deployment of this meta-language worked primarily to explain what Colin MacCabe, in discussing real-ism generally, describes as "the relation of object language to the real."[15] But again it is not clear that free indirect discourse is strictly a development upon epistolary silence or that the "metalanguage" of omniscience does not come from a different place altogether. Even as free indirect discourse would appear, in Austen's hands, to transcend all voices in the service of what MacCabe calls "perfect representation" (35), such discourse bears more in common with the dominant voice or point of view in an epistolary novel like Burney's *Evelina* than it does with any silence on which Burney was, by the imperatives of form, dependent. Rather than an advancement upon the silent or "unwritten" language (36) of epistolarity, the "wise and shrewd narrative voice" (Levine, 63) that we associate with Austen was a concurrent and an independent development in which the anterior silence of epistolarity, in being neither antecedent to the language that had replaced it nor necessary *now* for the purpose of verisimilitude, was liberated to an altogether different function.[16] Coming from a narrator, who is also a character in her own right, even as is she incapable, in strictly linguistic terms, of speaking *as* a character, the "voice" of Austen's novels turns out to be precisely that. It remains a disembodied omniscience whose service to "the real" is no longer sufficient to prevent either the voice itself or the residual silence that remains its accompaniment from jointly complicating the authority on which direct (as opposed to epistolary) narrative now depends.

Silence and the Real

In speaking of a surplus silence independent of the fictional conventions beside which it is somehow double-parked, I am not arguing for a wildly proleptic reflexivity on Austen's part. I am merely suggesting that, by no longer serving the "real" in the way that unwritten language had done previously, Austen's silence—a residual but profoundly functional silence in her case—was recruitable to other uses. These, I hope to show, were directed to an expansion, enhancement, or complication of a "real" that Austen was engaged, in the estimation of most critics, in rendering uniform and natural.[17] In his essay on realism from which I have been quoting, Colin MacCabe asserts that the chief function of metalanguage in realistic or free indirect discourse, the language that places speech in quotations, is to take up a position of "knowledge" of "how things really are" (37–38). In letting the "identity of things shine through the window of words" (35)—whose materiality vanishes in comparison to that of characters, their actions, and *their words*—the "real" in realistic fiction is no longer perceived as "articulated," arbitrary, or partial but as existing *tout court*. As a result there are "two essential features of the classic realist text" according to MacCabe: first, the "realist text cannot deal with the real as contradictory"; and second, "in a reciprocal movement the classic realist text ensures the position of the [reading] subject in a relation of dominant specularity" (39).

With these features in mind two other things may be suggested regarding the role of silence in Austen's narratives and the disposition of her narratives in conjunction with it. First the silence inherited from epistolarity complicates the dominant specularity on which the totalizing reach of a still-partial real depends. Second, and more important, the complications brought by Austen's silence involve a reconception of the ordinary as heterogeneous and susceptible to a level of difference that narrative and plot are unable to contain.

Such heterogeneity in Austen can be as subtle and seemingly slight as the recognition, most recently articulated by social theorist Anthony Giddens, that social structures and routines exert influence precisely because they are recreated and influenced by the conscious agents who comprise them.[18] As Giddens notes, "all social life is episodic," requiring the "reflexive monitoring by the agents involved of the conditions in which they make 'history' " (244–45). And contradictions in Austen also derive from social developments peculiar to her time and locale, which were sufficiently "dense" (in Foucault's formulation) or "complicated" (in Raymond Williams's)[19] to provoke "perfect representations" that are somehow imperfect—or, in an arguably conscious appropriation of the charge frequently levied against realism, representations in which some things are beyond the narrator's ken and comprehension. (In a fairly candid admission of the limits of realistic representation, even of apparently mundane materials, the Frank-Jane relationship in *Emma* is never represented in the novel or transparent to the narrator.) Or such contradictions may be as local as matters of style and tone in which, as Gary Kelly remarks, the metanarrative frequently changes from "unironic identification to ironic distance in the same sentence" (119).

But whatever their particular constitution, the contradictions in Austenian omniscience and the opacity in the real they corporately foster depend in large measure on a residual and recuperated silence—on a metalanguage independent of the metalanguage of realistic practice—which is at odds with the imperative to either clarification or dominance. Antithetical to the workings of plot, which are subordinated in Austen's fiction to the quotidian and its details, Austen's silence and the various complications to which her real is consequently rendered permeable have the effect of transforming her (as some of her contemporaries already recognized) into an historian of a dense and inscrutable present rather than an unwitting prophet of a dismal future.

Historical Mediation

To speak of Austen as an historian of her time is a good deal less whimsical than it sounds and in fact marks an important but frequently overlooked feature of her practice as a novelist. Two of her novels, *Pride and Prejudice* and *Mansfield*

Park, were pegged to what many believe were specific years on the calendar. Even more important, Austen's first three novelistic compositions were revised for a decade and a half in the course of which their "real" was sufficiently temporalized that it literally shifts from what might initially have been a matter of fact to a matter of retrospective and (as the fourth novel, *Mansfield Park*, makes clear by contrast) increasingly nostalgic appreciation. The uncanny dimension of this enhancement was not lost on Austen's contemporary readers, many of whom distinguished the ideological or explanatory work of her stories from the unexpected interest generated by her attention to quotidian detail and character. Annabella Milbanke, the future Lady Byron, described *Pride and Prejudice* to her mother as "the *most probable* fiction I have ever read" in rejecting as it did "the common resources of Novel writers."[20] And the dowager Lady Vernon joined a number of other contemporaries, including several acquaintances of the author whose opinions Austen later gathered, in describing *Mansfield Park* as "not much of a novel" but "more the history of a family party in the country, very natural, and the characters well drawn."[21] In 1833, marking the reissue of Austen's novels sixteen years after her death, the *Literary Gazette* echoed these observations in describing Austen's "delightful works" as "absolute historical pictures" (30 Mar. 1833, 199).

The notion that novels, especially early narratives, were engaged in a specific historical work is by no means new. But this notion has taken on greater importance with Michael McKeon's *Origins of the English Novel*, which explores in depth the ideological dimension of such historical mediation. According to McKeon an important function of the novel as it developed in the early eighteenth century was the adjudication and explanation of historical change in the aftermath of the English Revolution. In seeking to mediate this historical experience, narratives took on two essentially antithetical forms: the aristocratic form of circular romance and the more progressive form of linearity.[22] The aristocratic form strongly militated against status inconsistency in making any social upheaval, or upward mobility on the part of nonaristocrats and nongentry, a temporary aberration righted in a character's return to a prior and preordained status. By contrast the progressive or linear form of narrative worked to justify the upward mobility of the non- or differently entitled in "representing the downward mobility of unworthy nobility and gentry and the upward mobility of industrious and deserving commoners" (223) so that differences in status, though by no means abolished, were at the very least reconstituted.

Now in the dialectical constitution of the novel, as McKeon adduces it, these antithetical forms work gradually toward an equipoise—a conservative equipoise—whose measure is nothing less than the novel itself, which McKeon deems a "dialectical unity of opposed parts" in which "progressive ideology subverts aristocratic ideology, and is in turn subverted by conservative ideology" (267). Nevertheless his prior observation—that early novelistic narrative was taken up with, among other tasks, the "conversion of history to story" (232) so that "in the formation of novelistic narrative, the most important model was not another 'literary' genre at all, but historical experience itself" (238)—seems the more germane with respect to the "historical Austen." It is tempting (and in many ways typical) to view Austen's writing as a measure of the "unity" of which McKeon speaks, particularly regarding the conservatism to which progressive narrative is eventually susceptible in its own subscriptions to distinction and desert. However, the peculiar density (or temporalized dynamism) of Austen's "real," coupled with the ancillary character of her plots, bespeaks something else. It points less to a conversion of history into story by way of mediating change than to the very opposite: the emptying of story *into history*, or into a review of the actual, where retrospection and an horizon of possibility are largely interdependent.[23]

It is a truth universally acknowledged that Austen's narratives are arrayed on the scaffolding of the "marriage plot." But rarely appreciated by most critics, though it was plainly evident to many of Austen's contemporaries, is the marginal character of those plots, especially as vehicles for directed explanation of the sort that McKeon describes. Lady Byron may have noted that the "interest" in *Pride and Prejudice* "is very strong . . . especially for Mr. Darcy," thereby underscoring an aristocratic strain in that particular comedy. However, she is quick to observe that the novel's other characters, "which are not [as] amiable," are "diverting, and all of them are consistently supported" (159). If we assume that interest in Mr. Darcy is generated by and on behalf of a plot bent on underscoring his desirability as a mate for the principal female character, then we can also assume (along with Lady Byron) that the other—equally interesting— elements of the novel are not always consistent with this orientation and with the ideological function it performs. As we shall see, the competing interests in *Pride and Prejudice* are not just at crosspurposes with a plot that is aristocratic and circular thanks to the interest and desirability of its hero, whose renunciation of pride in the novel's latter phase works paradoxically (and retroactively) to justify his pride to begin with along with his other entitlements. The "diverting" aspects of *Pride and Prejudice* are equally at odds with a plot that is concurrently progressive in rewarding a heroine who is far less advantaged than the hero she inevitably and deservedly marries.

The coexistence of competing ideologies in a novel like *Pride and Prejudice* would seem to support the supposition that by the time of Austen and the "rise of the novel," progressive and aristocratic plots were dialectically poised in an explanatory function less easily parsed and thereby suited to the "middle-class aristocracy" in whose service Austen is presumed to have written. But equally crucial in *Pride and Prejudice* is all of the history that remains unconverted and unassimilable to story. Amid the synthetic formation of a plot that is alternately progressive and aristocratic, what *Pride and Prejudice* provides is less a subsumption, by way of story and explanation, of the conditions and elements of social change, than a tension between this kind of mediation on the one hand, and a diversionary "real" on the other, in which other possibilities are lodged.

That is, far from pointing to the dialectical unity of the novel as a genre in the service of a dialectically constituted middle class, the conflation in Austen's marriage plot of the linear and circular forms of narrative is also a way of displacing change in two fundamental ways. In the first the conservative shape of Austen's narrative marks a displacement of disparate accounts of change that, even at the height of the romantic movement in England, were seen by Austen as largely interchangeable despite what in many quarters was a fervently held progressive ideology. Second, and more important, such a conflation of forms represents a displacement of social change itself, which is simultaneously diverted to precincts, notably everyday life past and passing, where change was presumed to be ephemeral or nonexistent.

Historical Density and Change

It is important, then, to distinguish the change of a measurable and demonstrable kind that was transpiring at this time in British history, to which Austen's fictions were responsive, from a change that was somewhat less palpable and material but also less answerable to the discursive or explanatory structures that continue to bind most discussions of Austen's ideology. (Is she is a protofeminist? Is she a Tory? and so forth.) This latter change—one elaborately tied to Austen's eccentricities as an historian of the present—is a change that only partly serves the usual constituencies, progressive or conservative, whose vision of historical change, especially "improvement," is hypostatized in the marriage plot and—as the early response to *Pride and Prejudice* suggests—displaced.

The rise of what historian Randolph Trumbach terms the egalitarian family or what Lawrence Stone calls affective individualism, through and by such institutions as the companionate marriage with its growing interest in children and their nurturance, may have constituted a substantive development over earlier, more hierarchical structures of kinship and patriarchy.[24] Still, for members of the gentry who, by Austen's time, were the legatees of developments that took place first within the aristocracy, the benefits of such improvements, especially for women, were a good deal less clear-cut.[25] I have spoken already of the rise of domestic ideology, which provided women with a demarcated but sharply circumscribed area of existence within a male-dominated culture. Such asymmetry is equally evident in the egalitarianism that historians have identified, which was ultimately contingent upon the amount of money an egalitarian family could confer upon its individual members.

For families like the Austens it was increasingly the practice for all assets to be placed in the hands of the eldest male, who, though somewhat freer to dispense of them as he chose, could not in many instances do so in any functionally egalitarian way. In the Austen family the meagerness of the estate forced the oldest son to take a clerical living and the remaining brothers to seek careers either in the navy or in banking. Only one Austen brother, Edward, who became heir to a landowning family that lacked a male descendant, enjoyed anything like a life of genuine privilege or leisure. As for the daughters, Jane and Cassandra, the future was even more precarious. In the absence of marriage, a likely fate for many gentry daughters at this time, the future involved (barring any monetary reward from Jane's novel writing) dependency on one or several male relatives along with the ever-present specter of their employment as governesses.[26]

Many of these changes, notably the precariousness of women's lives in an otherwise affectionate family culture, are documented in Austen's fictions along with other changes that, as Raymond Williams reminds us, make Austen's society anything but "settled" and in fact a "most difficult world to describe":

an acquisitive, high bourgeois society at the point of its most evident interlocking with an agrarian capitalism that is itself mediated by inherited titles and by the making of family names. Into the long and complicated interaction of landed and trading capital, the process that Cobbett observed—the arrival of "the nabobs, negro-drivers, admirals, generals" and so on—is directly inserted, and is even taken for granted. The social confusions and contradictions of this complicated process are then the true source of many of the problems of human conduct and valuation [in Austen's fictions]. . . . An openly acquisitive society, which is concerned also with the transmission of wealth, is trying to judge itself by an inherited code and by the morality of improvement.[27]

To readers familiar with Austen's fictions, the picture that Williams paints of the society of which she wrote seems remarkably accurate. There may be some subtlety, for example, in the allusions to Mrs. Elton's Bristol connections in *Emma* and to her family's newly acquired wealth from what is likely (or connected in some measure to) the slave trade. But in general just about everything Williams lists takes up residence *somewhere* in Austen's novels.

The problem with Williams's assessment is not in his representation of Austen's society or of the society represented in her fictions. The problem is in his representation of Austen's function as a fiction writer regarding her milieu: his sense, which he variously shares with Armstrong and others, of Austen's regulatory role in discriminating among improvements. According to Williams, Austen's advocacy of improvements is partial and restricted, along with a "real" whose capacity for either change or difference is necessarily limited. Thus Austen has an "eye for a house, for timber, for the details of improvement" that "is quick, accurate" and "monetary" whereas "money of other kinds, from the trading houses, from the colonial plantations, has no visual equivalent" in her novels. Similarly "the visible order and control [of the land] are a valued product" in her writings "while the process of working [the land] is hardly seen at all" (115).

According to Williams, the partiality of Austen's realism, indeed her attention to detail, is an attention that sharply, even willfully, restricts the "material basis" of the life that she represents. This leads to the conclusion that change or "improvement is or ought to be improvement" in Austen's calculus and that insofar as she regards any development or change as an improvement, it will be represented in a necessarily narrow and conservative light. In "her remarkable unity of tone," writes Williams, "that cool and controlled observation which is the basis of her narrative method; that lightly distanced management of event and description and character which need not become either open manipulation or direct participation . . . [t]he working improvement [agricultural or capitalistic], which is not seen at all, is the means to social improvement, which is then so isolated that is seen very clearly indeed" (116). Yet the question remains: what could "improvement" have possibly meant to a woman like Jane Austen? If the answer to this appears to derive force from the inclusion of "woman" in the query, it is hardly accidental. While Williams may be right in criticizing Austen (or her narrator) for conveniently distinguishing some improvements from others, he seems altogether wrongheaded in overlooking the many cultural materials, particularly regarding the lives of women, to which the novels recur with no overtly regulatory aim in mind. Moreover, when it comes to the cultural production by and of women in Austen's novels, the question of improvement is, not surprisingly, moot. Improvement, sadly, is no more essential to Austen's vision regarding women than the marriage plots to which improvements in their lives are both relegated and—even as they may marry up—discounted.

Austen, as Williams correctly discerns, was no Marx. But this should not be taken to mean that Austen feared change or that she was unequipped to deal with it save by reinterpreting change to the advantage of her class, which for Williams and others implies stasis and regulation. Nor is it any surprise that it devolves upon a female character in *Mansfield Park*, the novel perhaps most alert to "money . . . from the colonial plantations," to make the definitive statement on the very matters that Williams addresses. Responding to an account of the various changes wrought upon the chapel of an ancient estate in which additional changes are already being contemplated, Mary Crawford, who is *Mansfield Park*'s villainess as well as its most absorbing character, makes the following observation. "Every generation," she asserts smilingly, "has its improvements" (77).

There are a number of ways to interpret this statement—the most obvious being a wholesale endorsement of the kinds of improvements, notably Reptonian landscaping, that the tradition-minded heroine, Fanny Price, who is an advocate of the picturesque, disapproves of. Yet beyond this already problematic debate, which aligns a certain kind of naturalizing practice (the picturesque) with traditionalism, there is the larger argument that for women, in particular, the prospect of qualitative change has a history too long and repetitive for there to be any hope that "improvements"—to paraphrase Williams paraphrasing Austen—"ought to be improvements." It is more that, in making this statement or in being allowed to make this statement, Mary is indicating two things: that change, especially social change, has been little more than a repetition of the same; and second, and more important, that genuine improvements or changes *have* occurred—albeit in forms unassimilable to the grander narratives of progress and melioration to which improvements may otherwise refer.

History, Oppositionality, Silence

In advancing this interpretation of a single statement in a complicated and sprawling novel, I am guided as much by Mary's behavior in the book—which is directed, albeit futilely, to a kind of change or "improvement" that is nonnarratable—as I am by an aspect of the novel as a whole that, in conjunction with the author's silent stance toward her materials, I call oppositional. In using the term "oppositional" I am referring to a practice of living and consuming, but also to a practice of writing (and reading), that Michel de Certeau describes as change by other means.

In his famous book, *The Practice of Everyday Life*, de Certeau enumerates a range of practices on the part of the weak or disempowered—laborers, average pedestrians, indigenous peoples in areas under colonial and ecclesiastical domination, but among whom we might also include women in the late eighteenth century—which entail the use of, and by that means a resistance to, various imposed systems. Such practices include activities like *la perruque* (the wig), where

French factory workers make items for themselves "disguised as work for [their] employer,"[28] the appropriation of European saints' tales by indigenous South Americans as a way to allegorize the miracles necessary to escape from domination, or even the practice of pedestrians to resist the mapping of cities, and the grids on which such places are organized, by jaywalking and other kinds of peregrination. Oppositional practices of the everyday have two things in common then: they are practices "that elude discipline," and they are practices that remain firmly within "the field [of discipline] in which [they] are exercised" (96).

That is, precisely by *not* aspiring to a position of exteriority, or to a revolution, or even to the status of a certain kind of improvement, oppositional practices eschew the various strategies or acts of power by which they would (as Foucault brilliantly demonstrates) be recruited to the work of dominion and control. If anything, the "improvements" attendant upon oppositional practices are achieved in the recognition that "every generation has its improvements" and that the more dramatic or noticeable improvements work largely to ensure the reach and sustenance of hegemonic formations. Oppositionality is more a way of getting on than a practice predicated on the revolutionary or utopian dream of getting out. And its practices are necessarily "outside the reach of the panoptic power" (95), which, as Foucault has shown, counts on the belief in progress or "improvement" to function as it does.[29]

De Certeau figures centrally in my discussion of Austen because of his theory of oppositionality and because the materials in which possibility resides in his reckoning are essentially the same materials on which Austen dilates. But de Certeau is equally important for his theory of writing, particularly history writing, from which his theories of everyday practice, and their uncanny aspects, derive.[30] Although de Certeau's theory of "heterology" is complicated and wide-ranging, most important is the otherness that, as de Certeau demonstrates, marks the "limit" of knowledge (*History*, 39) in most historical representation and is thus consigned in the name of the "real" to the realm of the "unthinkable" (4). While the protocols of historical recovery may continue to countenance it on the basis of its having happened, much of what has transpired in history is routinely excluded in most history writing. This exclusion occurs because the "real" is less an interest of historians than an institution that de Certeau tellingly terms an "orthodoxy." Both mystification and a *partialization*, the real is the means now by which history is consistently held distinct from fiction in the same way that any representation that did not hew either to precedent or to "things as they are" was in Austen's time discredited in the name of probability. Thus not only is the inclusion of the unthinkable, or the possible, unlikely in the "writing of history." Its exclusion is reciprocally enforced by the partiality or "fiction" that ironically "haunts the field of historiography," making genuinely " 'fictitious' discourse," as Jeremy Bentham notes, "closer to the real than objective discourse" (*Heterologies,* 219). The "real," then—and the real as Austen represents it—is real not just in the way it is comprised of the routines and detritus of the everyday; its reality is reciprocally measured by its vitiation of a practice—call it realism—that is probabilistic rather than possibilistic in making the merely thinkable all we know on earth. Unlike the histories that continue to serve the real by a comparatively orthodox belief in the intelligibility of things, the real in Austen's fiction, on which density and retrospection cooperatively converge, silently confirms that the very "things" most often deemed intelligible are the very things that, upon scrutiny, "resist [comprehension] most" (220).[31]

In the privileged entity that I call the "historical Austen," the novelist's status as an historical agent is ultimately indivisible from the history *in* her writing. For here, partly in consequence of the extended interval during which the real of Austen's narratives gradually *became* history, reality and temporality are admixed so that Austen's status as an historian of the everyday (as at least some of her contemporaries recognized it) turns out to be an unusually precise description of her achievement. Not only is there a palpable connection between certain developments and disappointments from which possibility springs at once retrospectively and nostalgically in Austen's representations. There is a concomitant link between a reality, where possibility and loss are to a large extent versions of the same, and a silence that just as imperceptibly casts any claim to comprehending that reality into critical relief. The silence that Austen derived from epistolarity is important precisely because it is something in the end that free indirect discourse can neither subsume nor resemble. Instead such silence works to highlight and compromise the novels' metanarrative, their position of dominant specularity or omniscience, where fidelity to the real is no less a fidelity to the merely probable—and in contrast to the inconceivable union of Frank Churchill and Jane Fairfax—the characteristically thinkable.

Thus there is a necessary link between *all* of the following: Austen's oppositional practice as a fiction writer about which a little more must be said; the history writing of which her fiction writing is both a subset and, following de Certeau's critique, an improved version; and the silence or metairony that is the both the linchpin in Austen's particular practice as a writer and the means through which story *becomes history* in its incomprehensibility, ordinariness, and promise. These links exist because even as "every generation has its improvements," there is in the practice of every generation a resistance to intelligibility that, as Austen discloses somewhat wistfully, is the mark and measure of resistance per se.

Oppositionality and Irony

I will turn, very shortly—and speculatively—to Austen's work as an historian, which involves in this instance her paradigmatically silent response to the arrest and subsequent trial of her aunt Jane Leigh Perrot for shoplifting. Taken with the various circumstances surrounding the crime and its eventual prosecution and resolution in trial, Austen's response to the "trial" of her aunt, both in and out of court, underscores the homology between her fictional practice, in which silence figures critically, and the peculiar historical practice, to which her "real"—in its "authentically temporal destiny"—is eminently suited. Before entering this, I want to turn first to the question of oppositional writing in general

Mrs. Leigh Perrot, from *Grand Larceny, Being the Trial of Jane Leigh Perrot, Aunt of Jane Austen,* by Sir Frank Douglas MacKinnon (Oxford: Oxford University Press, 1937).

regarding which Ross Chambers—a critic influenced by de Certeau—has recently offered a number of important guidelines.[32]

Recurring to narratological and reception theories (notably the work of Susan Suleiman),[33] which he combines with de Certeau's notions of everyday oppositionality, especially regarding consumption or use, Chambers draws an important distinction between the so-called narrative function of a story and the "textual function." The narrative function "respects the power structure" whereas the "textual function" operates "more covert[ly]" in "appeal[ing] to the 'readerly' activity of interpretation" (13). For a narrative, then, to become oppositional there must be "a split between the 'narrative' and 'textual' functions." In this split

the "narrative function," as the site of an address to the narratee in the position of power, comes to be relativized—or, more technically, *ironized*—by a "textual function" that distances the reader from the narratee position and requires the "narrative function" to become part of the text *as an object of interpretation.* Everything thus depends on the intervention of a reader capable of manifesting the discourse as a mediated phenomenon by producing the crucial split between "narrative" and "textual" functions. Discourse that is not, in this sense, read cannot be oppositional. (43)

A number of issues that I have already broached are restated here. What Chambers terms the narrative function, particularly as a position of power, corresponds to the dominant specularity of free indirect style and the realist text generally, which Austen, I submit, knew pretty much to be what Chambers describes. So too the textual function, which he grounds in reception theory, has its correlative in the peculiarly antecedent silence that haunts the metanarrative in Austen, forcing it into a position of being interpretable as another—and perforce limited—object language. Such interpretability in Austen is undoubtedly linked to a process of ironization. But it remains, following Chambers, a remarkably rich process comprising a text capable of foregrounding its narrative function and a reader to whom that function and its related partialization are fairly transparent.

With the introduction of irony Chambers raises an issue near and dear to Austen criticism, even if the irony that most readers detect in her writing remains, in its apparent distribution of praise and blame, rather closely aligned with the "narrative" or authoritative function. Still, in the movement to a less stable irony—and to the cultivation of a reader shorn of more conventional power—the issue, at least in Austen, comes to more than the liabilities, or even the rewards, of narrative authority and its absorptive operation. It involves, as Austen's earliest readers noted with some regularity, the conversion, or again emptying out, of story into history and the subordination of plot to detail.

Together these conversions provide a firmer link between oppositionality as readerly practice and a textuality whose inherent responsiveness to the otherness, opacity, or incomprehensibility of the real is additionally a reminder that every generation has its opposition.

The work, then, of a less stable irony, both in its disavowal of authority and unregulated yield, is directly tied in Austen to the silence of which I have been speaking. Undermining the narrative function, which inheres in among other places plot, such silence is additionally a model for the peculiar openness of what Chambers (after Suleiman) terms the "textual function." In this latter function oppositionality is not strictly a matter of resistance, of some antithetical and strategic manipulation of the regime to which narrative, in its regulatory commitment to rewarding virtue, is tantamount. It amounts now to a series of readable details that sooner or later disclose an otherness, something hitherto "unthinkable," where change or some other possibility is uncannily lodged. To be sure, Austen's fictions also lend themselves to a narrative function and to a textual function not always reducible to the readerly equivalent of flying under the radar. However, in the actual work of Austen's fictions, both the writing and the reading, these antinomies are more directly linked, giving readers with no particular stake in resistance—readers like the earl of Dudley[34]—occasion to pause, which for Austen is a means, perhaps the only means, to change.

Now all of these permutations of irony would appear to correlate in only the slightest way with a series of events to which Austen recorded no response (at least none that is extant) and regarding which her silence may be just as easily interpreted as tact or indifference rather than the paradoxically activist (dis)engagement that I have been discussing. Nevertheless the arrest and prosecution of her wealthy aunt Jane Leigh Perrot for stealing a card of lace was news—big news—at the time of its occurrence, making its virtual absence in Austen's correspondence, even by allusion or reminiscence, unusual.

There are explanations for this absence. The most important, apart from the posthumous destruction of letters that may have contained references to the incident, is that Austen was living with her sister and chief correspondent at the time of their aunt's arrest and incarceration and had no occasion or pretext to write candidly about it—this despite the fact that she and Cassandra were at one point offered as companions to Aunt Perrot during her incarceration. Another explanation for the absence of any reference, which might have been a way of allowing the facts to speak for themselves, may be found in Austen's treatments of "my Aunt" in letters written after the fact.[35]

Many of these letters are fairly critical in their representation of an apparently pompous, self-absorbed, and parsimonious woman. Yet on balance Austen's reflections yield a decidedly active (or activist) perplexity whose functional correlative is silence: with respect to the trial, most immediately, but with important bearing on a narrative-historical practice of which the trial as suppressed referent is emblematic. For as much as anything in Austen's actual fiction, "The Trial of Jane Leigh Perrot," as it was literally titled in the published transcriptions that appeared shortly after the verdict, was finally turned, with the benefit of Austen's "silent treatment," to an otherness that, as the novelist recognized, is always close at hand.

Part of Austen's reticence regarding her aunt owes to the fact that Aunt Perrot was a shared and already understood discourse between sisters, removing the need to expatiate in any great degree upon her faults and eccentricities. When Austen reports, in apparently good humor, Aunt Perrot's enthusiasm regarding the Austens' impending move to Bath ("it is an event which will attach her to the place more than anything else could do, &c., &c." [110]), we hear not only Aunt Perrot's hyperbole but also an inferable dread that Perrot should actually mean, and act on the basis of, what she says. With an irony so subtle that it was virtually a private language between sisters, Austen's treatment of their relative frequently deploys wit as a stand-in for thoughts that lie too deep for either laughter or tears. "My Aunt," she later tells Cassandra, "has a very bad cough; do not forget to have heard about *that* when you come, & I think she is deafer than ever" (132). The conflation of a presumably exaggerated infirmity with a more concrete problem—the loss of hearing—is complicated and enriched by the presumption that it is the prerogative and therefore the purpose of all others to be healthier than "my Aunt." Quite simply, the latter's demands for sympathy require auditory capacities that for reasons, physical and otherwise, exceed her own. This demand of health becomes especially problematic when these injunctions are sharply tried in the author's final days. Even here, though, in the midst of her very real infirmity, Austen remarks—with no overtly comparative purpose but simply to discourage any hope of an imminent inheritance from their wealthy, childless aunt—that "my aunt is very stout" (494).

Austen was right about her aunt's good health, which sustained the older woman for ninety-two years. Yet her conviction in her aunt's fortitude, despite years of chronic complaints regarding coughs and headaches, bespeaks something more than either irritation at having to endure such complaints or even the functional optimism that those closest to the complaining woman had to maintain so as to suffer her gladly. Austen knew and appreciated very clearly her aunt's strengths as well as her weaknesses and saw them, I would argue, as part of a dense and contradictory profile that defied containment, even by two sisters who could have easily pursued such a strategy between them. Perhaps the most remarkable feature of Jane's remarks to Cassandra regarding "my Aunt" is the way their relation twice removed routinely comes between true intimates, forcing a suspension or, at the least, a qualification of totalizing judgment.

Many years earlier, in recounting to Cassandra a connection that Aunt Perrot was fostering in Bath between the writer and a Mr. Evelyn, Austen writes: "She ought to be particularly scrupulous in such matters & she says so herself—but nevertheless . . ." (137). The ellipses with which Austen concludes discussion of her aunt, indeed of actions that contravene the latter's own better judgment, might seem a readable silence in which (like the earlier "&c., &c.") a more specific and fully understood criticism is lodged. At one level this surely is the case. Yet even as they point to a secret or unspoken language between sisters, the ellipses point also in the direction of the unsayable, which is more an empathy than a blank easily filled: a soundless echo of the inscrutable density of Aunt Perrot's historical reality. This position is equally in force in a letter seven years later when, recounting her mother's response to a letter from "my Aunt" fraught with numerous complaints, Austen adopts a more detached but not necessarily disengaged stance: "the discontentedness of it shocked & surprised [my Mother]—but *I* see nothing in it out of Nature—tho' a sad nature" (232).

It is likely that Austen construed the events, circumstances, and motives surrounding her aunt's arrest in 1799 for "stealing a card of lace" (as the court document put it) as pertinent to this "sad nature." Yet it may be argued that the very notion of "Nature," especially one lacking a possessive, moved seamlessly at that time, as it does in the later letter, from a conception of a single subject, however complicated, to a larger conception of the "real" in which the subject finds itself. In this latter notion of "Nature" we have, following the silence that attends it, a conception distinct from other conceptions like the picturesque, which continue to speak for nature in a partial, if eminently intelligible, way. The best way to communicate the full measure of Aunt Perrot's "real" is not to try to comprehend it nor to measure it; the best way is to let it be in a readable and fathomable density.

Story versus History

This is not, of course, how the incident of the putative theft was explicitly narrated, either by Jane Leigh Perrot in her defense or by most members of her family in aftermath. In fact the narrative that was proposed by way of explanation, coupled with what actually intervened between the alleged theft and the eventual resolution in trial, approximates many of Austen's own fictions, to the extent that these works can be reduced to plot and to the ideology enforced thereby. In this last, a woman of generally unimpeachable character is, by a conspiracy of some kind (or owing to some aspect of status inconsistency), removed from her proper place and transported to a social wilderness. There she heroically endures certain indignities while suffering the threat of lasting displacement, before returning to her original place or to a place proper to her. Her return is invariably accompanied by the (re)acquisition of wealth and by her (re)ascension to a position of relative ease. If this position is one previously denied the heroine, it is granted her according to a status that she has earned by specific actions or, as the case may be, forbearances. Conservative in shape and the sort of story that a "middle-class aristocra[t]" would presumably find appealing, this trajectory characterizes in one way or another the plots of *Northanger Abbey, Sense and Sensibility, Mansfield Park,* and *Persuasion* in addition to unfinished texts such as *The Watsons* and possibly even *Sanditon.* Yet in every one of these texts it is a trajectory also taxed by the *history* to which other elements attest.

And so it is, or was, in the case of Aunt Perrot, as Jane Austen knew all too well. Despite her assertion that the extra card of white lace that she was accused of taking was in fact inserted into her package by the man who sold her black lace for which she did pay, Jane Leigh Perrot went to great lengths not just to prove her innocence but more importantly to protract her victimization. Instead of resolving the matter quietly by making immediate restitution, which she could easily have afforded, Perrot denied stealing the material when confronted by the shopkeeper shortly after the alleged theft and allowed the matter to proceed to indictment and later to trial, which entailed perils far less supportable. The crime for which Perrot was charged was not petty theft but grand larceny, a crime punishable in the laws of the time by death. In his detailed, if somewhat biased, account of this incident Frank MacKinnon insists that Jane Leigh Perrot would not have been executed had she been found guilty. Her likely fate, in the event of a guilty verdict, would have been transportation to Australia for a period of about fourteen years, which would have been severe enough.[36]

Perrot's insistence on hazarding transport by going to trial was remarkable. But it was not nearly as remarkable—as Austen must have realized or intuited—as the fact that the decision to go to trial turned out to have been no risk at all. As much as any of her niece's heroines, in fact, Aunt Perrot was virtually destined, after an appropriate interval, of returning, and even ascending, to her proper place as a virtuous woman. True, she had to endure eight months' incarceration, followed by a trial that lasted nearly seven hours. But she was able finally to bask in a verdict of not guilty that took a jury, composed of tradesmen and workingmen, all of fifteen minutes to render. That these events constituted a "story" that Aunt Perrot effectively authored or allowed to take the only form it could take (down to the ostensibly classless or universal consensus regarding her innocence) could hardly have escaped the discerning eye of her niece, the novelist. But the real point of Austen's understanding, with bearing again on her practice as a different *kind* of author, is the history that was unconverted and unrecuperated by Aunt Perrot's "story" and to which Austen's silence, I argue, bore respectful, attentive, and, one might say, complementary witness.

Perhaps the most salient feature of this unconverted "history"—this history independent of story—is the fact that Perrot actually stole the lace. At least one of her attorneys, Joseph Jekyll, was of that opinion and was reported to have described his client as one of those rich ladies "who frequent bazaars and mistake other people's property for their own." This judgment was subsequently echoed by a relative, Richard Austen-Leigh, who, in recounting Jekyll's view, wrote privately that Perrot "did steal the material and probably meant to" (Honan, 150–51). In addition a commonplace book from the period contains a poem mentioning an undocumented theft of plants that Perrot allegedly committed in Ilchester, where she was jailed for the theft of lace.[37]

More telling still, a copy of *Northanger Abbey* belonging to the Reverend Alexander Dyce, a college friend of James Edward Austen—the novelist's nephew and the "young relation" to whom Austen famously described her fictional world as "a little bit of ivory, two inches wide"—contains a marginal comment suggesting that Perrot's kleptomania was well known, at least among members of her family. Prompted by the well-known anecdote, first published in Henry Austen's preface to *Northanger Abbey*, in which Austen playfully defends herself against the charge of having "pilfered the manuscripts of a young relation," Dyce remarks with his usual punctiliousness that the relation was indeed Austen's nephew.[38] Dyce then recounts that young Austen "read to me the very letter now quoted" when they were students at Exeter College, Oxford, and that "he is now (1844) the Reverend James Austen Leigh, having added the Leigh to his name since he succeeded to the property of his aunt, Mrs. Leigh Perrot." Having introduced, then, the subjects of both pilferage and Mrs. Leigh Perrot, Dyce's next bit of Austenia seems inevitable rather than gratuitous: "The lady last mentioned, Mrs. Austen's sister, had an invincible propensity to stealing, and was tried at Bath for stealing lace. The printed account of her trial is extant. Her family were dreadfully shocked at the disgrace which she brought upon them. For many years she lived in seclusion at Scarlets (a handsome place where she died)."

One could of course discredit this marginalia as mere hearsay. Nevertheless, Dyce's other annotations to Austen reveal him to be a reader of uncommon exactitude. In his copy of *Northanger Abbey*, for example, Dyce proudly identifies the

various gothic novels—the so-called Northanger novels—that Catherine Morland and Isabella Thorpe read with entirely too much interest, and even expatiates on the narrator's references to the works of Burney, noting that "Miss Austen
(as her nephew told me) thought Madame D'Arblay the very best of English
novelists; and she used to praise the character of Sir Hugh Tyrold in *Camilla* as
extremely well-drawn." In his copy of *Mansfield Park* Dyce makes note of an
"ungrammatical sentence . . . such as Miss Austen seldom writes" and later observes with a great deal of surprise that Austen has given in "to the odious vul-
garism of using 'lay' for 'lie' " in the query, "whereabouts does the Thrush [a
boat] lay at Spithead?" Dyce also corrects a typographical error in the novel,
substituting "hate" for "have" in the sentence, "You have politics of course" and
peppers his copy of *Emma* with similar observations and explanatory notes.

Perrot's culpability hinges on more than this pedantic commentary. While
some of the evidence of her penchant for stealing—for example, the poem in
the commonplace book—probably owes to the popularity of the trial, which
was reported in at least three newspapers and in the *Lady's Magazine* and was
transcribed in three separate published accounts, there is additional evidence
pointing to her guilt.[39] This latter evidence comes in the form of letters, both
signed and anonymous, that the Perrots received during Mrs. Perrot's incarceration, several of which attest to a conspiracy to extort money from the Perrots in
exchange for the suppression of evidence against her. These letters make it clear
that although attempts were indeed made at extorting money from the wealthy
Perrots, they were undertaken because, in the understanding of some of those
closest to the case, Perrot was in fact guilty and as such an easy mark. One unsigned letter, only part of which has ever been published, is especially forthright
in identifying the chief "villain" in the conspiracy as William Gye. In addition to
maintaining an interest in the shop from which Perrot allegedly stole the lace,
Gye sought to capitalize on her misfortune not only by apparently conspiring to
extort money from the Perrots to "buy off the Witnesses" (as the anonymous
letter indicates) but also by publishing one of the transcripts of Perrot's trial the
following year.

This letter, which is excerpted in MacKinnon's book about the trial, recounts (among other things) an overheard threat to "publish a Ludicrous Print
of your Crest, with a Card of Lace, & other Articles in the Parrot's bill" and
pretty much confirms the efforts of one or more people to bully the Perrots into
some form of compensation. But what MacKinnon's redaction typically leaves
out is the report in this same letter of Gye's efforts to solicit testimony from a
lady ("the wife of one of the most truly respectable inhabitants of this city") to
the effect that the shopman, who had sold Perrot the lace, had wrapped only the
black lace for which she had paid and not the white lace that mysteriously

appeared in Perrot's package minutes later. The letter goes on to observe that the woman, who was apparently in the rear of the store at the time of Perrot's transaction and had actually witnessed the shopman with Perrot's half-folded parcel, could not, upon application, "say what the paper contained." Still, it attests to initiatives that would not have been taken by someone who already knew that the lace had been secreted in Perrot's parcel, as the Perrots charged, or by someone who, as another letter rumored, had directed that Perrot be set up so as "to extort a sum of money to support the falling credit of that infamous set of fraudulent shopkeepers."[40]

Even with her aunt's culpability in view, it was not apparently to Austen's purpose either to discredit a narrative founded on her aunt's innocence and redemption, which the *Bath Chronicle* had endorsed, or to promote one founded upon Perrot's guilt and inordinate privilege, which the *Bath Journal* pursued in noting that the prosecution's witnesses gave evidence "in a clear and distinct manner, much to the satisfaction of the whole court." Instead the *effect* of Austen's silence, here and representatively, was to displace these narratives of praise and blame, and their respective ideologies, by taking seriously the particular incomprehensibility that Perrot herself introduced by way of her own defense. In a statement read before a packed courtroom and before many men and women who, like her husband, were reduced to tears by her recitation, Jane Leigh Perrot questioned her inquisitors:

Placed in a Situation in every respect the most Enviable—blessed with a Tender and most Affectionate Husband who is ever anxious to indulge my Wants and anticipate my Wishes and whose Supply of Money is so ample as to leave me rich even after every desire is gratified what inducement could I have to commit this offence? Depraved indeed must have been my Mind if with these Comforts I could have been tempted to this Crime. You will hear from my Noble and highly respectable Friends what has been my conduct, and what has been, and still is their opinion of me. Can you think it possible they have been so many years deceived? Is it possible that at this time of Life my disposition should so suddenly change and that I should foolishly hazard the well earned reputation of a whole Life by such Conduct, or endanger the Peace of Mind of a Husband for whom I would willingly lay down that Life?[41]

It goes without saying that some of this is transparent fiction, notably Perrot's solicitude for her husband, whom she allowed to accompany her during her entire stay in prison despite his being stricken with gout.

It is true that upon additional payment the prison was upgraded to the jailer's own home. But as Perrot's letters to her cousin Mountague Cholmeley during the period of her incarceration confirm, life among the Scaddings family was only a cut above actual prison, especially for one as fastidious as Mr. Perrot:

"My dearest Perrot with his sweet composure adds to my Philosophy [of God's mercy]; to be sure he bids fair to have his patience tried in every way he can. Cleanliness has ever been his greatest delight and yet he sees the greasy toast laid by the dirty Children on his Knees, and feels the small Beer trickle down his sleeves on its way across the table unmoved" (195). Although it was customary for letters to circulate among those close to the correspondents, there is no evidence that Austen had access to those written to Perrot's cousin. Letters, of course, passed between Mrs. Perrot and Mrs. Austen at this time, including one in which the latter offered her two daughters as companions to the prisoner, who heroically refused the offer as she also refused having her servants accompany her (205–6). Nor is it clear for that matter that the correspondence with the Austens was as weighted down by the narrative of self-legitimation as the letters to Cholmeley, which are routinely hyperbolic in documenting the "many Evils" the Perrots "unavoidably endure[d]" (193).

Whether Austen actually laid eyes on the various installments in her aunt's odyssey en route to vindication is not important. What is important is that such a narrative ultimately demanded more (and less) of her than either direct assent or direct rebuttal. If anything Austen was simply moved—pursuant to the one document to which she did have access since it was included in the published transcripts of the trial and had circulated in original form among various family members—to follow the lead of her aunt's self-defense in introducing the *unthinkable* into the text of the trial. She did so not by way of blame but to collaborate silently with her aunt in a way that, to borrow Perrot's own language, renders the probable, or what Perrot would have us believe *is* the real, a cover for what Perrot tellingly calls the "possible."

Such a collaboration flies in the face of a conventionally progressive interpretation of these events, where the unthinkable—that Perrot *stole* the lace—becomes thinkable in order to level a wealthy, indulgent woman. And it discountenances as well the conservative or regulatory narrative in which Perrot, by virtue of her privilege and her ability alternately to mask it, becomes a normative moral agent. For in riding the unthinkable to the borders of the possible, Austen is taking seriously the otherness onto which a reply to her aunt's questions—particularly as they become unmoored from the narrative they are meant to serve—necessarily verges.

Thus while Austen, I believe, took no apparent or progressive joy in her aunt's downfall, she remained, as her silence also indicates, just as wary of the particularly sinister character of the latter's vindication. For here, like the Jane Austen conceived by the newer historicisms, the entitlement essential to the ability to mount a successful defense, and to endure imprisonment in the certainty of being successful, is effectively masked by two things: the material indignities that Jane Perrot had to suffer and Perrot's ability to represent herself as somehow classless or as a moral example for all people. The same woman, then, who authorized a considerable sum to be spent in her defense (*Austen Papers* 206–7, 209), which included investigating the shady financial past of one her accusers (214), and may have also authorized additional sums toward the suppression of evidence against her, was quick to follow the advice of her counselors in producing and subsidizing character witnesses from all walks of life (206–7, 209). Consequently, while her defense, like her own speech, may have hinged on the fact of her entitlement, and on the preposterousness of her need to steal in lieu of actually purchasing what she desired, it was subsumed in an account of suffering where a woman of means became a model to which all women might aspire.

Whether Perrot's narrative had this particular effect on either the judge who presided at the Taunton Assizes or the jury that, all appearances notwithstanding, very quickly acquitted her, is another matter, and in many ways beside the point. Indeed the real question was not guilt or innocence or even jurisprudence but the yield released by the peculiar enhancement of the "probable" that admission of the "unthinkable" (specifically the prospect of an actual theft) ultimately provided. "Probability" was quite a charged word for Austen, as it was for her contemporaries, who routinely used the word in both approbation and recognition of Austen's unique accomplishment and, more broadly, to distinguish works of fiction that were realistic from works that were improbable and likely to imbue young women with false and potentially harmful expectations. Commenting on Mary Brunton's novel *Self-Control*, Austen herself notes that it was "excellently-meant" and "elegantly-written . . . without anything of Nature or Probability in it" (*Jane Austen's Letters* 344).

Such observations are, like those regarding Austen's own works, normally construed to refer to the exaggerated plots of fiction of the time, particularly women's fiction, to which Austen (as her "bit of ivory" indicates) was concertedly fashioning an alternative. Still, with the inclusion of "Nature"—a term also used in conjunction with the indeterminacy of one Jane Leigh Perrot—probability takes in a good deal more here than the equally partial vision that Austen's narratives of country life allegedly embraced in service of the real and in opposition to either fancy or imagination. Like all of the nature, in fact, that is also inadmissible in certain representations of the real, including representations operating under the aegis of the picturesque, probability extends in the example or "nature" of Jane Leigh Perrot to precincts that, suddenly permeable to the unthinkable, are a site as well of possibility.

Now by "possibility" I am referring to two related things: the possibility that Perrot stole the lace for good reason or in order to reclaim something taken from her in which questions of gender and entitlement figure prominently,[42] and the possibility—the more oppositional possibility—of a different, less contradictory social and psychological configuration, that the conflation of the probable and the unthinkable can, with an assist from Austen's silence, be said to serve. Although neither the theft nor the alleged efforts on the part of the shopman to secrete an extra card of lace in Perrot's package in the aim of eventually extorting money are themselves oppositional acts, the act of allowing history to speak in all its density or independent of plot certainly is. Such an act or tact on Austen's part constitutes a very real resistance because it counts chiefly on the intractability of the real—the "trial" of Jane Leigh Perrot before *and after* the fact—to changes and improvements of the more customary and narratable kind. This resistance, which is also an invitation to a special kind of reflection on the part of the reader, is in many ways the central work of Austen's major and still silent writings.[43]

2
The Picturesque, the Real, and the Consumption of Jane Austen

In a memorable, if cryptically brief, episode in *Emma*, Harriet Smith—the artless and vulnerable protégée of the eponymous protagonist—is accosted by a party of gypsies while out walking with "another parlour boarder" at Mrs. Godard's school for young women:

About half a mile beyond Highbury, making a sudden turn, and deeply shaded by elms on each side, [the road] became for a considerable stretch very retired; and when the young ladies had advanced some way into it, they had suddenly perceived at a small distance before them, on a broader patch of greensward by the side, a party of gipsies. A child on the watch, came towards them to beg; and Miss Bickerton, excessively frightened, gave a great scream, and calling on Harriet to follow her, ran up a steep bank, cleared a slight hedge at the top, and made the best of her way by a short cut back to Highbury. But poor Harriet could not follow. She had suffered very much from cramp after dancing, and her first attempt to mount the bank brought on such a return of it as made her absolutely powerless—and in this state, and exceedingly terrified, she had been obliged to remain. (300)[1]

Needless to say, the threat that the gypsies pose to Harriet, a girl of seventeen, is more imaginary than real. And the threat is enfeebled further by the sudden arrival of Frank Churchill, a man of twenty-three who, with the additional armature of class, immediately frightens the gypsies—"a woman and a boy"—into submissive retreat before returning Harriet to her regular protector, Emma Woodhouse.

"This was," notes Austen's narrator, "the amount of the whole story." Yet this seemingly dismissive reduction of Harriet's experience is quickly amended in Emma's subsequent response, where Harriet's "story" is made more "whole" by addition of fantasy. Impressed by the improbability of the incident—which in her memory had never "occurred before to any young ladies in the place" (302)—Emma is struck more by the appositeness of "Frank Churchill, with Harriet leaning on his arm" (299), which she resolves (having recently failed to unite Harriet with another eligible bachelor) to let "take its natural course"

(302). Emma's attempt to retroject this "very extraordinary thing" in a narrative that, as she conceives it, is altogether less extraordinary and more natural, is quickly thwarted by the titillation that the "frightful news" (302) bestows on the entire community. Emma's nephews, for example, adamantly oppose her narrative and naturalizing impulses in "asking every day for the story of Harriet and the gipsies, and . . . setting her right if she varie[s] in the slightest particular from the original recital" (303).

Now the full significance of the episode—its "amount" if you will—may be nothing more than Emma's incorrigibility: specifically her need to control other people in lieu of being controlled and to control in the process her own fantasies of union, which she routinely projects onto others. Or the episode's significance may extend, as one critic has recently suggested, into an exposure of the uses of stories and storytelling, where the "narratological compulsion to repeat," or to gossip, is alternately a way of containing "gypsy intransigence" and the "hysterical" reaction to it, both of which are inimical to the hegemony of an increasingly liberal society.[2]

But regardless of how we calculate the "whole amount" of this "story"—whether by narrative or authorial motive, or by a metacritical calculus of historicization and theory—one thing is inescapably clear: the alterity signified by the gypsies is arguably the last place in *Emma* where otherness takes on a dangerous manifestation or threatens in any way the controls administered by a civil society. Indeed, Frank's arrival on the scene, and the restoration of order he immediately brings, merely recapitulate what is already, in effect, *in* the scene: namely, a containment of the gypsies by process of aestheticization.

In speaking of aestheticization I am referring not just to the digressive aspects of the episode that render it something of a tableau. I am referring more to elements in and about the episode that bear directly on the aesthetic of the picturesque: the model of landscape organization and representation proposed by William Gilpin and subsequently elaborated by Richard Payne Knight and Uvedale Price, who actually recommended the inclusion of gypsies and beggars in picturesque representations.[3] A leading—perhaps *the* leading—aesthetic theory in the decades that Austen developed as a novelist, picturesque theory sought not only to reorganize the landscape according to certain aesthetic desiderata, which are pretty much adhered to in the inviting scene that Harriet and Miss Bickerton enter. In a reciprocal turn that was nearly tautological, picturesque theory sought also to encourage an aesthetic or representational order—an idea of nature to be precise—that was natural insofar as it resembled a landscape already governed by aesthetic rule. Gilpin hints at this tautological exchange when he remarks in a slightly earlier account that the aim of picturesque travel is to arrive at a station from which "natural scenery" conforms to "the principles of artificial landscape" (*Observations on the River Wye*, 2); and he later amends the tautology by observing, in his most sustained discourse on the subject, that what is picturesque or representable in nature are those aspects that lend themselves to being sketched and thereby represented (36–37).

It is tempting to credit Gilpin with the sophisticated, if strangely innocent, awareness that a landscape's originality or authenticity is inextricably linked to the fact that in experience, no less than in art, it is already a copy of something. And a number of commentators, notably Rosalind Krauss, have credited him with just this discovery.[4] Nevertheless a careful reading of picturesque theory, beginning with Gilpin and continuing on to his successors Price and Knight, reveals a naturalizing and partializing imperative to the theory overall to which Austen, I believe, was responsive but also opposed. Unlike the picturesque, which aestheticizes nature, restricting the real in either art or actual experience to a partial, regulated version of itself, Austen's narrative practice—her ostensibly realistic practice—presents a version of the real that, as many of her earliest readers understood, is effective because it eschews, in one way or another, the regulatory strategies that seek to cut reality down to size.

Picturesque Realism

The picturesque developed in the latter decades of the eighteenth century as an aesthetic alternative to the categories of the sublime and the beautiful articulated by Edmund Burke in his famous treatise on the subject. Objecting to the fact that Burke's conception of beauty as both uniform and smooth excluded many natural objects that were also beautiful for want of a better term, Gilpin came up with the idea of the picturesque, specifically the notion of "picturesque beauty," as an intermediate or extended category of taste. The ultimate object of Gilpin's modification was not, however, to redeem certain aspects of the physical world as beautiful. Rather, as Gilpin and his successors show again and again, the picturesque objective was to redefine and to recuperate beauty as a standard applicable to the roughness and variety of nature in its more adulterated, comparatively quotidian, manifestations.

Thus the privileged term in picturesque theory is not "beauty," which Price suggests be dispensed with altogether; the privileged term is "nature," which slides imperceptibly in picturesque theory (and as a measure of its privilege) into other totalizing terms such as "truth" or "reality." Unlike beauty, which is necessarily restrictive despite Gilpin's particular efforts to enlarge it, the concept of nature transforms in picturesque theory from a previously unappreciated aspect of the object world, into a totality—with picturesque nature becoming in

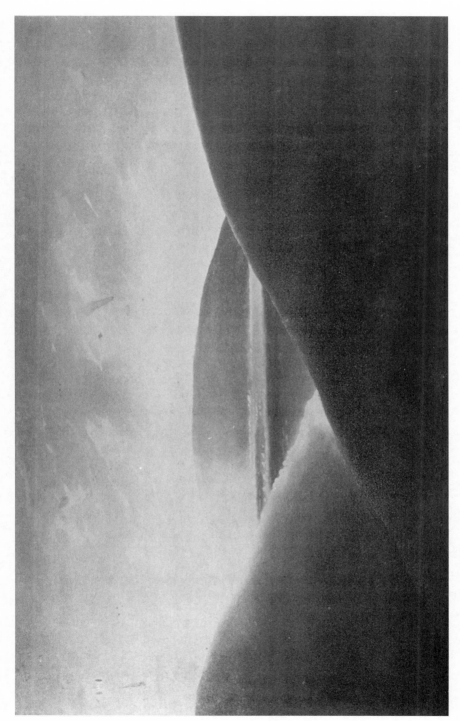

A beautiful landscape. William Gilpin, *Three Essays on Picturesque Beauty* (London, 1792). The Library Company of Philadelphia.

the process a synecdoche—in which a more comprehensive "real" is suddenly visible. An admittedly partial, hitherto marginalized, order of representable nature becomes under the aegis of the picturesque not just the only nature we know on earth; it becomes (to follow further with what may well have been Keats's critique of the picturesque muddling of beauty and truth) the only nature—or "all"—we apparently need to know.

Nowhere is the restrictive aspect of the picturesque more in evidence than in the analogies that picturesque theorists, notably Gilpin and Knight, make between landscape organization as they prescribe it, and narrative fiction, which they argue must be equally naturalized and made to conform to a similarly partial, if somehow accurate, conception of reality. The "naturalizing" tendencies of the picturesque (as Knight describes them [*The Landscape*, 159]) become in these analogies a virtual blueprint for realistic practice, both as it was becoming codified in narrative fiction at the time and, even more important, as it is increasingly understood in hindsight.

Theorists of the picturesque not only recommend representations of human and social life in narrative fiction that are natural yet limited; they also urge representations where the conflation of truth and subject matter serves specific social and ideological interests. In commenting on the correct procedures for sketching a landscape in the best of taste, Gilpin remarks, by way of analogy, that "correct taste cannot bear those unnatural situations, in which heroes, and heroines are often placed . . . whereas as a story, *naturally*, and of course *affectingly* told . . . tho known to be a fiction, is considered as a transcript of nature" (*Three Essays*, 53). In appealing to a consensus regarding what is natural in a given story or representation, Gilpin neatly transfers the burden of creating taste to a community already possessed of the taste to which Gilpin means somehow to enlighten them. Gilpin no doubt wants to strengthen his case by appealing to an already-established cultural authority, or to the community again that knows the difference between truth and falsehood. But he does this finally to normalize and obscure the limits already placed on the real by a now-mystified interpretive community, all of which is registered in the near (and characteristic) tautology that a story "naturally told" is "considered" by the community "a transcript of nature."

It is not my purpose to charge Gilpin and his colleagues with bad faith any more than I wish to credit him for exposing the fault lines in his theory so prominently that he may be enlisted, along with Kant, in the ranks of proto-postmodernists. Rather it is my purpose here to remark and to speculate on how an exposure to picturesque theory might have enlightened Austen to the uses and abuses of representation, particularly regarding any function that might be deemed realistic. Moreover, I suggest that Austen's well-documented

A picturesque landscape. William Gilpin, *Three Essays on Picturesque Beauty* (London, 1792). The Library Company of Philadelphia.

familiarity with the picturesque provoked her not only to a different *kind* of realism but also to a realism directed to a transformation of the very standards of
probability—the community standards, if you will—that both picturesque
theory and realistic practice alternately inculcate and uphold.[5]

I will have more to say about probability, as distinct from possibility, in the
next chapter. In the meantime it is worth noting that the consensus on which
the naturalness of a given representation depends, and to which Gilpin's theory
is directed, represents only *one* need of the community where matters of art are
concerned. As both Gilpin and Emma's nephews suggest, there is an appetite on
the part of many, including those who also know and respect the difference between truth and falsehood, for the extraordinary and the unnatural: for something so opposed to Gilpin's sense of nature or reality that he disparages it as an
intoxicant. "The *marvellous*," he writes, "disgusts the sober imagination; which
is gratified only with pure characters of nature" (53). Whether Gilpin is acknowledging a range of imaginative needs on the part of the individual subject, or
whether he means only to discipline the individual's imagination to essentially
one function and a single means of requital, is a secondary issue. At base in
Gilpin's discrimination is a hierarchy of orders and desires in which the probable is the only legitimate representation of life, whose privilege in turn is tied to
a suppression of the extraordinary and the improbable.

It would be acceptable, even desirable, for gypsies to be included in picturesque paintings, where they are composed of oil base and pigment and
have the value and the same "qualities" as "old hovels and mills" (Price, 76). But
it is completely unacceptable—given the limits placed by picturesque theory
on the improbable—for gypsies to materialize out of nowhere, especially in
surroundings that are themselves picturesque. Such a materialization accomplishes two things: it disrupts picturesque containment by addition of what
was otherwise improbable; and, as the Emma's nephews' resistance to their
aunt's narrativizing impulse shows, the gypsies' materialization contests the
consensus that apparently places limits on what is natural, expectable, and
properly desirable.

In practice the picturesque inoculates itself to such irruptions of the other,
and to such attenuation of the probable, by admission of tempered variety and
managed accident. "Picturesque composition," writes Gilpin, "consists in uniting in one whole a variety of parts; and these parts can only be obtained from
rough objects" (19). Something of the same obtains in *Emma*. While the irruption of the extraordinary in life infects the community in the novel, reducing
it to temporary juvenescence, such "roughness" simultaneously issues in what
Gilpin would deem a more salutary reaction: the "natural" fantasy of marital

union authored by Emma herself. That this narrative extension in the marriage plot resembles the kind of fiction that Jane Austen herself is usually assumed to have written—that is, domestic fiction "naturally told"—may also explain why the gypsies are no more a threat to the world of this novel than they are to the worlds in Thomas Gainsborough, George Morland, and others in whose images they frequently appear.

But Emma's more "natural" narrative also projects the gypsies' instrumentality in an order, or social hegemony, that requires, as surely as does the projected union of Harriet and Frank, that the gypsies be taken seriously: both as the extraordinary "other" that the community, like the picturesque, defines itself against; and as a potentially ordinary, more subjugated, other that the community, like the picturesque, wards off by somehow appropriating. Thus at the end of the novel—by which point Emma is herself subject to the very plot over which she had earlier contrived to exert control—the consummation of the story, and the strengthening of social hegemony through the consolidation of the Woodhouse and Knightley estates, is motivated by the reappearance of the gypsies. Although initially resistant to his daughter's marriage, as he is to almost any change in his everyday routine, Emma's valetudinarian father cheerfully consents to her marriage, and to the addition of George Knightley to his household, but only in the wake of a rash of poultry pilferages in his neighborhood, which Mr. Woodhouse is convinced are preliminary to housebreaking.

These pilferages—which are arguably the work of the gypsies (for there are no other suspects in the novel so far as I can tell)—are no more a threat to the social fabric of Highbury than they are likely to escalate to more invasive crimes that require, as the narrator puts it, a "son-in-law's protection" (440). Rather the thefts, however unanticipated, are a device, a contrivance really, by which a social whole, no less than an aesthetic one, perpetuates and legitimizes itself. Like the variety and activity that the picturesque composes into union, the gypsies' activities are in the end anticipated surprises: a feared and palpable "roughness" to which the community, no less than the realistic domestic comedy that Austen is alleged to have written (and to some extent *has* written here), is forever on the alert.

But this is not the "whole story," much less its "amount." As Austen's parting gesture in *Emma* also confirms, the social and aesthetic wholes in which the gypsies are required at some level to participate are clearly readable and transparent. They are readable to such effect thanks largely to the theories, at once aesthetic and political, whose injunctions regarding the other are a bulwark against change and against any practice that might be deemed oppositional.

The Politics of Picturesque

The analogy between picturesque landscape and realistic narrative was initiated, again, by the theorists themselves. But even in the absence of any direct commentary by Austen on these analogies, there is no doubt that such connections were both familiar and of real importance to her, if only in that she was developing a fictional mode very much akin to what Gilpin and Knight had

Engraving by John Wood after a lost painting by Thomas Gainsborough entitled *Gypsies.* British Museum.

urged writers to practice and contemporary readers to consume. As much as anything in picturesque theory itself, the analogies go a long way in explaining the many allusions to picturesque theory in Austen's fictions, whose prevalence has rendered her a witness on whom nearly every analysis of the picturesque draws in some way.[6] That the prevalence of picturesque theory in Austen's writings may also reflect a certain anxiety or dissatisfaction with some of the picturesque's more sinister operations (as I have touched on them) seems not to have occurred to anybody. This is so despite the fact that the picturesque is frequently an object of ridicule in Austen's fiction.[7] And it is so despite the fact that the contemporary response to Austen, by reviewers and common readers alike, was sharply divided between an endorsement of her realism in accordance with picturesque theory (for example, Scott's review of *Emma*) and a less disciplined recognition that her particular realism, far from domesticating or containing otherness, actually celebrated its uncanny prevalence in everyday life.

It is tendentious perhaps to assess Austen's accomplishments, much less her intentions, as a novelist on the basis of responses that are largely impressionistic. Nevertheless, the early responses to Austen's fictions, when weighed in conjunction with picturesque theory, constitute an important alternative to recent historiography, which increasingly regards Austen as a representative woman indelibly marked by the dominant discursive structures of her time.[8] A return to the original scene of reading Austen helps us better understand not just the contemporary response to her novels, particularly in conjunction with the more conservative responses that quickly followed, but also the various incentives to that response in the novels themselves. For if nothing else, the responses of Austen's earliest readers underscore her success in mediating and in resisting what was not only an imperative to fictions of probability at the time but also a charge that, for all its proclaimed neutrality or fidelity to nature, was directed toward the constitution of a society in which opposition, possibility, and novelty were to be contained.

It is one thing to claim, as some have, that Austen was astonishingly proleptic in her feminism and in her critique of both patriarchy and bourgeois hegemony.[9] It is quite a different thing to claim in hindsight that Austen's agency was oppositional at the time and quite deliberate. Such a claim does more than counter the tendency of the newer historicisms to limit the degree of agency that any historical subject can reliably claim or that we can claim on her behalf. It actually builds on these more sophisticated readings in making interpretation answerable to a history that in this case underscores Austen's oppositionality as we increasingly understand such matters.[10]

I have already mentioned the links that Gilpin makes between the representation of nature and what he regards as an equally natural representation of human life in narrative. But it is Gilpin's successors, Price and especially Knight, who make clearer what is at stake in their various injunctions for what Knight calls "poetical probability" (*An Analytical Inquiry*, 270). Although poetical probability appears to be nothing more than a quasi-formal or even practical injunction for consistency in language, sentiment, and action, it expands quickly into an argument for naturalization. In Knight's various appeals for naturalized productions, whether in improved nature or in the imitative arts, the proximity of a given embellishment to what he tendentiously calls "real nature" (329) accomplishes a double task. It succeeds in masking its motives and goals, most prominently the enclosure of property whose boundaries demarcating ownership are effectively drawn by nature itself in a properly improved landscape; and it obscures things, or at least how one looks at them, in the service of specific class and hegemonic interests.[11]

When Knight criticizes Samuel Richardson for having failed in *Clarissa* "to fill up properly and consistently those bold outlines of character," and singles out the character of Lovelace as "a vulgar tavern buck, who apes the more elegant and refined loquacity of the polished rake of fashion" (286), Knight is doing more than simply lamenting Richardson's bad ear and eye; he is also noting the author's insufficient familiarity with a certain class of persons whom Richardson can, as a result, only undermine or misrepresent.[12] To represent Lovelace accurately would introduce a level of admiration that is necessarily absent in *Clarissa* because its author simply does not know "the principles of good breeding or politeness" that are "the same in all ages and in all countries" (287). Thus what amounts in Richardson to an exposure and criticism of aristocratic libertinism is not an artistically or politically conscious decision on the novelist's part. It is chalked up to a deficiency of both knowledge and imitation that is subversive solely in the failure to recognize the transhistorical principles that only bad or unrealistic representations are likely to oppose.

The linkage of a representational practice with a hierarchy, where gradations of difference are suddenly coextensive with reality, or with nature properly rendered, is further shown in the similarities that Knight observes between fashions of landscape gardening, chiefly those followed by Lancelot "Capability" Brown and Humphry Repton, and certain French and English novels. In the same way that the new English garden does not always do a good enough job in uniting a great man to his property, usually by failing to obscure or to naturalize as effectively as possible his imposition on and control of the landscape, it is the case that certain modern fictions similarly attenuate their naturalizations.[13] Such fictions, that is, abandon their regulatory task of giving "useful knowledge and sound morality" (447) in the way they "relat[e], in intelligible language,

An estate landscaped in the style of the English garden. Charles Alphonse Du Fresnoy, *Art of Painting* (Dublin, 1783). The Library Company of Philadelphia.

events of familiar life"—albeit events that, as Knight cautions, are "not quite incredible, nor quite common" (445–46).

With respect to the landscape that bears too clearly the marks of enclosure and improvement, Knight recommends that novelty be replaced by intricacy and variety as picturesque theory warrants, adding that the function of proper gardening is to conceal the extent of a man's property by joining it to nature in the largest sense possible. In a landscape improved according to picturesque principles, "the spectator never knows when he has seen all; but still imagines that there are other beauties unrevealed" (442). Such a gesture does more than conceal the extent of a person's holdings; it effectively extends those holdings in making a person's specific property interchangeable with general nature. So too in fictions that embellish reality short of becoming unrealistic, the naturalizing imperative, which is adhered to in some measure (as it is in the comparatively "natural" gardens of Brown and Repton [see note 13]), does not provide sufficient protection against the tendency to fabulation that Knight deplores, and encourages a "sickly" or escapist "sensibility of mind . . . which cannot stoop to the tameness of reality, or the insipidity of common life" (446–47).

There would appear, of course, to be a real difference between "common life," as Knight urges its representation in narrative fiction, and the nature whose quotidian formation in landscape gardening is marked ideally by variety and contrast, thereby lending what Knight calls a charm of novelty (441). Yet these differences, however substantial, mark two routes to the same end. This end remains a society where universal deference is achieved either by masking the arbitrary gradations of authority and privilege, which other fashions of landscaping ostentatiously (even waggishly) expose, or by reconciling the mass of readers, many of them women, to a world of diminished expectations. Knight no doubt believes in the integrity of his social vision and its consistency with some natural or divine plan. But the increasingly problematic proximity of certain romantic or escapist fictions to "life" as he construes it, or of certain artificial improvements in the landscape to nature as such, expose a slippage in his position in which nature is pitted against a merely naturalized "real" limited to specific interests and needs.

It must also be observed, particularly in light of what Austen would have derived from picturesque theory, that the slippages in Knight's various conceptions of the natural do not materialize under pressure of an especially resistant reading of his commentary. They materialize because of the hegemonic disposition of the theory itself, where naturalization is part of a larger initiative for regulating change. This is made especially clear in a poem that Knight composed prior to his *Analytical Inquiry into the Principles of Taste*, whose very title—*The Landscape*—recapitulates picturesque theory in neatly eliding any difference

An estate landscaped according to picturesque principles. Charles Alphonse Du Fresnoy, *Art of Painting* (Dublin, 1783). The Library Company of Philadelphia.

between nature and naturalization. Recurring to the locus of (then) contemporary change, the French Revolution, Knight joins with Price, to whom the poem is addressed, in raising the specter of leveling to denigrate improvements in the landscape that, while probably undertaken by those with little stake in radical reform, are at odds with social hegemony.

Hegemony, as I am using it, is a profoundly functional mechanism precisely because, like either the picturesque or even the episode in *Emma*, it is sufficiently elastic to absorb and assimilate emergent and opposed elements.[14] In raising the specter of leveling as a reviled practice, picturesque theory installs itself as establishmentarian not by being reactionary (or opposed to displays of entrepreneurial gains) but by contradictorily claiming a truly progressive, more humane, affiliation. When Price decries the "levelling [of] all differences," by which landscape improvements currently in fashion manage to make "all places alike," and then likens this leveling to a "despotism" in which "selfish pride" holds unbridled sway in an ostentatious "parade of property" (381), he is doing more than enlisting the all-purpose pejorative of leveling to serve his argument. He is effectively working *both* ends of the political spectrum, declaiming against despotism as well as the "democratical" (380) tendencies that a more paternalistic stance, committed to the prerogatives of ownership, finds similarly anathema.[15]

This double move is repeated by Knight, who deplores the amount of blood spilled in the name of Christianity and, more recently, in the cause of revolution (235–36), but only as a prelude to inveighing against what he describes, with specific reference to landscape improvements, as the imposition of taste by rule (237). Knight's ecumenical history lesson necessarily obscures the difference between progressive and conservative initiatives (or even between different ideological initiatives within Christianity itself) in the service of what he calls "genuine liberty" (*The Landscape*, 73). By this he means something different from the apparently false liberty sought by those who also join him in their opposition to the vanity and pride of the wealthy. As a result the lengthy explanatory note on the French Revolution that Knight appends to *The Landscape*—describing it as the "most tyrannical, sanguinary, and atrocious, that ever desolated the human race" (73–74)—has only one function. This function is to shore up an order whose opposition to revolution is additionally mystified by its constitution as a libertarian whole composed of disparate parts. Like property improved in accordance with picturesque principles, humanity in Knight's seemingly democratic vista is no less a version of "true nature" in its variety and harmonious coexistence.

Much of what is contradictory in these ideological conflations may be explained by remembering the particular entitlements with which a liberal view, and thus the idea of liberty, consisted at this time. As John Barrell notes, the liberal view, and coincidentally the view of the picturesque traveler or beholder, is very much anchored in an "old sense" of liberal. Liberty, in this sense, is lodged in the franchise of the individual beholder, and holder of property, rather than in a more universal view, where the prerogatives of beholding are suddenly available to those subjects, often the erstwhile objects, who fall within the liberal beholder's ken and control.[16]

This connection between liberty and ownership is crucial in recognizing the political backgrounds of picturesque theory, which, as Barrell further notes, seeks to privilege the concerns of the gentleman (96). Nevertheless it is a connection sorely tried by the inclusion of revolutionary ideology in picturesque discourse. While there is no doubt that picturesque theory means to naturalize the claims of ownership following the needs of liberals in the "old sense," it also seeks, in attacking revolutionary despotism, to appeal to liberals or progressives in a somewhat newer sense. Even as picturesque theory may have looked less problematic or less contradictory to contemporary readers, it was tendentious in its claims and sufficiently opportunistic in occupying every high ground currently available, to give someone like Jane Austen pause. As Austen develops as a novelist she takes measures to oppose her style, particularly free indirect style, to a liberal vantage in the old sense and to the aesthetic directives that serve it. One of the ways she does this is by showing that not everything that is representable is immediately comprehensible to her narrator much less subject to that narrator's acts of containment or interpretation.

Reading for Particulars

An important task of the succeeding chapters in this book will be to outline the differences between Austen's oppositional and frequently uncontainable realism and the conventional or codified realism of which picturesque theory remains a blueprint. However, to return briefly to the episode with which we began, it is worth noting that the narrator's attention to Emma's narratological impulse, and the anatomy of picturesque realism this excursus offers, follows the main character in failing to achieve the sovereign intelligence and control to which it aspires. There are, in short, elements in this episode that plainly elude the narrator no less than Emma herself. They involve specifically the activities of Frank Churchill, who, though a crucial component of the real in this text, is not always comprehensible or transparent in the way nature or reality is supposedly to a realistic vantage. The majority of these incomprehensible activities, chiefly the shuttle diplomacy in which (as it is only later disclosed) Frank was presumably engaged at the very juncture that he is also unsuccessfully emplotted by Emma, are all directed toward his eventual marriage to Jane Fairfax. This is hardly a coincidence. In opposing social hegemony—and by implication the Emma-Knightley union—in its functional dispersal of property and power, Frank's eventual marriage to a woman in economic distress is additionally (and aesthetically) oppositional in its vitiation of the control figured jointly by an omniscient narrator and her decidedly less omniscient protagonist.

In other words, despite all that *Emma* provides the reader by way of understanding the world it represents, it does not extend or govern that understanding sufficiently to contain the practices of characters who are plainly less reconciled to society than are other characters. Numerous incidents and elements in the novel, including the famous Box Hill episode—which turns out to be a different "sort of gipsy party" than the one Mrs. Elton tellingly imagines (320)—yield up possibilities to which the reader is never directly guided by the narrator, yet to which, on subsequent readings, she is likely to be more attentive. In the very way that Frank Churchill is free to roam the prison house of the language of this novel, it is to Austen's purpose to make the experience or consumption of the text a practice as little oriented by control as either Frank's or even the novelist's.[17]

But there is also a difference between these various practices. In putting her writing at the disposal of readers in this way, Austen allows the reader to construe a work like *Emma* in whatever way the reader chooses, which not infrequently involves ascribing to her fictions a regulatory or didactic function. Far from always opposing the liberal vantage of a controlling intelligence, reading can also figure the field of discipline that the text in consequence must negotiate on its own, since it is the paradoxical feature of Austen's practice as a writer that her reader can, if he or she elects, give the narrator, who seemingly knows all, the last word. Correspondingly, to read *Emma*, or for that matter any text of Austen's, *oppositionally* requires that the narrator's words—and the reality they disclose—be reduced to words, or to particulars, rather than expanded to a more unified vision undergirded by plot. It is this reduction to particularity, and the uncanniness achieved through a largely antipicturesque highlighting of detail, that is reflected in much contemporary response to Austen's writing. In observation after observation, by reviewers and common readers alike, the uncanny experience of reading Austen—frequently by the designation "amusement"—is equally remarkable in refusing to credit the author with any aim beyond the interest she brings to an admittedly narrow sphere of life.

In presenting such a reality Austen would appear to have represented the very "real" that Knight urges when he complains of largely realistic fictions that wander into fabulation by gilding "familiar life" with "events" that are "not quite common" (445–46). Yet on the basis of those readers who knew very well the everyday aspects of life at this time, it is clear that Austen's fictions do not at all satisfy Knight's related injunction in also stooping to the "tameness of reality, or insipidity of common life" (447). This last, to be sure, involves some projection on Knight's part regarding the contempt in which ordinary life is seemingly held by many contemporary readers and writers. Still, when taken in conjunction with Knight's less ironic charge that such fictions are averse to "the acquisition of all useful knowledge and sound morality" (447), the stooping to reality, no matter how draconian or condescending, seems exactly what Knight has in mind for fiction and what Austen, in contrast, seems to have found a way around.

This difference should not surprise us. Although Austen's fictions, with their recourse to the ostensibly probable, can be read didactically, or as fictions that instruct women to live within their means, they can be and were read against the grain of those plots by which fictions of probability were to have persuaded readers to presumably better values than fictions of extravagance. Thus it is a measure of Austen's oppositionality as a writer, and of the reading practices that her writings encouraged, that she was able apparently to resist the realistic imperative, the imperative to probability, without also resorting to romance or the unreal.

On the contrary it was Austen's purpose to work the peculiar interface of probability and possibility, or what to her bemused readers often seemed an uncanny amalgam of familiarity and strangeness, in the most routine, everyday experiences. This becomes evident when we weigh Austen's accomplishment as a writer (as attested to by her earliest readers) along with and against theories of representation advocated not just by picturesque advocates but also by such proponents of realism as Frances Burney, Clara Reeve, and Anna Barbauld. These theories and the regulatory aims they serve are crucial to appreciating how, in recalling readers to the otherness that is near at hand, or to the variation that inhabits routine, Austen advocates change through the entirely disarming gesture of actually showing it: both in the practices of characters like Frank or even Miss Bates and, more important, in the recalcitrant practices of reading to which her writing is continually available.

Austen's Earliest Readers

If, for proponents of realism, it was the function of probability to inculcate deferential behavior of one sort or another, it was the *effect* of Austen's fictions to problematize the link between realism and social control. The reviews and comments regarding Austen's earliest published works, *Sense and Sensibility* (1812) and *Pride and Prejudice* (1813), seem almost split at times between the obligation to credit these works with a didactic purpose (which their prescriptive titles encourage) and a nearly transgressive attention to particularity independent of either plot or instruction.[18] The typically unsigned reviews of *Sense and Sensibility* in the *Critical Review* (Feb. 1812) and the *British Critic* (May 1812) are suspended between commending the "benefits" that female readers in particular will derive from "these volumes" (40) and a less determinate sense of the "satisfaction" (40), pleasure and interest (35) that owes to particular incidents and to the accuracy of their depiction. This view is echoed in the only known contemporary observation on the novel from beyond the Austen circle—that of Lady Bessborough—who, in a letter to a friend, recommended *Sense and Sensibility*, which she found "amus[ing]" despite what she described as its "stupi[d]" ending.[19] Assuming that this sense of an ending accords with a sense of plot— or with a trajectory that to one degree or other echoes the Richardsonian topos of "virtue rewarded"—Lady Bessborough sounds a theme repeated by reviewers and lay readers alike: the suasive or ideological work of an Austen text, insofar as it is achieved through story, is somehow at crosspurposes with other aspects and particulars, notably the vignettes of incidental characters that captivate by other means and to other, less immediately comprehensible, effects.

This pattern is particularly evident in the responses to *Pride and Prejudice*, which was more widely read than *Sense and Sensibility* and more variously appreciated. Nevertheless, in the unsigned notices of the novel in the two periodicals already mentioned, the disjunction of plot and character, or between a simple story of "no great variety" (*British Critic* [Feb. 1813]) and the various elements whose depiction yielded "satisfaction and amusement," is again paramount (41–42). Both reviews stress the representative nature of scenes and characters while remarking at the same time on the curiously exemplary nature of these same elements. The *Critical Review* (Mar. 1813) lauds the portrayal of characters (not "one [of] . . . which appears flat") and the "delineation of domestic scenes" (47), and the *British Critic* singles out the "result" of the Bennet sisters' visit "to the market town where officers are quartered" as being "exemplified in every provincial town in the kingdom" (42). While the last observation certainly implies a didactic function to Lydia Bennet's eventual flight with the young officer Wickham (which the *Critical Review* actually calls a "lesson" [46]), it attests, just as important, to the accuracy of the observation itself, subordinating any exemplum to the pleasure inherent in the novel's representation. The one other known review of *Pride and Prejudice* is less attuned to these virtues and to their variance from plot. In fact the notice in the *New Review* (Apr. 1813) is given over entirely to plot summary. Ignoring virtually everyone and everything in *Pride and Prejudice* beyond its two main characters, the *New Review*'s account typically narrows the fiction to its didacticism or instruction—specifically the praise and blame that are consistent with a "story" that, as the *British Critic* had already noted, lacks variety.[20]

This more conventional sense of *Pride and Prejudice*, tied to the interest generated by the novel's story and by the marriage plot, is registered in lay readings as well. Annabella Milbanke, soon to be Lady Byron, remarked that while *Pride and Prejudice* was "not a crying book," the "interest" in the novel is "very strong, especially for Mr. Darcy."[21] As Milbanke's notion of interest implies, the plot of the novel constructs Darcy as a desirable mate for the heroine so that their eventual marriage, in which Elizabeth is both rewarded *and* re-warded, concomitantly serves the landed or paternalistic interests for which "Mr. Darcy" (not to mention his picturesque estate) functions as an endorsement. Whether this aspect of the novel consists with the other virtues to which Milbanke also attests—its rendering of the everyday ("no drownings, nor conflagrations, nor runaway horses") and the "diver[sion]" that its less "amiable," if "consistently supported," characters also furnish—is another matter.

In fact the "diverting" aspects of the novel that Milbanke simultaneously commends are as she dubs them: they are *divergences* both from plot and from the interests that Darcy commands and serves. This view of the novel is reiterated by John William Ward, the earl of Dudley, who found the novel remarkable not for its hegemonic work but solely (or so it seems) for its representation of the obsequious, fawning Collins. "Have you had 'Pride and Prejudice,'" he wrote to Helen Darcy Stewart, "there is a parson in it quite admirable."[22] By "admirable" Ward differs from later readers, who universally loathe Collins and the upward mobility he embarrassingly figures, in referring only to the fact that his character is well drawn—and with an acuity sufficient to deflect attention from the novel's story line. In a similar vein Maria Edgeworth noted in a letter that she had been reading the novel while traveling, where she was interrupted only by "corn fields—broad wheeled wagons and gentlemen's fine seats."[23] Although such comments are, with specific reference to the novel, a little opaque, the peculiar contest of absorption and distraction seems as much a conflict between book and world as a tension alternatively stimulated by the experience of the text itself, which is continuous with the world in its fascination with detail.

A similar perplexity afflicts Jane Davy, the wife of Humphry Davy, who confessed her dislike of the novel to Sarah Ponsonby, one of the famed ladies of Llangollen. "Want of interest," she opines, "is the fault I can least excuse in works of mere amusement, and however natural the picture of vulgar minds and manners there is given, it is unrelieved by the agreeable contrast of more dignified and refined characters occasionally captivating attention."[24] Like

Milbanke, Davy notes a tension in *Pride and Prejudice* between the interest provoked by admirable characters (among whom she undoubtedly means Darcy)
and the distraction, the noncaptivating attention, provided by other characters,
who are functionally opposed to them. However, unlike Milbanke, who is happily struck by the tension of "interest" and "diversion" in the text, Davy decries
the novel's divergence from the more conventional task of instruction by "dignified" and "refined" example, which is the only proper end, she suggests, of
natural or realistic writing.

There is little doubt that of all of Austen's novels *Pride and Prejudice* is the
most interesting or persuasive in the way that Jane Davy recommends. Thus it is
a measure of Austen's unorthodox and unsettling practice as a realist that Davy
would be so put off by what is arguably Austen's most successfully conservative
work. Nor is it any less a sign of the errancy of Austen's technique, with its remarkable divergence from plot and from the interest that story sustains, that
her succeeding and ostensibly most didactic novel—*Mansfield Park*—elicited,
in the majority of recorded observations by contemporaries, a nearly opposite
reaction.

There are no known contemporary reviews of *Mansfield Park*, which is
somewhat surprising given both Austen's growing popularity and the fact that
her novels were now being brought out in quick succession. Nevertheless,
among the contemporary comments that have been recovered, including those
by relatives and acquaintances of the author whose opinions Austen actively
solicited, there is remarkable consensus regarding the source and nature of
the novel's interest, which is the "natural[ness]" (as Austen's brother Frank
put it [13]) of both characterization and depiction of incident.[25] Such appreciation of the novel's verisimilitude occasionally flattens into opinions, pro and
con, on the disposition of the novel's characters, notably Mrs. Norris. But
among those who hazard a more developed opinion, generally by contrasting
Mansfield Park with *Pride and Prejudice*, the novel's virtues center generally on
the density and inscrutability of its real, which plainly lacks the embellishments
of the earlier and (by most accounts) cleverer text. There are, of course, those in
the Austen circle who prefer the new novel on account of its moral theme. Yet
among the majority who admire it for other, less determinate reasons, it is the
attention to the everyday aspects of "common life" (as Lady Gordon discerned
[17]) or the accuracy of its representations—which, as Mrs. Pole noted, confirmed the author's "*belong*[ing] to the Society whose Manners she so ably
delineates" (17)—that remains the novel's strength.

Furthermore, among contemporary readers in general, there is surprisingly little admiration of the very didacticism that Jane Davy, despite designating it a work of mere amusement, found insufficient evidence of in the more

humorous *Pride and Prejudice.* Lady Vernon compared the novel favorably to one by Burney (it is unclear which), praising *Mansfield Park* as "not much of a novel" but "more the history of a family party in the country, very natural, and the characters well drawn."[26] Similarly, Anne Romilly, in extolling the novel's virtues to Maria Edgeworth, preferred it to Scott's *Waverley,* which she disliked for being too much a novel and too concerned with its hero rather than with "general manners." Romilly goes on to say that a good novel "must . . . be true to life, which this is, with a good story vein of principle running thro' the whole." Although also lacking in this vein of principle or in the "elevation of virtue" or "something beyond nature" that "gives the greatest charm to a novel," *Mansfield Park* remains, to its particular credit, "real natural every day life, and will amuse an idle hour very well in spite of its faults."[27] It initially appears that Romilly admires *Mansfield Park* for its realism and for its story, which she characteristically attaches to its "principle" or moral point. However, as she details her position, it is clear not only that *Mansfield Park* satisfies almost exclusively on the grounds of verisimilitude, but more importantly that the novel's effect—or pleasure—consists in something quite apart from realism as Romilly wants it practiced.

Contemporary observations seem alert, then, to the tendency of Austen's fictions to frustrate expectations without also losing interest. According to these accounts, interest in Austen's writings is invariably directed to aspects of everyday life, which are successful in diverting attention from the didacticism ordinarily upheld by "story" in its distribution of praise and reward. Jane Davy may have complained about the relative dearth of exemplary characters in *Pride and Prejudice* from whom the reader might take instruction. But she could not resist commenting on the "power of new character," as she termed it, which is "ably displayed" and shown to particular advantage in "Mr. Bennet's indifference" that "in truth" is "not exaggeration" (351).

Whether such muted social criticism as Davy derives from the more diverting aspects of *Pride and Prejudice* can be deemed oppositional is another issue and one that can be assessed only through a more detailed examination of the novel. Yet withal we must not forget that the defining condition of the everyday practice that de Certeau calls oppositional lies in its tactical ability to elude a discipline. Such practices are practices of the weak, which, even on the part of those as privileged as Austen's female contemporaries, appear to take the form here of a secret or guilty reading. Such reading, in other words, contrasts with the relatively empowered modes of response that de Certeau (following Karl von Clausewitz) terms strategic, where reading follows other practices of dominance in being regulatory and otherwise aligned with a disciplinary regime. The reading practices to which Austen's writing was available at its inception were palpably a counter, then, to more determinate practices, both social and aesthetic, that are almost never, on the evidence of much contemporary testimony, universally met. This becomes quite evident in the controversy that develops in the responses to Austen's fourth and (in her lifetime) most successful work, *Emma*. Not only does *Emma* occasion the first truly comprehensive assessments of its author's career to date; it also provokes certain readers, notably Walter Scott, who reviewed the novel anonymously but influentially in the *Quarterly Review* (Mar. 1816), to an assessment of domestic fiction and realistic practice generally, to which Austen's writing gives critical, if by no means consistent, testimony.

The Response to *Emma*

Unlike some of Austen's lay readers, who recognized her divergence from realistic practice as it had been prescribed and defined at the time, Scott may well have been the first to install Austen as the realist par excellence. In addition to noting the recent development of a "class of fictions . . . which draws the characters and incidents introduced more immediately from the current of ordinary life than was permitted by the former rules of the novel" (59), Scott is remarkably candid in outlining and privileging the present "rules" of the novel. These last demand a more faithful adherence to "probability" that had been previously "transgress[ed]" in favor of "possibility" (61), but which in the "[new] style of novel" is ably served by "presenting to the reader, instead of the splendid scenes of an imaginary world, a correct and striking representation of that which is daily taking place around him" (63).

In using "striking" to describe the daily life represented in fictions such as *Emma*, Scott comes very close to identifying the more diverting aspects of Austen's real, especially when measured against the aims of realistic practice and its vitiation of "possibility." Scott continues in this vein, explicitly crediting "the author of *Emma*" with "keeping close to common incidents, and to such characters as occupy the ordinary walks of life," as a result of which "she has produced sketches of such spirit and originality, that we never miss the excitation which depends upon a narrative of uncommon events, arising from the consideration of minds, manners, and sentiments, greatly above our own" (63–64).

With the admission of a notion such as "excitation," which is *apparently* a yield (albeit by different means) of Austen's uncanny attention to the "middling" walks of life (64), Scott approaches once again the divergent effects of Austen's representational technique. Yet the hierarchy he invokes in alluding to the minds and manners "above our own" is not simply at crosspurposes with the more original, less determinate, aspects of Austen's practice as he construes them. It is perfectly consistent with the regulatory or deferential ends of a practice in fiction that works less by a fidelity to life than by a process of naturalization, where representations are kept "close to common incidents" by a controlling *and controlled* authorial hand.

Thus it is a feature of Austen's fictions (and the realistic practice they embody) that they "inculcate" a "moral" that "applies equally to the paths" of what Scott—following Richard Payne Knight—patronizingly calls "common life" (64). At this point Scott departs from the acuity of Austen's depiction of common life to discuss her plots or what he calls the "narrative of all her novels" (64). This departure proves to be a telling move. In generalizing Austen's plots into one narrative, Scott implicitly places plot or story at odds with other elements that comprise Austen's originality. Furthermore, he actually widens the gap between the regulatory work of Austen's plots, which he endorses, and the uncanny possibility that also haunts the probable world in her novels, by getting at least two of the three plots he discusses wrong.

While Scott's description of the story of *Sense and Sensibility* merely reduces the novel to its basic elements in observing that Marianne Dashwood "is turned wise by precept, example, and experience" (64), he significantly misrepresents the plot of *Pride and Prejudice.* In remarking that "after some essential services rendered to [Elizabeth's] family," Darcy becomes "encouraged to renew his addresses, and the novel ends happily" (65), Scott elides the fact that the Darcy-Elizabeth connection is effectively resolved with nearly a third of the novel left to go and that the eventual happy ending owes largely to their joint containment of Lydia's sexuality and Wickham's roguery. Nor does Scott fare much better with *Emma* when, in summarizing the narrative, he implies that the concealment of Frank's "affair" is known to the reader—and, by implication, to the narrator—well in advance of its eventual disclosure.[28]

That these misrepresentations involve aspects of the two novels, specifically the transgressions of Frank and Lydia, that delimit and contest the regulatory reach of their story lines is hardly surprising. After all, it is one function of plot in Austen to work, as Sandra Gilbert and Susan Gubar noted some time ago, as something of a cover story. Still, as Scott demonstrates, it is also a function of Austen's highly unorthodox practice that her cover stories never adequately cover. This failure occurs because "the narrative of all her novels" is continually tried by the details of all her novels—what Scott calls the "minute detail"—from which, he contends, "the faults of the author," and of *Emma* in particular, "arise" (67–68).

In the case of *Emma* these faults center largely on the depictions of Emma's father and Miss Bates: two characters, it is worth noting, whose own preoccupation with detail effectively recapitulates the work of Austen's real overall in bringing the narrative of *Emma* to a grinding halt. In contrast to these faults, where the novel is reduced to words or to details that are readable yet ungoverned, the apparent virtues of "the author's novels" consist in an ordering of detail explicitly akin to a landscape improved according to *picturesque* principles. Austen's novels bear "the *same* relation" to improbable or sensational fiction "that cornfields and cottages and meadows bear to the highly adorned grounds of a show mansion, or the rugged sublimities of a mountain landscape." They bear this relation thanks to their largely naturalizing tendencies, where the "pleasure [of reading] is *nearly allied* with the experience of [one's] own social habits," allowing one to return from the act of reading (or from "promenad[ing]" as the picturesque analogy warrants) "without any chance of having his head *turned* by the recollection of the scene through which he has been wandering" (68, emphasis added).

In attesting to the invisible, yet profoundly coercive, work of naturalization, Scott offers an anatomy of realism as much as he offers a defense. In so defending realistic practice, and in this case Austen's practice, with the proviso that it be shorn somehow of its more troublesome complications, Scott does more than simply join with picturesque theory in making realism an armature of social hegemony. He departs from the majority of Austen's other readers either in discrediting or in seeking to appropriate the more antithetical aspects of her writing. This is not to say that other contemporaries are not similarly divided in their appreciation of the different registers and kinds of "interest" generated by Austen's works. It is just that virtually no other contemporary reader is as transparent as Scott in the effort to bend Austen's works—and the work of domestic fiction generally—to a purpose to which Austen's novels are, by Scott's *own* observations, opposed.

Scott would later change his views regarding Austen, opening them to precisely the elements he had touched on but had resisted in his initial appreciation. There were, in any case, a good many readers and reviewers of *Emma* for whom no revision of this sort would be necessary. The *British Critic* (July 1816) commented approvingly on the novel's contracted space of "unity," adding that "we know not of one [novel] in which the author has sufficient art to give interest to the circle of a small village." In addition, the unsigned review singles out for special commendation the very details—"the valetudinarian fathe[r]" and the "chattering village belles"—that Scott identified as the novel's faults, yet whose approval here is clearly of a piece with the review's other observation that the novel is neither moralistic nor "fanatical" (71). This praise is echoed in virtually all the reviews of *Emma*, where the "interest" generated by plot and theme is almost always subordinated to the interest given to everyday particularity in the novel.

One review in particular—that in the *Champion* (Mar. 1816)—comes closest to articulating the oppositional yield that Scott sought either to transfigure or to discredit.[29] As with most reviews of *Emma*, the *Champion* begins by commending Austen's "skill" in "representing objects of an ordinary, and at the same time so familiar a nature" (469). The review expands quickly to a more sustained articulation of the uncanny aspects of Austen's writing, where the familiar (as the initial observation already implies) is distinct from the ordinary, reflecting an otherness close at hand. Noting that the author "presents nature and society in very unornamented hues," the review resists crediting the novel for its naturalizing work, adding that the "force of nature" is "so strong" that "few can take up her work without finding a rational pleasure in the recognitions which cannot fail to flash upon them of the modes of thinking and feeling which experience every day presents in real life" (470).

In one sense the *Champion* is simply crediting the verisimilitude of *Emma*, where there is essentially no break between book and world. Yet it is clear that the power of verisimilitude, with its necessary structure of difference, admits a flash of recognition that transforms familiar experience into something seen and understood anew. Far from a strategy of containment, or naturalization, Austen's real—the "real life" to which her novel directs the reader—is (to borrow Scott's own image) a reality to which one is somehow wrenched or "turned" rather than reconciled.

The *Champion* describes this recognition as a "rational pleasure," which may well be a bit of damage control, given the irrational or uncanny pleasure of Austen's text as it is described here. Nevertheless such reflection as the novel apparently encourages is also severely rational in a critical sense: both in the kinds of insights it furnishes—for example, the sense that the utterly compliant Mrs. John Knightley is "just perhaps what a wife ought to be . . . sufficiently sensible—not at all clever—of a small mind which the ties and duties of domestic life abundantly fill" (473)—as well as in its opposition to an aesthetic practice that would divest details of the ability either to stimulate change through "rational pleasure" or, as the case may be, to exemplify it in everyday life. Thus the reviewer in the *Champion* moves from the example of *Emma* to a theory of the novel, specifically the new novel, which is described as "fictitious biography" in contrast to romance or what the review terms "fictitious history" (473).

In distinguishing the novel as biography from the novel as history, the *Champion* resorts to a fairly common distinction where the genre of history is aligned with epic in its representation of great events and figures and in being removed from the practice of everyday life. Even as the *Champion* contrasts the domestic novel with other representations taken up with events and actions that the majority of readers will never witness, much less initiate, it does not undervalue either what a novel like *Emma* necessarily chooses for its subject matter or the ultimate importance of that subject matter for contemporary and future readers.

It is more that the domestic novel figures a new and alternative history or what can be termed, once again, a history of the present. This new history is important both in its attention to the significance of individual lives (no matter seemingly insignificant) and in the related implication that such attention will—in a flash of recognition—disclose the difference that a given person can and often does make:

To the historian's generalizing eye, unobtrusive virtue presents few features of prominence or splendour;—but the novelist has the licence of ranging into the recesses of domestic life, and of distinguishing the *actions* of the mind, the temper, and the feelings. Surveyed in this microscopic detail, characters which, to a more sweeping observer, furnish only the uniform outlines of virtue and worth, will always be found to exhibit sufficiently distinctive traits of mental and moral individuality, to answer all an author's objects of giving them a personal identity and relief. (473)

On the face of it the *Champion* is making a typically humanistic connection between "historical" figures, whose "actions" are visible even in "a wide survey of events," and characters whose more internal actions are invisible to such a vantage, yet are by implication just as important. Still, the connection here between the agency of the ordinary person and the particular perspective in which that agency is brought into palpable relief, propels the argument in a different direction altogether. Among other things the writing of conventional history recapitulates the very realistic or picturesque practices—practices at once representational and social—that create order at the expense of detail and preserve hierarchies through the maintenance of deferential behavior.

By contrast the domestic novel, and *Emma* in particular, resist this containment through a different kind of attention wherein individual action, rather than the equivalent of great action, remains an activity whose effectiveness is not only invisible to and at odds with the "sweeping" survey but inextricably connected to a covert or microscopic formation. Far from leveling the distinction between great and ordinary action, the domestic novel ideally preserves their difference, and the relative prestige accorded each, in disclosing practices that other versions of art contain either by ignoring or by appropriating to more didactic and narratable ends. Or to put it even more pointedly: as a specimen of fictitious biography, *Emma* represents the oppositional practices of everyday life oppositionally.

The *Champion* may well be unique in its reasoned appreciation of the peculiar agency of Austen's characters and of her writing in general. However, it is no less representative in identifying the kind of work that, as other readers con-firm, *Emma* succeeds in performing, if not always to their delight and gratifica-tion. Maria Edgeworth, to whom Austen sent a copy of *Emma*, managed only to get through the first volume and passed the remaining two volumes to a friend unread, warning that "there was no story in it, except that Miss Emma found that the man whom she designed for Harriets lover was an admirer of her own—& he was affronted at being refused by Emma & Harriet wore the willow—and *smooth, thin water-gruel* is according to Emma's father's opinion a very good thing & it is very difficult to make a cook understand what you mean by smooth thin water gruel."[30] The movement here from plot—specifically the marriage plot—to detail, which Edgeworth, despite ridiculing, cannot resist re-hearsing with equal scrupulousness, is instructive. Her Miss Bates–like response actively recapitulates the novel's attention to the detritus of everyday life by showing the impact that such a focus, although unappreciated in this instance, necessarily makes.

This decided, if unwanted, impact of the novel is also noted in a letter to Edgeworth by her friend Anne Romilly, who after expressing sympathy with Lady Byron in the wake of her separation from Lord Byron, turns to the more mundane matters of *Emma* and another novel whose identity is unclear. "In the first [novel]," complains Romilly, "there is so little to remember, and in the last so much one wishes to forget, that I am inclined not to write about them" (*Romilly-Edgeworth Letters*, 143). Compared to the Byron affair, the quotidian details of middling gentry life in Austen's work may well seem forgettable. Yet Romilly manages, by a logic of negation where the forgettable is sufficiently memorable to be forgettable, to affirm the unsettling aspect of this kind of text. While put off by *Emma* as she is by bad romance (as the other, unnamed work purports to be), Romilly confirms *Emma*'s failure at the very processes for which Scott commends it, yet whose absence in this instance proves a challenge to both Romilly *and* her friend.

Finally, Susan Ferrier, a novelist in her own right, remarks in a letter that she has "been reading 'Emma,' which is excellent; there is no story whatever, and the heroine is no better than other people; but the characters are all so true to life, and the style is so piquant, that it does not require the adventitious aids of mystery and adventure."[31] In centering on the piquancy of Austen's style Ferrier is referring to what another Austen contemporary, Thomas Moore, praised as the "effect" in *Emma* achieved by the "method of describing things."[32] With its necessary connection to a narrative independent of story, Ferrier's "piquancy of style" points to the narrative in description, whose peculiar "truth," following the *Champion*, is more a flash of pleasurable recognition.

There are other reviews of *Emma* that I have not touched on, along with

other contemporary comments, including reactions to the novel that Austen solicited herself as she did those to *Mansfield Park*.[33] While some of these depart
from the more telling observations that I have been examining, they do not vary
sufficiently or substantially to warrant fuller treatment. The opinions that
Austen solicited range from the opinions of those who do not like the new novel
as much as the previous novels; to the opinions of those who, like Scott, admire
its naturalizing and moralizing tendencies; to those who join with the majority
of respondents in being put off by the many details (especially the particulars
recounted by Miss Bates) and by the relative lack of incident in the text; to those
who are struck by what Frank Austen, among his sister's most discerning
readers, called "its peculiar air of Nature" (*Plan of a Novel*, 19). In the end,
though, the majority of responses to *Emma* attest to a narrative practice whose
"effect," for better or for worse, is as striking in its attention and as it is frequently unsettling.

The Posthumously Published Novels

The joint publication of *Northanger Abbey* and *Persuasion* in 1818, shortly after
Austen's death in the summer of 1817, was met with responses freighted by a
sense of loss and by the premature obligation to put the author's accomplishment overall in a larger perspective. These initiatives, unfortunately, were too
well served by the preemptive biographical note appended to the volumes by
Austen's brother Henry. Criticism is rarely accurate or discriminating when it
must accede to such apparently authoritative observations as those with which
Henry concluded his brief essay: "One trait only remains to be touched on. It
makes all others unimportant. She was thoroughly religious and devout; fearful
of giving offence to God, and incapable of feeling it towards any fellow creature.
On serious subjects she was well-instructed, both by reading and meditation,
and her opinions accorded strictly with those of our Established Church."[34] While
Austen's regard for her "fellow creatures" accords well with her regard for the
activity of ordinary individuals as it had been noted by readers before, the deference by which her view of life was apparently directed made it difficult for
readers and critics to credit the less determinate effects of her writing in the
posthumously published works. Their response was hampered further by the
disparate character of the novels under consideration. The *British Critic* (Mar.
1818) did well under the circumstances in widening its notice to a general assessment of Austen's representational technique. Despite emphasizing Austen's preoccupation with everyday life—which the review insists must have been drawn
exclusively from her experience—the *Critic* is ultimately suspended between a

recognition of the uncanny power of Austen's verisimilitude, chiefly the "unaccountable pleasure" derived from her "simple imitation of [an] object," and the need to account for the notable absence of narrative in *Northanger Abbey* or, as the review puts it, for the unabstractable nature of that novel's contents (81–82).

Blackwood's (May 1818) fares somewhat better in underscoring the "singular," indeed alternative, "history" that the novels constitute, noting that "any one of her fictions" could "be realized in any town or village in England," so much "that we think we are reading the history of people whom we have seen thousands of times" (267). And yet "with all this perfect commonness, both of incident and character, perhaps not one of her characters is to be found in any other book, portrayed at least in so lively and interesting a manner" (267). In recognizing that Austen's "history" is not a matter of "simple imitation" but of an attention sufficiently heightened and microscopic to invest the probable with a greater range and possibility, *Blackwood's* follows very much on the heels of the *Champion* in noting Austen's singularity as a realist. In addition *Blackwood's* departs—predictably enough from observations made in the *Quarterly Review* by Scott and later Bishop Whatley—in noting both the absence of plot as well as the novels' failure to "display . . . religious sentiments and opinions" (268). Somewhat pressured by Henry Austen's biographical notice, which it paraphrases at length, the review concludes by asserting that Austen's novels are indeed shaped by "the spirit of Christianity" (268). But this last is clearly an occasional imperative at odds with the more incisive conception of Austen's unconventional and uncanny realism.

Not so Richard Whatley, whose anonymous review (Jan. 1821) of the last published novels three years after their initial appearance accords with that of his predecessor in the *Quarterly*, Walter Scott, in lauding their regulatory and naturalizing aspects. Beginning by actually quoting Scott on the "new style of novel," Whatley proceeds to an appreciation of the instructive elements in works such as Austen's that follow "the general rules of probability" (88). Reluctant, unlike either the *Champion* or *Blackwood's,* to credit Austen's as an alternative history, focusing on the unrecognized agents in the world, Whatley subscribes to the customary hierarchy separating the writing of history from that of narrative fiction in crediting Austen with having provided an exemplary "mode[l] of real life" (88) capable of producing the "instruction which used to be presented to the world . . . in moral essays" (92). Such emphasis on Austen's didacticism does more than divest both Austen and the "new style of novel" of the various effects wrought by a broadening or attenuation of everyday life and activity. It proves the basis of an even larger critique, where Whatley is disposed not only to discredit novels that bear insufficient relation to what he dogmatically calls " real life" (93) but also to echo Knight in describing as "pernicious" novels "which differ from common life in little or nothing but the improbability of the occurrences" (89).

Predicated on the assumption that novels that are all but probable will likely imbue people, especially women, with expectations that eventually lead to harm, Whatley's criticism also broaches that other structure of "difference," where ordinary life resists a merely probable constitution in producing a less determinate shock of pleasurable recognition. Although Whatley would like his readers to believe that the "probable" and the "real" are synonyms, he means ultimately to *render* them synonymous in a restrictive and restricted formation, and to enlist both Austen and the novel in that project.

Far from complicating the probable as other readers had observed, the novels' "distinctness of description" and the "minute fidelity of detail" are for Whatley part of a rhetorical and naturalizing apparatus. Operating in conjunction with free indirect style, this apparatus gives Austen's "fiction the perfect appearance of reality" and thereby aids its work of "deception" (96). While one might expect a moralist like Whatley to be troubled by such manipulation, he has no problem either in reducing fiction to a moral tract or in assuming that its most important purpose is to distribute advice in the form of praise and blame. (Miss Bates, he typically notes, is a fool whereas Knightley is an apogee of sense.) In fact Whatley differs from readers in our time such as Raymond Willliams only in being *untroubled* by the hegemonic and deceptive ends of a writing that combines, "in an eminent degree, instruction with amusement" (105).

Whatley's judgments, however proleptic, stand in distinct contrast to the observations of many of his contemporaries. And they contrast as well with the subsequent observations of his predecessor and guide, Walter Scott, who in the wake of repeated readings of Austen's novels was increasingly struck (as Anne Romilly had been earlier) by their divergence from his own writings. In a journal entry of 1826 Scott was moved, in remarking on the "want of story" in a novel by Lady Morgan, to thoughts of Austen, in this case *Pride and Prejudice*, which he admits to having read "at least" three times. Contrasting Austen's descriptions of the "involvements, and feelings, and characters of ordinary life" to his own representations in a genre that he gently disparages as the "Big Bow-wow strain" of fiction, Scott laments that Austen's "exquisite touch, which renders ordinary commonplace things and characters interesting . . . is denied to me."[35] While these observations recapitulate those in his earlier review, Scott appears also to have abandoned the "picturesque" interpretation of Austen in favor of a less decidable (and more humbling) sense of her "interest." "Interesting," of course, is not without its connections to the work of naturalization. Yet, as the comparison with the overbearing Scott suggests, "interest" in Austen is no longer necessarily consistent with the kind of control with which it was earlier aligned.

This "argument" is continued in journal entries from March 1826 and September 1827. In the former, Austen is compared favorably (along with Edgeworth and Ferrier) to Thomas Henry Lister, whose novel *Granby* is criticized for being too authoritative in its omniscience and too concerted in "put[ting] the reader exactly up to the thoughts and sentiments of the parties." The "women," according to Scott, "do this better . . . far superior to anything Man vain Man has produced of the like nature."[36] Scott is not discounting the suasive use of free indirect style, nor is he suggesting that women writers, including Austen, lack a specific aim or purpose. He seems, in fact—despite lumping these various writers together—to be pointing to a another kind of purpose, which is served by putting fiction at the disposal of a reader rather than by putting a concurrently empowered reader at the disposal of an authoritative text.

The entry of September 1827 brings up the analogy of painting to describe Austen, much as Knight had earlier deployed the analogy of narrative to describe the operation of the picturesque. "There is a truth of painting in her writings which always delights me. They do not it is true get above the middle classes of Society. But there she is inimitable" (*Journal*, 353). Scott's recourse to what is arguably the picturesque and to its particular commitment to "truth" is certainly understandable, especially given his observations twelve years earlier. Now the analogy is notable in the way it stresses Austen's "inimitable" practice as a writer rather than her adherence to certain representational conventions. This uniqueness is similarly reflected in Scott's refusal here to articulate the ends of Austen's writing beyond the capacity to "delight." For the more minimal, less determinate assessment of Austen's effect, brought on by repeated readings of the novels, follows the responses of other readers in self-consciously separating delight from the control or pedagogy to which it is traditionally linked in aesthetic theory.

Bentley's Edition

The reissue in 1833 of Austen's six novels in Richard Bentley's *The Standard Novels* not only marked Austen's formal inclusion in the canon of essential European fiction; it gave rise to reviews and assessments that are noteworthy both for their relative contemporaneity and for the fact that they are in the main considered opinions based, like Scott's, on multiple readings of the novels. It is especially interesting to note the by-now-familiar themes sounded in these responses. The *Literary Gazette* (30 Mar. 1833, 199) urged the "rising generation" to read Austen's novels for their "absolute historical pictures" of a way of life that was fast disappearing. As with previous efforts to reconfigure history writing through Austen's realistic practice, the *Gazette* typically directs its sense of history to the everyday—to "the delights of a tea-table" or the "animation of going down a country dance"—which, however belated, is important in recovering the significance of ordinary life and activity.

This significance depends, for the most part, on the uncanny effects of seeing the "common-place" as if for the first time or of seeing "our acquaintance[s]" in a more "entertaining" guise (*Gazette*, 5 Jan. 1833, 9). But such significance also involves, as it did for the *Champion*'s reviewer, a particular intelligence that a heightened or "complete[ly] tru[e]. . . . reality" makes available (9). Typically covered over by adjectives such as "amusing" or "interesting," whose vagueness overall is consistent with the nonprescriptive nature of Austen's fiction as readers had previously described it, the intelligence in Austen is by no means neutral or without point. Seemingly pointless observations—for example, that the "majority of [Austen's] actors are like those of real existence—silly, stupid, and ridiculous" (9)—are inflected in the *Gazette* by more specific observations, including one regarding Mr. Weston and Miss Bates: two characters who (to my knowledge) never have occasion in *Emma* to address one another directly. "Mr. Weston," remarks the reviewer, "with his gossiping, universal good-nature, is a copy of a thousand; and those who have not a Miss Bates among their acquaintance, are not like ourselves, who have at least a dozen" (199). The numerical differences, which multiply endlessly those who, like Mr. Weston, live securely, blithely, and without risk by circumstances of class and gender, place them in marked contrast to women who, by other circumstances, are familiar enough in their obsessive and alienated awareness of the world around them. Thus the *Gazette*'s coupling is also noteworthy in its implicit sympathy for Miss Bates and the dozen (at least) like her, whose precariousness and apparent deformation are too common yet worthy of more focused attention.

The review is much less direct about these matters than I am in rehearsing them. Indeed the union here of two relatively incidental characters—with a shared penchant for gossip (albeit to different ends)—follows Austen's own procedure in letting their "reality" perform a supplementary work of observation and explanation with special attention to the arbitrariness of their respective fates. Just as important, the otherness or defamiliarity by which the arbitrariness of things is disclosed in *Emma* remains, by a similar logic, the basis as well for a sense of possibility, wherein "life as it is" (to quote another contemporary review of Austen) is no longer life as it must or even may be. The uncanny effects of a reality seen and understood as perhaps never before accomplish two things therefore: they imbue "reality" with a "charm" of otherness so as to distinguish it from a less readable, more naturalized, "prototype" (9); and they manage, in presenting a reality that is also different from itself, to render what is "absolute" (199) and "true" (9), according to the *Gazette*, "absolute" in the more etymological—and destabilizing—sense exploited by Austen's German contemporary Friedrich Schlegel.[37]

It must be emphasized that the yield of the *Literary Gazette*'s appreciation of Austen is, commensurate with Austen's own practice, a matter of inference whose indices (in the reviews at least) remain the vague and indeterminate references to the "interest" and "amusement" of her novels and their particulars. Nor is every review of the Bentley edition as attuned to these aspects of Austen. The *Examiner* (20 Jan. 1833, 37) typically notes the "truth[ful] . . . delineation" of Austen's various characters and credits the author, who is synonymous here with her narrator, with having "thoroughly understood" them. This "understanding" of human character consists predominantly with judgment or blame, which the *Examiner*—in stressing Austen's narrative authority—eagerly renews. Similarly, the *Printing Machine* (19 Apr. 1834, 77–78), which actually describes Austen as a contemporary, follows Whatley in crediting her with having performed an educative function short of writing a conduct book. As in Whatley's notice, the review praises the naturalizing work of Austen's novels, specifically her ability to "paint scenes" that are not only "familiar" to her but also "thoroughly English . . . in the really good sense of the word" (78).

The regulatory or nonoppositional view of Austen's achievement would hardly die out with what at the time were the merely competing views of these journals, and of the *Quarterly* before them. The largely conservative conceptions of both Austen's achievement and the motives behind her writing would come, in fact, to represent something of a consensus that not even feminist criticism in our time has succeeded in overturning. Thus it is instructive to remember and to stress that for earlier readers, including those who, though chronologically proximate to Austen, were able with the benefit of only some hindsight to read her with the special attention that her novels attract and display, Austen's writing was palpably at crosspurposes with the hegemonic ends of what we have come to regard as realistic writing.

The *Atlas*, which like the *Literary Gazette* took special note of each of Bentley's reissues, recapitulates many of the responses where Austen's writing was found to be arresting rather than directive. Noting that the "great characteristic of Miss Austen's tales is their domestic truth" (20 Jan. 1833, 40), which greatly exceeds the imperatives of plot and suspense, the *Atlas* also hints at the oppositional reading practices encouraged by Austen's writings. Minimizing her narrator's omniscience by emphasizing that Austen's characters are somehow left to "speak and act for themselves" (40), the *Atlas* typically concentrates on the novel's effect, which is lodged in a "charm" of "style" so subtle that the reader is not "soon made aware of the spell that fascinates him" or of the "irresistible *vraisemblance* that animates the whole" and only "gradually wins upon the feelings" (40). That the irresistible similitude of Austen's representations encouraged readings that were in turn resistant, or independent of narrative authority, is less contradictory than it sounds. In the absence of any specific judgment, or sense of a position to which her representations lead, a "*vraisemblance*" that only gradually wins upon the reader represents a sharply critical recognition that, however stimulated by the text, comes ultimately from a respondent who, as it were, "acts for herself."

Rather than confirming a suasive tendency in Austen, "irresistible *vraisemblance*" refers to an ability to "chronicl[e]" what the *Atlas* coyly terms "life as it is" (40). With its particular if provisional constitution now, "life as it is" is less a sign of complacency on Austen's part than the result of a joint labor, or agency, where the reproduction of Austen's "real" in the act of reading is alternately provoked, as well as recapitulated, by the readable and increasingly possible world that adorns her pages.

Victorian Readers and the Janeites

In a recent essay that seeks similarly to excavate an oppositional or a "queer" tradition of appreciating the antinormative aspects of Austen's writing, Claudia Johnson recurs to Kipling's famous vignette of a group of World War I veterans and to the obviously homosocial aspects in the "Janeites'" joint enthusiasm for Austen's novels.[38] Johnson also notes an erotic register to these same-sex relations, whose covert or closeted disposition, beyond implicitly identifying the dominant culture as "hostile" and homophobic (153), finds a sympathetic chord in Austen's fiction, where the courtship plot is also a closet within which alternative lifestyles and ideologies are sustained and readable. Johnson is on especially firm ground in claiming that for the Kipling's Janeites, no less than for many of Austen's earliest readers as we have seen, the "atemporal aspects of narration, descriptive details, catchy phrases, and, especially, characterization"(152) stand variously in opposition to plot, with its heteronormative momentum, marking a countercurrent to the more conventional aspects of domestic fiction.

At the same time, the most remarkable feature of Kipling's Janeites involves their generalizations over character, pro and con, which accord with a far more conventional and naturalized conception of Austenian verisimilitude. In the very way that Austen's characters are, as one Janeite puts it, "just like people that you run across any day" (159), they are also stereotypes and vulnerable to a kind of prejudice that, beyond granting a legitimating status to the Janeite reader, reflects a protocol of reading that had long served the normative aims that Johnson, like many early readers, rightly understands Austen's fictions to oppose. The Janeites are by no means off base in describing the Reverend Collins as "always on the make an' lookin' to marry money" (159), or General Tilney as a "swine" similarly "on the make" (159), or in their recurrent hatred of Lady Catherine de Bourgh. Still, the Janeites tend not just to emphasize the blamable in Austen; they also anchor their blame in an unerring verisimilitude in which these caricatures are suddenly real people against whom a moral or ethical stand is imperative. This is something of a problem. For the way with Austen that Kipling describes points to a way of reading her that became increasingly common and increasingly possible only with the development of a readership that was on the whole less sophisticated about representational matters and in need of the very authority or entitlement that a partnership with Austen's narrator provided.

An especially salient instance of this Janeite way of reading is the 1852 essay on Austen that inaugurated *New Monthly Magazine*'s series on female novelists. Although B. C. Southam dubs this essay "the first considerable 'middle-brow' piece on Jane Austen" on the evidence of what he takes to be its introductory bent (131), it is striking in the way it reflects the more informed judgments of contemporary literary professionals like George Henry Lewes and Thomas Macauley for whom Austen's characters are similarly "real" and thus actual people from whom tangible lessons about the conduct of life can be derived. The fascination with Austen's verisimilitude was scarcely a Victorian invention. But where mid-century readers depart from their earlier counterparts is in the tendency to transform a reality effect, which earlier readers understood to be more an intervention than a transcription, into a real world shorn of all naturalizing props or techniques. When the *New Monthly* observes that the "figures and scenes pictured on Miss Austen's canvas" are "exquisitely real" so that what is "flat" and "insipid [in other hands]" is, "at her bidding, a sprightly, versatile, never-flagging chapter of realities" (134), and proceeds then to assemble among its list of "lifelike" characters the figures in her novels who are often closest to caricature and most vulnerable to judgment (138), the "everyday" as such has effectively moved from a locus of attention and appreciation in Austen to an aspect of her novels that, as the earliest proponents of probabilistic fiction had hoped, is immaculately folded into their regulatory operation.

But there is a difference now. Initially, regulation was perceived by Austen's contemporaries (and I would further argue by the novelist herself) as predominantly a function of the "virtue rewarded" plot, to which everyday detail frequently proved a hindrance more than an aid. By mid-century, however, the increasingly normative operation of Austen's fiction is lodged almost entirely in a disposition to judgment. Here *character*, especially blamable character, is sufficiently coextensive with the everyday that the quotidian is also the *means* now by which the reality of those under judgment, along with the judgments upon them in which readers are privileged to indulge, are reciprocally authenticated. To be sure, the cautionary characters in Austen are invariably compared in these assessments with heroes and heroines who are meant to serve as role models—so that the *New Monthly*'s adduction of characters, ranging from General Tilney and Walter Elliot to Mrs. Bennet, Mr. Collins, and Lady de Bourgh, is typically counterpointed by observations of Anne Elliot as "self-sacrificing and noble-hearted" or of Captain Wentworth as "intelligent, spirited, and generously high-minded" (138). But this hardly diminishes the fact that the authority of Austen's fictions and the values they putatively uphold increasingly derive their sanction from a reality—the real people whom both author and reader can look down upon in the act of blaming—which is rarely appealed to with the same urgency or enthusiasm with respect to characters who are merely praiseworthy.

Lewes, the most erudite and prolific defender of Austen's fiction at this time, and best known for having provoked Charlotte Brontë into her infamous critique of Austen as a writer lacking passion, sentiment, and poetry, is also typical in his tendency both to locate and defend Austen's "fidelity" (130) to real life in her "truthful representation of character" (153). Although Lewes's observations bear more than a trace of an earlier way with Austen in appreciating the degree to which Austen's characters are "at once life-like and interesting" so that the "good people" in her fictions "are . . . good, without being goody" (153), the density and inscrutability of character, along with the "every-day life" on which they bear, inevitably give way to an appreciation of Austen's "noodles" as so "accurately real" that "they become equal to actual experiences" (153).

To show this, Lewes summons the examples of Mrs. Elton and Mrs. Norris. "We have so personal a dislike to Mrs. Elton and Mrs. Norris, that it would gratify our savage feeling to hear of some calamity befalling them" (153). Lewes is being hyperbolic, both in the fantasies he admits to harboring and in the reality effect whose force has presumably provoked them. Nevertheless the keyword in his assessment is not "character" or "truth" or "fidelity," but "personal." This is so because the extension of Austen's fiction into "actual experience" is for Lewes, no less than for Kipling, a seduction whose interpellative reach is keyed directly to the status conferred in the ability to judge and ultimately to hate. It is often assumed that "Janeite" enthusiasm for Austen's novels reflects a nostalgia for and thus an endorsement of the gentrified world that the novelist brings so vividly to life. Nothing could be further from the position of those figures from whom the term derives. Unlike the disempowered but knowing readers who actually inhabited Austen's world, Kipling's Janeites, with their rather pitiful aspirations to power and enfranchisement, illustrate and deconstruct the protocols of reading that have over time mitigated our understanding of the difference that Austen's novels succeeded initially in making.

3

Why Jane Austen Is Not Frances Burney: Probability, Possibility, and Romantic Counterhegemony

"Let us not desert one another"
—Northanger Abbey

Austen clearly was not the first to have made such pronouncements. But make them she did. In a surprising digression in *Northanger Abbey*—surprising in that it appears to contravene the satiric drift of the narrative thus far—the narrator offers a defense of the novel that bears a more-than-casual affinity with the claims of some of Austen's male contemporaries regarding the importance of *their* moment as distinct, aesthetically and ideologically, from the literature of what Charles Lamb disparagingly termed the "past century." Observing that the novel's heroine and a friend manage a kind of solidarity by reading novels in each other's company, Austen's narrator loses little time in extending that observation into an assertion of the novel's rightful place in the canon of English literature. Uniformly male and generally conservative in its aesthetic and doctrinal affiliations, the canon, for the narrator, is also an institution so formidable and entrenched that its biases are routinely defended even by novelists themselves.

Yes, novels;—for I will not adopt that ungenerous and impolitic custom so common with novel writers, of degrading by their contemptuous censure the very performances, to the number of which they are themselves adding—joining with their greatest enemies in bestowing the harshest epithets on such works, and scarcely ever permitting them to be read by their own heroine, who, if she accidentally take up a novel, is sure to turn over its insipid pages with disgust. Alas! if the heroine of one novel be not patronized by the heroine of another, from whom can she expect protection and regard? I cannot approve of it. Let us leave it to the Reviewers to abuse such effusions of fancy at their leisure, and over every new novel to talk in threadbare strains of the trash with which the press now groans. (21)[1]

Then, in an appeal that modulates rapidly from women readers to women writers, and ultimately to a sense of reading as a version *of production*, Austen's narrator celebrates the novel's break from the established canons of taste on the basis of, among other things, the difference that such texts make: both in the minds of beleaguered female readers, who are able at last to read about themselves and their milieu, and in the more general conception of what literature is and does.

Let us not desert one another; we are an injured body. Although our productions have afforded more extensive and unaffected pleasure than those of any other literary corporation in the world, no species of composition has been so much decried. From pride, ignorance, or fashion, our foes are almost as many as our readers. And while the abilities of the nine-hundreth abridger the History of England, or of the man who collects and publishes in a volume some dozen lines of Milton, Pope, and Prior, with a paper from the Spectator, and a chapter from Sterne, are eulogized by a thousand pens,—there seems almost a general wish of decrying the capacity and undervaluing the labor of the novelist, and of slighting the performances which have only genius, wit, and taste to recommend them. "I am no novel reader—I seldom look into novels—Do not imagine that *I* often read novels—It is really very well for a novel"—Such is the common cant.—"And what are you reading Miss—?" "Oh! It is only a novel!" replies the young lady; while she lays down her book with affected indifference, or momentary shame.—"It is only Cecilia, or Camilla, or Belinda;" or, in short, only some work in which the greatest powers of the mind are displayed, in which the most thorough knowledge of human nature, the happiest delineation of its varieties, the liveliest effusions of wit and humour are conveyed to the world in the best chosen language. Now, had the same young lady been engaged with a volume of the Spectator, instead of such a work, how proudly would she have produced the book, and told its name; though the chances must be against her being occupied by any part of that voluminous publication, of which either the matter or manner would not disgust a young person of taste; the substance of its papers so often consisting in the statement of improbable circumstances, unnatural characters, and topics of conversation, which no longer concern any one living; and their language, too, frequently so coarse as to give no favourable idea of the age that could endure it. (22)

This lengthy excursus, which has long been regarded as a foundational moment in feminist literary criticism, chiefly in its promotion of a "literature of their own," seems relatively unambiguous in its claims. Although one purpose of the digression is to counter the objections of critics and reviewers by reminding them that the novel is an enthusiasm shared by readers of both sexes, its main purpose would appear to be the promotion not only of women's writing but also of a version of women's writing that is realistic or "probable" in scope and allied thereby with an ideology of domesticity.

But there is clearly a problem in mounting such an argument. It involves the schism between a legitimacy based on popularity, or on the range and degree of consumption, and a legitimacy based in ideology. That is, the solidarity forged by the institution of the novel, whose sudden respectability is confirmed by the proliferation of readers of both sexes, narrows in the narrator's polemic to an aggregation whose tastes and identity are sufficiently *restricted* to account for the novel's problems in the first place. Moreover, when one adds to this problem the narrator's insistence on the greater refinement of novels by and for women, a claim that virtually every literary movement or "modernity" from the late seventeenth century onward had waged on its own behalf, a fairly transparent defense of a particular kind of writing—exemplified in the productions of Frances Burney and Maria Edgeworth—seems suddenly opaque and pitched, if only rhetorically, toward a discursive field more extensive than either domestic fiction per se or the conventionally male canon, whose improvements and refinements are (the *Spectator* notwithstanding) a basis for its current prestige and ubiquity.[2]

If such circumlocution is preliminary to identifying this "discursive field" as "romantic," or on a continuum with a canonical break that the Romantics, more than any other of Austen's contemporaries, consistently claimed in their own defense, it is because there is no other way that Austen could possibly have indicated that affiliation. For just as the Romantics stand sufficiently on the other side of the gender divide to remain among the unnamable in the above polemic (and in Austen's writings generally), so there would seem to be little point in extending the romantic imperative into precincts—notably women's fiction—where the Romantics and their writings are ostensibly incongruous.

But if Austen's narrator has apparently avoided this particular incongruity, there are additional incongruities here that warrant attention since they bear ultimately on the alliance that dare not speak its name. The first of these inconsistencies, which I have only hinted at, is the satire in *this novel* on novels in general, which range from the gothic—the fictional genre for which *Northanger Abbey* reserves its greatest criticism—to the present narrative, whose own heroine, although gently debunked as too probable or pedestrian a figure for the purposes of readerly transport, never entirely shucks off a characterization meant to serve as a cudgel against "improbable" or sensationalistic fiction in general. Similarly, despite the narrator's effort to distinguish and demarcate the efforts of male and female writers to the benefit of the latter, it is unclear whether the narrator is also disparaging the "male" tradition as then currently constituted, or whether that tradition and the ideologies it sustains are in any way contradicted by the particular authors, Burney and Edgeworth, whose works are presumably exemplary in their "knowledge of human nature" and in their responsiveness to its "varieties" and possibilities. Nor is it clear, given the increasingly overdetermined character of this passage, whether the binarisms here, predominantly those of men and women, are as firm or as determinate as they appear at first glance, or as they seem in retrospect to readers intent on identifying Austen's commitments as a practitioner of domestic fiction: that what the narrator is striving for—to the degree that novels are being read by both men and women—does not also amount to a *hegemonic* compact, uniting the initiatives and imperatives of a fairly specific order of male writing (Milton notwithstanding) with the embellishments and charm of a female sensibility.

It is more the case that the remarkable consensus linking men and women here, both as readers and as conservators of a cultural inheritance in which Burney or Pope each has a rightful place, moves in two directions: toward a legitimation of the current group of women writers based on their entitlement to inclusion in a canon, whose principal deficiency appears to be its failure to have made a place for them and the novel to begin with; and toward a counterconsensus, in which the novel, far from according with canonical rule, would appear to contest the canon in the threat that the novel's catholicity, chiefly its responsiveness to the varieties of human nature, might well pose to a literary order that is also, needless to say, a political or doctrinal one. Or to put it another way: just as the narrator's defense of the novel imagines a general consensus consisting of both men and women, readers and writers, this horizon also mimes and exposes yet another consensus, whose avowed break with the past, and with the hegemony to be sustained by the inclusion of women novelists, is contrastively progressive.

The Romantics, it must emphasized, are not simply unnamed as adversaries in this passage; they are explicitly imitated rather than directly derogated. This affinity should give any literary historian pause. For short of declaring Wordsworth, or Coleridge, or Shelley the unacknowledged legislators of the narrator's polemic, it can be asserted that the *author* of *Northanger Abbey* was sufficiently familiar with a "Romantic school" to know that she was appropriating its particular claim to modernity and to being different in allowing her narrator to digress in this fashion. Moreover, Austen knew enough to know that the literary establishments named in the narrator's polemic, both the one composed of writers of the "past century" and the projected establishment in which Burney and Edgeworth would be added to their ranks, stand on only one side of a divide separating a canonical hegemony (such as the narrator projects) and another grouping that, with the inclusion of certain women writers and certain novels, is more akin to what we would today call a counterhegemony.[3]

The distinction I am making here, or that I believe Austen is making, between one pledge of solidarity and another appeal may seem overfine. Yet the divided character of the digression is part of a consistently larger conflict in *Northanger Abbey* between the manifest intentions of a narrator bent on debunking the gothic novel and the *yield* of *Northanger Abbey* overall, which actually validates the gothic to the degree that it is a genre obsessed with the imbalance of power that currently defines the relationship of men and women. It is certainly the case that the novel's nominal villain, General Tilney, does not resort to the kinds of physical violence represented either in the so-called Northanger novels that Catherine Morland reads avidly or even in a work such as *Udolpho*, which she also reads. Nevertheless, the brunt of the novel's satire on imaginative fiction, which rests finally with Catherine's fantasies regarding the violent treatment of the general's deceased wife, is sharply mitigated by the fact that Catherine is fundamentally correct in treating the general with apprehension. The narrator of Austen's novel may well continue to disdain the heroine for her suggestibility and naïveté. However, the "text" of *Northanger Abbey* makes available a perspective that, like the romanticism *embedded* in the narrator's polemic, essentially rejects narrative authority in recognizing that a work such as Radcliffe's *Italian*, while dependent for its interest on the prospect of some supernatural agency, is more important an enhancement of, and not a departure from, the "real" as such.[4]

Imagination, then, or that faculty that the gothic both cultivates and depends on, works in two different but complementary ways. In the first, imagination is simply an extension of ordinary apperception, which explains Catherine's seeming misrecognition of gothic elements in real life. In the second, the particular union of the quotidian and the extravagant that Catherine maintains under the influence of the gothic is recapitulated in imagination's other function: the equally escapist and *equally plausible* fantasy of a different configuration for both men and women. It is impossible, in other words, for Catherine to fantasize the various terrors visited upon women (and upon the general's wife) without indulging in a social fantasy where such afflictions would be literally fantastic.

Literary historians have long maintained that the gothic is the genre of prose fiction most clearly of a piece with the contemporaneous romantic project. The reasons for this claim are fairly obvious. In addition to being a popular genre, with antecedents in the folk or vernacular culture for which the very notion of "romanticism"—as distinct from classicism—was initially and polemically a shorthand, the gothic features and demands the exercise of that most sacrosanct of romantic faculties, the imagination. Thus even as Wordsworth and Coleridge seek also to dissociate their writings from gothic productions, as they do from virtually all novels, the effect of their protest is far from straightforward. Undertaken to differentiate the Romantics' commitment to a discourse of imagination, which follows the gothic in requiring and encouraging what Coleridge famously termed a "willing suspension of disbelief," or "a feeling analogous to the supernatural, by awakening the mind's attention from the lethargy of custom, and directing it to the loveliness and the wonders of the world before us,"[5] the somewhat derivative attacks on the gothic by both Wordsworth and Coleridge manage, by force of denial, to accomplish the very opposite. As several critics have noted, their attacks, however virulent, work in large measure to recall and to underscore the prevalence of gothic elements in a variety of their works, from "Christabel" and the "Ancient Mariner" to "Goody Blake and Harry Gill."[6] Most striking about Coleridge's "suspension of disbelief" is not only its proximity to a function that is recognizably gothic; equally striking is his characterization of a representational desideratum for which the fictional ideal embedded in Austen's polemic *also suffices*—and for which the gothic, far more than the works of Burney and Edgeworth, is a better index. It is the purpose, surely, of the narrator's digression in *Northanger Abbey* to make a case for the canonical status of domestic fiction in conjunction with the canon currently in place. But it is the function of that digression *in context* to introduce a canonical break, both in imitation of the "romantic" claim of modernity and in advocacy of a horizon of possibility, in literature as in life, to which the Romantics were demonstrably committed.

My aim, following Austen's telling silence in the *Northanger Abbey* passage, is not specifically to embrace the Romantics by taking their polemical word for their deed. Rather my aim—in construing romanticism through Austen's project *and not* the other way around—is more to recognize the degree to which romanticism is a movement and a moment, whose often conflicted (as opposed to merely contradictory) constitution allows also for certain possibilities in both individual texts, and the modes of reading they instill, in excess of the usual discursive parameters. While romantic writing, no less than domestic fiction, is governed by certain aims and teleologies, such governance is almost always a matter of generalization to which individual texts do not just prove a complication but can be said in fact to open a window upon and against.

While romanticism, then, is a species of the new that, as its more severe interpreters have noted, recalls the inherently repetitive and traditional conception of "modernity" as such,[7] there abides within this predictable rupture another break or errancy that is a good deal less accountable and less susceptible to the kinds of appropriations that the narrator of *Northanger Abbey*, no less than romanticism's most demanding critics in our time, are determined to see negotiated. It is *this recalcitrance*—or, following the digression in *Northanger Abbey*, this break *within* a break *with tradition*—that renders Austen so important and representative a writer. Her project, however circumscribed by discursive or disciplinary structures, or reduced to a routinized social landscape, remains in context—in conjunction with both women's writing of the period and the contemporaneous romantic movement—committed to horizons of possibility that, as noted previously, are productively hidden in plain sight.[8]

The remainder of this chapter is taken up therefore with a number of disparate but related issues, the majority centering on the historically crucial differences between Austen's fictional project and that of her influential contemporary Frances Burney. No one has of course argued that Austen and Burney are identical, and it would only belabor the obvious to claim that, at the level of craft and management of narration, Austen is a very different writer from the novelist whom she read with care and was influenced by. Even so, one of the ironies of historical recovery is that it is Austen, rather than Burney, who is generally credited (or discredited) with having successfully served the aims of domestic ideology, along with the fundamentally conservative or patriarchal ideology of which domesticity was a development.[9] And it is Austen too who, in naturalizing these aims in representations of authority and plausibility, is assumed not only to have furthered the cause of bourgeois hegemony in tracing and in promoting the evolution of the gentry into a professionalized middle class but in so doing to have virtually codified the genre of classic or "realistic" fiction as an armature of the newly constituted order.[10] There are, to be sure, competing versions of Austen, many of which seek to recover a feminist or comparatively subversive current in her work. Still it is the case that such subversion or complaint increasingly finds a less mediated expression in the writings of Burney, whose sprawling narratives, with their attention to what Burney dubbed "female difficulties," are credited with having dramatized, more directly and forcefully, the predicament of women and women writers in a patriarchal world.[11]

It is more than a little tempting to credit the narrator in *Northanger Abbey* with sharing this insight so that the encomiums on behalf of Burney, which rest chiefly with the latter's putative depiction of things as they are, may be also part of a more generalized complaint against the hegemonic force of masculinist culture, literary and otherwise. Nevertheless the defense of Burney, and of women's fiction generally, is consistent also with a claim for legitimation of which canonical judgments, past and passing, are the ultimate measure. Moreover, when one adds to this the fact that the gothic—the novelistic subgenre carrying the notion of "female difficulties" to a vertiginously sublime pitch—is deliberately excluded from what purports to be a defense of the novel generally, an altogether different picture begins to emerge: one in which the refinements of probabilistic fiction are complicit rather than at odds with the traditional order currently in place.

In reasserting the differences between Austen and the female novelist who was likely her most influential model, a return to history is necessary for two reasons: to complicate the historical judgments that increasingly count Burney as a feminist *avant la lettre*; and to appreciate the degree to which Austen's progressivism, her investment in an horizon of possibility rooted in the oppositional practices of the everyday, ultimately eschews identity politics on behalf of a more democratic vista in which "female difficulties" are symptomatic of human and social difficulties. It may well have been Burney's purpose, as Catherine Gallagher has noted, to emphasize and to exploit the fact that women are chiefly "nobodies." But it is Austen's achievement, following the enlarged or counterhegemonic romanticism on which her novels verge, to deconstruct the implicit binarism in Gallagher's formulation in consistently underscoring the degree to which nobodies are potentially sombodies and vice versa. Fitzwilliam Darcy in *Pride and Prejudice* may well be the Austenian hero or "somebody" par excellence. But his heroism, which consists in hewing to the prerogatives of rank and gender, is apparently insufficient to protect Darcy from being thoroughly interpellated or, reduced in Austen's rather piquant allegory (as we shall see), to the two-dimensional surface of a picture.

Burney's *Evelina* and the Fictions of Probability

There is no term more crucial to understanding the horizons of possibility in Austen's novels than "probability," a notion we encountered in our survey of the aesthetic of the picturesque and of the related representational practices that contrived similarly to speak in the name of either "reality" or "nature." As we saw, probability was a rather mystified term by the time that Austen was exposed to it: a desideratum where the charge for accuracy in representation—or for proximity to either "nature" or the "real"—was preliminary to a still larger aim, which was that readers, particularly women readers, would be sufficiently persuaded by probabilistic representations to consent to living within their means.

Thus it is no small matter that the imperative to probability remains the sum and substance of the preface to Burney's first and most successful novel, *Evelina* (1778), or that this preface, in anticipation of the narrator's digression in *Northanger Abbey*, offers a defense of the novel that prescriptively separates the genre into salutary and "depraved" orders. Conceding that the novel's reputation cannot be reckoned independently of the legitimating efforts of Fielding, Smollett, Richardson, Rousseau, and Johnson, Burney insists at the same time that both the fate of the novel and its much-needed recuperation rest with novelists like herself: novelists writing chiefly for women, whose responsibility it is to retrieve the genre from "the fantastic regions of Romance."[12] In place of the "Marvellous," which has had a deleterious effect on young women who, in reading novels, are imbued with unrealistic expectations that may likely lead to "injury," Burney urges both novelists and novels to seek "aid from sober Probability" (8). Burney, for her part, has sought this aid so that in the pages that follow the contagion to which the novel has become tantamount has been stanched by "characters [drawn] from nature" and by the novelist's depiction of "manners of the times" (7). Unlike "history," a genre devoted to accounts of the extraordinary in life, it will be the function of Evelina's "history" (a term used somewhat cheekily here) to inculcate truth rather than fantasy.

Burney may have been among the first female writers to urge the claim of probability as a representational desideratum. She was scarcely the last. Writing just seven years later in 1785, Clara Reeve took the bolder tack of describing and privileging the novel as a genre distinct from romance. Where romance, according to Reeve, is an heroic fable treating "fabulous persons and things," the novel "is a picture of real life and manners, and of the times in which it is written."[13] Where romance "describes what never happened nor is likely to happen," the novel "gives a familiar relation of such things, as pass every day before our eyes, such as may happen to our friend, or to ourselves; and the perfection of it, is to represent every scene, in so easy and natural a manner, and to make them appear so probable, as to deceive us into a persuasion (at least while we are reading) that all is real, until we are affected by the joys or distresses, of the persons in the story, as if they were our own" (111).

In admitting to the absorptive dimension of the probabilistic novel, Reeve points with striking candor to a potential problem or contradiction regarding the novel as a genre distinct from romance. If the novel stands in opposition to romance, it does so as much by an appeal to the probable or the natural as by resembling its counterpart. The novel, in other words, can oppose romance and the work of romance only by essentially assimilating romance through the mechanism of what, as Reeve describes it, is really naturalization. For in naturalization, as Roland Barthes and others have since shown, the everyday or the "real" is more a means by which the reader is deceived than a subject matter that, as Reeve suggests, is even accurate.[14] Less an index of what is really "out there" in the world, the probable remains a screen or overlay for what is still idealized. It is a typology by which the joys or distresses of persons in the story appear "as if they were our own" precisely because they are *not* our own: because "what never happened nor is likely to happen" to the reader has, with an assist from probability, been given a temporary reprieve from appearing merely fabulous.

Reeve does not enter this contradiction as thoroughly as I have made out. However, it is equally clear that she is not very good at protecting the novel in its commitment to the probable from the imprecation of bad faith. Reeve would no doubt argue that such a charge is beside the point: that the absorptive aspects of the novel, which require the overlay of what Burney terms "sober Probability," are there simply to counteract the more seductive aspects of romance, from which, as she and Burney contend, young minds may receive bad, and sometimes fatal, influences (Reeve, 115). Still, in arguing for a new institution of influence in place of an older and more dangerous one, Reeve and Burney find themselves awkwardly suspended between making probability a representational goal and their more dubious assertion that the new novel, however probable and thereby seductive, is also distinct from its more improbable and seductive antecedent.

This slippage between "realism" and "romance," which is also necessary to the aims and the cultural work of probabilistic discourse, clearly characterizes Burney's *Evelina*. Although the principal setting of the novel is, as its subtitle promises, the "world"—chiefly the London of 1776 or thereabouts—the narrative also conforms to the conventions of fantasy. Or to put the matter more specifically: what is improbable one moment in the novel—notably Evelina's acceptance by Sir John Belmont, the nobleman who allegedly abandoned her as a child and whose daughter she may be—is suddenly and even predictably probable by the novel's close. Worse still, it is almost as probable, or posited, for the purposes of readerly interest, as *becoming* probable, within twenty pages of Burney's prefatory manifesto. Expressing doubt that his ward, Evelina, will ever be accepted by her natural and noble father, Reverend Arthur Villars asks rhetorically, "is there any probability that he will *properly* own her?" (19).

Now to readers of romance, not to mention this novel, Villars's question cuts two ways, pressing the impediments of the real in what, within the first twenty pages of the novel, is already a trajectory of overcoming. Thus when Evelina attends a private assembly upon arrival in London and is immediately singled out for admiration by Lord Orville, a twenty-six-year-old nobleman of apparently unimpeachable character, the reader is not put on guard so much as invited to regard this unlikely pairing as desirable and, by turns, deserved. The sense of Evelina's desert owes a great deal to Burney's appropriation of the epistolary form in the service of what is basically a first-person account. The heroine's letters to her guardian, Villars, which constitute nearly 90 percent of the novel, are no doubt essential in preserving the surprise and embarrassment upon entry into the world that a retrospective narrative would be obliged to contextualize and thereby to blunt. But their function is at crosspurposes with this ironizing tendency.[15] In the absence of any counterperspective on the world, Evelina's letters create a compact between author and character, allowing the authority they share or the attributes on loan to Evelina—notably her powers of observation and facility with language—to justify marital and social expectations that are simultaneously deemed fanciful.

Such a conflation of the probable and the improbable, or the way the improbable (in response to Villars's question) is very quickly unmoored from the patently impossible, does double duty ideologically. On the one hand the circularity of Evelina's narrative, in which she travels to her rightful station as a noblewoman possessed of both a noble husband and a noble father, accords with the aristocratic function of romance in militating against any status inconsistency or disruption of the status quo. On the other hand the simultaneously linear course of Evelina's progress, by which her final ascension is somehow earned or perceived as the deserved consequence of attributes independent of lineage, accords with a more progressive or bourgeois ideology in which, as Michael McKeon has detailed, a hierarchy based on birth is effectively replaced with another based on excellence.[16] Thus just as the improbable, specifically Evelina's claim to nobility, gilds the probable in this novel by suggesting that the heroine's inherent or personal virtues are also consequences of birth, so the probable, through which Evelina's aristocratic genealogy is subordinated to Nature of whom she is "but the Offspring in . . . her simplest attire" (8), collaborates with the improbable in naturalizing what in other quarters appears undeserved and arbitrary. While it is the case, surely, that not all aristocratic people in *Evelina* are good and deserving of all that has accrued to them, it is also true that all good and deserving people in the novel are in the end aristocratic.[17]

That the probable was paradoxically instrumental in fostering the very "expectations" that fictions of probability were to "rectify" and subdue[18] was not exactly lost on Burney's contemporaries, some of whom were alarmed by the apparent breach in regulation. We can cite as one example Richard Payne Knight who, as noted in the previous chapter, not only agrees with Clara Reeve in his endorsement of naturalizing and regulatory practices but had recourse to narrative fiction by way of articulating his position regarding proper improvements of the landscape. Concurring with his colleague Uvedale Price that the newer English gardens did not do a good enough job in uniting a great man to his property—in this case by failing to obscure, or to naturalize as effectively as possible, his imposition on and control of the landscape—Knight summons the analogy of modern fictions as having similarly undone the work of naturalization in the act of performing it. Such fictions, he complains, abandon their regulatory task of giving "useful knowledge and sound morality" in the way they "relat[e], in intelligible language, events of familiar life, not quite incredible, nor quite common" (445–46).

Such a muddle is a far cry from the crude binarism that (following Burney's preface) locates the probable or the "common" at one extreme and the "incredible" or the "marvellous" at the other. Still, in the very way that this binarism routinely issues in a collapsing of difference—for the purpose of rendering the probable more palatable and absorbing to the reader—the effective blurring of the probable and the merely possible in fictional prose, beyond putting Knight on the alert, introduces a horizon of possibility that, as Knight's own remarks suggest, is unique and noteworthy in being remarkably close at hand. The interchangeability of the probable and the possible does more than simply compromise the aims and the apparent ends of probability, as Knight suggests; such an exchange refers to, or less determinately perhaps, *recalls* possibilities by which fictions of probability, no matter how regulatory their apparent function, are transformed willy-nilly into what another Burney contemporary, Charlotte Smith, coyly terms romances of real life.[19]

The permeability of a probabilistic fiction like *Evelina* to possibilities and expectations that it was the purpose of such novels to excise from their pages, undoubtedly registers a responsiveness to "female difficulties," of which possibility—the prospect of a *different* and better world for the heroine—is surely one effect. At the same time, Burney's subscription to an order of possibility more "incredible" than "common" (to borrow Knight's terms) constitutes a fault line in the probabilistic imperative that, when reckoned in conjunction with Austen's realism and *its* version of the possible, remains a bounding line as well. Unlike Austen, who is ever alert to possibilities that animate an ostensibly predictable and patriarchal society, Burney is disposed to marshal the (im)possibility of Evelina's advancement, which is also an endorsement of that society, against the more tangible likelihood of her heroine's social free-fall, for which the social order in place is no less responsible.

There is nothing wrong of course in attending to the potentially abject decline of a character, who by virtue of her sex is more vulnerable to the vagaries of social life than are her male counterparts. The problem in *Evelina* is that, beyond simply an object of fear for Burney, the likelihood of her heroine's decline is a probability or likelihood on which "probability," as served by the novel, is parasitically and tautologically dependent. The "uneven developments" that currently define the prospects of the respective sexes are in Austen, by contrast, reason to embrace the possibility of a different world as well as an impetus to begin making that difference. When Collins in *Pride and Prejudice* can, upon being refused by Elizabeth Bennet, walk across the street and have a proposal of marriage immediately accepted by a desperate Charlotte Lucas, it is plainly time for a change. For Burney the situation is more complicated, owing no doubt to the relative security she enjoyed in contrast to her successor. To her the vulnerability of women is less a symptom of a larger social ill, which also counts men among its victims and deformations, than a probability that must be accepted so as to be avoided or defended against: a social condition that some women, notably Evelina, can happily but not representatively overcome. The likelihood of injury or catastrophe becomes in Burney, and in eighteenth-century discourse generally, the very ground, then, of a probabilistic worldview. Far from transforming the probable, or conceiving it as a deleterious yet potentially vestigial set of contingencies, Burney and her contemporaries actually cling to the probable, and to the social order with which it is coextensive, in a strategy of containment and fear.

The tautology of fear, which not only drives the probable but requires in the process that the probable be transfigured, if only temporarily, from an aesthetic desideratum into an horizon of concern, is better understood in the context of contemporary thinking about probability, which was manifest in a variety of disciplines, including epistemology, jurisprudence, and mathematics. In his survey of the "conditions of knowing" in earlier eighteenth-century fiction, Douglas Patey stresses how the "world" was variously "understood to be composed of probable signs" that "must be sifted by a process of inference . . . designed to aid in [the] rectification of judgment."[20] This rectification is accomplished mostly by negative examples intended not merely to show bad judgment but, more important, to perform an "educative function" (200) that extends to what Patey calls the "rectification of expectations" (214). In this way the goal of much eighteenth-century fiction, including a work like *Evelina*, is not just a disciplining of the mind; it is also a disciplining or diminution of the world to the point where "rational expectations," formed or understood in light of mistakes, become diminished expectations, which are the guarantors in turn of happiness.

Since Patey's purpose is to coordinate the aims of eighteenth-century fiction with the rise of empirical thinking, he does not attend in any real way to the social work of the developing genre. This is unfortunate. For the dispensation he describes is especially pronounced with reference to women readers, for whom the end of forming "rational expectations" (215) is increasingly aligned with the foreclosure of all other possibility, or of any felicity apart from avoiding indigence. More than an epistemological goal, in fact, the "end" of forming rational expectations is, following such instruction as Burney hopes to administer to her readers, a wholly probabilistic world where, in the wake of expectations that are rational *by being diminished* (and vice versa), "whatever is" will rightfully abide.

The particular force of probability is especially evident in developments in the sciences, which followed those in the law (for example, "probable cause")[21]

in lauding statistical regularity over an earlier, more elite conception of probability as informed inference. The abiding ground of this development—that
"order was to be found in the mass and over the long run"—was largely deduc-
tive.[22] Less the "dream of a calculus that would convert judgment and inference
into a set of rules" (xv), probability was grounded more immediately in a world
that had evolved from being unpredictable into one that was becoming safer
and more stable (185). It was not that events previously taken as unpredictable—
for example, suicides and hailstorms—had ceased to exist. It was that they were
contained now by a statistical and probabilistic apparatus, which reflected in
turn a prevailing sense of stability based on the increased and real likelihood of
a safer life. Probability came increasingly, then, to characterize a condition, indeed a status quo, in whose *defense* mathematical likelihood was more properly
a tool, along with perhaps the greatest weapon against contingency: namely, insurance. Insurance, to be sure, became practical only at the very moment when
it was unlikely to be needed, or when it could be offered at a profit to cover
losses of "comparatively small probability" (185). At the same time, the more
important feature here is that the *rise* of insurance reflected the simple, if paradoxical, fact that the comparatively secure or probable life increasingly available
to people had succeeded in breeding "more fear than hope" (186).

In turning to Burney now, and to the seemingly proximate example of
Austen, some tentative conclusions can be offered, including ones that underscore Austen's filiations with her romantic contemporaries against her more apparent affiliation with practitioners of domestic fiction such as Burney herself.[23]
These differences center on the degree to which Burney's works, as works of
probability, are more complexly works committed *to* probability or to a world
where change comes only in the form of disruption and where the best defense
against change is an insurance policy of some kind. In the case of Burney, and in
Austen's writings at least structurally, insurance takes the form of marrying
happily and well. Even so there are fundamental differences where Austen is
concerned. To begin with, Austen contravenes the discourse of the probable and
its rational and empirical bases in three distinct ways. She allows readers to
draw *improbable* inferences from probable signs; she allows in more romantic
fashion for the irruption of "novelty" amid the probable or the "everyday"; and
finally, Austen allows that a "probable," comparatively safe world is insufficiently secure at present to be always worth preserving.

In addition, change in Austen's novels is not always to be feared any more
than the response to fear, particularly by women, is necessarily or ideally an insurance policy. The many single women, who abound in Austen's writing, from
Miss Bates to the more complicated example of Mary Crawford—not to mention the heroines, Elinor Dashwood, Emma Woodhouse, and Anne Elliot, who

are at one point or another all inured to remaining unmarried—are neither strictly cautionary nor characters whose unmarried condition is merely a pre- condition for an eventual union demanded by plot. Rather these characters, like so many other elements in Austen, including her remarkably indifferent or per- functory endings, are indices of an alterity that is (or, at the very least, was) close at hand: a capacity for change, or for resistance, that the world, no matter how probable, both admits and, more important, demands. Thus it is in the way that the probable provides a window on possibilities that, however fearful, are possibilities nonetheless, that the differences between Burney and Austen are most evident and, paradoxical as it sounds, most negligible. Even as the proba- ble is allied in Burney with a perpetuation of the status quo, especially in the face of deleterious change, it is the case too that deleterious change, which for Austen or Burney invariably centers on some catastrophe that women may likely suffer, is simultaneously a product of the very order from which change is never far removed.

Although the probable in Burney's novel is instrumental in a movement of containment, validating Evelina's eventual escape from danger/change by acqui- sition of an insurance policy to which she is entitled by at least two different standards of merit, the probable is simultaneously extended in *Evelina* (and in anticipation of Austen) in a nearly opposite direction. Setting a horizon of *pos- sibility* in the novel—and, by extension, a largely radical teleology—probability gradually bifurcates into two forms in *Evelina*, with the more conservative stand- ing in increasingly problematic relief. This is not to suggest that what Burney calls probability is in any way marginal to her strategy of containment. It is rather that Burney's strategy requires that Evelina's narrative and the hegemony it serves be somehow *isolated* from another narrative in the novel, with different possibilities and political valences, that by similar alignment with the probable— and with the historically recoverable—is increasingly uncontainable and op- posed to the novel's regulatory function.

Horizons of Possibility in *Evelina* and *A Sunday Ramble*

The site of the possible in *Evelina* is London or, in the designation of Burney's subtitle, "the world." And it is a "world" in a trajectory of descent, where differ- ent classes and types of people are routinely thrown together in reminder of their common humanity and in opposition to the hierarchizing imperatives that otherwise guide the narrative's deliberation. *Evelina* not only tracks its main character's decline from the upper-class company of Lady Howard and her daughter and granddaughter, down to the company of Mr. Branghton, a silversmith, and his family. The narrative recapitulates this movement through the various sites and places the heroine visits.

These visits begin with a private assembly, where Evelina is brought in contact with the eventual hero, Lord Orville, ostensibly her superior; and they continue in the several pleasure gardens that she visits accompanied by her various hosts. In addition to being sites of intermingling and leveling, these gardens also decline in prestige from the relatively exclusive Ranelagh to the more boisterous and pedestrian Vauxhall and Marylebone. In other words, just as the regulatory work of *Evelina* brings the claims of probability and improbability into contradictory compliance, so the radical or counterhegemonic work of Burney's "world" points up the more palpable, indeed radical, impossibility of fashioning a public place or sphere that, either by a tariff or according to custom, can regulate which members of the public it serves or the people for that matter who constitute the public. It is the case that the more the novel tightens its apparatus of containment the more it resembles a place like Ranelagh or Vauxhall in simultaneously exposing an alterity beyond its control or immediate purpose.

We see this alterity most clearly in certain scenes for which the novel, if not always justly celebrated, is at least notorious. I am referring specifically to the treatment of Evelina's French grandmother, Madame Duval, who is made the victim of a particularly vicious and humiliating prank by the Francophobic and misogynistic Captain Mirvan, and later, to the footrace run by "two poor old women" at the behest of some decadent and wealthy men. These moments, to be sure, have correlatives in both the theater and the novel at this time and, in the case of the women racing, in actual social practice. But their service to the regulatory bent of Burney's novel, which demands that certain persons (specifically women) be both abject and always vulnerable, is complicated in the way these fundamentally *misogynistic* tendencies are also foregrounded.

Such reflexivity is not restricted solely to the hyperbolic in Burney's text. Very near the novel's close, by which point *Evelina* has literally abandoned London and its possibilistic drift, Sir Clement Willoughby, an aristocratic rake and foil to Lord Orville, remarks to Evelina, whom he has pursued with unrelenting energy, that her friends, especially her female friends, are remarkable solely in their ordinariness. Lady Howard seems to him a "common John Trot style of . . . aged dam[e]," and her daughter and grandaughter, Mrs. and Miss Mirvan, are respectively characterized as "insipid" and "too insignificant for notice" (334). Such judgments may simply be part of a comedy intended to redound on a character who has been continually frustrated in his efforts, and who finds the mask of conviviality too cumbersome by half. Even so, the rake manages with uncanny perspicuity to describe both Evelina's *and Burney's* representation of these very characters: they are consigned to anonymity in order to contrast with

Evelina and her "history," which are the repositories in turn of probability—especially as a privileged category.

And yet by insisting on a fundamental distinction between the ordinary and the probable, *Evelina* not only marginalizes or contrives to do away with the former. It manages, in this very stroke, to enlarge the ordinary into a repressed of sorts, whose return is probable, or inevitable, in ways that, consistent with Willoughby's acuity, actively contest the fictions of the probable that predominate in the novel. Not only does the ordinary in the novel remind us that Burney's probable is, in its open endorsement of a glorious insurance policy for Evelina, quite extraordinary; the ordinary in *Evelina* simultaneously follows the extraordinary in creating an horizon of possibility that differs only in being less contained and less answerable to the novel's political and social work. While Evelina's narrative can be said to color and reshape the "world" it claims to represent, the everyday world that Evelina enters—the public places, for example—is to a great degree caught in a downward trajectory and remains, in the manner of the places that figure it, a site of leveling.[24] The difference is that where this leveling was a feature of everyday life in eighteenth-century London, it remains in its challenge to, as well as in its inflection of, Burney's "probable," the basis of both fear and denial.

Although exclusionary by design, the London pleasure gardens were by the time of Burney's novel open to anyone who could afford an admission fee of a shilling or two. Vauxhall was perhaps unique among the gardens in having always attracted people from all stations, which forced upper-class visitors to isolate themselves by arriving later in the evening. The tendency of the gardens overall is perhaps best illustrated by a place like Ranelagh, whose reputation as a fashionable place was continually tried by the "mixed" company that found its way inside, prompting "one fashionable lady" to complain of "many tradesmen's wives" on view there (Wroth, 206). The proprietors of Marylebone Gardens (spelled "Marybone" in *Evelina*) sought to remedy this problem by allowing genteel visitors to enter the grounds for free. Yet to those whose custom might have depended on the success of such a strategy, Marylebone succeeded in attracting only the gentry and not, as one contemporary observer put it, "the *haut ton*" (109).

Unlike the probable, which is annexed to a narrative and, by turns, a geography of increasing exclusivity in *Evelina*, the ordinary or the everyday in Burney's novel is affiliated with a world, whose projected telos, like that of Ranelagh, remains a society composed entirely of equals. This telos is readable not just in the leveling that is everywhere apparent in Burney's text. It is equally readable in the counternarrative that, following Villars's rhetorical question, is pitched toward the achievement of what—in contrast to these increasingly democratic possibilities—is initially identified as impossible: the heroine's escape to a condition of entitlement. In the end of course Burney narrates the impossible, retrieving her heroine from the social free-fall of London that both she and her character find equally repugnant. But the taint of their mutual snobbery lingers in a narrative structure that leaves a specific, and too-memorable, geography behind.

To clarify this last point, I turn briefly to the unsigned *A Sunday Ramble* (1776).[25] The relevance of this contemporaneous urban survey is not simply in the fact that it visits many of the public places of *Evelina*, including Marylebone, St. James Mall, and Kensington Gardens, in addition to many places only named in the novel. Its bearing resides more in the ideological gyrations provoked by these visits and by other cognate experiences. In resembling the currents of Burney's work as they do, these various moves shed light on *Evelina*'s investment in a narrative opposed to the reality it claims, prefatorily, to represent. For if it is the case that Burney's London is, in its peculiar extension of the probable, an inversion of what, to follow the novel's own geography, we can call the anti-London (in this case the fashionable spa Bristol Hotwell where the narrative reaches closure), it is only because the social possibilities broached by London demand some other apparatus of probability, some new direction for what is socially possible and presumably desirable, as a stay or bulwark. Despite setting itself against the discourse of romance or improbability, it is the ironic consequence of *Evelina* that this opposition is directed finally against a version of romance, or in this case a version of *romanticism*, that both parallels and exceeds the novel's dominant discourse in having at its base the probability or "worldliness" that the novel seeks ultimately to reclaim and reconstitute.

A Sunday Ramble recounts a single day's outing in which the narrator, not a Londoner, and his companion, a knowledgeable and well-connected pharmacist in the city, perambulate the city over a twenty-hour period, frequenting a range of public places and institutions. The outing commences at 4 in the morning, and within two hours the narrator and his friend are already taking drink with a number of late-night revelers, the majority of them servants, over whom the two men had previously been moralizing. This pattern of engagement is repeated throughout the ramble as positions of exclusion or elevation are routinely muddled in descent or leveling. The constitution of Bagnigge Wells as a public place, for example, is recapitulated in two stories of those in attendance, where individual mobility, both upward and downward, projects a collective or potential uniformity. The first is a lengthy account of a "menial servant" who had been "lately raised" to the "dignity" of being the "wife of an eminent tradesman" (21). This account is followed by the account of a young man "possessed of an independent fortune" who "appear[s] to be in a deep consumption"

(25) and whose physical decline—proceeding from his parents' resistance to his marrying a woman of inferior station—is reversed only through his social decline, which happens when he is permitted to marry the woman in a last-ditch effort to mitigate his disease. From here the two men adjourn to a coffeehouse, where this same dispensation bears on discursive formations that, however different in their topical interests or political allegiances, are instances of what Coleridge would later term "desynonymity."

The two men eventually visit the Pantheon in the Spa-Fields, a more advanced instance of the leveling that is everywhere taking place and described by "an arch wag" as a beehive containing "little else but *drones*" (49). This is similarly the case with "Marybone-Garden," whose wretched condition (in contrast to the advertisements lauding it as a "superlatively genteel place" [50]) prompts the narrator to question how this leveling could have happened when more fashionable places, such as Ranelagh, charge far less for admission. Nor is it coincidental that only once in the entire account do the author and his companion ascend to anything resembling a prospect or elevated vantage. Having "arrived at the top of Highgate-Hill," the two "stopped a few minutes to admire the beautiful prospect . . . and then proceeded, as it was rather late, to the intended ordinary; where, when we arrived, dinner being on the table, we immediately sat down" (42). Although it would be wrong to make too much of the downward trajectory of this anecdote, or of the range of the word "ordinary" in this context, the anecdote is typical in describing how the private as such, and the difference with which it is essentially associated, are routinely violated.

This violation is especially evident in the concluding stages of the day's ramble, when the two men enter Kensington Gardens—a place visited by Evelina and presumed, as another contemporary guidebook put it, to be "crowded . . . with persons of fashion."[26] The narrator initially confirms this exclusivity in noting the "servants . . . placed at the different entrances, to prevent persons meanly clad from going into the garden" (54) as well as the beautiful and private "alcoves" that are "contrived" to "command an agreeable prospect through the most delightful vistas" while "serving at once to repose the limbs and charm the eyes of the weary visitants" (54). Yet having observed this dimension to the gardens, the narrator follows the guidebook's counterclaim, in this case its allusion to the "crowd," in proceeding to a "generally complained of nusance [*sic*]" that also "prevails" there, "the removal of which . . . seems not to be attempted" (54). He is referring specifically to the "obscene verses on the glass of the green house" as well as to similar "hieroglyphicks" that "many apparently virtuous females" can be observed "poring over" (54–55).

The difference, certainly, between appearance and reality, or between people "of distinction" for whom the gardens are intended and those who have invaded the place, is a distinction that the narrator would like to see enforced for the general good. The likelihood of this happening is diminished by the recognition that the narrator and his companion, no less than the apparently virtuous ladies, comprise an audience whose interest in such representations far outweighs any universal condemnation. The likelihood of preserving distinctions is diminished even further upon learning from a man "of distinction" who soon accosts them, that the frequenters of the gardens, particularly the nobility in attendance, are whoremongers or, in the case of their informant, men of "rectitude" who have nothing better to do than gossip and pass judgment (55–56).

A Sunday Ramble comes to a close with a visit to a brothel "full of well-dressed persons . . . whose behaviour" is "ill suited with their habits" (64). Like either the gardens or the mall in St. James park that, all fashion notwithstanding, is similarly rife with "publickly-complying females" (62), the brothel is representative of a world where distinctions of all kinds are increasingly impossible. This fluidity provokes *A Sunday Ramble* to an observation, regarding the lofty and ultimately dangerous expectations with which young women are imbued by modern education, that is clearly an effort to reverse this tendency.

But there is a problem with this reversal. The antileveling initiative depends also, and problematically at this point, on the discouragement of *upward* mobility to which the *Ramble's* judgments ex bagnio give both testimony *and* the lie. The attempt, that is, to reinstitute value and discrimination follows the kind of mobility by which persons of "fashion" constitute a "crowd" in illustrating how judgment itself, like the judgment most recently of the man of "distinction," actually serves and illustrates the instabilities it laments: in this case, the leveling that, following the "fashionable crowd" again, is simultaneously an *upward and a downward* trajectory. After remarking on the heterogeneous company in the bagnio and on the fact that the women in attendance did not find their way there by a single path or inclination, the pharmacist observes (with the narrator's agreement) that the "vices and follies" that currently "disgrace the human species" have at their root the great expectations to "high statio[n]" that women in particular, brought up "by their fatally indulgent parents," carry with them into the world (67–68). Having been educated "in a manner superior to the station they may reasonably be supposed to fill" (69), they are, upon entrance into the world, seduced "by those that are full as artful, and more experienced than themselves" and by turns plunged into "the gulph of infamy" (68–69). The implicit distance that the pharmacist and the narrator interpose between themselves and the various people in attendance certainly figures the two men's claim to a position of distinction. Yet recapitulating as they do the "man of distinction" in Kensington Gardens who is similarly among whores and whoremongers, their aspirations here, though linked to a moral initiative, are not easily dissociated from the aspirations (or even the activities) of the women in their presence, whose fall, like the judgments that deplore it, is coextensive with efforts to rise in the world.

By now, in any case, we are a hairbreadth away from the preface to *Evelina* and from the related arguments for the efficacious work of probability as distinct from that of fantasy. The difference is that in *Evelina* the contradictory work of probability, where the status quo remains a desired end *and* an already-realized end under potential threat, succeeds in rendering Evelina a role model for the very women who, by the apothecary's argument, will end up in a bagnio. By contrast *A Sunday Ramble* grants the leveling that Burney fears a probability, indeed an inevitability, that only a distortion or narrowing of the probable can forestall or retrieve from a more radical proliferation. To the extent that Burney's work is contradictory or incoherent, it is on behalf of an order it wishes to preserve. This is in distinct contrast to the sheer hypocrisy of *A Sunday Ramble*, whose judgments, far from helping to preserve difference, work constantly to collapse it. Sufficiently a site of possibility to provoke both Evelina's and *Evelina's* removal from it, Burney's "world," like that of *A Sunday Ramble*, remains the site of change that Burney's text, as it asks to be read, is not.

The Anti-Romanticism of Burney's *The Wanderer*

In implicitly contrasting Burney's reluctant romanticism to Austen's more conscious investment in a world whose prospects are at variance with a typically probabilistic framework, I do not mean to recapitulate the long-standing appreciation of Austen as a writer whose achievement must be weighed in contrast to, and therefore at the expense of, her scribbling female contemporaries. I mean only to suggest that in characterizing a broadly nonessentialist strain of romantic writing, Austen's "romanticism" is concomitantly ecumenical in recognizing the degree to which a probabilistic worldview is inimical to women and men both. It is with attention to romanticism in this decidedly catholic sense that the comparison with Burney proves illustrative. For if Austen can be said to marshal a protofeminist position toward a greater romanticism to which other, more conventionally romantic documents frequently only aspire, it is reciprocally the case that Burney *at her most romantic*—in, for example, her 1814 novel, *The Wanderer; Or, Female Difficulties*—reproduces a romanticism that has been diverted *in the name of feminism* from a more expansive, less ideologically hidebound formation. That Burney's romanticism is in this sense a vitiation of romanticism, especially to the degree that romanticism is linked to a conventionally progressive or radical discourse, is far less paradoxical than it sounds.[27]

In making the aristocratic Juliet Granville, rather than the revolutionary Elinor Joddrel, the eponymous "wanderer" whose odyssey leads through a thicket of difficulties reserved for women, Burney does more than simply disrupt any potential or plausible link between women's issues and people's issues. Burney actively reconfigures a potential counterhegemony in granting equal and simultaneous priority to a largely residual discourse of aristocratic privilege and an increasingly emergent discourse of feminism. That Burney's "wanderer" is both a representative woman beset by "female difficulties" and a representative aristocrat who has been temporarily removed from her rightful and predestined station, is far from an exercise in victimology. It is the basis, rather, of a cunning, if somewhat perverse, negotiation in which the aristocrat, and the still-dominant culture she figures, are responsive without also being answerable to women's culture and its emergent concerns.

Burney seems aware of what is inherently problematic in such a negotiation, which she confronts or allegorizes rather late in the novel by having Albert Harleigh identify the revolutionary Elinor as possessing a "noble, though, perhaps, a masculine spirit" (862). It is true that Elinor's "masculinity" is, in Burney's calculus, instrumental in her attraction to totalizing systems of change like the revolution in France. Yet Elinor's masculinity is also the lens through which, as a woman, she perceives and enacts contradictions in such notions as the "rights of woman" that (as she both states and demonstrates) follow the largely solipsistic trajectory of the rights of man. These contradictions in turn lead both Elinor and the novel to authentically oppositional moments, in which the potential dominance of any ideology, progressive or conservative, encounters substantial resistance.

Early on, Elinor is provoked by the topic of the French Revolution, and the charge of barbarism levied against it by Harleigh, to a series of questions that slide perceptibly from an apparently rhetorical function:

Can any thing be so absurd, so preposterous, as to seek to improve mankind individually, yet bid it stand still collectively? What is education, but reversing propensities, making the idle industrious, the rude civil, and the ignorant learned? And do you not, for every student thus turned out of his likings, his vagaries, or his vices, to be new modelled, call this alteration improvement? Why, then, must you brand all similar efforts for new organizing states, nations, and bodies of society, by that word of unmeaning alarm, innovation? (18–19)

Drawing an analogy between the progress of the individual and that of society, Elinor's rebuttal of the anti-Jacobin position founders on its own rhetoric and does so, I would argue, quite purposively. The progressive narrative of wholesale change that she proposes as an alternative is no more compelling than, or even different from, the idea of "improvement," which is the only qualitative change that the anti-Jacobin position admits. Elinor's description of education, by which she hopes to sway Harleigh to her position, appears—especially with the interrogative—to be anything but enthusiastic. This is reinforced in her concluding image of society as a body, which underscores the discipline to which improvement or innovation is demonstrably tantamount. Far from agreeing with her interlocutor, then, Elinor is really one step beyond both Harleigh *and herself* in recognizing the counter-revolutionary implications in the progressive argument, which does not mean that she is not still an anti-anti-Jacobin. If anything, Elinor is mindful here of the contradiction inherent in a "collective" whose improvement (as her initial query announces) is effectively tied to the coronation of the individual.

It is important to remember that Elinor and her ideology are derogated almost from the beginning of *The Wanderer* and that it takes a pressured reading such as I have exerted to complicate what seems on the surface a simple identification of Elinor with the excesses of the age. All the same, the various dead ends and, with them, the alternatives regarding social change to which Elinor's observations routinely lead us—especially in the novel's early stages—underscore the theoretical reach of an identity we can call romanticism as it is informed now by a horizon of possibility to which the usual vocabularies of change and their attendant narratives are curiously insufficient. When nearly a hundred pages later Elinor, in a dialogue with the novel's mysterious heroine, protests that she is not an enemy of marriage between social unequals, her expatiation on the "liberty" gained through such leveling initiatives adumbrates a position or possibility, again, that is also mitigated by the narratives of change on which such prospects currently depend. "If you imagine me an enemy to what the old court call unequal connexions, you do me egregious injustice. I detest all aristocracy: I care for nothing upon earth but nature; and I hold no one thing in the world worth living for but liberty! and liberty, you know, has but two occupations,— plucking up and pulling down. To me, therefore, 'tis equally diverting to see a beggar swell into a duchess, or a duchess dwindle into a beggar" (110–11). As in her previous observation, Elinor's conventionally progressive claims for liberty are transformed midway into a critique of a conventionally progressive narrative. By the time that the word "liberty" is uttered a second time it has proceeded from something like authentic freedom to what, as Elinor suggests, remains a diversion from that end. To see a beggar become a duchess, or a duchess become a beggar, is not to witness (or be pleasantly diverted by) productive social change but to be *diverted from* liberty by maintenance of narratives that are interchangeably progressive and aristocratic. This world is one where mobility and change coexist comfortably and seamlessly with the usual and still arbitrary gradations of status and authority.

And it is a world, furthermore, with which *The Wanderer*, like the foreshortened romanticism it promotes, is largely comfortable. Even as Burney allows Elinor her critical function in this text, she is much more intent upon writing a narrative that effectively traces one woman's odyssey from beggar (indeed a beggar in blackface) to aristocrat. The only difference is that where Elinor's image of liberty diverted from its true ends involves the fantasy of what is at least a real beggar, Burney's narrative about a woman who merely pretends to be one, and whose sense of entitlement is readable throughout, is far more hidebound in effectively asserting—even while enumerating Juliet's female difficulties—that beggars should remain beggars. Where Elinor's is in many ways a deconstruction of a certain aspect of romanticism as having failed the very liberty toward which it ostensibly points, Burney's is a reconstruction of romanticism to hegemonic purposes. But Burney apparently knew better than always to accept her own authority or, as Elinor's appearance suggests, the authority of her own narratives. In these moments, including the "world" of possibility and change from which Evelina must finally be removed, Burney is more romantic, more a feminist, and more like Jane Austen than is generally appreciated.

PART II

Reading the Historical Austen

Lady Susan *and the Failure of Austen's Early Published Novels*

The title of this chapter is meant to be provocative. But it seems more outrageous with each passing day. Not only does the title ascribe "failure" to *Pride and Prejudice*, the best-known and most beloved of Austen's novels; it suggests the failure as well of Austen's first published novel, *Sense and Sensibility*, whose popularity—thanks to Emma Thompson's cinematic adaptation—has never been greater. At the same time, a look at some of the disparities between *Sense and Sensibility* and its cinematic counterpart will help explain what I mean by "failure," which I hold distinct, in any case, from the conditions that account for the success of these texts, particularly in terms of their popularity.

The principal disparities between the adaptation of *Sense and Sensibility* and the original text—chiefly, the smoothing out of the ostensible heroes, Colonel Brandon and Edward Ferrars, the transformation of Sir John Middleton from a middle-aged husband with a salacious eye into a toothless widower, and the further demonization of the ostensible villain, John Willoughby—are not disparities so much as efforts to make sense of a text that, as the film version shows by contrast, is something of a mess. Heavily revised for over a decade, during which time it was transformed from an epistolary novel into a third-person narrative, *Sense and Sensibility* presumably underwent other transformations as well. The novel seems also to have gone from a relatively direct parable in which the sisters, Elinor and Marianne Dashwood, avatars of sense and sensibility respectively, collaborate in teaching both Marianne and Austen's female readership the dangers that accrue to an uncompromising imagination, into a work that, as I will argue, was revised so as to expose (thereby limiting) this didactic function.

This is not to say that epistolarity and didacticism are commensurate where Austen is concerned. If anything, my point, again, as suggested in my title, would be the opposite: that Austen's first published novels, her first fully realized attempts at free indirect discourse, ultimately foreclose on certain aspects of epistolarity—what I again call its oppositional potential—which are evident in the only mature epistolary fiction of Austen's currently extant, the novella *Lady Susan*. In fact I suggest that the particular difficulties of *Sense and Sensibility*, in contrast to the didactic simplicity of the film adaptation, owe almost entirely to what Deborah Kaplan (with a rather different focus) has termed the "achievement of authority" in that text:[1] an achievement that, although marked by the stylistic and rhetorical triumph of free indirect discourse, is complicit with certain hegemonic formations to which *Sense and Sensibility*, *Pride and Prejudice*, and *Lady Susan* are in many ways unreconciled.

It is this resistance to authority, and to the regulatory work in which domestic fiction is plainly instrumental, that the cinematic adaptation of *Sense and Sensibility* neutralizes. This mitigation involves, most notably, the suppression of the novel's most memorable scene: Willoughby's surprise visit in the midst of Marianne's near-fatal illness. In discarding a scene that provides Willoughby, the quasi-libertine, with some measure of vindication, the film does more than follow the lead of many popular cinematic adaptations in depicting a morally ambiguous character in an unambiguous way. It identifies what is otherwise opaque in most interpretations of the novel: the simultaneous, and at this point belated, resistance to an authority that regulates in the guise of liberality and directs in the service of progress and change. For if nothing else, the missing scene with Willoughby resuscitates expectations that, regardless of their configuration, are reaction formations to the diminished expectations of women, which the "achievement of the authority" has failed on balance to enlarge or to transform.

Readers of *Sense and Sensibility* will remember clearly Austen's painful delineation of her heroines' vulnerability following their father's death and the subsequent transfer of his property, including the house in which Elinor and Marianne are living, to a son by a former marriage. They will remember too the sharply satiric account of how the two sisters, their mother, and younger sister, Margaret, are systematically deprived of all but a mere subsistence by their half-brother who, under the influence of his wife, reneges on every promise he had made to his late father regarding the support of the latter's second family. What readers may not remember so clearly, however, is the use to which this representation, indeed this allegory, of women's vulnerability is put in the ensuing narrative. They will forget this because *Sense and Sensibility* is suspended between a sensible endorsement of marriage—ideally a companionate marriage—as the only practical stay against the insecurity of remaining an unmarried woman, and a more radical or utopian position, figured principally in Marianne, which is appropriated to the initial position (and to its legitimation) both as a distension of sense *and* as a cautionary counterexample. Although the utopian position in *Sense and Sensibility* is precisely *that*—a register of the desire for an entirely different social and affective configuration for women and men—it remains limited, along with sense, to a marital teleology characteristic of domestic fiction in general.

Thus the desire for a different world in *Sense and Sensibility* is not only held hostage to the claims and expectations of this world (and this genre) by which Marianne would be happily married to Willoughby, a man of apparent wealth and independence. Such desire is subject to a displacement so powerfully normative that the only trace of dissent is in the eroticism that lingers even in the wake of Marianne's disappointment. Despite the apparent aim of *Sense and Sensibility* and the effect of its authority, which is to discourage desire in deference to a more measured, more pragmatic restraint, the novel accomplishes that discouragement only by affiliating Elinor, the proponent of restraint, with her more expansive and uncompromising sibling. The novel, in other words, sustains the binarism in its title and the opposition by which the first category—"sense"—is converted into a privileged term over "sensibility," but through a *hegemonic* negotiation in which the signifiers of "sense" and "sensibility," the two sisters, are perceived as victims in kind of an order that *would be dominant* save for the little prestige accorded it by the narrative. The privilege accorded Elinor (and "sense"), then, derives not just from an affiliation with an emergent order, indeed a sisterhood, whose resistance to a dominant order is allegorically implied and thereby endorsed. Elinor's prestige derives even more from an order whose *increasing* dominance (over the increasing residuality of what is nominally the dominant order) consists in an opposition that, while implied, is simultaneously muted in a practiced and narratable restraint. But what this also means is that the subordinate and increasingly repressed term in the novel—"sensibility"—although similarly contained by a narrative that limits change to the telos of marriage, is free to circulate in an eroticism that for the most part remains a harmless trope of resistance.[2]

That is, until the return of Willoughby late in the novel. With the return of the impulsive Willoughby, Elinor is not merely exposed to an eroticism that she has long suppressed regarding her own prospects, which are attached to the comparatively asexual Edward Ferrars (played winningly and cosmetically in the film by Hugh Grant). She is captive as well to a narrative—in this case Willoughby's narrative—that, beyond being somewhat self-exculpatory, has the more important function of recalling what has been gained *and* lost in Austen's achievement of authority and in the use to which the novel has put Elinor.

The key to Willoughby's visit involves far more than Willoughby's belated disclosures regarding either his cruel letter to Marianne (which he explains was dictated by his jealous fiancée) or the apparently consensual nature of his affair with the unfortunate Eliza, who is the ward of Colonel Brandon. The key to this

crucial episode lies rather in its positioning of the allegorical figure of oppositionality and change—the eroticism that bears powerfully on the rapt and
attentive Elinor as it had earlier on Marianne—against the hegemonic choices
with which the achievement of authority here, specifically the attempt via Elinor to direct change by also regulating it, is necessarily coextensive. With the return of the repressed, in other words, a reversal of sorts takes place. The erotic,
increasingly a mere figure of resistance in the novel, is suddenly narrativized,
indeed literalized, at the expense of narrative itself, which undergoes a reciprocal (or in this case allegorizing) process following certain disclosures that bear
directly on issues of omniscience and narrative authority.

I am especially interested in two details in Willoughby's exculpatory account whose import is plainly lost on both Willoughby and his interlocutor and
unmoored thereby from a purely narrative or diegetic function. The first of
these involves Willoughby's explanation regarding his sudden departure from
Allenham—the seat of a wealthy relative whose estate he will inherit—and from
the company of Marianne and her family, at a time when a formal declaration
of love from him was strongly indicated:

"At last, however, my resolution was taken, and I had determined as soon as I could engage her alone, to justify the attentions I had so invariably paid her, and openly assure
her of an affection which I had already taken such pains to display. But in the interim—
in the interim of the very few hours that were to pass, before I could have an opportunity
of speaking with her in private—a circumstance occurred—an unlucky circumstance, to
ruin all my resolution, and with it all my comfort. A discovery took place,"—here he hesi-
tated and looked down.—"Mrs. Smith had somehow or other been informed, I imagine
by some distant relation, whose interest was to deprive me of her favour, of an affair, a
connection—but I need not explain myself further," he added, looking at her with an
heightened colour and an inquiring eye,—"your particular intimacy—you have probably heard the whole story long ago." (281–82)[3]

The second detail involves a similarly unattributed disclosure, this time to
Willoughby's fiancée, Sophia, regarding his recent attachment to Marianne,
which proves the basis for the chilling letter to Marianne (who is of course ignorant of Willoughby's prior engagement) breaking off *their* relationship:

Your sister wrote to me again, you know, the very next morning. You saw what she said. I
was breakfasting at the Ellisons,—and her letter, with some others, was brought to me
there from my lodgings. It happened to catch Sophia's eye before it caught mine—and
its size, the elegance of the paper, the hand-writing altogether, immediately gave her a
suspicion. Some vague report had reached her before of my attachment to some young
lady in Devonshire, and what had passed within her observation the preceding evening had marked who the young lady was, and made her more jealous than ever. Affect-

ing that air of playfulness, therefore, which is delightful in a woman one loves, she opened the letter directly, and read its contents. She was well paid for her impudence. She read what made her wretched. Her wretchedness I could have borne, but her passion—her malice—At all events it must be appeased. And in short—what do you think of my wife's style of letter-writing?—delicate—tender—truly feminine—was it not? (287–88)

D. A. Miller, who has written perceptively on this episode and is virtually alone among critics in stressing the eroticism that binds Elinor to Willoughby during his recital, is just as perspicacious in identifying Willoughby as "as a figure of disturbance" here.[4] In Miller's view Willoughby succeeds not only in unsettling Elinor's convictions regarding his behavior prior to this moment; more important, Willoughby makes any resettlement of Elinor's convictions and, by implication, those undergirding Austen's narrative all but impossible. In retelling Willoughby's story as she is charged by him to do, Elinor is compelled, as Miller observes, to censor Willoughby's account (and the urgency of his appeal)—first to Marianne and afterward, to their mother—in ways that, while implicating Elinor in the imperatives of novelistic closure, work to expose or even to open "narrative" to Elinor's "troubled" and conflicted judgment.

Still there is a question regarding the nature of Elinor's judgment and its bearing on the narrative overall. It involves the degree to which Elinor's retelling of Willoughby's story is, even with the eroticism that drives her to a reluctant and reflexive monitoring of its protagonist, an extension of the figuration already initiated in the episode and into which her amelioration of Willoughby's narrative is folded. The real examination of narrative that transpires here has less to do with the "disturbance" that Willoughby introduces and that Elinor sustains even by containment. It has to do rather with the intelligence selectively and influentially disseminated to the women closest to Willoughby, the source of which ("some distant relation," "some vague report") is not just mysterious but sufficiently unapproachable (or uninterrogated in this instance) to figure an authority in excess of the subordinate characters in its sway.

Nor is it only the characters who are subject to this omniscient authority. Subjugation also informs the *reading* of *Sense and Sensibility* to the degree that readers must somehow follow Elinor's lead—in the way that Miller, for example, follows it—in recognizing that the novel is not a failure but simply a text that, at its most limited, fails only to answer our demands as twenty-first-century readers and to share, in retrospect, our more open value system. To virtually all commentators on the novel, no less than the two interlocutors, it is scarcely an issue that the source of the information to Mrs. Smith and Sophia can be *none other than Colonel Brandon* or that it is only Colonel Brandon, of all the possible characters in the novel, who has the motive, the resources (in other words, the information) and the mobility to effect this brilliant manipulation of character, event, and most important of all, closure.

For most readers, including Elinor, the avuncular Brandon with his flannel waistcoat is part of a well-meaning, if conservative, apparatus whereby moderation and compromise are urged as a basis for happiness and, worse, as constituting an actual strategy for change. I say "worse" because the only change effected by the compromise that Brandon at once orchestrates and figures, one summarized in what he earlier terms "second attachments," is not change in a substantive, much less an oppositional, sense. It represents change in what one would, again, have to call a hegemonic sense. It is a change that follows Elinor's edition of Willoughby in assimilating possibility and discontent, which are figured by eroticism in the text, to an order capable of adequating itself to specific discourses of change and of redirecting those discourses in the process.

Thus while Brandon is assuredly possessed of erotic feeling, which drives him (in the manner of the lecherous Sir John Middleton) to an insistent, if sinister, pursuit of Marianne, he recognizes from the very first the compromised eroticism that would characterize their union should it somehow take place. In a conversation with Elinor early in the novel regarding Marianne's demonstrated belief in an all-encompassing—and, for the purpose of the novel's allegory, utopian—love, Brandon unhappily notes Marianne's evident disapproval of what in contrast are "second attachments":

> "Your sister, I understand, does not approve of second attachments."
> "No," replied Elinor, "her opinions are all romantic."
> "Or rather, as I believe, she considers them impossible to exist."
> "I believe she does. But how she contrives it without reflecting on the character of her own father, who had himself two wives, I know not. A few years however will settle her opinions on the reasonable basis of common sense and observation; and then they may be more easy to define and justify than they now are, by any body but herself."
> "This will probably be the case," he replied; "and yet there is something so amiable in the prejudices of a young mind, that one is sorry to see them give way to the reception of more general opinions." (47–48)

Putting aside for a moment Brandon's proleptic, even confident, nostalgia regarding the Marianne who will eventually cease to exist, the exchange with Elinor makes clear the significance of Marianne's demands. The "romanticism" of Marianne's opinions pertains less to the solipsism that allows her to fixate unabashedly on Willoughby (as usually assumed) than to the institution of male privilege that this seeming solipsism opposes: an institution, whose prevalence, or familiarity in this case, seems to Elinor even more than Brandon reason to proclaim its legitimacy. Demonstrating the dynamics of legitimation, specifically the ease with which the commonplace will slide into the normative and even the natural, Elinor does not echo Brandon so much as she casts him in sharper relief. For Brandon's more ambivalent construction of himself as a compromise candidate (or second attachment) follows and exposes the work of hegemony in deriving sustenance from the very discourses—the utopian or plenitudinous discourse of "first attachments"—that it seeks, by its own admission, to contain and to assimilate.

Thus Brandon's strangely anticipatory nostalgia is more than a perfect figure for hegemony, which necessarily values the emergent, comparatively disruptive energies that it deploys to dominant ends. It is the perfect figure for the rhetoric of *Sense and Sensibility* overall, which depends similarly on a loss, specifically the foreshortening of "sensibility" into "sense," so as to validate its appeal for compromise and restraint. The nostalgic residue of sensibility (and its implicit wish for a different, more equitable world) is more than just a means by which compromise is disingenuously held distinct from capitulation here. It is the very instrument, following Brandon, by which the narrative urges the reader's capitulation in turn.[5]

The case against Brandon and the disposition of his authority is not restricted to these figurings of omniscience. In fact Brandon's peculiar instrumentality, particularly when the narrative relocates to London, is a steady reminder that, regardless of its impossibility in purely linguistic terms, the very apparatus of free indirect discourse, or what Ann Banfield again calls "represented speech and thought," is an extraordinarily powerful *device* on which the novel's coercive capacity depends. The most notable example of this coercion, as it continues undetected, remains Willoughby's astonishing inability to link the mysterious, and to his mind unrelated, disclosures to Mrs. Smith and Sophia Grey to Colonel Brandon, whom Willoughby also identifies amid his recitation as one likely to be biased in any representations of him. "Remember . . . from whom you received the account," he exhorts Elinor just seconds after reporting on the intelligence "of an affair" that had been conveyed to Mrs. Smith and subsequently to his interlocutor. "Could it be an impartial one?" (282).

Nevertheless the real exposure of the authority now vested in Brandon comes in other, more concrete gestures, notably his refusal to inform Marianne directly of Willoughby's behavior at a point when disaster could have been averted and his seemingly benevolent offer of a living to Edward upon hearing of the latter's estrangement from his wealthy mother. In the case of the decision to withhold information, all of which suggests that he has elected to disseminate it by other, more calculated means, Brandon justifies his behavior with a daring that should give any reader pause—even as it fails to unsettle Elinor's sense of his rectitude. "My behaviour must have seemed strange to you then," he reminds Elinor of the time he had to leave Barton "so suddenly," "but now you will comprehend it. To suffer you all to be so deceived; to see your sister—but what could I do? I had no hope of interfering with success; and sometimes I thought your sister's influence might yet reclaim him. But now, after such dishonourable usage, who can tell what were his designs on her?" (182–83). It is possible that Brandon was initially hopeful of Willoughby's rehabilitation, which would have saved Marianne from the potential degradation to which Brandon has already been suspiciously proximate on two other occasions. But there is little question that the expectations relevant to his inaction bear at least as much on his own "success," which would have been interfered with as directly as Willoughby's had he been the messenger of such tidings. Willing, that is, to expose Marianne to almost certain risk in the "hope" of eventually claiming her as his own, Brandon not only says nothing when saying something might have made a difference. He also compounds his default in monitoring the deleterious results of his inaction (along with his more covert actions) during his numerous visits to the Dashwoods in London.

There is also, of course, the matter of Edward's living. Brandon offers the Delaford living to Edward not so that Edward can marry Lucy Steele, to whom he has been engaged. He offers it to Edward under the condition that Edward *not* marry and in a manner that discloses Brandon's real aim, which is to have Elinor and her sister at arm's reach. Although Brandon eagerly excoriates the "impolitic cruelty . . . of dividing, or attempting to divide, two young people long attached to each other" (246), his outrage is lodged less in a disinterested concern than in the structural similarities between Edward's dilemma and his earlier disappointments with the first Eliza from whom Brandon was similarly parted by parental edict. This is of a piece, then, with the decision to have Elinor deliver the offer to Edward, in lieu of making it himself. In charging Elinor with this task, Brandon sets about accomplishing two related things. He seeks to strengthen Edward's and Elinor's attachment at the expense of "long attach[ment]" with Lucy on whose behalf his intervention is supposedly based. And he lays the groundwork for ensuring that Marianne, who must presumably accompany Elinor on any eventual visits to Delaford, will shortly be in close proximity.

In making Elinor the envoy of good news, Brandon also makes it clear to her, then—and by extension to Edward—that the Delaford living will be insufficient for the purpose of supporting a wife. " 'This little rectory,' " he advises Elinor, "*can* do no more than make Mr. Ferrars comfortable as a bachelor; it cannot enable him to marry. I am sorry to say that my patronage ends with this; and my interest is hardly more extensive. If, however, by any unforeseen chance it should be in my power to serve him farther, I must think very differently of him from what I now do, if I am not as ready to be useful to him then, as I sincerely wish I could be at present. What I am now doing indeed, seems nothing at all, since it can advance him so little towards what must be his principal, his only object of happiness. His marriage must still be a distant good;—at least I am afraid it cannot take place very soon." (248)

The narrator goes on to note that the "sentence," by which she presumably means the last in Brandon's recitation, was sufficiently misunderstood by Lucy's cousin—the meddling but well-intentioned Mrs. Jennings—to "offen[d]" the latter's "delicate feelings" (248). Nevertheless a careful reading of Brandon's "sentence," including the conditions under which additional support may be forthcoming, suggests that Mrs. Jennings has understood him far better than is allowed. At the heart of Brandon's convolution, with its mixture of vagueness and stridency, is the thinly veiled promise of extended interest—or what for Brandon is never far from self-interest—depending on Edward's actions regarding Lucy. Such actions, if they are to work materially in transforming Brandon's opinion of Edward, must involve the rejection of Lucy (and her consignment to what at this point seems certain indigence) in deference to some other, comparatively distant marital goal.

As a figure for narrative authority, Brandon is disposed to "foresee" and micromanage the progress of the characters in his sway. But here, as a coercive device, he is more immediately a gatekeeper whose insistence on Edward's continued bachelorhood is designed to give Elinor access to the rectory that she would not enjoy otherwise and cannot enjoy lest she be accompanied by a companion such as Marianne. Even worse, Brandon initiates a sequence of events whose projected disposition, on which any transformation of his thinking and generosity will depend, is clearly an incentive for Elinor to aid in their achievement. If Edward can be persuaded to forsake Lucy and to remain single long enough for the other likely visitor to Delaford to cast off any lingering attachment to Willoughby, which her visits there (and to Brandon) will abet, Elinor will be rewarded in a myriad of ways.

None of this is stated very explicitly in Austen's narrative or more explicitly, say, than Brandon's cryptic directives as I have interpreted them. Even so, it is by no means incidental that while Elinor embraces Brandon's generosity to a degree that the narrative appears also to endorse, other recipients of the good news, including Mrs. Jennings, think differently. Much fun is made of Mrs. Jennings, who quickly misconstrues Brandon's intentions as pertaining to Elinor and *their* impending marriage at which the newly ordained Edward would likely officiate. Yet, Mrs. Jennings cannot also help noting the oddity of the colonel's refusal to write Edward directly on these matters, including the disposal of the Delaford living. Edward, needless to say, is truly perplexed. Informed by Elinor of Brandon's offer, he is notably dumbstruck—even as he performs exactly as Brandon has directed.

Edward's astonishment over Brandon's apparently random act of generosity is especially key, as is his continued astonishment in the wake of Elinor's attempts to explain the colonel's generosity. Despite Elinor's justification of Brandon's behavior as reflecting an altruism alien to Edward's "own relations" (253), Edward's only response is to credit Elinor in a way that alternately fulfills and exposes Brandon's intentions. In his demonstrable gratitude over an initiative that Elinor has undertaken by mere proxy, Edward is more than simply unpersuaded by her defense of Brandon, whose generosity remains paramount in Elinor's opinion. He implicitly rejects an illusion of Brandon that his "own relations," whose unkindness Elinor deems exceptional and antithetical to Brandon, find similarly implausible. Informed in due course of the bequest that has suddenly relieved his brother-in-law of any obligation to their family and its imperious matriarch, John Dashwood, the selfish and satirized half brother of the Dashwood sisters, introduces a question regarding Edward's good fortune that the narrative, like Elinor, must necessarily discountenance:

> "It is truly astonishing!"—he cried, after hearing what [Elinor] said—"what could be the Colonel's motive?"
> "A very simple one—to be of use to Mr. Ferrars."
> "Well, well; whatever Colonel Brandon may be, Edward is a very lucky man!" (258)

It is easy to construe John Dashwood's implicit skepticism as pertaining more to his own motives under comparable conditions than to Brandon's. Still, as this is at least the third separate register of surprise over Brandon's actions in fewer than ten pages, and one that is unambiguous in identifying Brandon as suspiciously motivated, it works both individually and cumulatively to exert pressure on Elinor, especially to the degree that she is figured throughout as a repository of knowledge who can be trusted.

Such faith in Elinor's trustworthiness is held by no less an adversary than Lucy Steele, who, calculatedly or not, entrusts Elinor with the knowledge of her secret engagement to Edward, knowing full well that Elinor will neither disclose nor jeopardize that arrangement. And it is held just as strongly by modern readers of the novel, who regard Elinor as a repository of restraint that the narrative strenuously promotes and as someone akin to "the mediating narrator," whose judgments, like Elinor's, are apparently rendered from a detached perspective rather than on the basis of self-interest.[6] The most notable manifestation of such disinterestedness probably comes in Elinor's spirited defense of Lucy as "a woman superior in person and understanding to half her sex" (229), whom she is willing at that juncture to consign to Edward's care.

At the same time, Elinor's proximity to Brandon in the occasion of serving as messenger to Edward complicates *her role* as the narrator's surrogate by exposing and complicating the narrator's function. Although Elinor's complicity with Brandon is consistent with her tendency to accommodate rather than to oppose, it is readily exploited by Brandon, and by at least one other author now, whose meditation on the achievement of authority in *Sense and Sensibility* is ultimately extended to a character who also differs from Brandon in being, as Barbara Benedict has recently suggested, the narrator's virtual double. In the case of Brandon, as I have been arguing, the machinations of authority are sufficiently recoverable and self-serving to inculpate him as a troublemaker who, more than Willoughby himself, recalls the meddling Clement Willoughby of Burney's *Evelina*. However, with respect to the other author here—in this case Austen—the implications surrounding Elinor's pliability are part of an abiding reflexivity, whose effect is to render Elinor an instrument and, by turns, a pivot on which the narrative wavers from its manifest function. In the very way that Elinor remains instrumental in Brandon's unrelenting quest of Marianne, so she remains, as a repository of value in the narrative, both a screen and a figure for a narrative practice whose affinity with her on the basis of either disinterestedness or omniscience remains, following Brandon's rather open manipulation of her, the basis of a more encompassing critique.

This use of character does not mean that *Sense and Sensibility* is necessarily wrongheaded in deploying Elinor in defense of a kind of praxis or course of action that is subversive (for want of a better term) in a different register. Elinor's ability to compromise also anticipates much contemporary thinking about resistance in its chameleonlike adaptability, all of which gives Elinor (in anticipation of such characters as Jane Fairfax and Frank Churchill) the advantage of being completely inscrutable to the very orders and their adherents to whom she would be as obvious and as unsuccessful in resisting as her younger sister. The problem rather is in the slippage between the orders to which Elinor arguably feigns capitulation, and the capitulation to her example, or to a course of action, on which the narrative insists—and of which her capitulation *to Brandon* remains a further and symbolic register.

In fact there turns out to be only one fundamental difference between the regime to which Elinor, in sisterhood or in solidarity with Marianne, offers opposition, and the hegemony to which her opposition is in the end adjunct. It is that the latter regime, as the capitulation to Brandon shows, is able to assimilate the cause of opposition to the end of self-legitimation whereas the former order—exemplified in the hopelessly status-conscious Mrs. Ferrars—is self-subverting for failure to do this. But what this also means is that "sense," whether as a figure for change or for the means to change, imposes limits on sensibility and the possibilistic horizons that Marianne, for one, has been fixated upon.

It may be argued too that sensibility declines in prestige through its insistence that change be amenable to a relational order, namely marriage, which is arguably the last place (witness the Palmers and the Middletons) where change is either likely or structurally permitted. But this particular error, as the novel itself suggests, is not Marianne's problem, or sensibility's. It is at this stage in Austen's writing a problem of both genre *and society* and thus a problem that can be laid directly at the "achievement of authority" here, which entails the deployment of domestic fiction replete with a marriage plot in the service of social improvement. Marianne's eventual marriage to Brandon is more than an event that readers have long lamented in light of its compromised disposition, particularly following Willoughby's tenth-hour disclosures. It is a figure as well of Austen's marriage to a literary form and to an authority—or an hegemony again—that forecloses on change in seeming to value it.

Epistolarity and Opposition

The use of Brandon to allegorize the politics of novelistic authority, particularly in the aftermath of epistolarity, would appear to counter certain critical commonplaces regarding both the political unconscious of "realistic" fiction and Austen's complicity, as a practitioner of domestic fiction, with certain social formations. However, when we look to *Lady Susan*, the only mature epistolary fiction of Austen's still available, Austen's peculiar mitigation of the "rise of the novel," of which her writing is often deemed a culmination, becomes a good deal clearer. This generally overlooked work not only provides a sense of what epistolarity entailed for Austen, both at the time and in retrospect; it actually anticipates Austen's achievement of authority by looking even further ahead to the adjustments that Austen would make by way of transforming both the rhetoric of her fiction and its related social work. Chief among these transformations, as I have indicated previously, are certain limits to narrative authority, specifically the metamorphosis of an omniscient narrator into a character with biases and limitations. This characterization, which follows upon the figuring of narrative authority in Colonel Brandon, complicates the directive aspects of a given fiction by effectively restoring what is lost (and was lost, I would argue, in *Sense and Sensibility*) in the movement from epistolary instability, where there is only silence separating the letters by fictive hands, to the relative stability of free indirect discourse.

I am not suggesting that all epistolary fiction is somehow permeable to an indeterminacy that the metalanguage of represented speech and action—the language that places speech in quotations in explaining its relationship to the real[7]—necessarily eliminates. I am suggesting only that for Austen, or more precisely *in Austen*, the "rise of the novel" is not without its demonstrable and acknowledged costs. While it is customary to argue that Austen's fiction is regulatory in its function, the epistolary legacy suggests that this was not always the case and that, if anything, the achievement of authority was always conflicted in ways that Austen's continued practice of free indirect discourse has managed to obscure. Austen never returned to the epistolary style. Yet it is almost surely the case that with the exception of her first two published novels, which B. C. Southam has concluded were the only major works of hers originally in letters, Austen was never in the position of having to *abandon* epistolarity and its potential enfranchisement of the reader for the sake of something more authoritative.[8]

The aspects of *Lady Susan* that bear immediately on Austen's fiction, chiefly its accessibility to certain oppositional reading practices, are numerous and obvious. The most obvious by far is the way the topos of the manipulative or scheming woman (à la *Les Liasons dangereuses*) is removed in this brief narrative from its otherwise didactic function. Although it is virtually impossible to regard the recently widowed Lady Susan Vernon as a role model for a presumably female readership, it is just as impossible to perceive the cultural order, which seeks to contain and to thwart her, in a more positive light. It is more the case that the various challenges that Lady Susan poses to the normative cultural order, notably the culture of domesticity that places a premium on the affective ties uniting husbands and wives and parents and children, go largely unmet in this text.[9]

Austen is perhaps being satiric, or hyperbolically waggish, in permitting her heroine, who is writing to a friend, to describe her daughter Frederica as a "stupid girl" with "nothing to recommend her" (215).[10] But Austen is doing more than playing for laughs in her of treatment of Lady Susan's sister-in-law and foil, the apparently virtuous Catherine Vernon, who is quick to observe in a letter to her mother-in-law that Lady Susan "has no real Love for her daughter and has never done her justice, or treated her affectionately" (232). Catherine Vernon may appear justified in this obvious, if self-serving, observation. However, she is even more noteworthy in failing in the course of her twelve letters (which comprise about a quarter of the narrative) to mention any of her own children by name. Even worse, her disapprobation may be unwarranted. As *Lady Susan* carefully delineates, the eponymous character's apparent—and, as it turns out, unnecessary—contempt for her daughter simply reflects an anxiety over Frederica's ability to survive in a world where women are indeed "worthless" and acutely vulnerable.

Thus Catherine Vernon serves a more complex function than the promotion of the ideology of domesticity in response to Lady Susan's negative example. If anything, she joins with her antagonist in demonstrating the deficiencies in the burgeoning ideology: from the lack of gratification that drives Catherine to mother other children in lieu of her own to the overarching patriarchy to which domestic ideology is always adjunct. If the patriarchal order can be said to marshal Catherine as its armature, reducing her in the process to a sanctimonious deformation, it is just as instrumental in reducing Lady Susan, recently removed from the benefits of both marriage and entailment, to dependency on her friends and relatives. That Catherine turns out to be *as manipulative* as her amoral counterpart, and as capable of dissimulation when the occasion warrants, is surely no surprise then. Even with their mutual antagonism, the sisters-in-law perform the more important function of demystifying and deconstructing the purchase on virtue that women are granted according to domestic ideology—and by which at least one of them is found wanting—in its rather obvious containment of them.

And contained the women are, whether as proponents of virtue like Catherine Vernon or seeming victims like Frederica or as openly transgressive figures like the main character, who, prior to her eventual remarriage, manages (in the course of fewer than eighty pages) not only to captivate the attentions of three men simultaneously, and to wreak havoc among their respective families, but to bring chaos as well upon her own family in competing with her daughter for the interest of a potential suitor. Austen's novella does not explicitly endorse the disruptive, if wickedly funny, activities of its main character. But it is quite explicit in refusing also to endorse their condemnation. Mindful rather that the "extraordinary fate" of women under patriarchy (as it is ironically dubbed in *Sense and Sensibility* [333]) is undoubtedly punishment enough, the novel is at pains to trace the various ways that the normative order reasserts itself. In addition to seeing to it that both Lady Susan and her daughter are married off, the normative order crowns its reestablishment by also silencing both the main character and, tautological as it sounds, the indeterminate, if readable, silence that Lady Susan's vocality—or ability to communicate according to the conventions of epistolarity—is instrumental in sustaining.

It is no accident surely that this novella—composed of letters that have apparently been retrieved by an editor—chronicles a period in Lady Susan's life demarcated by the death of her previous (and older) husband and by the acquisition of a new husband. Among other things, this bracketing of Lady Susan transforms the marriage plot from a vehicle of pure ideology into a different sort of plot. Marriage is a conspiracy now. And its purpose, at least in this text, is to remove women to a place where they are inaudible, invisible, and where their only agency is in serving the landed and patriarchal interests in which they are presumably subordinate and, like the eponymous character who is also homeless, continually vulnerable.

The eventual silencing of Lady Susan is accompanied, then, by the sudden audibility of the hitherto silent editor. This editor's concluding observations in *propria persona* introduce a form of omniscience that, in contrast to free indirect style, is akin to an earlier, Fieldingesque mode of authority:

Whether Lady Susan was, or was not happy in her second Choice—I do not see how it ever can be ascertained—for who would take her assurance of it, on either side of the question? The World must judge from Probability. She had nothing against her, but her Husband, and her Conscience. Sir James [Lady Susan's new husband] may seem to have drawn an harder Lot than mere Folly merited. I leave him therefore to all the Pity that anybody can give him. For myself, I confess that I can pity only Miss Manwaring, who coming to Town and putting herself to an expence in Cloathes, which impoverished her for two years, on purpose to secure him, was defrauded of her due by a Woman ten years older than herself. (272)

In reverting finally to a form of authority that is also misogynistic, both in its condemnation of Lady Susan and in the solace that it derives from the humiliation to which the women in this narrative are exposed, Austen is doing two things. She is looking ahead to her own achievement of authority, which is of course different; and she is looking even further ahead—which is to say backward—to the indeterminacy or the epistolary silence that, as Austen's greatest triumphs make clear, is indispensable to a literature directed, however nostalgically, toward prospects of change.[11] Omniscience undoubtedly provided an empowerment, in which Austen took enormous pleasure as a practitioner of fiction. Nevertheless, as the major fictions that she was working on at this time confirm, such empowerment was also incommensurate with the kinds of changes, or interventions in this case, that demanded more of the writer than a capacity to direct and more of her reader than the readiness to agree.

As a result, there remains a direct, if nearly paradoxical, link between the inability to ascertain the response that Austen had hoped to elicit in this occasion, or to which her text can be said to have directed its readers, and the various incentives to discretionary reading that abound in its pages. The most important of these aids, in addition to the epistolary apparatus, is the fact that the women of *Lady Susan*, regardless of their affiliations, are very nearly the sole agents in a world, indeed a social text, to whose margins they are also relegated. More than any specific yield of *Lady Susan*, including the suggestion that the protagonist's friendship with her coconspirator, Mrs. Johnson, is far from conventional, such figurings of agency, from Lady Susan to Catherine Vernon to Frederica's own, altogether masterly handling of the Vernon family, attach to certain protocols of response that Austen's initial readers and contemporaries routinely practiced.

But this again is only part of the story. As the editor's injunction to "Probability" indicates, the ability of Austen's contemporaries to read independently, and in active disregard of the deserts, good or ill, that were the hallmarks of value in the novel at this time, underscores a tension finally between certain possibilities that reading effectively limns and the probabilistic—indeed representational—order increasingly in place. Thus it is to the history of opportunities *missed*, rather than to possibilities necessarily abroad, that reading Austen in a certain way refers and—in a more nostalgic register—manages to recapitulate.

The View from Pemberley

Although *Lady Susan* was probably written no later than 1795, its survival in a copy made no earlier than 1805 implicates it in the spate of revision that characterized Austen's career from the earliest version of *Sense and Sensibility* ("Elinor and Marianne"), begun at almost the same time as *Lady Susan* (1795–96), to the versions of both *Pride and Prejudice* and *Northanger Abbey* that were begun in 1796 and 1798 respectively and revised over the next decade and a half. While the nature and extent of these revisions will always remain a matter of speculation, the evidence suggests that the changes in *Pride and Prejudice* were more extensive than those made to *Northanger Abbey* and, even more important, that the changes to the former, undertaken at several junctures, may well have involved the transformation of the novel initially titled "First Impressions" from a "novel in letters" into a "direct narrative" (Southam, 59). It is common knowledge that *Northanger Abbey* was the first novel of Austen's actually sold for publication. It is not generally argued that it was submitted to a publisher because *Northanger Abbey* (or "Susan" as it was then called) was also the first novel that Austen may have deemed salable or in appropriate form. An early version of *Pride and Prejudice* was offered to a publisher in 1797 by Austen's father only to be rejected. Nevertheless the sixteen years separating this public offering from the publication of the novel in revised form suggests that there may have been some wisdom in the publisher's decision that Austen eventually concurred with.

At all events, by reexamining the hierarchy, which reduces both *Northanger Abbey* and to a lesser degree *Sense and Sensibility* to fledgling exercises in deference to *Pride and Prejudice*, we accomplish two related tasks. We effectively join Austen in recognizing the eminent revisability of a work whose courtship plot (if the initial title is any hint) probably remained unchanged through its various revisions; and we follow her lead in reading *Pride and Prejudice* as yet another working testimony to what was gained and lost in the movement from epistolarity to the relatively stable operation of direct narrative. If nothing else, *Pride and Prejudice*—the *revised Pride and Prejudice*—follows *Sense and Sensibility* in also thematizing the achievement of novelistic authority, which is marked by the abandonment not just of epistolary form but of the indeterminate silence that goes with it on which a work like *Lady Susan* depends. It is not that epistolary fiction is necessarily less serviceable for the purposes of authority than direct narrative or that this discussion is predicated on a taxonomy of narrative forms where epistolarity is always more subversive to the degree that it is potentially less determinate. As I will speculate shortly, the epistolary version of *Pride and Prejudice*—to the degree that one might be extrapolated from the final version—was likely more didactic in explicitly measuring the liabilities of the character who became Elizabeth Bennet against the virtues of her forbearing sister, Jane, whose role is diminished in the version of the novel that has survived. The problem rather is with the achievement of authority in the surviving text and with the cultural hegemony to which narrative practice is once again fitted.

A matter of revision and retrospection as it is in *Sense and Sensibility*, the reflexive bent in *Pride and Prejudice* begins as early as the famous first sentence. It may be "universally acknowledged," and by that sanction a truism, that "a single man in possession of a good fortune, must be in want of a wife" (1).[12] However, this truism does not obscure the fact that an altogether normative scenario such as the inaugural sentence offers is simply that. It represents an imposition where the coercive weight of public opinion ("*must* be in want of a wife") is virtually synonymous with the wish-fulfilling fantasies of women, whose affirmation of "truth" is a by-product of their vulnerability and subordination. For the probabilistic scenario to thrive, there must be not only wealthy single men and unmarried women available for emplotment in a narrative of eventual and necessary union. There also must exist something on the order of "universal" inequality since only in such a climate is there sufficient pressure on both single men and women to produce a phenomenon so widespread that it wears the mantle of truth.

The mere fact that this truth must also be universally acknowledged, that it cannot stand alone without the continuous prop of opinion, custom, and fantasy, raises another possibility, which all the weight of coercion and probability cannot suppress. This of course would be a condition wherein women no longer need or want to be married and where men, accordingly, are no longer obligated, much less entitled, to rescue them (as Collins, for example, will succeed in doing to Charlotte Lucas). Such a view presupposes that conventional marriage, especially in its mystified form as the telos of narrative or romance, is also an impediment to women and on a continuum with the subordination that drives them to desire marriage as a respite in the first place. However, taken in context—namely, in conjunction with an observation that identifies both men *and* women as both the objects *and agents* of cultural imperatives—the prospect of things being otherwise, however far this may be from the "truth," is surprisingly close at hand.

In suggesting the *potential* revisability of truths universally acknowledged in *Pride and Prejudice*, I am drawing in some measure on the theories of Anthony Giddens and others who urge that structures are not simply impositions but testimony paradoxically to the agency of the individuals who make and abide by them. Such agency or "structuration" may often look like an imposition. Yet as the novel's first sentence implies, it constitutes a structure that can theoretically be altered at any moment.[13] That such changes are almost entirely a matter of abstraction in *Pride and Prejudice*, that the famous first sentence quickly modulates from an unstable observation with intimations of possibility to the more stable irony characteristic of an authoritative narrator to whom the marital prospects of unattached women and the anxiety of their parents are components of the human comedy, does not diminish either the prospect itself or its power in retrospect to contest what is asserted to be universal and true. Nor does it diminish the fact that here, as throughout the novel, a world of possibility shadows the probable and representable world in Austen, which in the manner of the novel itself is paradoxically open to the very revision on which it also forecloses. (This uncanny dynamic is an aspect of the novel to which Austen's earliest readers were especially sensitive.) There is rather a necessary link in *Pride and Prejudice* between a narrative whose central love story and delicious ironies have long beguiled readers and the work in progress whose revisions exceed in some measure the alterations by which an authoritative narrator may have superseded an editor of letters. In the course of her revisions, as I hope to show, Austen came to recognize and to intimate what was lost or sacrificed in what was still a considerable achievement.

Pride and Prejudice does not have a figure on the order of Colonel Brandon in *Sense and Sensibility*, by which novelistic authority and its relationship to social formations can be figured and identified. Yet what *Pride and Prejudice* lacks in terms of a reflexive locus it more than compensates for in other ways and by other means. We can take as one example Elizabeth's visit to Pemberley in the final volume, which rehearses a scenario sufficiently familiar to recent theories of spectatorship to give contemporary thinkers pause. "Ascend[ing]" to a "considerable eminence, where the wood ceased," Elizabeth's "eye" is "instantly caught by Pemberley House," the home of the wealthy *and single* Fitzwilliam Darcy, whose declaration of love she has recently spurned:

> It was a large, handsome, stone building, standing well on rising ground, and backed by a ridge of high woody hills;—and in front, a stream of some natural importance was swelled into greater, but without any artificial appearance. Its banks were neither formal, nor falsely adorned. Elizabeth was delighted. She had never seen a place for which nature had done more, or where natural beauty had been so little counteracted by an awkward taste. They were all of them warm in their admiration; and at that moment she felt, that to be mistress of Pemberley might be something! (215)

Elizabeth's fantasy of ownership, it is worth noting, is provoked not by nature but by naturalization: by the way that picturesque gardening allows Pemberley House to complement the landscape at the same time that the house remains an organizing center. This improvement in the landscape recalls the inaugural sentence of the novel. Like truths universally acknowledged, "nature" at Pemberley is a prescribed or partial phenomenon by which Elizabeth confuses artifice— the strictures to which nature conforms in the present instance—with something that is presumably endless and uncontained.

Thus even as she imagines herself "mistress" of the place (indulging once more the fantasy of a single man in search of a wife), Elizabeth is visibly in thrall and mastered by the scene. Her eye is "caught" by the sight of Pemberley House, whose allure involves both its naturalization and its equally metonymic relationship to its "handsome" master. Moreover, like the edifice itself, whose very infringement on the environment makes it vulnerable in like manner to fantasies of control, Elizabeth is herself annexed in the act, and as a condition of, her imaginary imposition.

This paradox, where ownership or control betokens one's cooptation in turn, becomes more of an issue as Elizabeth tours Pemberley from the inside. Here she is given further opportunity to survey nature, this time from the prospect of Pemberley's windows:

> The hill, crowned with wood, from which they had descended, receiving increased abruptness from the distance, was a beautiful object. Every disposition of the ground was good; and she looked on the whole scene, the river, the trees scattered on its banks,

and the winding of the valley, as far as she could trace it, with delight. As they passed into other rooms, these objects were taking different positions; but from every window there were beauties to be seen. The rooms were lofty and handsome, and their furniture suitable to the fortune of their proprietor; but Elizabeth saw with admiration of his taste, that it was neither gaudy nor uselessly fine. . . . "And of this place," thought she, "I might have been mistress! With these rooms I might now have been familiarly acquainted! Instead of viewing them as a stranger, I might have rejoiced in them as my own, and welcomed to them as visitors my uncle and aunt." (216)

Although Elizabeth's fantasies of ownership are indulged with more specificity and conviction once she is inside, there is a slight difference in their motivation. Previously this indulgence was a function of the way the house, in blending with the environment, provoked Elizabeth to imagine herself as one of its privileged inhabitants. Now her role playing, chiefly her stewardship of "place," involves following Pemberley's lead. No longer merely natural or sufficiently naturalized to submit to ownership, Pemberley actually deconstructs the work of naturalization in becoming a "space" of what Foucault has called "constructed visibility": a site from which things are seeable but in specific and restricted ways.[14]

In other words, for all her imagined authority, Elizabeth is even more contained than before. Not only is she enclosed by the house and by domestic space (and ideology); her gaze, although seemingly unrestricted, remains restricted by the vantage of Pemberley's windows, which vouchsafe some sights and not others. The more that Elizabeth asserts her authority, or acts on the presupposition of being free here, the more she resigns that freedom in discovering a nature beyond her ken and the reach of her fantasies. The particular control of the landscape earlier masked by the naturalizing techniques of picturesque gardening, so much as to invite fantasies of possession, is exposed from the vantage of Pemberley's interior in all of its limitation.

Such conclusions, needless to say, are consistent with picturesque practice as Austen understood it, and as it was marshaled by her contemporaries, whether as a desideratum in gardening or in defense of what Walter Scott termed "the new style of the novel." As we have already seen, it was the function of gardening, for proponents of the picturesque, as it was the purpose of the kind of novel Austen was supposedly writing, to make the necessarily limited and enclosed holdings of a landowner—and, in the novel's case, the probable world of domestic life—continuous with the real in general.[15] It is of considerable note, then, that this regulatory initiative fails at Pemberley. The synecdochical reach of picturesque gardening, and the legitimation that attends its enclosing practices in the initial sighting, are pointedly undone as the adjacent landscape recedes uncontainably beyond all control. Nor is it any less noteworthy that Elizabeth's fantasies of ownership proceed in this same interval from a control of the environment to a more mundane fascination with the material possessions that adorn the room before her. In the homology that increasingly characterizes Elizabeth and the world where she discovers herself at home, there is not only something partial and increasingly contained; there remains, in a reciprocal turn, the prospect of something that either *has been* or is about to be.

Finally, in the crux of Elizabeth's visit, the heroine enters a picture gallery where she is again "arrested," this time by a portrait of Darcy himself:

> In the gallery there were many family portraits, but they could have little to fix the attention of a stranger. Elizabeth walked on in quest of the only face whose features would be known to her. At last it arrested her—and she beheld a striking resemblance of Mr. Darcy, with such a smile over the face, as she remembered to have sometimes seen, when he looked at her. She stood several minutes before the picture in earnest contemplation, and returned to it again before they quitted the gallery. Mrs. Reynolds informed them, that it had been taken in his father's life time. (220)

Feminist critics will have little quarrel with Austen's representation of the "to-be-looked-at-ness," in Laura Mulvey's phrase (11), which Elizabeth connotes by performance of what Mulvey calls the woman's "traditional exhibitionistic role"; and they will appreciate as well Austen's subtlety in uniting this otherwise passive function with a more aggressive disposition in Elizabeth's experience of visual pleasure.[16] Where these same critics will likely encounter a problem is in Austen's refusal to allow the alternation between these "positionalities of desire" (de Lauretis, 143) simply to characterize what has been variously deemed "the instability of the woman's position" (Doane, 19). Although clearly sensitive to the split identification by which Elizabeth is simultaneously autonomous and subordinate, it would seem to be Austen's purpose, in staging the paradox of "mistressy," to use the "woman's position," as it has been theorized in our time, to represent the man's position as well.

This returns us to the novel's first sentence, where in asserting the differences between men and women, and the imbalance or inequality they produce, there is sufficient similarity between the genders (chiefly in the positionality to which they are relegated respectively) for other, more liberatory possibilities to emerge. No one will dispute that in the present configuration (and pursuant to the inaugural sentence), Elizabeth is more precariously positioned than Darcy. Where Darcy is "master" of the place, literally and symbolically, Elizabeth at the height of her imagined authority is no better than a mistress. Nevertheless, what we have already observed to be the paradox of mistressy says something about mastery as well: it too is purchased at the cost of a more authentic freedom.

This paradox, which recalls the structural origins of individual freedom in land ownership or in property freely held, is sharply underscored in the metonymic function of Pemberley. Although the "handsome" building "standing well on rising ground" is a virtual stand-in for its current occupant, the physical structure transcends in name, stature, and longevity the person it represents. The container may well signify what it houses or contains; but it is the containment of the contained, the chiasmic writing over of Darcy *by* Pemberley that the metonymy "instantly" discloses. A similar containment is also implied in Mrs. Reynolds's seemingly offhand (but to Austen vital) observation that Darcy's picture "had been taken in his father's life time." Here the peculiar authority with which the approving, smiling Darcy has been invested is revealed to be a pose taken at his father's behest and no less subject than either Elizabeth or her sisters to the ordinances of patriarchy and entailment.

Nowhere is the parallel between Elizabeth and Darcy more evident, or more crucial, than in the experience of the portrait itself. In Elizabeth's fantasy of the picture, Darcy's gaze is not simply activated and controlled by another, in effect "male," gaze; these gazes in turn have the cumulative effect of reducing and circumscribing the two beholders. In Elizabeth's case the circumscription is revealed (*pace* Lacan) in her compliant passivity at the prospect of the Other's regard. And Darcy, despite being physically and psychologically absent from this encounter, is equally circumscribed or "taken." At the very apex of his authority and superiority, Darcy is not just contained by the frame itself and the patriarchy with which it is explicitly associated; he is reduced simultaneously to the two-dimensional plane of a picture. By metamorphosis from "face" to "resemblance," Darcy reveals as dramatically as does Elizabeth the denaturing dispensation of a culture whose apparent sanctions to the individual and to individual freedom are flattening rather than enlarging.

Shuttling in this way between a probable world and a more uncanny or repressed world of possibility, *Pride and Prejudice* continually serves warning that it remains a work in progress. This is so even as the narrative, in seemingly underwriting the wish-fulfilling fantasies on which universal truth depends, is visibly aligned with the hero, the heroine, and the recoverable order they embody. Although some preliminary gestures are made toward admonishing Darcy for his pride and Mr. Bennet for his somewhat undeserved claim to being the genius of *his* household, it is clear by the Pemberley episode that Darcy and Elizabeth deserve one another, and that Elizabeth, whose inherent value has rightfully earned Darcy's affection, has been altogether wrong in discouraging him. Or, as Mary Poovey observes, "in *Pride and Prejudice*, the most idealistic of all of her novels, marriage remains for Austen the ideal paradigm of the most perfect fusion between the individual and society."[17]

Needless to say, I am less convinced than Poovey of Austen's ultimate investment in the marriage plot and in the society that such a plot promotes. But Poovey is certainly right in suggesting that the vindication of Darcy as an ideal husband, along with the particular social order at whose pinnacle he stands, is at one level fairly obvious and unnecessary to detail. At the same time, Austen's seeming endorsement of the constitution of society, and with it the asymmetrical relationships between genders and classes, opens onto a host of antithetical possibilities, which are adumbrated in the way the marriage plot, the prime vehicle again for the enforcement of universal truth or probability, achieves resolution considerably in advance of the novel's ending. With Darcy's declaration of love to Elizabeth and his subsequent letter to her justifying his actions at the close of volume 2, what the narrator has long given the reader to understand becomes the product at last of Elizabeth's understanding. In her well-known self-reproach—"How despicably have I acted. . . . I, who have valued myself on my abilities! who have often disdained the generous candour of my sister, and gratified my vanity, in useless or blameable distrust.—How humiliating is this discovery! . . . Had I been in love, I could not have been more wretchedly blind" (185)—Elizabeth achieves in consciousness, and by assimilation of humility and love, what remains only to be achieved diegetically by procession to the altar.

That this procession is deferred for almost the entire final third of the novel may be reckoned, as it has been, something of a liability aesthetically. But there is more to this deferral, and to the aesthetic liability, than the awkwardness that may have obtained from rewriting a novel for more than a decade after its inception. What suffers in this deferral is the narrator's unambiguous and conventionally ironic defense of the status quo. From the satiric portrait of Mrs. Bennet in the opening chapters, which all but justifies her husband's misogyny, to the deployment of Wickham, Collins, and Bingley as foils for Darcy, to the heroine herself, whose only real failure remains her insufficient appreciation of Darcy (and the related misjudgment of Wickham), *Pride and Prejudice* is arguably unique among Austen's fictions in its admiration of a man (and all that he represents) at the cost of everything else in it, including the main character.

But not so in volume 3. Beginning with the visit to Pemberley, the novel follows the gyrations of its very first sentence in destabilizing—or in ironizing more plainly than before—all that has transpired under the aegis of narrative authority. The hero's promotion, which had been tied to the demotion of other characters, is suddenly a more costly proposition and no longer negotiable at the expense of others. During the tour of Pemberley attention is directed not just at the naturalized imposition of the house itself. Attention is directed simultaneously on the naturalized status of its inhabitants—Darcy and potentially Elizabeth—whose mystification by the narrator seems increasingly arbitrary and dependent on the reader's ability to remain equally within and committed to the social order that Pemberley represents. The very stature to which Darcy seems naturally entitled, or the entitlement with which the narrator concurs in transforming Darcy's house and grounds into a metonymic echo of the hero's inherent worth, is encumbered now by a material—and in effect deconstructable—base that no amount of naturalization can fully mask. It is hardly a coincidence that the first encounter with Darcy in the final volume modulates quickly from the metonymic and material sanction of Pemberley House to the shrunken, circumscribed plane of "resemblance." In this the hierarchies and correspondences that have been endorsed as universal are, like Pemberley itself, made or naturalized to appear as such.

And what of "nature" itself—that increasingly fathomable, comparatively possible order, in which a resistance to the novel's argument and the truths it upholds, is currently grounded? One answer, beyond its utopian figuration as a site of possibility and change, would be to echo Freud and Lacan in designating this order "woman"—if only in that it is a woman now (and a particularly visceral one), Elizabeth's younger sister, Lydia, whose erotic escapades throw the narrative into a tailspin. This answer, needless to say, is problematic—albeit less for denominating woman as "other" than for denominating Lydia as "woman." After all, to grant Lydia the function of "feminizing" Austen's text, beyond the fact that it is simply another naturalizing practice, ultimately misrepresents Lydia's function here, which is to refer us by the sheer force of her resistance to a less apparent, if still possible, alternative against which the Elizabeth-Darcy narrative remains a bulwark.

I scarcely join with the majority of commentators in dismissing out of hand Lydia's frequently maligned energy and conversational style, which proves a critique of, rather than a concession to, the novel's defense of the dominant cultural order. Nor am I suggesting by the same right that Lydia is an alternative locus of value in the text. What I am suggesting is that Lydia's flight with Wickham, along with their eventual union, in which Lydia will presumably have other officers at her disposal, follows the Pemberley episode in serving as a signpost for the barely fathomable referent of Austen's work. This last, like the nature barely visible from Pemberley's windows, centers on the uncanny, if imperceptible, possibilities to which Elizabeth's older sister, Jane, and her on-again-off-again suitor, Bingley, gradually refer us in their ameliorative compliance with the world and with other people. In other words, the irruption of the feminine in *Pride and Prejudice*—by which nature and naturalizaton are set in opposition—is less an end itself than a beginning in the spirit of the novel's real beginning. It is Lydia's function now to make Jane and Bingley *readable* so as to contrast with the phenomena in the novel's first sentence, whose universality is gradually weighted down by a certain arbitrariness and partiality. With the emergence of "woman" the novel is more than simply jolted out of complacency. The hero and heroine, following the probable order they embody, are effectively united and, along with the narrative of volumes 1 and 2, *exposed* in their regulatory function.

The common complaint, voiced by Reuben Brower and others, that the final third of *Pride and Prejudice* lacks the amusing and confident irony of the first two sections is well taken since it recognizes a shift (long intimated) from a stable, authoritative irony by which the reader may align herself with the narrator to a far less stable irony in which the narrative is gradually placed at the reader's disposal.[18] Where the first two volumes of *Pride and Prejudice* are by and large successful in showing that the normative order, whatever its lapses, is somehow worth preserving, the third volume discloses all that is at stake in the hegemonic negotiation by which Darcy, a distinguished avatar of the old aristocratic order, is united with Elizabeth, whose merit (over and against the remonstrance of Lady Catherine de Bourgh) is inherent rather than inherited. By exposing the hierarchy that Darcy and Elizabeth serve, both individually and jointly, or that they exemplify thanks to a narrative that stresses their respective superiorities, volume 3 makes their coupling—and the resolution based upon it—a consolidation in which compromise plays a small and misleading role. By contrast the union of Jane and Bingley is truly a compromise. And it follows their generally compliant behavior in both confounding and—in the rapid and easeful settlement of their marriage—*eluding* the kind of narrative indulgence reserved for the hero and heroine. Jane and Bingley, in other words, work to isolate hegemony, which uses compromise as part of its mystification (Darcy is chastened for his pride and Elizabeth for her prejudice), from a compromise so thoroughgoing that even structures such as marriage attest somewhat mysteriously now to the transformative power of a still-inscrutable human agency.

Thus while *Pride and Prejudice* does not openly endorse Lydia's flight with Wickham, it deploys the flight toward something other than a simple renunciation of "the moral anarchy epitomized in Lydia," which would likely be motivated, as Poovey argues, by the reader's "experiences and values" (206). In fact, with these very "experiences" in mind—including the experience of volumes 1 and 2—Lydia's actions are instrumental in discovering a virtually inconceivable and, until this point, unwritable possibility. Beyond the extremities of willful sexuality and the equally powerful morality that would regulate Lydia (thereby rescuing Elizabeth from shame), there emerges—following Lydia's variation on the marriage plot—an alternative to *her alternative*, which differs from the main narrative (as from Lydia's) in being merely (or barely) readable. Significant in its insignificance—or by the resistance of the "complying" (309) characters to the customary terms of description, by which they would appear other than what

134 Reading the Historical Austen

they seem to an observer like Darcy (who typically regards Jane and Bingley as diminished in one way or another)—this alternative, like those broached in the inaugural sentence, is appropriately poised on the margin of verifiability.

As an illustration of this marginality, we can cite the seemingly innocuous inability of Jane Bennet to "know what [she has] written," as she so describes it in her letter to Elizabeth recounting Lydia's scandalous behavior (241). This gesture is neither hyperbolic nor a demonstration of female consternation. If anything, Jane's act of "disowning knowledge" (to borrow Stanley Cavell's term) signals a resignation of authority characteristic not only of her compliance as a character but of the compliance as well of another "Jane" with the terms and scope of her own work. The ability or authority to know and to represent the truth, that is, attests to one's simultaneous subjection as *one who knows* and to a regime of truth as the "universally acknowledged" of which the novel has been in large part a representation.

To be sure, the novel's push toward resolution or to what, following Elizabeth, we may call the "happiest, wisest, most reasonable end" (308) is perfectly consistent with the regulatory drift of the marriage plot as developed in volumes 1 and 2. But it remains, on the very strength of this consistency, as much a protest to those truths, whose universality and probability is more properly a regime of truth. By accession to the ideological demands of the universally acknowledged and the always knowable, the superlative ending of *Pride and Prejudice* parses, even as it unites, artistic or narrative authority on the one hand and the authority of what the knowing artist (or the narrator in this instance) is condemned to recapitulate on the other. Effectively resigning her authority as a writer in deference to the already written and conceived, Austen satisfies the demands of her art, but in a way that the knowable and the true—and the omniscient authority that attends them—are already a prelude to dissociating writing from the already written and, following Jane Bennet, to writing and becoming the unknowable.

The Epistolary *Pride and Prejudice*

With Jane's tentative emergence as an alternative site of value, the question of epistolarity—of what was lost and gained in the transformation of the epistolary version of the novel initially called "First Impressions"—must be broached one last time. Any claim for the preexistence of an epistolary version of *Pride and Prejudice* is no more than speculation, of course. Nevertheless, of the only Austen novels that could have been epistolary narratives at some point, *Pride and Prejudice* appears the more conducive by far to the epistolary mode. Where the letters that undoubtedly passed between "Elinor and Marianne" (in the epistolary text originally so titled) require a geographical separation of the two sisters that is largely collapsed in the final version of that novel, *Pride and Prejudice* maintains that separation and even preserves a number of Jane's letters to her sister from which the yield of the epistolary version may be inferred.

Such a yield or effect, as I have already intimated, probably differs from that of *Lady Susan*, where the indeterminacy of form stands in provocative relation to the belated attempt by the letters' editor to rein in and contain the narrative's attack on the culture of domesticity. It is more than likely that the original *Pride and Prejudice*, with Jane as the "Elinor" character, was openly didactic in granting Jane's probity and generosity a primacy that her younger sister's rashness works antithetically to promote. What this suggests, especially in conjunction with *Sense and Sensibility* where Elinor is a repository of value with marked affinities to the narrator herself, is that the emergence of Elizabeth Bennet as the delightful exponent of individualism was achieved at some cost. Mounted on the back of her older sibling who, far more than Marianne, is relegated to the margins of the final text, Elizabeth's centrality is similarly indivisible from a courtship plot to which Jane and Bingley *and their plot* are not only ancillary now but, to the degree that the Darcy-Elizabeth coupling is necessarily fraught by contradictions endemic to the ideological and regulatory work of their story, also opposed.

This opposition brings us to the hegemonic function of *Pride and Prejudice*, which follows fairly directly on the heels of Colonel Brandon's character in *Sense and Sensibility* in valuing certain emergent discourses and practices that it appropriates to dominant ends. In this configuration the rewards that Elizabeth is granted as a measure of her inherent worth are, in the marriage plot and by the conservative ideology it serves, coordinated to an aristocratic conception of entitlement by birth, which is sustained rather than vitiated in Darcy's decision to take Elizabeth as his wife. Regardless of the apparent threat that marrying Elizabeth may pose to an order that would maintain strict divisions on the basis of birth and lineage, the hierarchized view of society that such an order presupposes is maintained by Elizabeth's demonstrable superiority to every other character in the novel with the exception of Darcy. *Pride and Prejudice* may well gesture in the direction of ecumenicism, chiding Elizabeth for her prejudice and Darcy for his pride. However, in the narrative form that Austen has ultimately settled upon, by which events and circumstances are registered primarily through Elizabeth's consciousness, the latter's mortification at having misjudged Darcy and the concomitant embarrassment that she feels for herself and her family with respect to him create an atmosphere of deference that serves aristocratic interests far more than the progressive interests that depend similarly (and ironically) on Darcy for legitimation. There is little doubt that the crowning measure of Elizabeth's worth and the standards of merit she upholds is to stand the test of Darcy's judgment and to bask in the glow of his approbation. Nor does it matter really whether Darcy is similarly promoted on the basis of characteristics that appear inherent rather than inherited. For it is the function of the marriage plot—as a vehicle again of pure ideology—to shore up the aristocratic and paternalistic order in two ways: by showing Darcy's particular efficacy in rescuing Lydia from ignominy *and* by indicating his receptivity to emergent and alternative criteria of value in his selection of a wife.

But there is also a problem with the melioration over which Darcy presides. It involves the fact that the particular stability that obtains from the union of the two most exemplary characters here is continually tried by certain continuities that expose the contradictions on which their political work, or the political valence of their marriage, is predicated. It is all very well that individualism, and the progressive ideology to which it is connected, are promoted by the altogether winning example of Elizabeth Bennet, who does not scruple to go where she wishes even if that means returning home soiled and muddied. But when similar (or at least related) initiatives are undertaken by her younger sister, Lydia, the pursuit of happiness that stands at the core of the novel's—and Darcy's—seeming ecumenicism becomes an orientation requiring regulation and correction. So too when the narrative—in perhaps its crowning moment of accommodation—pits Elizabeth lopsidedly against Lady Catherine de Bourgh in a debate over the prerogative of choosing one's mate regardless of rank or birth, the still-dominant social order, which is otherwise recuperated and promoted thanks to Darcy, is suddenly exposed as being oppressive and outmoded. The point is not that Darcy and Lady Catherine are one and the same any more than Lydia and her sister are identical. The point is that these two sets of characters are on enough of a continuum that the novel's accession to and presumptive endorsement of certain emergent practices and discourses in Darcy's marital choice cannot be advanced—or advanced through the marriage plot—without also coordinating these practices to an order where democracy is plainly false democracy.

That *Pride and Prejudice* is at base a conservative novel, with only grudging acceptance of the culture and ideology of individualism that was gathering prestige during the interval of its composition, is hardly a revelation. But what is less immediately evident in the novel is not only the degree to which its conservatism is anchored largely in an ideal of compromise that is contradictory but the degree as well that such conservatism and the hegemony of which it is accordingly a blueprint remain, as they do in *Sense and Sensibility*, a consequence of form. It does not matter whether the heroine of Austen's novel is a forbearing Elinor or an irrepressible Lizzie. The result, specifically the political result, is at this stage—and in the transition from epistolarity to direct narrative—always the same. Thus in the very way that Brandon operates as a reflexive reminder of the peculiar fall to which the rise of the novel in the movement from epistolarity is unfortunately equivalent, it devolves upon the epistolary legacy of *Pride and Prejudice*, to the extent that one may be inferred from Jane's letters, to perform an analogous function.

In the case of Brandon this reflexive operation involves specific acts of manipulation and control, which figure narrative authority in its omniscient form, particularly as an instrument of cultural dominance. Jane's function is more prospective than reactive or reflexive. To the degree that she may be read as an alternative to Elizabeth and her narrative, which involves reading Jane in a way that Darcy or the narrator cannot, Austen is recurring in a way to what was once there. The only difference is that where Jane's significance was presumably linked to a didactic apparatus in which the indeterminacy of form may have been helpful in keeping readers usefully suspended between the imperatives of individualism and those of sociability and accommodation, her importance in the version of the novel that survives, if such a notion can be conceived, would be diminished even more were it not for her *letters*. The several letters by Jane that appear in *Pride and Prejudice* do more than provide a trace of the novel's epistolary legacy to the degree that one may have existed. They work, in conjunction with that presumed legacy, to suggest other values and possibilities in the world of the novel in which Jane's former prestige as an alternative to her sister is once again freestanding and sustained without the props of either narrative indulgence or authority. Jane's recuperation is an uncanny development in *Pride and Prejudice*: a recursion to the future, in which certain anterior values and orientations, notably compromise and consent, assume an oppositional complexion *in retrospect* and in consequence, for better or for worse, of Austen's most enduring achievement.

5

Narrative Incompetence in Northanger Abbey

Longing for Balls

In a book that is widely cited, but whose implications are just as widely overlooked, B. C. Southam offers the following speculations regarding the chronology of Austen's early novelistic compositions. "By the time *Northanger Abbey* was commenced in 1798," he notes,

> Jane Austen had written three works besides the juvenilia: *Lady Susan* and *Elinor and Marianne* in letters, as also may have been the third, *First Impressions*. Assuming that her decision to employ direct narrative dates from the conversion of *Elinor and Marianne* in November 1797, it is almost certain that from its beginning *Northanger Abbey* was conceived in this form, though in other respects the original must have differed slightly from the text we have.[1]

Although Southam's reconstruction of Austen's development as a novelist is partly a matter of speculation and open to debate, its implications for *Northanger Abbey*, routinely regarded as the clumsiest and least controlled of Austen's novels, are considerable. Chief among these is the suggestion that, unlike *Northanger Abbey*, which required comparatively little change, the first published novels, *Sense and Sensibility* and *Pride and Prejudice*, underwent an extensive and (for Austen's part) much-needed process of revision.

Moreover, when we recall that all three novels remained unpublished for well over a decade, during which time the first published novels were presumably subjected to any number of emendations, the comparative completeness of *Northanger Abbey*—in contrast to the revisability of the companion works—takes on even greater significance. Unlike the changes to both *Sense and Sensibility* and *Pride and Prejudice*, whose conversion to direct narrative was a fairly early transformation according to Southam and a prelude to still other embellishments and additions (including those on which I have speculated in the preceding chapter), the relative stability of *Northanger Abbey* would seem to indicate that there were in fact two issues confronting Austen at this time. The first was the generic and stylistic improvement that free indirect discourse, in contrast to epistolarity, represented. The second was the incompetence (for want of a better term) that these improvements had also mitigated and for which, as I have tried to show, they had somehow to be held accountable.

In speaking of incompetence I am referring to something that coextends with, even as it surpasses, both the indeterminacy of epistolary narrative (which the transformation to direct narrative effectively redresses) and the peculiar inconsistency that invariably marks *Northanger Abbey* as a repository of techniques that, as A. Walton Litz notes, "never coalesce into a satisfactory whole."[2] I am referring, in fact, to an abiding failure of narrative authority from which Austen's remarkable achievement as a practitioner of free indirect discourse in the works after *Northanger Abbey* has managed to distract attention.

It is a virtual commonplace of literary history that Austen brought the novel to a place (or an eminence as Ian Watt would have it) from which the great realistic achievements of the nineteenth century could proceed. This development took place apparently because Austen's narrative practice, as an ever-growing number of critics now contend, was also a regulatory apparatus in which the real was routinely partialized or plundered on behalf of specific values and ideologies in whose service the novelist was working at once diligently and unconsciously. The exact disposition of the values will shift according to the political and theoretical orientation of a given critic. However, with the exception of certain feminist readings, which enlist the novels in a subversive project that is often anachronistically framed, the political assessments of Austen's achievement differ only in the degree to which they emphasize the author's alignment with an increasingly residual discourse of class-based entitlement on the one hand and an emergent and progressive discourse of merit-based entitlement on the other.[3] When George Levine, in discussing *Northanger Abbey*, locates Austen's "moral commitment" in the way she "adjusts personal needs to social order," he is not only referring to the "ordered," always "legible" world in Austen, which is the cornerstone in turn of all realistic practice. He is also identifying such practice as being coterminous with both a social hegemony, whose dominance resides in the ability to absorb the emergent discourse of individualism, *and* a probabilistic order in which any attempt "to stretch beyond the limits of the quotidian" is in the end "beyond the limits of language to name."[4]

Levine's treatment of *Northanger Abbey* is unique, and of particular use, in its willingness to confront head on what the majority of commentators routinely regard as the novel's chief liability: the unevenness of tone, ranging from parody to sentimentality, which Levine rightly contends is hardly "an accident of Austen's immaturity at the time" of the novel's composition (69). If anything, the narrator's proclivity to parody, particularly in the novel's early phase, is part of a nearly reflexive apparatus insofar as it "gives us an opportunity to observe directly the not quite hidden literary sources of her characteristic voice, and of the characteristic forms of [Austen's] major novels" (69).

Levine begins by asserting that reality for Austen, and for the discursive tradition she helped inaugurate, is "society and its relations" so that the aim of any realistic text is to represent or in Austen's novel to "discover what is essentially and validly communal"(68). He then goes on to show that the narrator's ham-fisted parody of both romance fiction and the expectations such fiction inculcates is an attempt at a crucially early juncture to prevent "us from falling away into the private sensibility of our uniqueness and energy" (68). Parody, in other words, protects us from a monstrous introversion that by its very constitution is antisocial and inimical to the legibility that is also the hallmark of both realism and social stability. Thus there is a necessary connection between the world's legibility in Austen (and in the realistic tradition generally) and the ability of its inhabitants, both real and imagined, to curb their expectations in recognition of—and in deference to—what Levine, perhaps too confidently, terms "quotidian reality" (71). A realistic text is no doubt capable of addressing and crediting an individual character's needs or problems. However, the legibility of the world, without which realism would not be realism, requires that personal ambition, in readers and in characters alike, also be curbed to coincide with "social need" (75) and with the particular discipline that a society of selves requires. In hewing to the imperatives of the courtship plot, *Northanger Abbey* does not contradict itself according to Levine. Indeed the novel's subscription to romance effectively reminds us that the legibility essential to the realistic project is costly even as it is flexible: that expectation and desire, and the selfhood in which they consist, are *also* realities—albeit ones that *make* the "social order" and its protocols of representation eminently necessary.

The dynamic of subversion and containment, by which Levine is able to account for *Northanger Abbey*'s inconsistency and, in doing so, to revisit and deconstruct the institution of realistic representation at its ostensible foundation, is a double stroke of considerable ingenuity. But it is an intervention and, with respect to Austen's novel, a recuperation that is historically compromised by a number of features. The most important of these features is the fact that the imperative to legibility—or what Levine, quoting Bishop Whatley, calls "probability" (71)—had been a commonplace in critical and aesthetic discourse at least since the 1770s or for a duration sufficient to have divested that imperative of the particular urgency that, in Levine's historiography, drove Austen to a nearly reflexive exposure of her novel's political unconscious. Furthermore, when we recall that the various strictures against the fantastic or the marvelous in fiction were directed primarily on behalf of women, to whom such possibilities were deemed sufficiently appealing to provoke actions that might lead to ruin, the containment of the self endemic to the realistic imagination seems more a postromantic retrospection here than a prospect to which Austen's fiction is immediately answerable.

This is not to suggest that the prerogatives of the individual or the imagination were entirely alien to the novel at the time that Austen was first formulating her fictions. It is only to recall that the deleterious possibilities to which proponents of probability were continually on the alert had ultimately less to do with any impulse to self-determination on the part of either men or women than with an already restricted or probable condition *from which* fantastic fiction or romance—with its prospect of a different world—provided an enticing escape. To the extent that Austen would endorse—or appear to endorse—the "sense of order" (66) whose probability is necessarily prior to any effort to discover "what is essentially and validly communal in the text" (68), she was doing so in the knowledge that such regulatory aims were directed toward women in particular. And "women in particular," as Austen knew as well as anyone, required precious little instruction in either the constitution or probability of "things as they are." Levine is right in maintaining that "parody is the instrument out of which" Austen's seemingly "confident realism is born" (67). For the "wise and shrewd narrative voice" that the parodist of *Northanger Abbey* adopts in the narratives following this one is more than simply a development in either form or function. It is a development that, given its origins in parody, never completely erases either its genesis as a disciplinary apparatus or the regulatory limit that distinguishes the purely legible in Austen from another kind of actuality that, far from stretching "beyond the limits of the quotidian," merely extends beyond the "wise and shrewd" narrator's ability to countenance and comprehend.

The failure to control either the materials from which the narrative of *Northanger Abbey* is fashioned or the irony by which control is continually exerted in the novel is there from the beginning. The novel's first sentence—"No one who had ever seen Catherine Morland in her infancy, would have supposed her born to be an heroine"[5]—is plainly an attack on readerly expectation or on the appetite for heroines who are extraordinary in every way. However, by the time that Catherine is described as "a strange, unaccountable character"(2), or as a character whose apparent lack of interest in normal sexual relations is "strange indeed"(4), the irony, which is initially stable, quickly attenuates to an instability where the "strange" or "unaccountable" is sufficiently prevalent and readable to complicate the probabilistic—and ironic—attack on fictions of the marvelous. Far from being reducible to the ordinary, or immediately translatable to the quotidian, the "strange" in these initial pages also figures alternatives amid ordinary circumstance to which the narrator is simply inattentive.

Chief among these possibilities is Catherine's boyishness, specifically her "love of dirt" and "hat[red of] confinement and cleanliness" (2–3), all of which eventually "g[i]ve way," in the narrator's self-confident description, "to an inclination for finery" and to other proclivities and developments:

She began to curl her hair and long for balls; her complexion improved, her features were softened by plumpness and colour, her eyes gained more animation, and her figure more consequence. . . . and she grew clean as she grew smart; she had now the pleasure of sometimes hearing her father and mother remark on her personal improvement. "Catherine grows quite a good-looking girl,—she is almost pretty to day," were words which caught her ears now and then; and how welcome were the sounds! (3)

It is easy to regard this as a witty description of the inevitable course of a young woman's growth. Still, with the history of Catherine's initial resistance already in view, her gendering, which the narrator sees as entirely natural, hence inevitable, opens onto an horizon of possibility that works to denaturalize and to deconstruct Catherine's development. Becoming a woman seems as much a "consequence" of external motivation here—notably the sporadic even sadistic praise attendant to the regulatory work of intermittent gratification—as the result of certain innate longings that cannot, in any case, be divorced from the incentives and rewards following which persuasion as coercion, as Austen was always mindful, becomes "internal persuasion" (*Persuasion*, 207) or conviction. The "inclination" to be a full-fledged woman tends, in the narrator's accounting, to conflate personal improvement and the improvement of the person so that the coercive force behind the imperative to gender is entirely a matter of biology.

I am hardly suggesting that Austen's narrator is preternaturally mindful of the nonequivalence of sex and gender to undertake a knowing and somewhat sinister strategy of both obfuscation and containment. I am suggesting rather that there is enough slippage between the narrator's claims and the materials from which these claims are fashioned so that narrative authority, or incompetence as the case may be, is marshaled on behalf of certain possibilities that it was the manifest aim of fictions of probability, along with free indirect discourse, to discountenance and erase.

An omniscience that actually founders on its knowingness, the narrator's authority is just as paradoxically a means here by which the aims of probability are systematically stripped bare to reveal a naturalizing and regulatory imperative. This is true even of such seemingly innocuous observations as those regarding the preparations for Catherine's departure for Bath in which the sheer ordinariness of circumstance is again underscored:

Every thing indeed relative to this important journey was done, on the part of Morlands, with a degree of moderation and composure, which seemed rather consistent with the common feelings of common life, than with the refined susceptibilities, the tender emotions which the first separation of a heroine from her family ought always to excite. Her father, instead of giving her an unlimited order on his banker, or even putting an hundred pounds bank-bill into her hands, gave her only ten guineas, and promised her more when she wanted it. (6)

The narrator returns, following this description, to her characteristic irony, re-marking on the notable absence in the ensuing journey of the "robbers" or "tempests" typical of sensationalistic fiction in its departure from real life. Still, it is in the description that I have cited, with its parsing of the "common" and what might be called the representable, that the exposure of the probabilistic order is most evident. Unlike the ironic attacks on the fantastic, which are directed against the manipulative aspects of escapist narrative, the more measured description of the Morlands' parting refers to more than the ordinary circumstances that delimit the Morlands' ability to produce a heroine worthy of interest. It refers almost as pointedly to the naturalizing techniques on which "romances of real life" (as Charlotte Smith again termed them) are no less dependent. The particular ordinariness of Catherine's circumstance cuts in two directions at once: it stands in contrast to gothic embellishment, of which it is plainly a critique, and simultaneously, or it seems, to realistic practice as well, which, as Clara Reeve was among the first to note, makes use of embellishment for its absorptive effects.[6] The prospect here of a tender parting, not to mention the receipt of a hundred-pound bank note, may be sufficiently excessive to be ridiculed on the grounds of verisimilitude. But they are sufficiently modest, in comparison again to robbers, tempests, and the like to direct readers to the real point of the description: that Catherine and her family are as unsuited for the purposes of romance as they are for the purposes of novelistic narrative generally.

Northanger Abbey goes on to remedy this situation by removing Catherine to Bath, and almost immediately upon arrival, to a courtship plot involving Henry Tilney. Yet with every effort of the narrator to coordinate Catherine's life to the interests of both narrative and normalcy, there is a concomitant resistance on the part of both Catherine and her world to being so coerced and made a part of the probabilistic agenda. Such resistance may be as slight as the inscrutability that provokes the characteristically knowing narrator into an uncharacteristic—but important—admission of ignorance when, in considering

Catherine's response to Henry in the aftermath of their initial meeting, she concedes that nothing could, in fact, "be ascertained" (15). But it is a resistance that, on balance, manages to compromise the courtship plot, whose protocols, the narrator blithely assumes, are immaculately fitted to Catherine's "inclination." This is far from a seamless or coherent operation. There are occasions when Catherine's interest in Henry is presented as incontrovertible. Early in the second volume we are told flatly that Bath held little interest for Catherine "beyond the pleasure of sometimes seeing Henry" (107) and that "her passion for ancient edifices" such as Northanger Abbey "was next in degree to her passion for Henry Tilney" (110). Coming as they do from a narrator who presumably has access to the minds and feelings of the characters, such assertions do indeed carry weight. But it is often the case that such claims, or ones like them, are just as capable of missing their mark. In the pages immediately following the observations just noted, a nearly identical set of convictions over the disposition of Catherine's affections is sharply disputed by the heroine herself. Responding to John Thorpe's assertion that she had given "him the most positive encouragement" (112), Catherine remarks to Thorpe's sister, to whom John has already confided his assumptions, that she has been "describing what never happened" (114). The same, I would maintain, can generally be said of the narrator herself.

Nowhere are the limits of authority more evident than in the narrator's obtuseness regarding same-sex relations among women in the novel, which variously circumscribe and direct Catherine's affective life, including her relation to both men and the male-dominated culture at large. Nor is it a coincidence that the first relationship of this sort in the novel, the ultimately short-lived friendship with Isabella Thorpe, is initially cemented by a shared interest in novels, specifically gothic novels, whose function was to represent, if allegorically, the condition of women at the time they were written. This last point, of course, is revisited much later in the novel when, in his famous correction of Catherine's gothic fantasies regarding his father's ill treatment of his late wife, Henry Tilney effectively rewrites the gothic by instructing Catherine in the difference between "the country and age in which we live" and the gothic anterior, whose only referent, in Henry's jingoistic calculus, is a world elsewhere. In the meantime the task of disabusing the gothic—chiefly the Radcliffean gothic—of any explanatory function with respect to the present is taken up by the narrator, who, without even mentioning the nature of the novels that Catherine and Isabella "shut themselves up . . . to read . . . together" (21), uses the occasion of their joint reading to launch a paean to the novel that, as I have already argued, has little bearing on the specific reading habits of which it is ostensibly a defense. If anything it is the effect of the narrator's pointed defense of probabilistic fiction—particularly in conjunction with the subsequent disclosure that this is not the kind of fiction that Catherine reads or enjoys—to perform two functions: to situate the narrator still more firmly in the probabilistic or regulatory camp and to introduce a protocol of reading that follows the example of *readers in the novel* in opposing the narrator's strictures and aims.

One mode of reading in this manner involves the possibilistic orientation that the narrator's polemic, in specifically imitating certain romantic discourses, vouchsafes for the novel (and for contemporary writing in general) over and against the canonical space that the narrator explicitly reserves for regulatory narratives for women. But the more important mode of oppositional reading, for the purposes at least of understanding *Northanger Abbey*, involves the degree to which reading against the grain of narrative authority, and against the suasive aspects of free indirect discourse, exposes and enacts the very possibilities that same-sex solidarity, in its resistance to the normative momentum of the courtship plot, harbors and sustains. It does not matter whether the relationship that binds Catherine first to Isabella and later, and more important, to Henry's sister, Eleanor, is explicitly eroticized in the manner of similar relations in Austen's other novels, including the relationship of Mary and Fanny in *Mansfield Park*.[7] What matters is that such reading as I have described follows the scene of reading *in* the text—and the protocols of reading practiced by many of Austen's contemporaries—in several related ways. Reflecting a wariness about "things as they are," and an impatience by implication with the particular ideology of which the marriage plot remains a vehicle in the novel, such reading allows commensurately for certain alternatives that, like those realized by Catherine and her friends, reside firmly, if inscrutably, in the *durée* of both textuality and control.

There are many examples of same-sex desire in *Northanger Abbey*, almost all of which take priority over both Catherine's heterosexual relations and the narrator's effort to marshal those relations in a developmental narrative where Catherine's growth is marked by the discovery that what she wants is what every girl wants.[8] These examples range typically from the scene of reading with Isabella, which undercuts the defense of the novel it provokes, to a more inferable resistance that works similarly to expose other narrative impositions, including the suggestion that the normative reach of Catherine's desire is sufficient to mitigate her dislike of Isabella's boorish brother, John: "Little as Catherine was in the habit of judging for herself, and unfixed as were her general opinions of what men ought to be, she could not entirely repress a doubt, while she bore with effusions of his endless conceit, of his being altogether completely agreeable" (48). Nevertheless it is in Catherine's attachment to Eleanor Tilney, which beyond any question of decorum is the motivating factor in her attachment to the Tilney family, that the narrator's incompetence, however masked by irony, is most evident.

This particular incompetence begins with the initial sighting of Eleanor accompanying her brother, where Catherine's demonstrable "interest" in the female Tilney is, in the narrator's opinion, adjunct to the latter's "relationship to Mr. Tilney" (38). And it continues in a host of examples and narrational missteps in which the details of Catherine's attachment to Eleanor effectively conspire with the misrecognition of their significance to produce an horizon of possibility in a world, at once textual and social, where anything beyond the merely probable is usually invisible or unavailable.

One of the earliest examples of the narrator's blindness to the dimensions of Catherine's enthusiasm regarding Eleanor occurs quite early in the novel, when on the morning following her initial encounter with both Tilneys, Catherine awakes from "a sound sleep which lasted nine hours" with the instant and unregulated "wish to improve her acquaintance with Miss Tilney." The narrator ascribes this wish, which Catherine moves immediately to fulfill in resolving "to seek [Eleanor] ... in the Pump-room at noon" (42), to a characteristically "female intimacy," whose "secret discourses," far from subversive, are sufficiently trivial and restricted to "confidence[s]" about men and marriage to require no additional exploration. But for the reader, who has been given little reason to take seriously any attachments of Catherine's apart from those to her female friends, the narrator's dogged pursuit of Catherine's interest in and involvement with *Henry* Tilney may well seem almost perversely beside the point. Even as we are told that "Catherine's resolution of endeavoring to meet Miss Tilney again continued in full force the next morning" (51–52) and are informed subsequently of Catherine's "joy" at the sight of Miss Tilney "entering the room" not with her brother but with a female chaperone, we are strenuously disabused of any inferences regarding the significance of this developing relationship by the narrator's patently condescending—but importantly unverifiable—claim that in the conversation between Catherine and Eleanor that ensued there was "in all probability not an observation ... nor an expression used by either which had not been made and used some thousands of times before, under that roof, in every Bath season" (52).

It scarcely requires repeating that the narrator's investment in the "probable" is such now that any generalizations regarding what women do and say in each other's company will be necessarily dismissive. But what cannot be emphasized enough is the *apostasis* of the world *on view* in *Northanger Abbey* from the normative framework to which the narrator is determined to make that world conform. It is undoubtedly, and importantly, the case that Catherine's reported interest in Henry owes a great deal to the latter's unorthodox interest in things feminine, from muslin to novels. But it is the case as well that their developing relationship is given a particular primacy by Austen's narrator that counter-mands the recoverable *facts* of Catherine's affective disposition in failing to weigh sufficiently the degree to which Henry's "feminization" is alternately a possibility of real significance and a signpost (as such) to the relationship with Eleanor, which is always primary.

The entire drama regarding Catherine's commitment to an outing with the Tilneys, which Isabella subverts by arranging another outing in the aim of unit-ing Catherine and her brother, John, is an especially salient instance of the nar-rator's failure to present the facts of the narrative with full attention to their bearing. Although Catherine makes it clear on at least three separate occasions that she is intent on honoring her commitment to Miss Tilney in particular ("I cannot go indeed, for you know Miss Tilney may still call" [62]; "I cannot go be-cause . . . I expect Miss Tilney and her brother to call on me to take a country walk" [63]; "Stop, stop, Mr. Thorpe . . . it is Miss Tilney; it is indeed" [65]), the episode is mined for little more than Catherine's exposure to manipulation and the embarrassment to which her malleability leads. That the nearly obsessive preoccupation with the female Tilney might well signify something else, par-ticularly as it stands poised between the comparatively normative trajectories represented by John Thorpe and Henry respectively, is simply unavailable to the narrator, who is disposed again to look the other way. It scarcely matters to the narrator that the first real instance of self-determination for Catherine—the correction that she resolves to administer to the misrepresentation of her plans and interests that the Thorpes have calculatedly tendered to the Tilneys—is in-spired entirely (or so it seems) by Eleanor: " 'This will not do,' said Catherine; 'I cannot submit to this. I must run after Miss Tilney directly and set her right.' "(77). The image of Catherine "running after" Eleanor may appear a far cry from the resistance with which I have freighted it. But there is little doubt that, by comparison to the other pursuit that has preoccupied Austen's narra-tives thus far, namely the pursuit of a "single man . . . in want of a wife," the fol-lowing of Eleanor marks an alterity that the narrator seems unable or unwilling to recognize.

"My real power is nothing"

If the narrator's blindness to certain possibilities within her ken works to di-minish her authority, particularly as that authority is vested in parody, the re-moval of the novel's action to the Tilney estate in volume 2 would appear to reverse this tendency. The broadly satiric attack on the gothic, which is mounted on Catherine's ridiculous suggestibility while in residence at Northanger Abbey, manages in a single move to diminish Catherine as an agent and, by implication, the antithetical reading habits that she practices and provokes. This is the case, of course, only if we take seriously the narrator's main presupposition here: that the gothic—and for the novel's purposes again the Radcliffean gothic—is unrealistic and thus typical of escapist literature in being both improbable and without instruction.[9] It goes without saying that Radcliffe's novels (not to mention the other "Northanger" novels) are distinct from those fictions of probability in whose defense the narrator, like Burney and others, is unrelenting in her support. Nevertheless the additional arguments here regarding the irrelevance of the gothic, in comparison to the seeming relevance of probabilistic or domestic fiction, are valid only in the sense that it was the principal function of probabilistic writing not just to represent a social order already in place but, more importantly, to promote the order in place as the best of all possible worlds.

A sensationalistic novel such as Radcliffe's *The Italian* (1797), which Catherine plans to read just as soon as she finishes the earlier (and more famous) *Mysteries of Udolpho* (1794), may appear to have little to do with its English audience apart from providing women readers with some diversion and, to the degree that the heroine Ellena Rosalba remains a paragon of virtue and steadfastness, some fairly obvious instruction. But this is largely a superficial reading. The real function of Radcliffe's fiction, as its initial chapter underscores (and as Austen could not but have been aware), was probabilistic in an altogether different register. In deliberately emphasizing the distance separating the Italy of the novel, with its church apparatus of convents, confessions, and inquisitions, from the England of 1764, Radcliffe introduces a structure of difference by which the gothic anterior, however useful for the purposes of self-legitimation, operates as a typology for England in the present time. This is so much the case that there is invariably a bifurcation in Radcliffe's novels between a social or ideological program, supporting cultural developments currently abroad—in particular the "affective individualism" by which the hero and heroine seek one another by choice independent of rank or parental edict—and a protofeminist circumspection regarding the underside of such seeming improvements.

In Radcliffe's *The Italian*, no less than in any of Austen's novels to date, the precariousness of women's lives in a culture whose extensions of franchise have apparently rendered it more ecumenical and less class bound is a recurrent theme. It is *figured* in two specific ways: in the manifold dangers that continually befall Radcliffe's heroine and in the peculiar sympathy for the eponymous "Italian," the Confessor Schedoni, which only a reader tone deaf to the nuances of Radcliffe's allegory, particularly as it bears on the inadequacy of the nominal hero, Vivaldi, would confuse with an unabashed paternalism. Deflecting attention from Vivaldi, whose protective agency is diminished by the carceral world into which he vanishes for a hundred pages, and focusing on Schedoni, whose villainy is increasingly mitigated by numerous trials of conscience, Radcliffe is doing more than heightening the drama by exposing her readers directly to the apparent origin of terror here. She is expressing nostalgia for the paternalistic order that she earlier and initially demonizes. Radcliffe undertakes this reversal not because she necessarily subscribes to or wishes to recuperate an order that, as the novel makes clear, is irretrievably moribund and incapable of exerting responsible agency in the present. Rather the nostalgic turn to "the Italian," no less than the nostalgia in either her *Romance of the Forest* (1791) or her *Udolpho*, is enlisted to express anxiety over the failure of newer social formations to furnish women with anything resembling the security they may have previously enjoyed. There is no real difference in Radcliffe's calculus between the gothic as such, with its anterior or displaced setting, and the here and now of which the sensationalistic apparatus is primarily a figuration.

Northanger Abbey differs dramatically from novels like *The Italian* in its patent unwillingness to idealize patriarchy—represented here by General Tilney—even by way of registering its discontent over the condition and security of women in the present. But it clearly follows Radcliffe's text in collapsing any distinction between an alarmist or hyperbolic world elsewhere and the way we live now. This last point is literally enacted in a gesture taken by Austen's narrator as evidence of the suggestibility that Catherine must discard en route to becoming a woman and (she hopes) a wife. After patiently taking instruction from Henry on the constitution of the picturesque—an aesthetic with inescapable relevance to the narrative technique at issue here—Catherine responds, with no apparent bearing on Henry's demonstration, that "something very shocking indeed, will soon come out in London" (87). This "something very shocking" turns out, as Henry quickly surmises, to be "nothing more dreadful than a new publication . . . in three duodecimo volumes, . . . with a frontispiece to the first, of two tombstones and a lantern" (88). And he hopes with this information to relieve his "stupid sister" (as he instinctively calls her) of any fears to which Catherine's "expressions" may have given rise at that moment. Nevertheless the point of the episode, particularly as bracketed by Henry's instruction, is not merely to prepare for Catherine's similar missteps in volume 2. The point—and there is scarcely an episode in Austen without point—is to dramatize the degree to which the gothic, as a species of writing for and about women, has a *relevance* that is perfectly warranted: that gothic dread, although seemingly contained by genre, is sufficiently justified by experience, even in so benign an event as "a very nice walk" with "two very nice young ladies" (84), to remain uncontainable and immediate.

The immediacy of Catherine's dread is carried to comical extremes during her visit to the abbey, whose "modern[ity]," it is worth noting, is emphasized and displayed by the general himself (147). While Catherine's fearful fantasies regarding the fate of the general's late wife are, as readers have long recognized, plainly the stuff of parody, they are sufficiently bracketed by the general's chilly aloofness and by her growing intimacy with Eleanor, which is explicitly a stay against the general's behavior, to identify and thereby blunt the aggressive force of the narrator's satire.

This is just as true of Henry's well-known correction of Catherine, which admits an antithetical response thanks in part to its interrogative form:

Dear Miss Morland, consider the dreadful nature of the suspicions you have entertained. What have you been judging from? Remember the country and the age in which we live. Remember that we are English, that we are Christians. Consult your own under-standing, your own sense of the probable, your own observation of what is passing around you—Does our education prepare us for such atrocities? Do our laws connive at them? Could they be perpetrated without being known, in a country like this, where so-cial and literary intercourse is on such a footing; where every man is surrounded by a neighbourhood of voluntary spies, and where roads and newspapers lay every thing open? Dearest Miss Morland, what ideas have you been admitting? (159)

If there is a link here between Henry's comfort in the "probable" and his ten-dency to read the gothic literally, there is, as the terms (and form) of his correc-tion indicate, a concomitant connection between Catherine's allegorical reading of the gothic and the regulatory or, as Paul Morrison has put it, "carceral" world in which she now finds herself.

The "country and the age in which we live" is doubtless the apogee of civil-ity and goodwill for a man such as Henry. For Catherine, by contrast, it is an en-vironment whose prospects range from the figurings of the probable entertained by the gothic, from which reading the gothic is also (and paradoxically) an es-cape, to the *other* possibilities of empowerment, whose foreclosure—whether by the replacement of same-sex relations with normative ones or in the way women must accede to male prerogative and control—is equally "probable" and "very shocking." While Catherine (in anticipation of Emma Woodhouse after Box Hill) is plainly affected by Henry's instruction—or affected sufficiently to be able to parse the more obvious differences between Radcliffe's fictional world and her own—such instruction does not, by either its terms or form, work im-mediately to the benefit of her teacher. If anything, Catherine's transformation into a suitable partner for Henry owes less to any direct action on Henry's part than to Catherine's ultimate recognition—in the wake of Eleanor's inability to prevent her removal from Northanger Abbey—that normative relations, or more precisely marriage to Henry, are her *only* means of security.

That Catherine's "development" owes far more in the end to Eleanor's *lack* of agency rather than to any of Henry's interventions and corrections is an aspect of the novel to which most readers—thanks chiefly to the narrator's direction—are generally inattentive. Even Claudia Johnson, who rightly stresses the novel's preoccupation with women's power and regards the parody of Radcliffe as more properly an homage to the gothic and its discontents, gives surprisingly short shrift to the events leading up to Catherine's dismissal from the abbey, which is ordered upon the general's discovery that she is not in fact the heiress he had imagined.[10] These events, involving the general's and Henry's removal from the abbey and the intimacy with Eleanor that flowers in their absence, are especially key. Although intimacy among women was a feature of domestic-romantic friendship, and on a continuum with marriage and the ideology of normative sexual relations, the particular intimacy between Catherine and Eleanor clearly exceeds, and for a brief duration subsumes, any affective ties between Henry and the novel's heroine.[11]

Such intimacy is as much a palpable fact of Austen's narrative as it figures the possibilistic space amid the "country and the age" in which the two women "live." For even as this space is quickly annexed by Catherine's dismissal, and by the fantasies of rescue her vulnerability provokes, its annexation necessarily proves that such space has *existed*. And with the existence of such space, however fleeting or temporalized, there is also (and with no small irony) enough traumatic slippage between a recoverable and *readable* condition of everyday life, and Eleanor's aggrieved observation that her "real power"—and by implication woman's power—"is nothing" (182), to reduce Catherine to the benumbed and flattened state from which Henry eventually rescues her.

The oft-noted shift in tone, by which the narrator ultimately exchanges irony for sentimentality in sympathetic identification with the rejected Catherine, requires some comment then. In addition to being a much-belated, even disingenuous, attempt at solidarity with her heroine, the narrator's sudden shift from the third to the first person in the wake of Catherine's dismissal—"I bring back my heroine to her home in solitude and disgrace" (188)—is a pointed reminder that the narrator of the novel has been a device and a complicated one at that. Although clearly a prototype for the less cumbersome versions of omniscience in the novels that succeeded *Northanger Abbey* and, if we accept Southam's chronology, in the first published novels that underwent substantial revision, the narrator also hearkens *as a device* in a direction apart from either the novel's rise or the regulatory practice with which both Austen's development and the rise of the novel consist.

That this latter, oppositional direction has been largely erased from critical memory is a consequence no doubt of the proliferation and prestige of the real-istic imagination in the nineteenth century. But it owes mostly, or more specifi-cally, to certain reading practices to which novelistic (and indeed Austenian) practice, in its authoritative distribution of praise and blame, was nicely fitted. To Austen's contemporaries, by contrast, whose interest in the novel was, like Catherine's, reflective of practices that the novel was being urged at that same moment to discipline and contain, the situation was a little different. As Cather-ine's interest in and subscription to the gothic view of things suggests, the pecu-liar adjudication attendant to fictions of probability was tried less in the end by other kinds of fictions, which were nevertheless charged with having inculcated irrational and dangerous expectations, than by probability's "other" status as a term for "things as they are." There is a difference obviously between a nomi-nally escapist novel such as *The Italian* and probabilistic fiction such as Edge-worth's *Belinda*, whose oppositional tendencies, or in this case characters, pay dearly for their opposition. But whether the world to which readers are invited in the former is any less the "country and the age in which [they] live" than the world that they are prevented from leaving in the latter is highly debatable.

As a result the *possibilities* that Catherine realizes in the course of Austen's narrative, and that readers are permitted to recognize thanks to the narrator's misrecognition of them, work to make reading a measure—and arguably a more sustainable measure—of other practices that do not exactly jibe with the courtship plot. These possibilities, from "base ball" (3) to same-sex relations, bear urgently, if retrospectively now, on the sinister and powerful arm of a probabilistic—or again representational—order where the legibility of a thing or person or practice, with its potential for blamability and control, is some-how proof of its authenticity. The transparent irony of the novel's concluding statement—"I leave it to be settled by whomsoever it may concern, whether the tendency of this work be altogether to recommend parental tyranny, or reward filial disobedience" (205)—is sufficient to convince most readers that despite an apparent partiality for the latter position the narrator (whoever or whatever she is at this point) is by no means convinced of their nonequivalence.

However, the "effective meaning" of the final statement (to borrow a Kris-tevan notion)[12] marshals the oedipal circularity uniting fathers and sons in a critique of the legible under the aegis of the probable. Here the totalizing circuit of "tyranny" and "disobedience" turns out not only to be a partialization of hu-man practice and progress along an axis of masculinist conflict. It remains also a partialization that, by compliance with the probabilistic order, typically regards resistance as a counterpart, indeed a doublet, of the very "tyranny" it opposes. One meaning of the final statement is undoubtedly that the novel has been about many things, including other kinds of "disobedience," apart from the two practices whose endorsement is comically in abeyance. But the rather explicit charge to "whomsoever it may concern" is in the end an invitation to consider what is, or rather *was*, at stake in arriving at this latter meaning. In other words, just as the novel's concluding statement can be said to recall another world that has been rather abruptly foreclosed upon so the world onto which it opens is remarkably and poignantly proximate. It is as close, in fact, as the hand that holds the book or as the reading subject who can recall what she has just read. The oedipal circle of tyranny and disobedience may remain, for the narrator of *Northanger Abbey*, all we know on earth. But for Austen and for readers like the Catherine who cannot wait to read *The Italian*, it is scarcely all we need to know or all that there *has been* to appreciate and to honor.

6

Jane Austen's Future Shock

A Novel Unreviewed

Like *Northanger Abbey* before it, *Mansfield Park* was conceived as a direct narrative from the beginning. But unlike Austen's first two published novels, *Sense and Sensibility* and *Pride and Prejudice*, it did not enjoy the benefit of any reviews. The causes for this nonevent, ranging from the lassitude of individual reviewers to the relationship of Austen's publisher, Egerton, to the periodical press, are probably manifold. At the same time, there is ample justification to view the neglect of *Mansfield Park* as an historical limit rather than a goad to further (and probably fruitless) excavation. What the contemporary reaction to *Mansfield Park* underscores, particularly in light of the novel's proximity to two novels that were generally well received and to which potential readers were alerted on the title page, was the new work's inaccessibility. It is the history of this inaccessibility—including the history on which the novel's inaccessibility is largely founded—that I explore in this chapter. I do so for two related reasons: first, because many recent efforts at understanding *Mansfield Park* adopt some aspect of historical method so as to correct what, more than in any other interpretive occasion in Austen, seems fraught by anachronism; and second, because such efforts at recovery tend also to compound the problem in contriving to situate *Mansfield Park* in a *context*, be it individualism at home or slavery abroad, from which the novel, as its public reception indicates, was somehow displaced or disengaged.

Thus it is not merely twentieth-century detractors such as Marvin Mudrick or Kingsley Amis, who may be called to account for failing to appreciate the values and ideologies that animate this perplexing and dour narrative, any more than the defenders of *Mansfield Park*, notably Lionel Trilling.[1] Historical critics too, among them Marilyn Butler, Alistair Duckworth, and Edward Said, are equally challenged by the object of their investigation, even as they seek to return the novel to its time.[2] Although the historical way with *Mansfield Park* differs considerably from treatments of the novel that are unabashedly anachronistic, the act of recovery customarily practiced in this occasion is also vexed by the presumption to have discovered what those most able to recognize it—the novelist's contemporaries—had for their parts difficulty recognizing. This would be the bearing of Austen's narrative on the *moment* to which it was written.

Mansfield Park was indeed read and commented upon. Yet as we noted in Chapter 2, the contemporary response to this novel, including the responses that Austen solicited from her family and their acquaintances, rarely impinges on issues near and dear to historicizing critics, who insist on their urgency for both Austen and the culture in whose interest(s) she was writing. If *Mansfield Park* is militantly anti-Jacobin as Butler and Duckworth argue, or modestly ecumenical in the hope of making the Tory gentry the core of an increasingly middle-class hegemony (as Avrom Fleishman contends),[3] these points seem to have eluded those immediately affected by the conflicts and developments on which the novel apparently reflects. Such opacity may well register what Frederic Jameson has famously called the "political unconscious," which is as much a feature of the novel itself in, for example, its presumably instinctive subscription to plantocratic paradigms at home and abroad, as it informs and directs the invariable response to *Mansfield Park*, where ideology, so to speak, is masked in the name of the novel's verisimilitude.

There is a problem, however, with this largely interpellative view of the formation and reception of Austen's novel. It has to do with the fact that *Mansfield Park*, more than any other novel of Austen's, is far from opaque, especially in the Manichaean struggle to which the narrative is continually pegged. The repositories of value in the novel, no matter odious or inscrutable to postmodern sensibilities, are just as obvious today as they were to readers such as Walter Scott, who were inclined, often against their better instincts, to tap a polemical strain in Austen's writing where none was immediately compelling. The tendency of Austen's contemporaries to laud the *Mansfield Park*'s mimetic force in its delineation of manners (as Mrs. Pole notes), or in its representation of "real natural everyday life," as Anne Romilly observes, resides in something more than a "reality" so immaculately contained by the dictates of ideology as to make "nature" and culture synonymous. It reflects, if anything, a particularly infelicitous cooperation of ideology and detail, prompting Romilly to observe that while *Mansfield Park*, like "all good novels," is necessarily "true to life," it somehow "lacks" a "good story vein of principle running thro the whole."[4] The separation of the "everyday" and the particular guidance usually administered in conjunction with a "story" does not, in this case, produce wonder or delight for Romilly. Rather it presents a conflict between specific protocols of reading that, here and elsewhere in Austen, are cultivated and satisfied, and a narrative overwhelmed by elements that, for Romilly, are something other than a naturalizing apparatus.

It is not enough to say that the various details of *Mansfield Park*, ranging from the humorlessness of those characters in whom virtue and value are vested to the sheer interest of those who are also grist for the narrator's ideological program, are sufficient to countermand or, as was the case in *Northanger Abbey*, to problematize the particular view of self and society to which the narrator, no less than the novel in this case, is plainly committed. It is rather that in lacking a "story vein of principle," in which a character's desert is invariably tied to some development or moral education, the novel, following a heroine who already knows all she needs to know and whose signature action is to say "no" again and again, works entirely—or so it seems—by process of subtraction.[5] It is true that Fanny begins as a frightened ward of the Bertram household and ends triumphantly as the wife of the second son, Edmund Bertram. But it is the case too that Fanny's material and temporal progress is disjoined from her moral development, which essentially precedes the narrative and from which all other developments and actions in the novel are largely an *apostasis*. It is scarcely necessary to detail the various traits and tendencies that render Fanny an especially odious figure, who continually serves notice that the masochist, in her unrivaled capacity to endure pain, will invariably prevail in a given situation. Still it must emphasized that just as Fanny is already fully formed as an ethical subject so she also differs from an idealized, but two-dimensional, paragon such as Edgeworth's Belinda in being remarkably *deformed* and—in arguably the high point of Austen's practice as a realist—all too human.

To be sure, the actions of all the characters in *Mansfield Park* are assimilable to a moral lesson that the narrator means to inculcate and in which Fanny, despite her faults and jealousies, abides as a paragon of virtue. But it is no less a fact that the practices of these characters, and the details and circumstances by which their practices are shaped, double not only as negative examples in the novel but also, and more crucially, as figurings of a real that, in contrast to Fanny—or to the real that *is Fanny*—looks familiar if strangely insubstantial. This strangely negative versimilitude would appear to account for the perplexity of the novel's earliest readers, who, in the face of a work whose plot is almost nonexistent as a vehicle of ideology, were furnished with a naturalizing apparatus without anything to naturalize much less to contest. The invariable response of readers such as Mrs. Pole, who commends the novel's accuracy of representation, is really a subset, then, of the silence with which the novel was met by professional readers upon publication. For the novelistic apparatus, consisting entirely of episodes where Fanny's firm but unimpeachable sense of things is assaulted or offended by the practice of everyday life, from the theatrical at Mansfield to the greasy plates in Portsmouth to Mrs. Norris's parsimony, makes recoverable reality—or all we know on earth—a plenitude that, with no small irony, is also ancillary to what we apparently need to know or to a system of values about to be.[6]

The History and Futurity of *Mansfield Park*

It is well known that the composition of *Mansfield Park* between 1811 and 1813 marked the resumption of a novelistic career that had been suspended for over a decade during which time the Austen family had moved from the parsonage at Steventon, where the first three novels were drafted, to Bath and later to Southampton before finally settling at Chawton Cottage, which was made available to Mrs. Austen and her two daughters by her son Edward, who was now heir to the Knight family. During this notably fallow period Jane not only witnessed the death of her father; she also experienced a number of other personal setbacks and disappointments, from the untimely death of a potential suitor whom she met briefly on vacation at Cornwall to the rejection that she was obliged on at least one occasion to tender to a proposal of marriage that she briefly (and embarrassingly) accepted.[7]

Then of course there were the Napoleonic Wars and the even larger imperial prospects they evoked, to which Austen was alert in consequence of her brother Frank's participation, both as a naval officer under Nelson and as a captain in the East India Company. Compounded with her arrival at the very spinsterhood and state of dependency that had remained and would continue to remain a dreaded eventuality in her novels, these developments bore cumulatively on the narrative she produced after so long a duration. While family interests may have directed Austen to issues and prospects that had been of no concern in her works thus far, it was the *coincidence*, I am arguing, of certain personal expectations, which had gradually diminished over time, along with other, greater expectations regarding the future of England both abroad and at home that proved the motive for the novel she eventually produced.

The relative absence of history or macropolitics in Austen's earlier novels owes to a number of factors from the author's immaturity to her pragmatic decision to write about what she knew and, as her earliest readers suggest, what the audience for the growing genre of domestic fiction had come to expect. But the insularity of these texts owes just as much to a different (and relatively new) conception of history as something that, as the reviewer in the *Champion* stresses, ordinary agents were capable of making. As her early readers attest, Austen was not just in the business of satisfying expectations in her novels. She was, these readers show, committed also to *recalling* expectations of which reading, and the prospects it limns, would be largely a recapitulation. The protocols

of reading, ostensibly satisfied by the scope and object of Austen's novels' attention, were simultaneously extended, then, in recollection and in imitation of
certain practices, and in alignment with certain teleologies of change, that domestic fiction was increasingly enjoined to discountenance. That such prospects
inhabit and animate the probabilistic order in a novel like *Northanger Abbey*,
more than they actively subvert the status quo, is neither a problem nor a contradiction. Rather it bespeaks the sophisticated, if increasingly nostalgic, recognition not just that all politics are local but that in "the country and the age in
which live" (as Henry Tilney puts it) the politics that *matter most* are sufficiently
local that anyone, from Jane Bennet to Catherine Morland, may have made a
genuine difference.

It probably bears repeating that, in addition to their formal advancement
over the epistolary mode in which at least one of her early novels was conceived,
Austen's first three novels were preoccupied in various ways with the instrumentality of domestic fiction in the constitution of society: both as a regulatory
mechanism and as a means, more important, of revising the particular social
work that writers and readers undertake in the call and response that is also the
work of fiction. Nor can it be emphasized enough that for Austen, at this relatively early stage, the work of revision and the world of possibility onto which
such efforts opened were motivated by "gender troubles": with respect to women
who, like Austen and her peers, were manifestly second-class citizens and with
attention as well to men, who are deformed or flattened not despite—but more
often *by virtue of*—the privilege they appear to enjoy. A world where Collins can
command the acceptance of a marriage proposal only moments after being rejected by Elizabeth; or where the seemingly amiable and responsible Colonel
Brandon is a manipulative scourge with the nearly identical abjection of a former lover and a daughter to his credit; or where Henry Tilney is an attractive
marital prospect only in the wake of Catherine's discovery that her own "power
is nothing"; or where Edward Ferrars can talk blithely of dabbling in a variety of
careers even as his female interlocutors are struggling, thanks to the harassing
actions of his immediate family, to make ends meet; or where Mr. Bennet is forever Mr. Bennet is a world, plainly, that would benefit from transformations
that, as characters such as Jane and Bingley indicate, are or *were* conceivable
even as they have become inscrutable and, by the lights of novelistic convention,
unrepresentable. For with possibility of her own marriage still in view, and the
even more immediate prospect of a society, where social and sexual relations
had in many quarters proven resistant to more astringent modes of codification,[8] it is hardly surprising that the Austen of the 1790s would have alighted on
the domestic sphere as much for its familiarity and congeniality to her aspirations as a novelist as for its conflation, in again focusing on the "history" that in-

dividuals make, of the micropolitics of quotidian life and the macropolitics of social progress and melioration.

But by 1813, with the prospect of marriage behind her and with England's future marked increasingly by imperial and military prospects to which class inequality, much more than gender imbalance, was clearly inimical, Austen was far from sanguine about the efficacy of domestic life in the larger work of improvement and change. In fact, as *Mansfield Park* makes clear, practices that might likely serve a meliorative function—for example, the private theatricals undertaken in Sir Thomas's absence—are, along with the characters who support such activities, systematically discredited. They are discredited not just by a narrator who, like her counterpart in *Northanger Abbey*, is clearly predisposed to certain values and institutions; they are discredited by a narrative this time in which detailism of the sort that proved a bulwark against the normative drive to closure in the earlier text is now wrenched to accommodate a didactic pattern. It is not that *Mansfield Park* fails altogether to admit either oppositional practices on the part of certain characters or such contrary elements to which contemporary reading practices might be responsive. It is that these recalcitrant or resistant elements are no longer on a continuum with substantive change. This is as much an issue for social practice in the novel, in particular the behavior and destiny of a character like Mary Crawford, as it is for novelistic practice, which is wedded suddenly to a worldview and to a conception of character that Austen's immediate readership found inscrutable rather than compelling.

Austen's contemporaries were not the only readers that *Mansfield Park* succeeded in perplexing. Subsequent readers in the nineteenth century, who did not scruple to transform Austen's other fictions into conduct manuals, were far from enthusiastic or precise in their estimation of Austen's so-called Victorian novel. The novel had its admirers of course, notably George Henry Lewes, who typically concentrated his praise on the representation of the blameworthy Mrs. Norris, for whom Austen's "sad" aunt, Jane Leigh Perrot, is believed to have been a prototype.[9] But the response in general to Austen's novel, even as late as midcentury, reflects a perplexity akin to that registered by its earliest readers. The *New Monthly Magazine* fell back, as did initial readers, on the novel's verisimilitude, or its "Dutch-school accuracy of detail." But when this same review, under pressure no doubt from what the review terms the "moral of the tale," takes special and enthusiastic note of "what a bewitching 'little body' . . . Fanny Price" is (138), the reviewer's stance seems doggedly dutiful rather than discerning.

It is easy to see why readers in our time, from Julia Prewitt Brown to Ruth Yeazell, continue to identify *Mansfield Park* as a novel more immediately suited to the tastes and values of the generation of readers that would succeed Austen's.[10]

Even here, however, there is a failure to realize or to appreciate sufficiently the explanatory power vested in the anachronistic designation "Jane Austen's 'Victorian novel' " (Yeazell, 147), which speaks precisely to the novel's historic and continued inscrutability. Neither a Victorian novel in any practical sense nor a romantic-period or late–eighteenth-century novel of the kind that Austen had already produced, "Jane Austen's Victorian novel" was only the thing that a Victorian novel by Jane Austen could possibly have been, which is to say a novel about the future.

Here *Mansfield Park* differs from a nearly contemporary work such as Mary Shelley's *The Last Man*, whose meditations on futurity are reflections primarily on the present. Where *The Last Man*'s future is largely typological (balloon travel and so forth), Austen's novel is less a work "about the future" in this customary sense than a novel *of* the future in whose function the present of the early 1800s is effectively pressed. Unlike Dickens, who might have actually transformed Fanny into the alluring sprite that the *New Monthly* strenuously misrecognizes, Austen's representation of her "Victorian" heroine is suffused by a sense of what bids fair to be lost, particularly for women, in a culture and a nation to whose self-legitimating rhetoric of freedom the domesticated female was increasingly efficacious. This representation would explain as well why Mary Crawford, the novel's villainess, is at once the most interesting character here and a cautionary counterpoise to the novel's heroine. Enforcing a set of values that the novel doggedly upholds, Mary's derogation reveals at that same time, and in a somewhat longer view, that the novel's heroine, following the discourses she extols in her rare flights of enthusiasm, is a repository of certain developments that collectively impinge on any structural or practical transformation in the social life of women and men.

Both a domestic icon such as Thomas Gisborne would have promoted and a romantic character, whose autonomy, sincerity, and apparent depth are continually inferable, Fanny Price's character unites an ideal of womanhood marked by propriety and restraint *and* a conception of self suffused with the spilt religion for which the discourse of romanticism was, amid the tide of evangelicism, largely responsible.[11] Unlike the problems of the first published novels, which devolve largely upon imperatives of form, it is this discursive sedimentation, where current developments serve in imagining a future and in projecting, as it were, the *imagination* of the future that accounts for the enduring difficulty of *Mansfield Park*.[12] There is no question that *Mansfield Park* is more answerable to conservative interpretations, and that a rehabilitation of the Crawfords, and of Mary in particular, is virtually impossible: both from the narrator's perspective and from the sequence of events and circumstances that make up the narrative itself. Nevertheless there abides, in the treatment of Fanny and her antagonists, a more reflexive and nostalgic sense that the conceptions here of character and womanhood have, under pressure from without, been systematically deformed. It is not that Mary is charged, like Milton's Satan, with attracting the reader's fallen nature, any more than her attractiveness and perspicuity work to compromise and to expose Austen's commitment—here and elsewhere—to a fundamentally conservative program that usually benefits from better packaging. It is that such reflexive elements as *Mansfield Park* contains, including Mary's remarkable attachment to Fanny,[13] are notable not for their provisional success (as was the case in *Northanger Abbey*) but for their utter futility—or in recognition of what the future, in Austen's dystopic reckoning, has *already* foreclosed upon.[14]

Reading Austen's Reading

I will return in a moment to the reflexive effect of *Mansfield Park*, particularly as it bears on questions of character and identity, both individual and national. It is important first to explore more specifically the developments, at home and abroad, from which Austen extrapolated a future at this juncture and from which her novel became an exercise in what British fiction was unfortunately to become. This formulation will undoubtedly strike some as a convoluted evasion of the novel's apparent endorsement of a traditional or Burkean position; and it will strike others as a critical retrospection based primarily on the recent and rather gloomy historiography of Catherine Hall, Leonore Davidoff, and other feminist historians. But such a formulation remains the only way finally to account for the difficulty of a text that, by common and transhistorical consent, is too often its own worst enemy. I have already indicated some of the developments, public and private, on which *Mansfield Park* was compelled to reflect. The nexus of these developments in the novel that emerged is perhaps best understood through an examination of Austen's reading in the years preceding and encompassing its composition. Together the various works of nonfiction on which Austen made a point of commenting in her letters, notably the writings of Charles Pasley, Claudius Buchanan, and Thomas Gisborne, paint a picture of an England about-to-be in which the imperial reach of British culture, militarily, commercially, and ecclesiastically, is underwritten by a society whose claim to freedom and equality, and whose impending constitution as a middle-class hegemony, are also purchased at the cost of suffrage at home.

Part of the problem involves the structurally incompatible constituents of the liberal, bourgeois culture such as Britain is imagined in these texts. In representing what Pasley terms a "pure democracy,"[15] leveling (or something like it)

is presumed to coexist seamlessly in Britain with a kind of franchise or autonomy. Unlike the antithesis to slavery in, say, the Jacobin conception of freedom,[16] this franchise is an entitlement whose lineaments extend to ownership
and thus to a society where some people are freer and more equal than others.
Such inequality has been a recurrent theme in Austen, from the empowerment
of Collins by practice of entailment in *Pride and Prejudice* to Elinor's remarkably spirited defense of the nearly indigent Lucy Steele in *Sense and Sensibility*
"as a woman superior in person and understanding." Still, the more immediate
problem for Austen—even as she was plainly taken by the books she was
reading as she was conceiving *Mansfield Park*—involves the idea and ideal of
womanhood propounded therein. Whether it be Gisborne's model wife and
mother, who is virtually classless save that she is not poor, or Pasley's discrimination of political initiatives on the basis of being either "manly" or "woman-
ish" (120, 127), the constitution of society, as well as its survival and progress, is
variously pegged to a discourse of sameness (and difference), which is also a
sanction, in the name of democracy and a better world, for the containment of
women in ways that Austen would have found difficult to countenance.

We must remember that the possibilistic orientation of Austen's fictions to
date, and the probabilistic imperatives it contests, bespeak a certain privilege in
which a gentry woman imagines a world where adulthood might resemble
childhood in retrieving brothers and sisters from the uneven stations that they
are relegated to as men and women. Although far from Wordsworthian in its
material rather than metaphysical focus, such projective regression bears comparison with its romantic counterpart in the particular privilege that underwrites it and to which its horizons of possibility return. This is not to diminish,
by any means, either the sophistication or importance of Austen's initial (and
increasingly retrospective) belief in the significance of individual lives and in
the peculiar dynamism of everyday life. It is simply to emphasize that such
change as Austen *could* imagine, or that her equally privileged readership could
somehow fathom in reading her, was not just change by other means; it was also
change *according to means* or by (and for) those who would benefit most immediately from a loosening and reconfiguration of probable social practice. The
middle-class hegemony that the future holds in store, then, and on which
England's ambitions as a sovereign and civilizing force are apparently to be
predicated, is objectionable not only for its insistence on firm and unalterable
functions for people based exclusively on their sex. It is equally problematic for
the peculiar sameness by which the democratic ideal, in leveling all distinctions,
militates as much against differences of station, from which Austen's social
imagination paradoxically takes flight, as against the peculiar otherness or "internal difference" of a person or practice *from itself*, where (to borrow from

Emily Dickinson) the "meanings" for Austen "are." Fanny Price's stolidity, however assailable or deconstructable, stands as a register of a culture, and by turns
a future, where any change, apart from mobility in the most monolithic sense, is
plainly out of bounds.

Austen mentions Capt. Charles W. Pasley's *Essay on the Military Policy and
Institutions of the British Empire* (1810) in a letter to her sister, where the essay
stands as an example of the high seriousness that women readers in Chawton
eschew even as they "want to establish a Book Society" (*Letters* 294). While such
observations appear to contradict earlier statements, notably the paean to
women's writing in *Northanger Abbey*, Austen has a point in that Pasley's essay
articulates a program for British dominance in the world by way of reducing the
threat currently posed by France and Napoleon. Austen is plainly absorbed in
Pasley's study, which she reiterates "is too good" (304) for a certain type of
woman reader. However, his discursive saber rattling has a masculinist and normative dimension that Austen cannot help ridiculing. Confessing that she had
"protested against" reading the book "at first," Austen admits to "find[ing] it delightfully written & highly entertaining" and confesses even more that she is "as
much in love with the author as [she] ever . . . was with Clarkson or Buchanan"
(292).[17] I will be turning in a moment to Claudius Buchanan, whose popular account of the difficulty and necessity of bringing Christianity to India undoubtedly made good companion reading with Pasley's speculations and directives.
What must be stressed first, pursuant to Austen's declaration of love at this
juncture (or at a point in her life when prospects of "love" had vanished), is that
her interest in these works, though surely provoked by a jingoistic investment in
the success of their projected narratives, was insufficient in dispelling her initial
aversion. This aversion was based on the intuition that such success, as Pasley
promised, also spelled trouble: both for those not yet swayed by British culture
and for those *already* swayed, for whom a man in uniform, as Mrs. Palmer says
of her memorable spouse in *Sense and Sensibility*, "is just the kind of man [to]
like" (101).

Begun 1808 during the Napoleonic and Peninsular Wars and published in
1810, Pasley's essay pursues three interrelated theses, moving briskly from the
immediate threat of Napoleonic France to a projection of British hegemony in
the world. The first of Pasley's arguments is that naval dominance alone, even in
the wake of Nelson's victory at Trafalgar, would be insufficient in removing the
"menac[e]" currently "directed by the energy of one of the greatest warriors
that has appeared"(1). In addition to arguing for the expansion and cultivation
of a land force "capable of resisting a powerful invasion" (2), Pasley argues for
the deployment of that force in the "conquest . . . of such great fertile, and
populous ultramarine possessions, whether insular or continental, as will add

considerably to our strength and resources" (104). Only by becoming a "warlike people" (114) or the "military nation" (458), whose development Pasley urges as his third and final thesis, will Britain be able to dominate enough "lesser states" (151) to avoid the current "probability" of being "conquered" in turn (114).

It goes without saying that Pasley has a potent ally in Napoleon, whose numerous conquests in Europe and continuing war with Britain made the prospect of an invasion and of having to defend against one especially urgent. Yet striking in Pasley's account is not the threat of France, which is perhaps a given, but the prospect of an England capable of dominating a host of secondary European powers and of extending her control to other parts of the world whose resources, military and otherwise, are conducive to British interests. Even amid fears of an impending invasion, Pasley's attention is invariably directed elsewhere and toward the future, which he regards rather unproblematically and with a surety that seems somewhat out of place. In discussing the various encumbrances that strategically useless colonies such as the West Indies currently present, Pasley breezily observes that the "establish[ment]" of a "colonial empire . . . has been, and will probably still be, a favourite object of this country" so that Britain's aim "should be to grasp at great possessions"— including Egypt—"that would add to our resources and military force, instead of annihilating a great portion of both" (65). Pasley takes as his paradigm for such initiatives the British East India Company, whose success thus far, or "in every contest with their neighbours," may be traced to "the necessity of conquering, or of being conquered," in light of which they "have never made war by halves" (335). And with the East India Company as a template for a European policy yet unrealized, Pasley moves sufficiently afield so that what began as a call of alarm proceeds in remarkably short order to the prospect of world dominance leading to "a safe, . . . permanent and honourable peace . . . with France" (452).

Such prospects, both in Europe and beyond, depend in the end on Britain's transformation into a military nation. In this decidedly domestic prospect Pasley spoke immediately to Austen. Assuming that Austen was not surprised or especially offended by the gendered discourse that I have alluded to, which Pasley does not scruple to deploy in attacking the "unmanly timidity" (176) of Britain's refusal to dominate its European neighbors and allies, the consequences for women, specifically gentry women, in the military nation that Pasley proposes were not terribly hard to infer. Although Pasley alludes thankfully to the existence of an "hereditary nobility and gentry," particularly as they provide a "useful and necessary check upon the mercantile body" (477), the military nation he describes, and on which Britain's expansion and authority depends, is sufficiently consistent with a "pure democracy" to mandate a leveling of distinction that, for all its apparent virtue, is hegemonic in both form and function.

The proof of this—certainly for a reader like Austen—lies as much in the disappearance of class from Pasley's social landscape as in the division of labor he effectively prescribes, in which women have two functions only: to participate directly in the production of males and to figure forth, in their already projected domestication, the currently abject state of military policy.

It is essential to Pasley's argument to resolve an apparent contradiction between a system of conquest and a polity that values "freedom," which he regards as indispensable to the loyalty and patriotism of those in uniform. Yet with ancient Rome as his principal analogy, coupled with his abiding distaste for commercialism, Pasley's "democratic vistas" take on a Malthusian cast: in "thus affording greater employment for men of all ranks of society," the military nation "will find her population greatly augmented" and able consequently to "carry on war for ever, sometimes losing more, sometimes fewer men annually, without its population being in the least diminished" (506–7). Such "employment for men," needless to say, involves employment for women in the production of more men who can be sacrificed freely given the prevailing birthrate. At the same time, the silence encompassing this monolithic view of domesticity, wherein all women are essentially collapsed, along with social classes, into a fertile, endlessly reproductive, aggregation must have been deafening to Austen. There is little doubt that Austen's family was sufficiently influenced by the larger military and imperial prospects in Britain to be a template for the Price family in *Mansfield Park*, specifically Fanny and William. But it was a family too where (unlike the Prices) station and distinction fostered certain expectations to which Pasley's program is fundamentally opposed. The naval career that Frank Austen aspired to would have had some connection, of course, to the expanded military culture that Pasley projects. The same can hardly be said of the relationship of Pasley's reproductive nation to Jane's own writing and milieu, where possibilities and transformations—at least for those women privileged enough to imagine them—are nowhere in evidence. As Austen's dubiously hyperbolic affection for Pasley indicates, his essay was of use to the author of *Mansfield Park* in the projection of a future that at the very least stood in stark contrast to the present of her novels to date.

Claudius Buchanan, whose *Christian Researches in Asia* (1812)[18] Austen was also reading during the composition of *Mansfield Park* and whom she claimed to love as much as she did Pasley, would seem worthier of her affection, thanks to his chivalric horror at the sacrifice of women and children according to certain religious practices in India. In contrast to Pasley's fears, which are ruthlessly pragmatic, Buchanan's dismay at the pagan rituals he observes, and his concomitant hopes for the conversion of the East to the British type of Christianity, are inspired by a more mystified sense of mission in which the burgeoning reign of imperial Britain is apparently the latest chapter in biblical eschatology. There is a piquant fascination to Buchanan's firsthand accounts of Indian pagan rituals, in particular the procession of the Juggernaut, where pilgrims, as Buchanan describes them, are routinely sacrificed and crushed to death. This is similarly true of his discovery of an actual inquisition in Tanjore, replete with torture chambers, which the "Romish Church" actively supervises "within the boundaries of the British Empire" (78). Although they constitute the majority of Buchanan's account, these scenes of horror and surprise (which undoubtedly made for engaged reading) are prefatory to his ultimate advocacy of British hegemony as the only means to mankind's redemption. Unlike a novel such as Lewis's *The Monk*, where Manichaean strife is a generic sanction for a range of antinomian indulgences and transgressions, Buchanan's "gothic" works to nearly opposite effect. With its catalog of religious perversions, from paganism to Catholicism, Buchanan's "researches" uncover what was already obvious and in plain sight to his readers: the superiority of British Christianity and justification for its influence abroad.

It goes without saying that few British readers, including Austen, would have doubted the reasonableness of Buchanan's jingoism, especially when confronted with scenes of infanticide, torture, and simple ignorance. Still only the most self-infatuated Briton could subscribe wholeheartedly to the mythopoeic arc of Buchanan's expatiation, which climaxes in his tour of the Holy Land. Here, as Buchanan imagines it, a translation and circulation of the New Testament in Hebrew under the aegis of Britain will likely provoke a "conversion" of the Jews as prophesied in the Bible, leading (as promised) to a renovated world in time. The probable consequence of such active mitigation of "Papal and Mahomedean powers" (115) by discursive means "will be a long time of general holiness and peace, which will succeed to the present reign of vice and misery . . . during which righteousness will be as common as wickedness is now" (129). With that horizon in view, Buchanan ends on a note at once pious and bombastic: "Let Great Britain imitate the example of the Chaldean King; and send forth to all the world, her Testimony concerning the True God. She also reigns over many nations which 'worship idols of wood and stone;' and she ought, in like manner, to declare to them 'the sights and wonders of the Almighty' " (154).

Buchanan was scarcely the first writer in English to advocate the dissemination of British religious practice abroad. But he is of interest here—and was of interest to Austen—less for his reiteration of a centuries-old commonplace than for his articulation of a position that, despite its aversion to the "imposi[tion] of rule by the sword" (151), is in many ways the ideological complement to Pasley's unadorned materialism. The two books share, individually and together, a totalizing vision of British dominance that is decidedly proleptic in flavor.[19]

If Buchanan represents the ideological underpinnings to Pasley's expansionist fantasy, Thomas Gisborne's *An Enquiry into the Duties of the Female Sex*,[20] which Austen had read several years earlier after avoiding it for nearly a decade, provided the domestic counterpoint to the prospects of British hegemony in the world by giving a vision of what lay in store for women in a nation committed increasingly to homogeneity and conformity. Beyond its immediate relevance to the novel Austen would shortly commence writing, in this case regarding the propriety that Fanny displays in contrast to the ostentatious transgressions of her cousins and their friends, the broader relevance of Gisborne's companion treatise to his inquiry into the duties of men lay in its projection of a division of labor and identity in which *any* variation on the part of either men or women from their designated roles is discouraged.

The domestic roles that Gisborne assigns to women, and on which his inquiry expatiates, will be familiar to most readers, even if they have never read Gisborne or a similar conduct manual such as the earlier one by James Fordyce that Austen makes a special point of mocking in *Pride and Prejudice*, which she was also revising at this time.[21] They will be familiar because the domestic duties that Gisborne outlines, from the "comfort" of family and friends "in the intercourse of domestic life, under every vicissitude of sickness and health" to the "improv[ement] . . . of the other sex, by society and example," to "the modelling [of] the human mind during the early stages of its growth" (12–13) became something of a standard in the nineteenth century, especially in the decades following Austen's death. Domestic ideology was already well entrenched by the time of Austen's generation. Yet it remained, as Gisborne himself argues, a contested category to which *An Enquiry into the Duties of the Female Sex* means to lend stability over both competing accounts and the actual practices of those who should be reading them.

The critical features of Gisborne's text for the author of *Mansfield Park* involve something beyond the standard prohibitions and directives with which Austen had been long familiar and, on the evidence of both her novels and letters, had remarkably little patience. Such directives, including those against inappropriate conversation, dangerous amusements such as gaming, and the proclivity of young women to take part in theatricals, were no doubt relevant to the society whose tendencies Austen was chronicling. But Gisborne's various imperatives, and the codification of domestic ideology in which they issue, are far from coterminus with the varieties of difference to which Austen was also responsive and on which her view of everyday life had been predicated. Not only does Gisborne implicitly inveigh against differences of class and station, which it is a woman's proper function, in deportment, dress, and overall sociability to mitigate; he explicitly opposes any difference in either practice or motive that might remove a woman from what amounts, in his reckoning, to her ideal progress from cradle to grave.

Like Austen's more discerning contemporaries, Gisborne recognizes the importance of everyday activity in contributing to "human happiness," which is "affected [much less] by great but infrequent events . . . than by small but perpetually recurring incidents of good or evil" (11–12). Still his project overall is to regulate everyday practice to a specific, indeed single, model so that the positive difference that women make will be proportionate to the various differences in class, bearing, or behavior they must forsake in service of the "good." In addition to the usual prohibitions directed at young women in particular, or at those who are at the very station of the majority of Austen's characters in *Mansfield Park* and elsewhere, Gisborne devotes most of his account to describing a hypothetical housewife to whom "readers of every description," including those in both "the higher" and "middle classes of society" might well conform (1–2). The generalized character of this figure scarcely masks the fact that she is also a specific type—a gentry housewife to be precise—whose example women everywhere are instructed to imitate. Rather than urging a return to a version of country life that, as even Gisborne realizes, is ever less a synecdoche for British life in general, the effect of his normativizing drive is the projection of an England about to be. Here the welter of metropolitan and commercial life will be neutralized by emergence of a type of woman whose behavior and other characteristics render her both classless and class bound and an ideal from which both middle-class identity and hegemony can spring forth.[22]

Such a woman is not very different from the "middle-class aristocrat" in whose development and legitimation Austen's fiction was, according to Nancy Armstrong, particularly instrumental. Even so, such a view confuses the function that Austen's fiction would eventually perform for subsequent generations with the quite different function that Austen's particular attention to both gentry life and the practices of its younger female participants effected for its immediate readership. As a practitioner of domestic fiction in expectation of monetary gain from her efforts, Austen had little choice or inclination but to write about young women of marriageable age. Yet withal, her focus in *Mansfield Park* on women at the stage when, by Gisborne's lights, they are most easily swayed from the correct model of behavior cannot, even with narrator's bias against them, be understood simply as a fictional counterpart to Gisborne's inquiry. If the "real" of *Mansfield Park* turns out to be a falling away from a model of behavior that is understood by both narrator and protagonist to be the only proper mode of conduct regardless of its unpopularity, it was a reality sufficiently familiar to Austen's readership and proximate in bearing to the (then) present, that the novel's "vein of principle" was inscrutable to many readers.

Whether this accounts, even in part, for the fact that the novel was published to the ultimate inattention of the periodical press can only be speculated upon. What should be clear by now is that the novel's currency, on which the attention of periodical reviews and reviewers would presumably have been based, is diminished by the fact that the present, from which the novel's real is largely culled, is essentially a negative way.

In underscoring the negativity of *Mansfield Park*, I mean to dissociate the novel's obvious commitment to an idea of character, on which an inferable future appears to bear, from a metareflexivity in which the novel, to amend Susan Stewart's formulation, is self-consciously a false prototype.[23] Even as the novel is something of a dud, or a text whose manifold difficulties have consistently impeded its admiration, *Mansfield Park* is not, as I have perhaps implied, a rigorously managed exercise in representing the future and the role of fiction in ensuring it. There are certain aspects of the novel, in particular its management of narrative authority, where a demonstrable and unsubtle bias plays conveniently to Austen's abiding preoccupation with the novel as a social and ideological instrument. But even here, it is not enough to say, as it was in treating *Northanger Abbey*, that narrative incompetence is to the novel's purpose in its steady mitigation of a regulatory program.

I have already noted that the actions and attitudes of the more vibrant and dynamic characters, of whom the narrator and her protagonist consistently disapprove, are notable both for the real they comprise and for their demonstrable futility in directing readers to an alternative system of values. What must be emphasized is that this relentless doubling or negativity, whereby life in the present remains as wanting as the vantage(s) from which such practice is both observed and judged, indicates the genuineness of Austen's engagement at a moment when both the everyday and the prospects to which it had previously given rise belonged increasingly to an England that was disappearing.

We can even take this a step further by suggesting that the three novels Austen had completed prior to *Mansfield Park*, all of which were drafted in the late 1790s, tend variously to anticipate the latter in marshaling an anterior England on behalf of improvements and meliorations that were recognizable only to readers with enough privilege and hope to believe in them still. Unlike these earlier texts, whose history of composition was literally an exercise in making the present answerable to the past, or to a conservatism that was by no means conservative in a strictly ideological sense, *Mansfield Park*, written at the time of its publication, pursued a nearly opposite tack. Here the novel's present, which is the future by comparison with the present of Austen's works thus far (including the two novels she had just published), extends its mandate in making a residual real answerable to a future that, based on Austen's investigations and intuitions, holds nothing comparable in store. Or to put it in a way that is even more consistent with the double consciousness of the novel: there is no longer any difference between what the future holds and what the present, however assailable by standards that are apparently gathering force, may still harbor. Both the residual real and the emergent real are, in different ways and in different registers, dead ends.

Lovers' Vows and the Performance of the Narrative Authority

There are multiple ways to explore the double consciousness of *Mansfield Park*, beginning indeed with Fanny herself. Both a heroine such as Gisborne might have imagined *and* a manipulator who seems always to recognize her main chance, especially in her rejection of Henry Crawford, Fanny is not just a character whose particular purchase on virtue is negotiated at the cost of self-knowledge or in a way that masks her nearly metastatic ambition. Fanny is also a character whose claim to superiority is simultaneously deferred to a host of morally charged discourses that work, in characteristically Austenian fashion, to make "internal persuasion" or conviction a constant echo of persuasion from without. Such duality is evident in the treatment of other characters as well—for example, Mrs. Norris. An odious parasite who is constantly "spunging" in one way or another, Mrs. Norris is also the product of a misogynistic economy whose transparent delectation in the deformation of women (notably Lady Bertram) works disingenuously to absolve both the culture at large and the male agents, who are its beneficiaries, of any concomitant blamability. Then, of course, there are the Crawfords, particularly Mary. Although plainly implicated in the unsavory (but by no means unambiguous) business of marrying Fanny off to her brother Henry, Mary is probably the most complicated character in all of Austen, a woman whose perspicuity and charm are exceeded only by the integrity of her decision to remain unmarried—this despite Edmund Bertram's self-serving belief that his obvious attraction to her ("I cannot give her up" [384])[24] is entirely reciprocal. Indeed there is not an aspect of *Mansfield Park*—from the heroine's virtue to the moral deficiencies of Henry Crawford to the selfish indolence of the Bertram sisters—that does not also inculpate domestic ideology, along with the related notions of both character and national character, to which the future, in literature and in life, appears wedded.

The question of national or English character, and the particular duplicity it introduces, comes to crisis and attention in the *Lovers' Vows* episode where Fanny's memorable response to being pressured by the other characters to take part in the private theatrical—"No, indeed, I cannot act" (131)—performs two related functions. First, Fanny demonstrates (in conjunction with her behavior thus far) that sincerity, of which her demurral is a virtual definition, is more properly the inability to know one is always acting. Second, Fanny's response follows nearly all of her actions in the novel, along with the demonstrations of the narrator, whom the observant and detached heroine also figures, in underscoring the particular bias to which an imputed objectivity or fairness is always connected.[25] This duality would explain, more than anything else perhaps, the uncanny reflexivity that haunts *Mansfield Park* even as the novel is pitched toward a future in which the difference of a subject or practice from itself, on which change or possibility has depended thus far, seems increasingly inconceivable. For, as the *Lovers' Vows* episode indicates representatively, the emplacement of the subject *into* discourse, be it Kotzebue's or Gisborne's, is more than a thoroughgoing act of interpellation. It produces, by its very constitution, an "internal difference" that actually transforms the negativity or doubleness of *Mansfield Park*, in which narrative bias and incompetence are plainly one component, into a nostalgic echo of an increasingly lost present.

I am aided in this view as much by the peculiar difficulty of the novel overall, which continually cries out for some acknowledgment that the author and her narrator are not in fact one and the same, as by a number of elements in the theatricality episode that, while seemingly incidental, are quite crucial. Several of these involve the translation of *Lovers' Vows* that the performers, led by Tom Bertram and his friend John Yates, have settled on. While there were a number of English translations of the German play available at the time of the novel's publication, the version used by Austen's players is, by common acknowledgment, the 1798 translation of Elizabeth Inchbald whose "altered" version of the play was performed at Drury Lane, Covent Garden, and the Theatre Royal in Bath, where Austen would have been able see it. Unlike the other, more literal translations of *Lovers' Vows*, the most salient feature of Inchbald's translation is its avowed Englishness, which is especially evident in references in her version to the British that were not in the original.[26] Inchbald comments on this aspect of her translation in the introduction, noting (rather cryptically) the "discordanc[e]" of Kotzebue's "original" with "an English stage" and then observing somewhat more specifically that the "forward and unequivocal manner" of the young heroine, Amelia, particularly when "she announces her affection to her lover, . . . would have been revolting to an English audience" had Inchbald not changed it (5). Thus Inchbald has endowed Amelia "with manners conforming to the English, rather than the German taste" (6).

It can be argued, certainly, that morality, whether introduced by the translator or simply highlighted in the play's preoccupation with "*conscience*" that Inchbald approvingly lists among its author's "virtuous concern[s]" (7), focuses what is meant by Englishness. However, two of Inchbald's more notable emendations indicate that her nativism has more complex and far-reaching lineaments with respect to both character and national character. The additions involve references to England made by Count Cassel who, as the most decadent of the play's characters, is a repository of antiaristocratic feeling. Commenting on the many characteristics he has assimilated in his "travels," Cassel claims to have "learnt delicacy in Italy—hauteur, in Spain—in France, enterprize—in Russia, prudence—in England, sincerity—in Scotland, frugality—and in the wilds of America . . . love" (28–29). Regardless of the appositeness of these characteristics, or their resonance for an English audience, important is the way a nationalistic view of self depends (no less than in Buchanan or Pasley) on a prejudicial view of the non-native. While the other characteristics named, including love, are attributes or techniques that can be learned or appropriated, the fidelity to one's essence (whose claim to virtue is presumably self-explanatory), would seem to militate against the count's "epitomization" of "the world" as he describes it (28). Unless, of course, sincerity—and the particular integrity it presupposes—is a role or, worse, a legitimating identity that can be cast off or compromised like any other.

If Inchbald refrains from commenting more conclusively on this point, she manages, despite her evasiveness, to make sincerity and the internal difference to which it ironically refers a central concern in Kotzebue's play, whose every character, or so it seems, has wandered from another identity or essence. Where the original *Lovers' Vows* may be regarded as a play in which a more natural and authentic identity asserts its claim over a selfhood forged by culture and society, chiefly in the baron's acceptance of his "natural" son, Frederick, the "English" *Lovers' Vows* is far less sanguine about a selfhood seemingly impervious to anything but itself.

It is more the case that the virtue we call sincerity, and the sincerity that is reciprocally a mark of virtue, is as unnatural and as much an imposition as the virtue traditionally ascribed to rank or privilege. Inchbald indicates as much when, later in the exchange, she has Count Cassel expatiate on human goodness:

Count. Who is Mr. Anhalt?
Amelia. Oh, a very good man.
Count. A good man! In Italy, that means a religious man; in France, it means a cheerful man; in Spain, it means a wise man; and in England, it means a rich man.—Which good man of all of these is Mr. Anhalt?
Amelia. A good man in every country, except England.
Count. And give me the English good man, before that of any other nation. (30)

Without dismissing the comic effect here, there is in the summary rejection of English goodness (thanks largely to Cassel's approbation) an implication regarding sincerity that—given the proximity of Inchbald's two "English" interpolations—is hard to overlook. The implication is that sincerity or English goodness is an entitlement in the same register as social rank and material wealth. Hence when the identity of the baron's natural son is disclosed in Inchbald's version of the play, the effect is not only the perpetuation of an ever more dubious virtue in the way natural affection finds its nearest register in the baron's unnatural or patrilineal designation of Frederick as his heir; the effect extends to the dismantling of sincerity, or its essential ground, in having the baron exclaim upon learning of Frederick's "true" identity: "Who am I? What am I? Mad—raving—no—I have a son—A son! The bravest—I will—I must—oh!" (61).

While it is important to note the dramatic effect of these and similar emendations, the baron's reaction serves two other purposes. First, it demonstrates, in conjunction with Frederick's disclosure, that identity, like sincerity, is a matter of being compelled not from but *toward* a fundamental duplicity in which one literally performs one's inability to act. And second, the baron's reaction shows that the only essence to which one may legitimately lay claim amid this doubleness is one's own corporeality or boundedness by what Charles Lamb, in complaining of the theater, called "straitlacing actuality".[27] This point (or one cognate to it) is made in the novel at the episode's climax when Yates is confronted by the newly arrived Sir Thomas in the latter's closet, which had been made into a theater, and proceeds to pass from one identity (the entitled baron) to another essence (the almost equally entitled Yates). It is a point and, even more, a *prospect* that—all futurity notwithstanding—is central both to the theatrical episode in *Mansfield Park* and, in its abiding negativity, to the novel as a whole.

At the beginning of the theatrical episode the narrator is especially direct (and very much a character in her own right) in charging young Tom Bertram with idleness and vanity. She is harder still on his friend Yates, whose fathomable self-irony is almost irretrievable in the blame visited upon him: "He came on the wings of disappointment, and with his head full of acting, for it had been a theatrical party; and the play, in which he had borne a part, was within two days of representation, when the sudden death of one of the nearest connections of the family had destroyed the scheme and dispersed the performers. To be so near happiness, so near fame . . . and being so near, to lose it all, was an injury to be keenly felt, and Mr. Yates could talk of nothing else" (109). Then, of course, there are the observations in which it is impossible to differentiate Fanny and the narrator, or where the narrator does *her* work simply by being

Fanny. In recounting the group's deliberations over which play to perform, the narrator melds with Fanny, observing how the latter "looked on and listened, not unamused to observe the selfishness which, more or less disguised, seemed to govern them all" (118). Several pages later—in noting Julia Bertram's distress in not being assigned the role of Agatha—Fanny, who is described again as having "been a quiet auditor of the whole," is also described as unable to "think of [Julia] as under the agitations of *jealousy*, without great pity" (123).

No one will dispute the acuity of Fanny's observations here. Yet their point, following the doubling to which no one is apparently immune, involves Fanny's presumption to omniscience or exteriority, which is reversed and "brought down," in Lamb's apt description, to "the standard of flesh and blood" (98). It is one thing for Fanny to be correct in surmising Julia's condition; it is quite another for her to stand apart convinced that her difference or privacy is an escape from selfishness and a measure thereby of her superiority.

It is possible that Austen is doing something more here and that her narrator's sympathy is neither sufficient nor so total to preclude a more critical rendering of her pitying heroine. But the greater possibility by far, all the more in that it returns us willy-nilly to the possibilistic horizons of the earlier novels, has little to do with any circumspection or control on the narrator's part. It involves, if anything, an objectification so severe, and so successful in rendering Fanny unattractive, that critics are nearly (and rightly) unanimous in deeming *Mansfield Park* the least objective of Austen's novels: a work whose oppressive literalness is more a testament to the author's obduracy than to her ability to hold two ideas in her head at once. The consensus regarding the novel's literalness is one with which I concur, although not for the reasons most frequently cited, which associate Fanny's unimpeachability with an unambiguous moral stance. I concur because the literalness, particularly as a reflection of things to come, remains (like English character itself) a doubled or displaced field into which both narrator and narrative are also cast and set in critical relief.

This dimension to the novel becomes evident in the instances where the inability to act, or to be anything but transparent, bridles against the very duplicity that sincerity must, by definition, deny. In returning to her room and ruminating over her refusal to act in the play, Fanny is assailed in private by a number of speculations: "She had begun to feel undecided as to what she *ought to do*; and as she walked round the room her doubts were increasing. Was she *right* in refusing what was so warmly asked, so strongly wished for? . . . Was it not ill-nature—selfishness—and a fear of exposing herself? And would Edmund's judgment, would his persuasion of Sir Thomas's disapprobation of the whole, be enough to justify her in a determined denial in spite of all the rest?"

(137). It may be tendentious to insist that Fanny's self-interrogation here is an interrogation of the self, whose "undecidability" is registered in the failure to adopt a more forthright stance. After all, Fanny is responding at one level to a good deal of pressure. Nonetheless, as her ruminations make clear, the separate position that Fanny would adopt, and has already adopted, is something of a compelled activity whose constructedness is registered both in its connection to Edmund (and to the way Edmund's integrity is linked in turn to the authority of his father) as well as in the indecision to which she is compelled now in consequence.[28]

This dynamic is echoed several pages later where Edmund's resistance to the play similarly dissolves in a disingenuously stated concern for the feelings of Mary Crawford to whom he has decided to play opposite: "Put yourself in Miss Crawford's place, Fanny. Consider what it would be to act Amelia with a stranger. She has a right to be felt for, because she evidently feels for herself. . . . Her feelings ought to be respected. Does it not strike you so, Fanny?" (139). Apart from the instability on which sympathy and sociability are based in Edmund's nearly deconstructive calculus, there are other aspects to his appeal that directly compromise the literalness of this demonstration. To the narrator—who at this juncture is omniscient—Edmund's concern for Mary marks a sliding from a self that is also a better and truer self, and is plainly a default that must be masked (through an act of conscience and perhaps fidelity to Fanny) by some mechanism of denial. Were Edmund's feelings true feelings, or the result of something other than Mary's wiles and the role playing they induce literally and figuratively, they could or would be readily admitted.

This position on Edmund—and positions like it in the novel—is hardly the most interesting in Austen's canon, as critics have long opined. Nevertheless the insufficiency of narration owes as much, at this juncture, to an overweening morality as it does to a "real" that is inaccessible to narrative control or understanding, save as a material phenomenon. It is Fanny, once again, who registers this effect: "To be acting! After all his objections—objections so just and public! After all that she had heard him say, and seen him look, and known him to be feeling. Could it be possible? Edmund so inconsistent. Was he not deceiving himself? Was he not wrong? Alas! it was all Miss Crawford's doing. She had seen her influence in every speech, and was miserable" (141). More than her previous ruminations over the decision not to act, the questions here do more than broach possibilities—chiefly Edmund's "inconsistency"—that are no longer inconceivable and easy to contain rhetorically. In fact these speculations, which also use Edmund to focus the pervasiveness of acting, and the concomitant impossibility of an authentic or consistent selfhood, go a step further in showing how the very position of authority from which Mary is then charged—whether by Fanny or the "miserable" narrator in her image—is also a matter of denying an altogether "possible," if duplicitous, sense of human identity in general.

Where Edmund's denial is used earlier to signify his delinquency or abandonment of a true self, denial in the example of Fanny now is the equivalent of that self, or of "true acting" as it is later dubbed, and a means, accordingly, by which the narrative participates in the very duplicity it discredits. For while denial, most particularly of inconsistency (" 'No, indeed, I cannot act' "), continues to drive Fanny in the narrative, issuing in an apotheosis of "consistency" in the marriage to Edmund and in the greater entitlement that union entails, the stance of *Mansfield Park*, however fashioned to the shape of things to come, is also compromised by the very possibility or errancy currently under siege. In fact, in the very manner of the antitheatricality it both promotes and deconstructs, the position of authority from which, as Thomas R. Edwards notes, "we are told less in this novel than in [Austen's] others" (55) is fundamentally a position beside itself: a denial *of the denial* that consists with sincerity and—to the extent it remains committed to a conception of character to which character itself gives the lie—with narrative authority as well.

This via negativa, where the blamable undergoes something of a recuperation at the expense of blame or value itself, is shown to particular effect, and with theatricality and sincerity as its focus, in the episode's climax, which involves, not coincidentally, the violation of Sir Thomas's privacy:

[Sir Thomas] stept to the door [of his room] . . . and opening it, found himself on the stage of a theatre, and opposed to a ranting young man, who appeared likely to knock him down backwards. At the very moment of Yates perceiving Sir Thomas, and giving perhaps the best start he had ever given in the whole course of his rehearsals, Tom Bertram entered at the other end of the room; and never had he found greater difficulty in keeping his countenance. His father's looks of solemnity and amazement on this his first appearance on any stage, and the gradual metamorphosis of the impassioned Baron Wildenhaim into the well-bred and easy Mr. Yates, making his bow and apology to Sir Thomas Bertram, was such an exhibition, such a piece of true acting as he would not have lost upon any account. It would be the last—in all probability the last scene on that stage; but he was sure there could not be a finer. (164)

If the meaning of this encounter defies a more precise articulation by either the narrator or Tom, it is not for failure to fathom or to transmit "what" a "theatre," to quote Henry Crawford, "signifies."

Following the narrative, and the doubling it cannot contain much less synthesize, Tom's notably cryptic delectation may be traced to the way the encounter between the "baron" and the baronet makes truth or sincerity a condition now of the particular text in which the subject quite literally discovers himself. The "true acting" that has an indelible if strangely benign effect on Tom pertains less to Yates's natural good manners than to the way this performance, actually this metamorphosis, highlights the theatricality of true being in general. For by passage from Wildenhaim to Yates, the body to which either "Wildenhaim" or "Yates" has been assigned does little more than shift roles, exposing the equally theatrical, equally duplicitous arrangement in which it is obliged as Yates to show deference to the seemingly ingenuous Sir Thomas. Beyond the oedipal strife, which might appear to justify Tom's amusement at his father's unease (and may likely owe to Tom's recent experience with his father in Antigua), there is something in this encounter that not only gives Tom pause but has the more important effect of joining him in a position beyond or opposed to the one that Sir Thomas and the performing Yates are compelled, in different ways, to sustain.

So far as one can tell, Yates's performance here is remarkably self-conscious, implicitly acknowledging (in conjunction with Tom's response) the acting that ordinarily passes as natural behavior. In this Yates is undoubtedly representative of the majority of the play's advocates, whose enthusiasm for this putatively decadent diversion also may be traced to impulses that, in their necessary complication of the judgments rendered upon them, are not entirely self-serving. It is frequently remarked that the role that each of the characters adopts in *Lovers' Vows* corresponds to his or her role in the novel.[29] This is true, but not necessarily in the way that most commentators mean it. Far from simply enabling characters such as Henry Crawford and Maria Bertram to give expression to their barely masked affection for one another (or anticipating in one way or another their respective fates in the novel), role playing in *Lovers' Vows* is, from another perspective, an occasion for self-scrutiny, allowing each player to observe herself as if she were in literature. A matter, then, of reading one's writtenness, which allows for the unwriting of a self that has been unreadable or readable only according to the narrator's (and Fanny's) reductive protocols, playing oneself—or what every character in *Mansfield Park* does regardless of their participation in the play—has a rather different significance for the actors and agents who do so consciously. And no two characters are more exemplary in their efforts both to read and unwrite themselves than Tom Bertram and Henry Crawford, who typically bear the brunt of Fanny's and the narrator's opprobrium.

The significance of Tom's performance in *Lovers' Vows* is made clear in his protean function, involving the performance of three different roles: the landlord, the butler, and the cottager. By this function Tom manages at least two things: he confronts directly, and within the same space, the inequities that social privilege has conditioned him to take for granted; and he exposes the arbitrariness of a system in showing (in the spirit of Inchbald's translation) its ability to endow the same person with different social value. Not only would Tom expose a world that makes players of its inhabitants; he would literally embody another world (to which intoxication also brings him) wherein the natively or naturally human—Tom's body, as it were, shorn of value—can resist circumscription.

A similar—and shocking as it will sound to some—similarly *utopian* impulse informs Henry Crawford's role playing, which, like Tom's desire to be anything but Tom, follows the doubled disposition of the novel in appealing to a nostalgic or again possibilistic retrospection. This is evident in Henry's enthusiastic response to the prospect of undertaking a theatrical at Mansfield:

"I really believe," said he, "I could be fool enough at this moment to undertake any character that ever was written, from Shylock or Richard III. down to the singing hero of a farce in his scarlet coat and cocked hat. I feel as if I could be any thing or every thing, as if I could rant and storm, or sigh, or cut capers in any tragedy or comedy in the English language. Let us be doing something. Be it only half a play—an act—a scene; what should prevent us? . . . and for a theatre, what signifies a theatre?" (111)

I have already appropriated and (admittedly) distorted Henry's final question for the purpose of exegesis. Yet it is the context of the question—a protheatrical initiative—as well as the enthusiasm of this exhortation that justifies my putting it to such use. "What" a theater "signifies" is not only "what" is always visible but never quite objectionable to our eyes, be it ambition or anti-Semitism or simply the role playing to which selfhood and character are equivalent. A theater also adumbrates what, here and throughout the novel, generally prevents that signification from taking place: the authority or impulse to discriminate to which the theater, in its openness to "every thing," remains resistant in turn.

Henry's "signifying" theater is in many ways an objective correlative for the novel itself. Although unattractive and seemingly unironized, the various representations of *Mansfield Park*, both pro and con, are also a means—the only means—to regress from the novel's relentless and dystopic negativity to the peculiar plenitude or "every thing" that acting "any thing" makes possible. Nor is *Mansfield Park* very different from the theater (and its advocates here) in the capacity, or incapacity as the case may be, to recognize the significance of these representations. It is the pathos of the novel, as it is the pathos of certain of its characters, that the urgency of its representations maintains precedence over any stable or consistent significance to be derived from them. Much like Henry, in fact, whose compulsive role playing—notably that of Fanny's sincere and genteel suitor—involves performing what his detractors are convinced is *not* simply another script, the novel can do no more at this point than stage the history that is being written or seems ever more writable. While the real of Austen's earlier novels, particularly *Northanger Abbey*, is increasingly inconceivable by 1813, its unrecuperability in *Mansfield Park* is a measure not only of its passing or unwritability but of its nearly simultaneous resurrection as a negative way. The real, despite its constitutive duplicity, is an armature now of the particular authority and moral commitment that domestic fiction must comply with, however miserably.

Nostalgia in Emma

Emma, generally regarded as Austen's most accomplished novel or, as Reginald Farrer terms it, her "Book of Books,"[1] is also responsible for more misconceptions about its author's achievement overall than any of her other works. The reasons for this misrecognition are manifold, but they stem in the present instance from two fundamental features that mark *Emma* as character-istically Austenian. The first of these is the practice of free indirect discourse, particularly as it directs our response to Emma, whose foibles are readable at the same time that they are unavailable to the heroine herself. The second of *Emma*'s representative features involves its country village setting that readers from Mary Mitford onward have deemed either an oasis, delightfully removed from the bustle of metropolitan life, or a sharply demarcated social space in which a normative, increasingly partial idea of Englishness is postulated on be-half of specific class and ideological interests.

That *Emma* is bracketed by two novels that are far from insular in the worlds onto which they open, making it more of a retreat than business as usual, is of little interest to most commentators.[2] Beginning with Walter Scott, whose review of the novel remains the most sustained and influential assess-ment of Austen's writing in her lifetime, *Emma* has stood as a synecdoche of Austen's oeuvre—Scott, for example, used the occasion of its appearance to comment on what he tellingly dubbed "the narrative of all [Austen's] novels"— and proof of the consistency of its author's achievement overall. It hardly matters, apparently, that the vaunted omniscience of the narrator, on which Austen's practice as a realist is founded, breaks down throughout the novel or that the novel's hero, George Knightley, is old enough to be the heroine's and his eventual spouse's father or that Emma's apparent blindness to Mr. Elton's atten-tions may have less to do with her self-centeredness and more to do with an interest in her protégée, Harriet Smith, that is pointedly eroticized. Nor does it seem to matter much that the world of the novel, as the condition of Crown Inn's ballroom makes clear, is irretrievably moribund and otherwise removed from both the present and near future of the novels between which *Emma* stands poised. In commentary after commentary the many things that are wrong with *Emma,* complicating its narrative momentum sufficiently that Maria Edgeworth gave up reading it after only one volume, are usually overlooked in deference to all that is right with the novel. And what is right with *Emma* involves, with varying degrees of endorsement, the adjustment of self and society, to which Emma's *bildung,* along with her setbacks, is often deliciously tantamount.[3]

The culminating lesson in Emma's education is delivered, or more precisely team taught to her, at Box Hill. But the road to Box Hill is by no means direct or clear. And by the time we get there enough has been set in motion under the surprisingly uncomprehending view of the narrator that *Emma's* narrative arc—and the growth or education it involves—seems ever more an exercise in foreclosure or misunderstanding than a vehicle of ideology successfully buttressed by circumstantial detail. Indeed it is not too much to say that the various details that, by the testimony of Scott and Edgeworth, mitigate the force and efficacy of Austen's achievement in *Emma,* work ultimately to retrieve realistic practice—or what was *becoming* realistic practice—from a tendency to make regulation and representation coterminal. Far more than in its seeming endorsement of a way of life that as recently as *Mansfield Park* was fast disappearing, it is in the details, so to speak, which remain inscrutable to the narrator even as they are increasingly readable and significant on second and third encounters, that *Emma* maintains its representative status in the Austen canon. This is so even as *Emma's* compulsive readability (pace Edgeworth) renders it something other than the novel, or the *kind* of novel, that readers like Scott assumed they were reading all along. Where Austen's earlier novels, particularly the first two published novels, are preoccupied with what is gained and lost in the practice of free indirect discourse as a formal innovation, *Emma* is more an attempt to make the formal constitution of the novel, from which there is clearly no turning back, answerable to a legacy that allowed for—or, better still, mandated—a *competency* in the act of reading that narrative authority effectively usurps.[4]

The legacy to which I am referring, and to which *Emma,* more than any of Austen's other novels, strenuously recurs, is the legacy of epistolarity. Its principal manifestation in *Emma*—beyond the nearly allegorical importance that letters are granted in the text—remains the novel's uncanny allegiance to the Richardsonian technique of writing to the moment. It is this aspect of the novel, more than any lapse on Austen's part, that explains *Emma's* most astonishing feature and, in the estimation of at least some readers, its chief liability: the suppression of the courtship narrative regarding Frank Churchill and Jane Fairfax. Where previously the omniscient style of narration represented the antithesis of epistolarity in matters ranging from control of character to the guidance that this practice exerts on readerly response, Austen appears intent here on exploring and exploiting the affinity of the two narrative modes. This affinity—one that to my knowledge no commentator has yet noticed in *Emma*—resides in the fact that narrative, however plotted *avant la lettre*, may be turned, following the very practice of writing, to the event itself, of which the written (here, as in a letter) is scarcely more than a recapitulation.

This is not to suggest that *Emma* somehow lacks the irony or knowingness which, even in so dour text as *Mansfield Park*, is characteristic of Austen's narrative voice. It is rather that the interval necessary for the narrator to opine on a given character or circumstance is no longer sufficient—at least in *Emma*—for the purposes of comprehension. There exists in *Emma* a perceptible and bewildering tension between an acuity everywhere in evidence, even in so slight an observation as Mr. Knightley standing in "tall indignation" upon learning from Emma of Harriet's refusal of Mr. Martin (54),[5] and a failure to grasp the full scope of the novel's many elements (including the one just cited). Reginald Farrer, whose unequivocal praise of the novel is regularly quoted despite its 1917 imprimatur, is only partly right in observing that *Emma* "is not an easy book to read" and that its "infinite delights and subtleties of workmanship" are appreciable "only when the story has been thoroughly assimilated".[6] For "the manifold complexity of the book's web" by which twelve readings of the novel provide "twelve periods of pleasure . . . squared and squared again with each perusal, till at every fresh reading you feel anew that you never understood anything like the widening sum of its delights" never quite succeeds in uncomplicating, much less in removing, the "dens[ity]" and "obscur[ity]" that abide "until you know the story" (266). It is the case rather that repeated readings of *Emma*, which the obscurity of the Frank-Jane counterplot initially invites, open onto a difficulty that, to borrow Farrer's own hyperbole, is "squared and squared again" in excess of those "delights" that bear directly and more explicably on what W. J. Harvey nicely terms the "shadow novel-within-a-novel."[7]

Part of the problem is that subsequent readings of *Emma* fail on balance to include the narrator among those who, for want of a better term, we may call the comprehending. Unlike the narrator of *Northanger Abbey* who, for all her excesses, is plainly mindful, especially on rereading, of the misunderstanding over Catherine's "fortune" that prompts General Tilney to invite her to the abbey in the first place, the various details surrounding Frank and Jane, from the former's chronic attention to the Bateses and their needs to his own need to speak constantly of Jane even if it means derogating her, are duly noted by the narrator without so much as a glimmer of recognition. Other characters, to be sure, are less ignorant than the narrator. But even these characters, notably Knightley and his brother, John, are led to their suspicions less by a complete and generous understanding of things than by a regulatory impulse that reflects their commitment to (and to maintaining) the status quo. Their speculations regarding Frank are, if anything, far closer to the "lucky guess" (*Emma*, 10) that Knightley characteristically charges Emma with having made in identifying Mr. Weston as a likely match for her former governess, Miss Taylor, than they issue from the "penetration" (122) that Emma, with far more generosity, credits the two brothers with possessing. Knightley is more than simply lucky in seeming constantly to understand how things really are here. However, with narrative authority in abeyance, or restricted to an acuity over the local and the contingent, it is left increasingly to the reader—or in this case the rereader—to evaluate the terms and bases of Knightley's apparent rectitude. To this reader the Knightley brothers' "penetration" may seem more the result of allowing the probable—for example, Mr. Elton's aim and prerogative of marrying to advantage—to hold sway in *all* judgments than the effect of anything particularly imaginative on their part.

The burden of imagination, as any reader of *Emma* knows, is borne chiefly by Emma herself, who is pointedly dubbed an "imaginist." With the probable or the status quo as a baseline for being right and lucky in understanding the way things are, the errancy of Emma's various speculations, particularly as they focus on the plight of unmarried yet still-marriageable women, takes on a thicker, more compelling cast. At the heart of Emma's fantasies is less a vision of the world as it is where, as the novel makes clear, women are continually at risk. Driving Emma's imaginings, at least initially, is a vision of the world as it should and perhaps can be, where women, who may have already enjoyed a modicum of security, can be confident of retaining it indefinitely. These worlds, to be sure—the probable world that routinely claims people like Miss Bates as victims, and the possible world in which a Harriet Smith will be guaranteed security independent of her circumstances—are not so easily parsed, particularly if separating them means granting Emma any agency in actually having things her way. This becomes clear in the case of Miss Taylor, whose marriage to Mr. Weston in the prehistory of the narrative appears, with the weight of information that gradually accumulates, less the result of any machinations on Emma's part than an exit strategy from quasi-servitude at Hartfield in which Miss Taylor is likely the more active and interested mover. Any luck that can be attributed to Emma in identifying Mr. Weston as a likely protector for her former teacher owes mostly to that teacher's desperation in the first place. It owes to a world where contingency and good fortune are routinely answerable to things as they are.

The reading of *Emma* here, which takes seriously the imperative to reread the novel that the failure of omniscience invites, presupposes more than a foreknowledge of the relationship of Frank and Jane. I am not diminishing by any means the importance of that relationship, both as an alternative to the marriage plot linking Emma and Knightley and as a union whose sheer out-of-boundness, at least in representational terms, tells us a great deal about the possibilistic horizons that govern Austen's project here and elsewhere. I am suggesting rather that once rereading becomes the protocol of reading *Emma*, there is no way that this reading can amount solely to a careful monitoring of the elements regarding Jane and Frank to which *all* of Highbury, with the characteristic exception of its chief magistrate, is apparently quite blind. It is more the case that (re)reading *Emma* is an uncontainable process or, in what may seem a paradox, a process restricted only to the world of novel. Although circumscribed in ways that critics from Charlotte Brontë to Raymond Williams have long lamented,[8] *Emma*'s is a world where, as Miss Bates reminds us over and over, there is always something more. Indeed there is no novel by Austen where reading is less controlled, less innocent, or more traumatic in its recursive operation of making something seeable and fathomable only after it has already been seen than this one.

"She would improve her"

The reading practices that *Emma* inculcates at some peril are evident as early as the novel's first volume. This is so despite the fact that this segment of the narrative, involving Emma's failed effort to unite Harriet Smith and the newly arrived vicar, Mr. Elton, along with Knightley's superior judgment in this matter from the beginning, is the most stable, least problematic, aspect of the novel. Here, as nowhere else in *Emma*, we see clearly the protagonist's various missteps in advance of the embarrassment she suffers on discovering that Mr. Elton's attentions have been directed toward her and not her protégée, whom she has succeeded now in placing at risk. But this is the case only on the first reading. With the foreknowledge of what transpires in the remainder of the novel, beginning with the appearance of Miss Bates and her niece Jane Fairfax in volume 2 and culminating in the former's eventual humiliation in volume 3, the elements of volume 1 are increasingly less easy to fix or to read within the framework of a consistently stable irony. Where Emma's blindness may initially be laid at the doorstep of her vanity and irresponsibility, it is indivisible on rereading, or potentially so, from her somewhat traumatic awareness of the subordinate and often abject position of women in her milieu for whom marriage is the only available lifeline. Thus Emma not only is content, for her part, *not* to marry, which she regards quite plausibly as a necessary evil in mitigating the "real evils" of "situation[s]" apart from her own exceptional independence. She is determined to marry Harriet off in a manner that renders this project less a prosthesis for her own marital expectations (as often argued) and more a protest to the disproportionate privilege that the men closest to Emma—her father, Mr. Knightley, and most tellingly, Mr. Weston—all enjoy relative to their female peers and associates.

Such an interpretation of Emma's matchmaking initiative, as against the prosthetic interpretation of her impulses, here and in the prehistory of the narrative, would be impossible without the specter of Miss Bates and, just as important, Jane Fairfax. Jane's proximity to Emma in age, ability, and bearing, coupled with her proximity to Miss Bates in the indigence and vulnerability to which she also appears destined, achieves a remarkable condensation in Emma's reckoning that only her contempt for them makes clear or the least bit accountable. So great is Miss Bates's influence on Emma that even before the spinster's stunning appearance in volume 2 Emma's early efforts to prevent Harriet from following in Miss Bates's tracks do not ultimately redound on the matchmaker as an initial, conventionally ironic reading of Emma's behavior here might lead one to conclude. Rather the effect of Emma's early actions, especially on rereading, is to foreground—if only as a dreaded prospect—the spectacle of indigence that drives her machinations in the first place and to which Emma's continued incorrigibility in seeking more matches for Harriet also refers. The charitable contrivance to secure a safe place for someone sufficiently different from or beneath Emma, in other words, operates under the same, largely unconscious motivation in volume 1 as does the subsequent loathing of two women who are equally vulnerable but also a good deal more like Emma and thus too close for comfort.[9]

This circuit, linking Harriet to Emma by way of Miss Bates and her niece, is also instrumental in the peculiar eroticism that binds Emma to Harriet. More than any vanity, or solipsism of the sort with which Emma is routinely charged, this libidinal investment would explain Emma's remarkable but quite genuine surprise in discovering that she, not Harriet, has been Mr. Elton's real interest:

She was a very pretty girl, and her beauty happened to be of a sort which Emma particularly admired. She was short, plump and fair, with a fine bloom, blue eyes, light hair, regular features, and a look of great sweetness. . . . She was not struck by any thing remarkably clever in Miss Smith's conversation, but she found her altogether very engaging. . . . Encouragement should be given. Those soft blue eyes and all those natural graces should not be wasted on the inferior society of Highbury and its connections. . . . *She* would notice her; she would improve her; she would detach her from her bad acquaintance, and introduce her into good society; she would form her opinions and her manners. It would be an interesting, and certainly a very kind undertaking; highly becoming her own situation in life, her leisure, and powers. . . . She was so busy in admiring those soft blue eyes, in talking and listening, and forming all those schemes in the in-betweens, that the evening flew away at a very unusual rate. (19–20)

The issue of same-sex desire here, particularly as it may oppose the normative order in the manner of Catherine's attachment to Eleanor in *Northanger Abbey*, is undoubtedly a secondary issue in *Emma*. The real issue, hinted at in the pronominal style where the referents "she" and "her" shift sufficiently in Emma's usage that what is "becoming" for Emma is largely inseparable from the project and prospect of Harriet's "becoming" Emma herself, is narcissism. Not narcissism in the pejorative sense or as a weak term for vanity, but in the register of what Freud means when he speaks of "self-regard"[10] which is indispensable to one's survival or, more immediately, one's detachment from "the inferior society of Highbury." The society deemed inferior by Emma is as much a particular class or type of society as it is a redundancy. Inferior not just in certain quarters, from which Emma can presumably demand severance, "the inferior society of Highbury" is precisely as designated. It pertains as much to specific types of people—for example, the Coles, who are in trade—as it does to the web of attachments and connections by which "Highbury," "inferior," and "society" are virtual synonyms: both in the practices and rituals that bring Emma into chronic contact with those whom she would prefer not to see and in her more subliminal or transferential connections—from the frightened and always prudent Mrs. Weston to the always hysterical Miss Bates—that in rendering Highbury a synecdoche for "society" at large make the prospect of detachment from it a nearly utopian dream.

That this dream or plenitude is to be fulfilled in marriage, making the detachment envisioned for Harriet an act of inclusion, is not a contradiction. Nor does it compromise, at least for the moment, the possibilistic horizons against which the probabilistic order in *Emma*, from the abiding hierarchies of class and gender to the contemptibly blithe and tyrannical regimes of Mr. Weston and Mr. Woodhouse, remains both an obstruction and a powerful incentive. At stake in Harriet's projected future, or in what Emma is convinced are Harriet's superior claims, is really a leveling of distinction where, to quote Elinor Joddrel in Burney's *The Wanderer*, "plucking up" has the same transformative effect as "pulling down."

This is not to minimize the narcissistic economy, in which Harriet's imagined success is connected perforce to Emma's own will to survive and to the self-regard figured in, among other places, Emma's portrait of Harriet, where in making her subject "too tall" (42) Emma is again portraying herself. It is to stress that, like Emma's self-regard, the telos of Harriet's marriage to someone nominally her superior is no longer strictly local, or blamable, but a prospect that connects the local and mundane to longer and larger horizons of equity and social change.

These prospects would explain Knightley's extraordinary reaction to the news of Harriet's rejection of Mr. Martin, where the former's vaunted pragmatism is on a continuum with the fear that makes *any* change in Highbury, from marriage to the weather to the evening's menu, a nearly apocalyptic event for Emma's father:

What are Harriet Smith's claims, either of birth, nature or education, to any connection higher than Robert Martin? She is the natural daughter of nobody knows whom, with probably no settled provision at all, and certainly no respectable relations. She is known only as parlour-boarder at a common school. She is not a sensible girl, nor a girl of any information. She has been taught nothing useful, and is too young and too simple to have acquired any thing herself. At her age she can have no experience, and with her little wit, is not very likely ever to have any that can avail her. She is pretty, and she is good tempered, and that is all. My only scruple in advising the match was on his account, as being beneath his deserts, and a bad connexion for him. I felt, that as to fortune, in all probability he might do much better; and that as to a rational companion or useful helpmate, he could not do worse. But I could not reason so to a man in love, and was willing to trust to there being no harm in her, to her having that sort of disposition, which, in good hands, like his, might be easily led aright and turn out very well. The advantage of the match I felt to be all on her side; and had not the smallest doubt (nor have I now) that there would be a general cry-out upon her extreme good luck. Even *your* satisfaction I made sure of. . . . I remember saying to myself, "Even Emma, with all her partiality for Harriet, will think this a good match." (54–55)

Emma will eventually concur with Knightley on the desirability of Harriet's marriage to Mr. Martin. But it is a measure of their difference at this stage that the pronominal style that previously marks Emma's solidarity with her protégée is marshaled by Knightley to nearly opposite effect. Where Emma's self-regard issues in a sympathetic confusion of subject and object, Knightley's sense of entitlement is expressed in reducing both Harriet and Mr. Martin to object and nearly material status. Both people go largely unnamed in his recitation, and what personalization they enjoy as pronouns gives way to a typically lopsided taxonomy in which Harriet is a "girl" and Mr. Martin a "man."

The relative privilege that Mr. Martin enjoys here by virtue of his sex (and the prerogatives of financial capability that devolve upon it) is consistent with Knightley's probabilistic worldview, where whatever is is right. But the differences between Harriet and Mr. Martin are also minuscule in Knightley's calculus compared to those that separate these infantilized figures from the likes of Mr. Weston and Mr. Elton. In discussing the Westons' recent marriage and

Emma's supposed role in helping to bring it about, Knightley cautions Emma against any additional meddling in their lives by reminding her that a "straight-forward, open-hearted man, like Weston, and a rational unaffected woman, like Miss Taylor, may be safely left to manage their own concerns" (11). Several para-graphs later, regarding Emma's apparent schemes for the new vicar, Knightley re-minds Emma that "a man of six or seven-and-twenty can take care of himself" (11).

The maturity and self-possession that members of the gentry enjoy relative to the childlike lower orders works, in Knightley's adduction, to naturalize spe-cific, if still arbitrary, power relations among classes.[11] Where Martin is appar-ently encouraged to solicit Knightley's wisdom in matters of marriage—this despite the fact that the latter is unaccountably unmarried at the age of thirty-eight—the reverse is plainly inconceivable. This asymmetry is especially strik-ing in the case of Mr. Weston on whom Knightley happily confers maturity and autonomy despite a history of chronic irresponsibility. In the summary of Weston's life that follows tellingly on the heels of Knightley's probabilistic pro-nouncements, we learn that upon "succeeding early in life to a small indepen-dence," Weston eschewed the "homely pursuits" of his brothers and instead joined the militia. The "chances of military life," which were entirely social and did not include any other action, eventually "introduced him to Miss Churchill, of a great Yorkshire family," whom Weston marries against the wishes of her brother and his wife, and with whom he lives, more or less unhappily if extrava-gantly. The marriage ends quickly with the early death of Mrs. Weston, provid-ing Weston with still another opportunity to avoid responsibility—this time regarding his infant son, Frank, whom he readily consigns to the care and nomenclature of his in-laws. At this point Weston quits the military and joins his brothers in trade, where they are already "established in a good way," and proceeds to pass the "next eighteen or twenty years of his life . . . cheerfully," gaining enough wealth to be able to marry the "portionless" Miss Taylor and to "live according to the wishes of his own friendly and social disposition" (12–13).

There is no similar account of Mr. Elton to justify more directly the level-ing or redress that Weston's curriculum vitae cries out for here and that his marriage to a portionless woman—particularly as an event Emma has con-trived to bring about—would appear to facilitate. But the point, already under-scored by Knightley's linkage of Weston and Elton as men capable in kind of taking care of themselves, is that these capabilities are a matter of privilege in the same way that the incapacity of certain women, or such characteristics as Knightley enumerates in describing Harriet, are the result of privilege withheld. This reminder is crucial not simply as a motive for actions and initiatives on Emma's part that are discountenanced by both Knightley and her father, who hates "change of every kind," especially "matrimony" (5). It is crucial as a circumstantial background that, significantly in advance of the appearance of Miss Bates and Jane, and in advance too of any rereading of the text, makes the entire episode culminating in Elton's profession of love for the protagonist, an over-determined business rather than a simple scene of instruction.

The difficulty in regarding the courtship episode in volume 1 simply as a mechanism of comeuppance for Emma owes to a number of factors, not the least being the eroticized attraction to Harriet that (as I have suggested) makes the prospect of normative relations—much less any relations with Elton—unthinkable to Emma. Readers may delight initially in Emma's failure to discern Elton's obvious interest in her. But even here Emma's blindness jibes uncomfortably with her alacrity in other matters, making her single-mindedness in this section something more than the simple flaw that many readers reduce it to. Furthermore, when coupled with Elton's disparagement of Harriet in terms that echo and exceed Knightley's in so reducing Harrriet that it scarcely matters to Elton "whether she were dead or alive" (118), it is not only easier to see why Elton's disappointment passes more or less without sympathy or any real significance apart from its bearing on Emma. It is also easy to see that the satiric force of Emma's apparent incorrigibility in continuing to imagine similar matches for her friend is actively mitigated, especially in subsequent readings, by the way her "relapse" (as she herself describes the resumption of such fantasizing) is directly linked to a "more serious, more dispiriting, cogitation upon what had been, and might be, and must be" (124). As the generalized referent of "what" suggests, along with the pointed opposition of the possible and the probable in the antitheses "might" and "must," there is a good deal more to Emma's sponsorship of Harriet than the particular "evil" that, for the narrator's part, accrues to her "having rather too much of her own way, and a disposition to think a little too well of herself" (4). Such "evils" and their consequences may well suffice for Knightley's interpretation of the events involving Harriet as readers such as Wayne Booth have often opined. But such an interpretation of those events, and the female difficulties they refer to, is—to borrow Emma's own thoughts on Knightley at the conclusion of volume 1—"unworthy" of "the real liberality of mind" (136) that (re)reading *Emma* both cultivates and presupposes.

Miss Bates and Mr. Knightley

With Emma's development at an impasse at the end of volume 1, the function of the novel's subsequent volumes, as readers have long maintained, is presumably to reenact the drama of Emma's willfulness, blindness, and inevitable embarrassment until she manages to get it right. Still, in the very way that Emma's growth is already crosshatched by an abiding, if subliminal, resistance to "what" she fears "must be," her progress en route to getting it right—particularly in conjunction with the various additions to the social landscape in volume 2— turns out to be a more complicated and in the end a more dubious development. The most significant of the additions in volume 2 is undoubtedly Hetty Bates. Miss Bates's remarkable appearance in this volume seems on subsequent readings to have been purposefully delayed to emphasize her importance in the novel, par- ticularly in relation to Emma's "development." Virtually anyone who has tried to teach *Emma* to a group that has never read it before can attest to the perplexity and anxiety produced by Miss Bates and by the other new characters in her wake. These elements generally prove a hindrance to understanding Austen's work not because they are manifestly irrelevant to what has transpired thus far but for the opposite reason: because, as even beginning students intuit, the addition here of Miss Bates, Mrs. Elton, and both Frank and Jane works to complicate the already complicated developmental trajectory established in volume 1.

Things are considerably different on the second reading, the most immedi- ate difference being the foreknowledge of Frank and Jane and the ironies such knowledge fashions from what has been a field of charged opacity. Even so, such relatively stable irony, where (as Wayne Booth describes it) "we join" with the narrator "in looking down on other men's follies"[12] is far from a limit point in rereading *Emma*. Just as the ironies surrounding Frank's courtship of Jane are unmoored from narrative authority or intelligence, so a retrospective reading of *Emma* is additionally free to range into other precincts where the narrator is equally disabled by a lack of understanding. Such readings may come to an alto- gether different view of Miss Bates herself, whose indelible representation of the world "before" her, which at the very least is a world according to someone *other* than the narrator, was thought, as early as Walter Scott, to be a real liability, hin- dering the novel's narrative momentum. While Scott's verdict has been echoed time and again in the reading practices of students (and their instructors) who routinely gloss Miss Bates's extended monologues on the real, her character and its remarkable verisimilitude also have been counted among the novel's virtues. A decade or so after Scott's pronouncements the *Literary Gazette* pointedly re- marked that "those who have not a Miss Bates among their acquaintance . . . are not like ourselves, who have at least a dozen." Doubtless the *Gazette*'s is more a commentary on the virtues of characterization than on those of character. Nor is there much question that with one or two exceptions the readings of *Emma* that actively engage Miss Bates recapitulate Knightley's defense of her in the wake of Box Hill in recognizing Miss Bates's inability to defend herself, both as a character and, more generally, as a social formation.[13] To these readers, no less than Knightley himself, it rarely matters that Miss Bates is a powerful, and one could argue progressive, counter to the novel's "other" hysteric, Mr. Wood-house. Where Mr. Woodhouse lives in perpetual fear of everything to which he is nonetheless attentive—from dining habits to the weather to the disposition of family life in Highbury—Miss Bates marshals the same pathological respon-siveness in a more expansive, less repressive outlook.

The lack of repression that governs and liberates Miss Bates, frequently to the discomfort of her interlocutors and readers, is most evident in her mode of speaking, which ranges promiscuously from one association to the next in virtual imitation of Hartleyean subjectivity as Austen would have known and recognized it. Although such vertiginous activity bears the marks of fear and in-security, it is just as remarkable for its openness and uncanny sensitivity. Mr. Woodhouse pays undue attention to the detritus of the everyday in the aim of bringing it under control whereas Miss Bates's response to and recapitulation of "what" she "see[s] . . . before" (157) her is palpably alive to the dynamism and depth of life's most routine occurrences.

We can take as one example Miss Bates's expatiation on the apples that she and her mother have received from Mr. Knightley and have baked to specifica-tions slightly different from Mr. Woodhouse's:

Indeed they are very delightful apples, and Mrs. Wallis does them full justice—only we do not have them baked more than twice, and Mr. Woodhouse made us promise to have them done three times—but Miss Woodhouse will be so good as not to mention it. The apples themselves are the very finest sort for baking, beyond a doubt; all from Donwell—some of Mr. Knightley's most liberal supply. He sends us a sack every year; and certainly there never was such a keeping apple any where as one of his trees—I be-lieve there is two of them. My mother says the orchard was quite famous in her younger days. But I was really quite shocked the other day—for Mr. Knightley called one morn-ing, and Jane was eating these apples, and we talked about them and said how much she enjoyed them, and he asked whether we were not got to the end of our stock. "I am sure you must be," said he, "and I will send you another supply; for I have a great many more than I can ever use; William Larkins let me keep a larger quantity than usual this year. I will send you some more; before they get good for nothing."

So I begged he would not—for really as to ours being gone, I could not absolutely say that we had a great many left—it was but half a dozen indeed; but they should be all kept for Jane; and I could not at all bear that he should be sending us more, so liberal as he had been already; and Jane the same. And when he was gone, she almost quarrelled with me—No, I should not say quarrelled, for we never had a quarrel in our lives; but she was quite distressed that I had owned the apples were so nearly gone; she wished I had made him believe we had a great many left. Oh! said I, my dear, I did say as much as I could. (214–15)

With Jane's propensity for dissimulation as perhaps a goad, Miss Bates goes on to relate how the additional apples she receives subsequently from Knightley turn out to be all of the apples that Knightley has. While this disclosure—learned typically from his servants—performs a rather complex function in the way its author is manifestly flattered by the special attention she receives from Knightley, in contrast to the Woodhouses' generosity for which she is always too decorously grateful ("You are extremely kind. . . . So obliging of you" [140-41]), it has the more immediate effect of reminding the reader that things are not always as they seem in *Emma*, especially to the narrator. The baked apples, for example, are no more cooked to specification, or according to the dispensations of authority, than Knightley's generosity is as modest as its appears, or as Miss Bates's understanding is as limited as Knightley and others surmise.

One point of this lengthy monologue, to which I will return presently, involves the peculiar intimacy between Miss Bates and her benefactor, whose solicitude here and throughout the novel, from the provision of transportation to his admonishment of Emma at Box Hill, is echoed in the care that his beneficiary takes in ensuring that he remain ignorant of all that *she knows*: " 'I would not have Mr. Knightley know any thing about it for the world! He would be so very . . . I wanted to keep it from Jane's knowledge; but unluckily, I had mentioned it before I was aware' " (215). The ellipsis regarding Knightley's imagined response to her discovery of the extent of his generosity is especially noteworthy, given Miss Bates's tendency to load every rift with more. It bespeaks an intimacy that follows upon their current method of communication in operating almost as a private language. Regardless of whether they communicate directly, it is already clear that Knightley will inevitably discover what Miss Bates has, for her part, already learned, but in a way that the ellipsis, or the response that Miss Bates puts under erasure, will remain in tact along with the tact or intimacy of which their joint silence remains testimony.

All of this information is provided to the reader with virtually no narrative intervention apart from the accuracy with which Miss Bates has presumably been rendered. This is much to Austen's purpose. For in the very way that the most ordinary of events becomes vertiginously abysmal in Miss Bates's rendering, disclosing possibilities and nuances that would remain hidden, so there is a link between the information she discloses and the tactical resistance to regimes, at once representational and social, that her disclosures effectively rehearse. It may be an exaggeration to claim that baking the apples only twice and withholding knowledge from Mr. Knightley regarding his own supply of apples are somehow oppositional in their resistance to regulatory imperatives. But it is worth noting that where Knightley and Mr. Woodhouse serve the interests of probability in attempting to ensure that things will remain as they have been and ought to be, Miss Bates serves the interests of possibility and change in proving that their purchase on the real, particularly as something predictable according to either precedent or injunction, may be compromised by practices unavailable to them and to those like them, who are intent on controlling, rather than in seeing, "what" is in fact "before" them. Knightley may very well infer some intelligence between Jane and Frank that has apparently eluded everyone, the narrator included. But he is no more successful in marshaling *his* intelligence in either penetrating or preventing their liaison than Mr. Woodhouse is in ensuring his culinary directives or than the narrator is in assuming that Miss Bates is altogether self-explanatory in her own words.

Nor is it a coincidence that Miss Bates also provides the most comprehensive and ecumenical account of Highbury society. Were it up to the narrator or to her principal character, much of Highbury would remain invisible and unnamed. It is through Miss Bates's familiarity with Knightley's servants—William Larkins, Mrs. Hodges, and Patty—that she has learned of their master's paucity of "keeping apples," just as it is Miss Bates—and not Emma, who is characteristically present but also silent—who later salutes "Dr. and Mrs. Hughes," inquires after Mr. Richard, and is moved to enthusiasm in encountering still more "friends" from "good Mr. Otway, and Miss Otway and Miss Caroline" to "Mr. George and Mr. Arthur" (290–91). The yield of this information, which depends in any case upon Miss Bates's excessive acuity, is another matter, especially as a mode of sociability alive to and aligned with what, for Emma, is increasingly an inferior and contemptible alterity. But what cannot be denied is that without Miss Bates, the partialized view of reality that Austen herself is routinely charged with endorsing in her seemingly narrow conceptions of social life and decorum would appear even more partial than it is.

It is the view here, needless to say, that things are always more complicated in this, as in other novels by Austen. One such complication—and another way of getting at the simultaneously expansive and receding horizons on which *Emma* as a whole reflects—is the invitation to speculate on a matter that, much like the world *according* to Miss Bates, is recoverable without the narrator's attention or understanding. I am speaking again of the attachment of Miss Bates to Mr. Knightley, which refers to events and contingencies in the prehistory of the narrative that no commentator has really noticed or explored. These contingencies circulate around the obvious, if significantly suppressed, fact that Miss Bates, a vicar's daughter, was at one time, and in the context of Highbury society, a conceivable mate for Knightley himself, who has managed instead—and under far less penalty than his same-aged counterpart—to remain unmarried in the decade and a half he has been eligible to wed.

This possibility, or retroprospect, is broached with startling, if unwitting, directness by Emma herself. In a debate with Mrs. Weston over the likelihood of Knightley's marrying Jane Fairfax, in whom he has taken an interest, Emma reminds her former governess of an aspect of life with Jane that would make marrying her "a very shameful and degrading connection" for Knightley. "How," she asks,

> would he bear to have Miss Bates belonging to him?—To have her haunting the Abbey, and thanking him all day long for his great kindness in marrying Jane?—"So very kind and obliging!—But he always had been such a very kind neighbour!" And then fly off, through half a sentence, to her mother's old petticoat. "Not that it was such a very old petticoat either—for still it would last a great while—and, indeed, she must thankfully say that their petticoats were all very strong." (203)

Apart from the foreshadowing of Box Hill that the ridicule of Miss Bates performs here, along with the nearly inadvertent gothic of her "haunting the Abbey," there is the telling image of Miss Bates "belonging to" Knightley and the equally telling observation regarding Knightley's particular kindness to the Bateses. Even as these serve as a clinching point in Emma's argument, her scenario of the spinster's obsequiousness, as any reader will recognize, is more immediately characteristic of Miss Bates's invariable response to Emma herself rather than to Knightley with whom Miss Bates maintains a contrastively measured, if cryptic, familiarity. (This familiarity is never more evident than in her instinctive "turn" to Knightley following her insult at Box Hill.) Thus for all of Emma's efforts to separate Knightley and Jane through the ghastly proximity of the latter's aunt, the prospect of Miss Bates's "belonging" to Knightley is introduced in a way that Knightley's uncommon solicitude, on which that very prospect may conceivably exert some explanation now, connects them over Emma's intentions or understanding.

This is not the only time that either Knightley's neighborliness toward the Bateses or his connection to Miss Bates in particular are issues. Very early in volume 2 Miss Bates is surprised to discover that Mr. Knightley will be accompanying her and Jane, whose arm she urges him to take in an injunction notable for its economy and in allowing her to depart from her customary servility: "Oh! Mr. Knightley is coming too. Well, that is so very!—I am sure Jane is tired, you will be so kind to give her your arm" (158). Furthermore, in a cluster of related observations that stand in close proximity both to Emma's prospect of Miss Bates's "belonging" and the extended monologue on the gift of apples, we are given additional incentives to consider the origins and importance of Knightley's neighborliness. In describing the efforts to transport Jane and her aunt from the party hosted by the Coles, Mrs. Weston is struck by the fact that "Mr. Knightley's carriage had brought, and was to take them home again" (200–201)." "I was surprised," she confides to Emma, "very glad, I am sure; but really quite surprized. Such a very kind attention—and so thoughtful an attention!—the sort of thing that so few men would think of. And, in short, from knowing his usual ways, I am very much inclined to think that it was for their accommodation the carriage was used at all. I do suspect he would not have had a pair of horses for himself, that it was only as an excuse for assisting them" (201). This observation immediately gives rise to the "suspicion" of a possible a match between Knightley and Jane, and proves the motive for Emma's rich and indexical rebuttal. Taken with her "surprize," which is sufficiently exaggerated to give the reader pause, Mrs. Weston's "suspicions," and the debate with Emma they provoke, collectively introduce information from which other suspicions may now derive.

Finally, in perhaps the most dramatic example of a connection that is typically inconceivable to all but its immediate participants, Knightley gets Miss Bates's attention in a manner that should give any reader—certainly any reader of Austen—pause. Angry with Frank's management of the Coles' musicale, particularly with his insistence that Jane continue singing despite her increasing hoarseness, Knightley remonstrates over Frank's vanity "[a]nd *touching* Miss Bates, who at that moment passed near," urges her to intervene: "Miss Bates, are you mad, to let your niece sing herself hoarse in this manner? Go, and interfere. They have no mercy on her" (206, emphasis added). Both the touching and the injunction that follows would appear, again, to signal an intimacy in which such reflex actions are admissible. But its function overall, in conjunction with the other details that bear on the narrative's prehistory, involves more than a further marshaling of Miss Bates as the unfortunate jilt of Highbury. Knightley's gesture actually shows Miss Bates as someone who, by consequence of her rejection, shifts dramatically between the roles of subject and object. Miss Bates is a figure now whose uncanny perception of "what" is "before" her stands in nearly inverse proportion to her diminished status as someone who can be physically corralled and admonished by Knightley in public. Where the world according to Miss Bates nearly collapses under the weight of variousness and possibility, the social world to which she herself must conform is one where any possibility or prospect of change for someone positioned such as she is clearly out of bounds. Is it any wonder, then, that Miss Bates's sense of the world would be notably, if irritatingly, opposed to specific representational or novelistic protocols wherein the part and the whole, or the seen and unseen (to borrow Miss Bates's own terminology), are presumed synonymous? For her life, on which virtually all possibility, from marriage to suffrage, has been foreclosed, is a powerful reminder that the probabilistic order, however partial and thereby assailable, is sufficiently aligned with the way things are that the narrator of *Emma* is as fated to be right in *her* representation of those things as Miss Bates, following her own example, will be necessarily proven wrong.

By "wrong" I do not mean that Miss Bates is incorrect or inaccurate in re-calling a world whose invisibility might be taken to signify its fundamental nonexistence. What I mean is that the world as viewed by Miss Bates remains, for all its dynamism and range, a world whose out-of-boundness is also strangely temporalized. The aspects of Highbury available to Miss Bates but unavailable to either the narrator or her protagonist constitute possibilities that are not just increasingly ephemeral—as opposed to either oppositional or subversive; they are possibilities commensurate with an horizon of change, and a basis for hope, that is receding ever more noticeably into the past. Even as the business of rereading *Emma* is permitted to focus on the lapses and limitations in narra-tion, the overwhelming sense of *Emma*, as any number of readers have either intuited or understood, is *nostalgic*: both for the England that is disappearing, of which both Highbury and its happily married stewards are in the end tokens, as well as for the England that *was*, from which Emma's early social imagination and its possibilistic horizons, like the transgressions of Mary Crawford in the preceding novel, have arguably sprung.

Mrs. Elton's "sad story"

The issue of nostalgia, to which I will return more specifically, is raised and un-derscored by the other notable additions in volume 2: Augusta Hawkins Elton, Jane Fairfax, and Frank Churchill. Mrs. Elton, to be sure, is among the most re-viled of Austen's creations, matched only by *Pride and Prejudice*'s Lady Cather-ine de Bourgh, who manages to elicit the hardly complementary impulses of misogyny and antiaristocratic feeling. Such "regulated hatred," to borrow D. W. Harding's famous phrase, never quite works to immaculate effect in Austen's novels. In the case of Lady Catherine, for example, it spells trouble for the novel in which she appears, if only to the degree that Lady Catherine remains a hy-brid, in effect, of both the independent-minded heroine and the aristocratic hero. Something similar happens with Mrs. Elton who, for all her odiousness, manages to expose and ultimately to compromise the worldview—and the nar-rative viewpoint—that also sanctions her derogation. It is noteworthy that long before they are in agreement on all crucial matters, Mrs. Elton remains the sin-gle issue on which Knightley and Emma concur, even as they come to this by separate routes. Knightley's dislike of Mrs. Elton recalls his systematic denigra-tion of Harriet in reflecting both misogyny and snobbery whereas Emma, while surely echoing Knightley in her contempt of Mrs. Elton's social aspirations, has the more difficult task of disliking someone who is like herself—or would be—

were Emma also not *unlike* Mrs. Elton in the distance she increasingly inter-poses between herself and the "inferior society of Highbury."

This distancing, which actually follows Emma's matchmaking initiatives as a protest to things as they are, also differs from that initial position in being ever more compromised by trepidation, for which Emma's much-noted snobbery turns out to be a resource more than a motivation. It is not that Emma is any less reconciled to the world in volume 2 than she was in volume 1. It is that the very world that may have seemed susceptible to change—even so ephemeral a leveling as the marriage of Harriet to Mr. Elton—is increasingly a locus whose intractability, as prophesied by Knightley and demonstrated by Elton himself, bids fair to overwhelm Emma. We see this transformation in the way that Har-riet gradually disappears as a social project in the remainder of the novel only to return as someone manifestly inferior to her sponsor. The change is even clearer in Emma's dislike of Jane Fairfax, who should be her friend and confidante and who, with no small irony, becomes the reluctant protégée of Mrs. Elton.

The default in which Emma's growing disenchantment finally issues, and of which her fear and loathing are a measure, is stressed at the very end of the second chapter in volume 2, whose concluding sentence regarding Emma's frus-tration over Jane's reserve and aversion to gossip—"Emma could not forgive her" (151)—is repeated as the inaugural sentence of chapter 3. In addition to maintaining a narrative momentum linked obviously to Emma's consciousness, Jane's incorrigibility is stressed in a way that makes Emma's anger toward her symptomatic of something larger and, as I have already speculated, a good deal closer. It is easy perhaps for Emma to reject out of hand the pitiable spectacle of Miss Bates whom she nevertheless underestimates, observing to Frank at one point that Miss Bates "will be all delight and gratitude, but she will tell you nothing" (229). Jane is another matter. A gentrywoman who, but for a run of bad luck, might easily outstrip Emma as the "queen of Highbury," Jane is unfor-givable for two related reasons: because she embodies "the difference of woman's destiny" (348) that Emma has recently tried and failed to mitigate; and because she collapses, in this case by negative example, Emma's presumptive difference from that destiny. Jane remains a steady and unforgivable reminder of the good fortune without which Emma would find herself on the slippery slope already unfooting Harriet, Miss Bates, and countless others.

Knightley is ready with a much simpler explanation for Emma's antipathy to Jane. In his view, as the narrator describes it, Emma sees in Jane "the really accomplished young woman" that Emma "want[s] to be thought herself" (148). But, as is so often the case, the ensuing information offered in support of Knight-ley's pedagogy complicates and undermines his claim. Implying that Emma necessarily concurs with Knightley in "moments of self-examination" when "her conscience could not quite acquit her," the narrator also describes Emma's various evasions of conscience to an effect that transcends the proof they are meant to furnish:

But "she could never get acquainted with her: she did not know how it was, but there was such coldness and reserve—such apparent indifference whether she pleased or not—and then, her aunt was such an eternal talker!—and she was made a fuss with by every body!—and it had been always imagined that they were to be so intimate—because their ages were the same, every body had supposed they must be so fond of each other." These were her reasons—she had no better. (148)

The narrator is undoubtedly right in marshaling these rationalizations and the blankness onto which they open to show that Emma neither understands nor can acknowledge the real basis for her antipathy. But it is clear too, if only with the inclusion of Miss Bates—along with the pronominal equivalence that Jane and Emma are relegated to in Emma's thinking—that the dislike of Jane is connected to something more encompassing than either her proximity or even her superiority to Emma. While there are undoubtedly numerous practical reasons why Miss Bates and Jane are almost always in each other's company and why Frank, in particular, is so eager to involve Miss Bates in activities that include Jane, the most important reason, as Emma's rationalizations indicate, is that Jane and her aunt are something of a condensation, figuring by either abjection or melancholy the very "destiny" from which Emma urgently demands severance. We will never know whether, under other circumstances, Miss Bates might have avoided her dubious constitution as the anti-Emma or, as the narrator somewhat viciously describes her, "a woman neither young, handsome, rich, nor married" (17). What *is* clear is that to find oneself in what the narrator, describing Miss Bates again, deems "the very worst predicament in the world" (17) is, with Jane's arrival in Highbury, a prospect no longer inconceivable to Emma and, on the basis of her immediate acquaintances, from the former Miss Taylor to the three teachers at Mrs. Goddard's school to the more prominent examples of Harriet and Miss Bates herself, nothing short of a "destiny" for women generally.

Augusta Elton may seem little more than a satiric distraction to the identificatory mechanism by which Emma discovers herself linked to a spinster whom she is eventually disposed to insult unfeelingly and, in some measure, unconsciously. But there is a crucial connection between the various additions to the novel's second volume, not the least involving the misogyny that is liberally visited on Mrs. Elton, as upon Miss Bates, as if it were a public resource always to be tapped.[14] A wealthy heiress whose family has risen in trade and, it is maliciously hinted, in business aligned with the slave trade, Mrs. Elton descends on Highbury with the apparent purpose of making herself a pillar in the community. Her attempts to achieve a legitimacy commensurate with her wealth and the wealth of her family, whose holdings and possessions she crassly advertises, are transparently ridiculous, signaling an upward mobility that Knightley, Emma, and the narrator are only too pleased to discountenance.

In one sense Mrs. Elton figures, far more prominently than do the Coles, certain transformations in English society—notably the rise of a trade-based versus a family- or land-based social hierarchy—that Emma, Knightley, and the narrator find deplorable. But her function is finally a good deal more complicated. The transformations in British society that Mrs. Elton represents are not just changes that are inevitable. They are transformations from which Mrs. Elton *herself* seeks refuge, particularly as they are coextensive with a burgeoning domestic culture that proves delimiting to those women who are paradoxically its beneficiaries. In the very way that Mrs. Elton represents certain developments, which Emma resists by hewing ever more strenuously to residual, class-based discriminations, so she contrives, with some justification, to follow or even join Emma in a trajectory that answers to more than a desire for social advancement. For the status that Mrs. Elton aspires to here, of which Emma remains the principal representative, is also a station by which she too seeks to hold both the present and the inferable future at bay.

The irony surrounding Mrs. Elton's aspirations to legitimacy, which the satire on her arriviste mentality obscures, involves two things, then. It involves the possibly galling fact that, like Fanny Price in *Mansfield Park*, Mrs. Elton represents a middle class sufficiently on the rise that she may usurp Emma's unchallenged supremacy. And it involves the degree to which Mrs. Elton's efforts to become something *like* Emma are increasingly subverted by a domestic culture, whose comparatively limited horizons mitigate the social imagination that Emma's early initiatives are based upon, and her early determination, pursuant to that imagination, to remain unmarried. As the novel makes clear, the woman's culture currently gathering force, where marriage and family are sovereign institutions, stands massively opposed to women generally: both in the division of labor and station that the culture of domesticity proscribes for them (witness Emma's married sister, Isabella, and the always accommodating, and now gestating, Mrs. Weston) and in making marriage the only refuge in a "society" where unmarried women, no matter how educated or privileged or beautiful, are (to quote Lady Susan) "worthless."

This is scarcely the place to recount in detail the various cultural developments, specifically the rise of the nuclear family and the winnowing of paternalistic protectivism on which *Emma*, as much as any other Austen novel, obviously dilates. What cannot be stressed enough is the structural irony that sends Emma and Mrs. Elton spiraling backward toward a past where such developments are less pressing and dispiriting. Mrs. Elton's seemingly incidental—but for Austen crucial—observation of the "sad story against" married women who "are but too apt to give up music," and her suggestion that she and Emma "establish a musical club" (249), is more than a transparent and assailable effort to insinuate herself into the highest reaches of Highbury society. It marks an attempt really to join Emma not only as part of the gentry world to which Austen's heroine so manifestly belongs but also in the erstwhile world of gentrywomen that, to borrow Matthew Arnold's phrase, increasingly "belongs to a different part of England."[15] The real problem that Mrs. Elton encounters has less to do with Emma's unresponsiveness to her than with Emma's growing unresponsiveness to the former's curiously brave scenario. Emma's response to Mrs. Elton's "sad story" is no longer to rewrite the story, in this case by resuscitating a woman's world that, as Emma's early actions signify, had presumably existed in some form. Her response, motivated by the fear of becoming of an even sadder example like Jane, is to retreat to the still-friendly—and, thanks to Mrs. Elton's aspirations, still-honorable—precincts of class and class-based discrimination that have been cleansed suddenly, in Emma's calculus, of any connection to women apart from condescension and aversion.

Augusta Elton's aspirations to the very "situation" or station on which, by Emma's example at least, a death knell has begun sounding, is additionally signaled—and further ironized—in her ostentatious sponsorship of Jane for whom she eventually finds a position as governess. In addition to highlighting the various social developments in which someone like Jane finds herself dependent on a woman who, by comparison to her charge, is merely another "daughter of nobody knows whom," the sponsorship of Jane, however meretricious, has an additional effect. It underscores the transformation marked by the difference between Emma's early sponsorship of Harriet, and the leveling (at least among genders) that that initiative imagines in the novel's first volume, and Mrs. Elton's current project, which is limited by the ever limited options for women generally. By no means is this to disparage Mrs. Elton or her attachment to Jane. In the absence of any similar initiative in volumes 2 and 3, not to mention Emma's own interaction with Jane, which consists entirely of trying to ferret information regarding an affair with Mr. Dixon that never took place, Mrs. Elton's project is consistent with her prospect of establishing a music "circle" in its nostalgia both for a milieu and its prospects of melioration that she would like to revive and be part of.

Nostalgia, needless to say, is a fairly broad category and an issue of long-standing relevance in discussions of Austen's writing. Long before Raymond

Williams cautioned readers on the many developments in England from which Austen's novels advert their attention, or before Nancy Armstrong remarked on the nostalgic appeal of Austen's social vision for a growing middle class in search of a legitimating discourse, the novelist's near contemporaries, from Mary Russell Mitford to the reviewer in the *Literary Gazette,* recognized that the social world Austen had rendered with remarkable fidelity was increasingly unavailable to readers and the more valuable as a result. Mitford's well-known encomium on her pleasure in sitting down "in a country village in one of Miss Austen's delicious novels,"[16] on which her own account of the seemingly timeless rhythms of village life is modeled, is echoed in the *Gazette*'s sense of Austen's educational value. Generalizing from the example of *Emma* itself, the *Gazette* commemorated the novel's reissue in 1833 by remarking that with "every hour" Austen's "delightful works . . . are becoming absolute historical pictures," which the "rising generation" should attend to if they want to know about the excitement of "a country dance, or the delights of a tea-table." Where for Williams nostalgia is something that Austen determinedly practices in airbrushing her English landscape so that, as a locus of value, it is remarkably free of precisely those developments on which its synecdochic reach depends, nostalgia for other readers, and for readers of readers such as Armstrong, remains something imposed on or seemingly provoked by Austen's writings rather than a specific feature of the works themselves.

There is little question that *Emma* is especially serviceable for nostalgic readers such as Mitford whose own account of "the talking lady" in *Our Village* echoes—albeit with less precision and sensitivity—the representation here of Miss Bates. Nor is there much doubt that the social vision the novel's narrative subtends echoes and exceeds the *Gazette*'s sense of the past in recalling a world still organized by the responsible stewardship of Mr. Knightley and his eventual spouse, whose entitlement to their function is also an entitlement by birth. Where questions do arise, thanks predominantly again to Mrs. Elton's somewhat different and overdetermined retrospection, is in the nostalgia that, by contrast, is a retrogression from, and a resistance to, the regimes here of both probability *and change.* For in the very way that this latter nostalgia, as Mrs. Elton makes clear, is a nostalgia for horizons of possibility that may have existed once, so it stands opposed to what is more immediately at issue in *Emma.* Such nostalgia, in other words, opposes the probabilistic order, which is either blind or averse to possibilities and transformations currently abroad, as well as *certain prospects,* in particular the ever expanding culture of bourgeois domesticity that, no less than the world that Knightley, Emma, and the narrator all endorse, is far from a utopian space.

In her recent study, *On Longing,* Susan Stewart comments somewhat dourly on the indeterminate longing to which nostalgia, or a certain kind of nostalgia, is equivalent. "Nostalgia," she writes, "is a sadness without an object, a sadness which creates a longing that of necessity is inauthentic because it does not take part in lived experience. Rather, it remains behind and before that experience. . . . Hostile to history and its invisible origins, and yet longing for an impossibly pure context of lived experience at a place of origin, nostalgia wears a distinctly utopian face, a face which turns toward a future-past, a past which has only ideological reality."[17] Stewart's sense of the "future-past" toward which nostalgia hearkens, along with the utopian valence that differentiates this imaginary or "ideological" future from the future that, here as in *Mansfield Park*, may be extrapolated from "lived experience," nicely describes Mrs. Elton's increasingly impossible aspirations. Mrs. Elton aspires to a past whose belatedness or removal from experience is linked to a horizon of change or futurity that is increasingly a matter of false consciousness (what Stewart calls ideology) rather than of "what" Mrs. Elton necessarily sees "before" her.

On the face of it there may appear to be little difference between Mrs. Elton's longing, which looks to the past as a site from which hope and the particular future it cherishes can somehow spring anew, and the longing of Mr. Knightley or Mr. Woodhouse for whom the past, or what has been the past, is ideally a template for the future about to be. Except for one thing. The reverence for the past that the probabilistic regime maintains pits lived experience (precedent) against living experience (change) in the aim of containing the latter whereas nostalgia, such as Mrs. Elton and the Emma of volume 1 harbor it, finds solace in a past that, as Stewart's formulation implies, is plenitudinous or utopian precisely because it does not count on experience, whether lived or living, as having any significance other than the obstruction it currently poses. The devaluing of lived experience is a risky business to say the least, and it is the cause of Emma's woes in volume 1. What the initial volume also suggests, however, along with Mrs. Elton's initiatives in volume 2, is that nostalgia, while perhaps hostile to experience, is by no means hostile to history, particularly if the history it embraces, as Emma's early actions indicate, is a history in which some prospect for change, or for some alteration in "woman's destiny," had appeared—however illusorily or ideologically—close at hand.

Stewart is surely right in describing nostalgia as "the desire for desire" (23). Where her concise and probing formulation requires emendation, at least for our purposes, is in its deconstructive dismissal of the historicity of desire itself: the position from which desire is or was possible. As Mrs. Elton serves notice, nostalgia in *Emma* is more than an inchoate longing. It is a longing for an interval (the recent past) as well as for a milieu (the world of educated gentry and aristocratic women) in which desire and possibility were abroad in advance of their subsequent disappointment.[18] It does not matter therefore whether nostalgia has become displaced or is as indeterminate in its constitution as Mrs. Elton's longing signifies. What matters is that regardless of whether desire, much less the desire for desire, is ever requited or requitable, the history of hope on which it bears is, even more concretely, a history of opportunities missed and, punning slightly on Stewart's own notion of impossibility, very nearly a future *passed*.[19]

A Young Man Bent on Dancing

All of these issues surrounding nostalgia, and the shadow or utopian space of possibility of which Miss Bates and Mrs. Elton are, in different ways, exponents, are crystallized in the last—and most sustained—of the additions to volume 2: the typically joint arrival in Highbury of Frank and Jane. We have already explored Jane's significance, both as an object of fear and loathing for Emma and as cause célèbre for Mrs. Elton. What remains to be examined is the nature and meaning of Jane's attachment to Frank, which has been ongoing and, until its belated disclosure with the news of their impending marriage in volume 3, invisible to all of the novel's characters, the narrator included. I am not especially concerned at this moment with the bearing of the Frank-Jane shadow narrative on either narrative authority or even the metanarrative in *Emma* in which, by invitation to reread the novel, thereby reading against the narrator's narrow conception of things, the shadow narrative (and the couple on whom it is based) are plainly instrumental. It is not that these are irrelevant in understanding what I am perhaps too boldly urging as the *meaning* of Frank and Jane. It is that the yield of rereading *Emma*, where their coupling is again instrumental, has an analogue, and a sharply qualifying analogue, in the indeterminacy that surrounds their relationship, which none of the characters, including Knightley, can fix sufficiently even as they are willing to judge it.

It bears observing, certainly, that Frank's marriage to a portionless gentrywoman, who happens also to be his own age, performs an ecumenical service that Knightley, regardless of any prior attachment to Miss Bates, deliberately eschews in eventually choosing Emma for his mate. Nor should we overlook the fact that the famous lesson that Knightley administers to Emma following her insult to Miss Bates in volume 3, and the "turn" toward a more responsible, if old-fashioned, condescension it provokes, depends equally on Frank's simultaneous attempt to instruct Emma to altogether different ends. Nevertheless, I take as perhaps the most representative moment in assessing Frank and Jane, Frank's initiative in organizing a ball, which is his inaugural gesture in the novel and generally disparaged as evidence of the young man's foppery.

One motive for the ball undoubtedly is Frank's desire to create an opportunity to be with Jane. Nevertheless, to the degree that "being with Jane" is hardly innocent where politics are concerned, it may be noted that the preparations for the ball, from Frank's encouragement to Emma to the gathering he imagines will take place, are typical of his and Jane's function in the narrative in underscoring an horizon of change that is palpable or "before" the reader's ken and simultaneously, to follow Stewart's notions, indeterminate and out-of-bounds.

The extended episode of the ball begins characteristically at the moment of Frank's arrival in Highbury and his initial encounter with Emma. His inquiries regarding Highbury's social life and disposition, which are seemingly exclusionary and restricted to the "several very pretty houses" and their likely inhabitants, culminate on two related issues: the frequency of balls and the accuracy of describing Highbury as "a musical society" (171). Without dismissing the causal relationship that links music and dancing, there is also, following matters we have already touched upon, another linkage to these activities that we are referred to in Frank's notable reversal of their relationship. Not only does dancing precede music in Frank's list of curiosities; the prospect of a musical society in general, on which Mrs. Elton will shortly opine, is given pride of place as the last but not the least of Frank's projected interests. This is immediately followed by a flurry of observations where Frank's extreme unction regarding his father's new wife is insufficient in obscuring an awareness of the particular imbalance by which Mr. Weston (in anticipation of Knightley) can always claim a much younger spouse: " 'Elegant, agreeable manners, I was prepared for,' said he; 'but I confess that, considering every thing, I had not expected more than a very tolerably well-looking woman of a certain age; I did not know that I was to find a pretty young woman in Mrs. Weston" (172). Emma contrives to correct Frank in suggesting that her former governess would object to being described as a "pretty young woman' " (172). Yet neither this correction nor the exaggerated surprise it seeks to chasten can dispel a sense that Frank's "compliments" here, to follow Emma's own thinking, are "proofs of defiance" more than "marks of acquiescence" (173). Ultimately there is little difference between Frank's mode of resistance and his mode of acquiescence. But before we get to this and to the ways in which such conflation of practices may be understood, it is important to examine further the way Frank's defiance, here and elsewhere, is purposefully hidden as perhaps the only way of being undertaken.

Both the covert aspect of Frank's actions and their oppositional complexion are readable in his enthusiasm for the Crown Inn where nostalgia—in this case for the "brilliant days" that have "long passed away" when Highbury "had been in a particularly, populous, dancing state"—again figures prominently:

He saw no fault in the room, he would acknowledge none which they suggested. No, it was long enough, broad enough, handsome enough. It would hold the very number for comfort. They ought to have balls there at least every fortnight through the winter. Why had not Miss Woodhouse revived the former good old days of the room?—She who could do any thing in Highbury! The want of proper families in the place, and the conviction that none beyond the place and its immediate environs could be tempted to attend, were mentioned; but he was not satisfied. He could not be persuaded that so many good-looking houses as he saw around him, could not furnish numbers enough for such a meeting; and even when particulars were given and families described, he was still unwilling to admit that the inconvenience of such a mixture would be any thing, or that there would be the smallest difficulty in every body's returning into their proper place the next morning. He argued like a young man very much bent on dancing. (177–78)

It is difficult to determine whether it is from Emma's or the narrator's point of view that Frank is apparently a young man bent on dancing. This confusion extends to the fact that "dancing" is sufficiently politicized in the course of Frank's reported recitation to cast aspersions on anyone, including Emma and the narrator, who regards Frank's interest in terms of mere appearance. Even the narrator, to whom surface and depth are largely synonymous where Frank is concerned, uses the occasion of Emma's astonishment, particularly her silence in witnessing Frank's enthusiasm, to permit the inference that there is more at stake here than dancing. All the same, the real and radical irony in this passage is that dancing—albeit in a more expansive and historical sense—is precisely Frank's bent, contradicting Emma's perplexity, where Frank's apparent interest is suspended between dancing per se and dancing with her, and the narrator's position, which is in many ways a disavowal of what is also in plain view.

In view is the fact that dancing, in Frank's imagination, opens onto a horizon of possibility that has been displaced over time. In the transformation of which "dancing" is a register and, in Frank's nostalgic view, a mode of recovery, the "good old days" refer to a time when people are perhaps not as separated on the basis of either class or wealth or even gender and in which, as Mrs. Elton eventually concurs, someone like Emma might conceivably make a difference. That there are simply not enough people to attend such an occasion, according to Emma, indicates a deplorably growing ratio of property to people, whose inequities must inevitably be felt elsewhere. These inequities, on top of Emma's own, increasing recourse to class-based discrimination in shunning the presumably newer inhabitants of the "good-looking houses," are precisely what a "dance" will mitigate—up to and including the fact that the projected participants, as Frank ostentatiously assures Emma, will return to their proper place the following day. With such assurance, then, the notion of propriety, of what is right or natural, bridles—in the image of the once and future dancers—against naturalized notions of propriety (with their additional echo of property) that Emma, "who could do any thing," wishes to uphold.

The nostalgia that drives Frank's machinations here is obvious enough. But what must be acknowledged, again, is "the authentically temporal destiny" to which his machinations in their covert and oppositional formation are strongly susceptible. If it is the case that Frank's interest in dancing signifies a larger commitment to change or melioration, such a reading is as insubstantial or ironic or as much an effect of desire (to follow Stewart again) as Frank, in his unique endorsement of dancing, is irreducibly a figment of the past. The possibilities that Frank is arguably committed to, and to which the idealized past provides comparatively unmediated access, work in a rather complex but important way. In addition to defining desire as an anterior wish for a version of the future on which the present (or erstwhile future) has subsequently foreclosed, Frank's initiative and the peculiar *readability* of this initiative work to expose and to demonstrate the "desire for desire," if only in the way "dancing," once ironized, is indivisible from its *indeterminacy* as an activity signifying change. It is not that Frank is ultimately uncommitted to making a difference however tactically or covertly. It is that, in the absence of anything concrete or verifiable or essentially "lived," the nostalgic distinction between Emma, "who could do any thing" and does nothing, and Frank, who is "doing something" (like Henry Crawford) that merely looks like nothing, remains sadly moot.

Nowhere is this difference, and just as important perhaps the nondifference it may finally amount to, more crucial than in the relationship of Frank and Jane, which both shadows and proves a contrast to the principal courtship narrative involving Emma and her eventual husband, Knightley. The major difference between these narratives is that the former is carried on in secret and is unavailable to the novel's other participants, including the narrator, whereas the latter is indivisible from the developmental trajectory that the narrative scrupulously tracks and celebrates. This difference has had the cumulative effect of making Frank and Jane both a counterplot to Emma and Knightley and an entity of diminished value where otherness at once marks and explains their—and especially Frank's—culpability. But there is a problem too with the derogation that their invisibility, particularly as a relational unit, must somehow justify. While most of the novel's characters, along with most commentators, have few scruples in taking Frank at his word in condemning his apparently insensitive treatment of a woman whom he has also rescued from virtual servitude, there is no independent account to confirm any real wrongdoing toward Jane beyond the secrecy with which Frank, with Jane's presumable concurrence, has enshrouded their attachment. The absence of such an account, along with the tenth-hour disclosure of their engagement, which surprises even the narrator, has sparked a lively debate. Yet here too the debate has been more a competition in exerting damage control over the novel's function as a regulatory instrument than a controversy over the success or failure (as the case may be) of the narrative's system of values.

The debate, at least in recent years, has sprung from Wayne Booth's unhappy observation that Austen's choice of "mystery at the expense of irony," specifically the stable irony by which Emma's development may be monitored and judged, is "the weakest aspect of the novel" (*The Rhetoric of Fiction*, 255). While readers have tried to retrieve the novel from what Booth understands to be a deficiency, at least in matters of form, regarding its ostensible and (in his view) felicitous purpose as a narrative following and celebrating Emma's development through Knightley's tutelage, they are somewhat less anxious to follow Booth's lead in exploring the compromise that "mystery" exacts upon the novel as a rhetorical and an ideological tool. Adena Rosmarin enlists Wolfgang Iser's reception theory, specifically his notion of the "advance retrospection" that obtains on second or third reading, in arguing that the "mystification" at *Emma*'s core makes "hermeneutic suspicion" a perennial effect of the novel rather than a one-time experience.[20] *Emma*'s "repeated quixotic unveilings," she writes, "not only develop our interpretive skill and discover us to ourselves but give us the impression of reaching ever deeper to an underlying reality" (336). W. J. Harvey, who anticipates Rosmarin in the value he ascribes to mystery and inaccessibility in the novel, argues similarly that "the invisible presence of the Jane Fairfax-Frank Churchill relationship . . . allows Jane Austen to accommodate the apparent randomness of existence to the precise elegance of her form." The "shadow novel-within-a-novel," he asserts,

enables Jane Austen to embody that aspect of our intuition of reality summed up by Auden—"we are lived by powers we do not understand." One of the powers we do not understand is the incredibly complex pressure put upon us by the actions and interests, dreams and desires—the mere existence, even—of our contiguous or remote fellow human beings. It is something we simply accept as there though invisible, just as the private lives and passions of other people are not to be tamed by the domineering egoism of a blind and blinkered Emma. (456)

If there is a necessary link in these arguments between a learning curve on the one hand and a reality on the other, to which the reader, in imitation of the protagonist, is initially and repeatedly unequal, it is hardly accidental. The particular reality-effect in which the "invisible" is clearly instrumental in these accounts is also consistent with a pedagogical trajectory where "mystery" becomes a nearly disciplinary apparatus in the way it humbles and compels both the reader and Emma to honor the incomprehensible. This is a somewhat

grandiose view of the problem. While mystery may be marshaled to the formation of a hierarchy in which reality performs as a sovereign and inviolable
entity, Booth is surely right in intuiting that not all mystery is insoluble or sufficiently opaque to prevent other meanings and effects from proliferating and
from compromising the cultural work in which Emma's evolution is key.

   Both Harvey and Rosmarin correctly recognize that the Frank-Jane narrative, rather than a lapse on Austen's part, remains the proverbial tip of the ice-
berg here, representing a reality in which the novel has more than a casual
interest. But their paeans to the novel's reality, and to Austen's seemingly generous conception of its sublime impenetrability, have the paradoxical effect of
transforming the real into a monolith upon which no one, least of all the reader,
can presume to exert explanatory power or control. Nor is it any accident that
when Harvey speaks of authority or of some governing intelligence, he speaks of
"Jane Austen" and not the narrator of *Emma*, who more than anyone must
transgress—if only as part of her job—the peculiar deference that the real
would appear to warrant. In other words, for all of the mystified density that
Harvey and Rosmarin ascribe to Austen's real, there is, beginning with the narrator and her necessary incompetence in fathoming what is before her, a concomitant transparency in *Emma* or *drive* to transparency to which the reader, or
the rereader in this case, is directed. The yield of this directive will naturally
vary from reader to reader. The point to stress, though, is that while the density
or mystery of the real in *Emma* is, as these critics note, a limit point beyond
which there may be nothing that can be grasped fully, there is plenty along the
way that is sufficiently comprehensible, particularly on multiple readings, to
lend a more specific meaning to the novel over and against the narrator's comparatively limited sense of her materials.

   I have tried to indicate "where"—to borrow Emily Dickinson's phrase
again—the "meanings are" in *Emma*. What must be stressed is that even *these
meanings*, and the oppositional strain they introduce, are ultimately insufficient
in dispelling the indeterminacy on which they and the practices they refer to
necessarily founder. In fact, just as the mystery of Frank and Jane redounds on
the narrator, whose hindsight is sufficiently limited in this instance to cast aspersions on whatever wisdom it presumably underwrites here and throughout
Emma, so it also redounds on any reading under which this mystery effectively
dissipates or proves a cover for something substantial and completely understood. Regardless of whether we share Knightley's or the narrative's interpretation of Frank and Jane, the fact remains that even by following the incentives
according to which the disposition of their relationship and its continued invisibility prove a challenge to the dominant order and the narrative that serves
it, we end up in roughly the same place as those, like Knightley, who think dif-

ferently. We end up in a welter of mystery and indeterminacy that supersedes all surmise. The only difference is that where a probabilistic reading of Frank and Jane, and of Frank's behavior in being less than forthright, is continually challenged by information that is simply unavailable or available only through Frank's ultimate letter of explanation and apology, a possibilistic reading of their relationship, in which they occupy what amounts to a utopian or unregulated space, proceeds more or less from a position where their alternative abides solely as a condition of its constitutive unrepresentability. To read Frank and Jane in a way that directly challenges conventional wisdom therefore or in a way that makes their relationship a register of an otherness that is both ongoing and close at hand is to read them *nostalgically*. It is to engage in a practice that the novel, in its fundamental discontent, encourages, but only by reminding us that the "good old days" are sufficiently in arrears that any attempt at their resuscitation, whether by dancing or by marriage or by the establishment of a musical society, is also a wish-fulfilling fantasy.

"Emma could not resist"

That the mystery at *Emma*'s core necessarily ends in mystery or in an alterity that, in figuring "the desire for desire," is indeterminate and unrealized is far from a lapse on Austen's part. Rather it is instrumental—following the reading practices that this mystery provokes—in the sobering recognition that substantive change, particularly as a prospect on which the present and the impending future have apparently foreclosed, is entirely a matter of theory rather than actual praxis. The resistance that Jane and Frank figure forth, or that Emma, however unsuccessfully, contrives to initiate in the novel's first volume, or that Miss Bates and Mrs. Elton represent in their different but oddly complementary versions of possibility amid routine has no real place or purpose in *Emma*'s final volume, save as a measure against which the novel's culminating developments may be evaluated. Although this may seem a rather meager initiative on Austen's part, particularly given her previous novels where certain alternative possibilities (in other words, the relationships of Jane and Bingley and of Catherine and Eleanor) are at least marginally represented, the gradual dissolution of a certain kind of "lived experience" into theory has the important effect of recuperating nostalgia as a utopian dream and a locus of value even "when," as Anne Elliot puts it in *Persuasion*, "existence or . . . hope is gone." If it is the case that Emma's development proceeds along a trajectory in which her desire modulates, in the face of disappointment, to a more conventional nostalgia where the traditional protections of class are the only stay against the abject "difference of woman's destiny," it is also true that the act of (re)reading her development remains a reading rife with desire: specifically for the "brilliant days" when, as both volume 1 and Mrs. Elton suggest, Emma's desire for change may have had some basis in fact.

The extended episode at Box Hill, which occupies the center of the novel's third volume and upon which Emma's development into a seemingly responsible social being turns, is just as important, then, for the nostalgias that it juxtaposes. Readers have long recognized this episode, from the competition Frank initiates, to Emma's insult to Miss Bates, to Knightley's climactic admonishment in defense of the mortified spinster, to be the crux of the novel's narrative, which is primarily one of Emma's education. But what commentators seem not to have noticed sufficiently is the tension or competition of ideologies that abides throughout the episode.[21]

We can begin with the game itself. Like his interest in dancing, Frank's game is easy to dismiss as a self-indulgent undertaking with necessarily painful consequences for Miss Bates as well as for Jane, who must witness what the narrator regards as an excessive flirtation between Frank and the protagonist. Still, Frank's initiative is typical of his performance in the novel in counterpoising one version of nostalgia, which is decidedly oppositional in the prospects and possibilities it recalls, and a more customary version that is merely conservative in its endorsement of the particular stability that only social stratification, and the roles such difference presupposes, furnishes. Thus Frank's initial announcement to the gathered company that he has been "ordered by Miss Woodhouse (who, wherever she is, presides) to say, that she desires to know what you are all thinking of" (334), looks in two directions simultaneously: to the Emma who earlier "could" aspire to "do any thing" and to the Emma whose special prerogatives are increasingly an invitation to do nothing. Moreover, Frank introduces this distinction in ways that are consistent with his tactical performance elsewhere by referring to Emma in a way that evokes (without enumerating) the abuses to which her power has been put. That Emma fails to take Frank's instruction in this regard, which he typically delivers under the cover of indulgent play, should come as no surprise. But for the reader, who may be already mindful of Frank's intimacy with Jane and familiarity with *her* predicament, the particular intent onto which Frank's imperative waggishly opens, suggests, first and foremost, that the thoughts and motives most worthy of reflection on this occasion are probably Frank's own.

It is Knightley, typically, whose immediate threat of disclosure—"Is Miss Woodhouse sure that she would like to hear what we are all thinking of?" (334)—forces a revision in the proposed festivities. Yet not even the revised game, where, allegedly under Miss Woodhouse's order, Frank "demands" from each member of the party "either one thing very clever, be it prose or verse, original or repeated—or two things moderately clever—or three things very dull in-deed" (335), is sufficient in dispelling the competition, however lopsided, between his rather open-ended initiative, where play is arguably a pretext for reflection on Emma's part, and Knightley's closed project, which appropriates play to con-ventionally pedagogical ends. No matter how much Frank, in the guise of either flirtation or frivolity, contrives to make Box Hill a scene of self-instruction for someone sufficiently empowered to "do" more than she has evidently been do-ing, his initiative has the effect of playing to Knightley's purpose in giving Knightley the occasion to inform Emma what he is "thinking of" and, on the evidence of his previous query, has been chafing to relay for some time.

This occasion, which occurs only with Frank's provocation, remains Emma's well-known insult to Miss Bates, whose seemingly abject but plainly self-ironic response to Frank's second proposal—"Oh! very well . . . then I need not be un-easy. . . . I shall be sure to say three dull things as soon as ever I open my mouth, shan't I?"—has the memorable consequence of provoking Emma's witty but cruel rejoinder: "Ah! ma'am, but there may be a difficulty. Pardon me—but you will limited as to number—only three at once" (335). Forgetting for the moment any prior obligation that may impinge on his motives here, Knightley is per-fectly justified in coming to Miss Bates's defense, especially in light of her im-mediate (and typically generous) response where Emma's insult is initially mistaken as something benign and less cutting. Nevertheless, both the disposi-tion of Knightley's instruction and, even more, its remarkable efficacy are nicely framed by the simple, declarative sentence that precedes Emma's riposte: "Emma could not resist." With this observation, which for the narrator simply underscores Emma's continued tendency "to think a little too well of herself," the "resistance" that Emma eschews at Box Hill and in response to Frank's provocation takes on a thicker, more nostalgic cast (335).

The most crucial moment in Knightley's remonstrance over Emma's lack of feeling toward Miss Bates comes in response to Emma's defensive insistence that Miss Bates did not understand her insult and, even worse, that the woman's constitutive ridiculousness made the insult justifiable. Knightley will have none of this. Chiding Emma for her insensitivity to Miss Bates's "character, age, and situation," he elaborates his position eloquently and, on the evidence of the tears it will elicit, persuasively:

Were she a woman of fortune, I would leave every harmless absurdity to take its chance, I would not quarrel with you for any liberties of manner. Were she your equal in situation—but, Emma, consider how far this is from being the case. She is poor; she has sunk from the comforts she was born to; and, if she live to old age, must probably sink more. Her situation should secure your compassion. It was badly done, indeed!—You, whom she had known from an infant, whom she had seen grow up from a period when her notice was an honor, to have you now, in thoughtless spirits, and the pride of the moment, laugh at her, humble her—and before her niece, too—and before others, many of whom (certainly *some,*) would be entirely guided by *your* treatment of her.—This is not pleasant to you, Emma—and it is very far from pleasant to me; but I must, I will,—I will tell you truths while I can, satisfied with proving myself your friend by very faithful counsel, and trusting that you will some time or other do me greater justice than you can do now. (339–40)

Like Henry Tilney's lecture to Catherine Morland in *Northanger Abbey*, which raises as many questions as it resolves, Knightley's lesson—though more crafted and avuncular—raises a host of issues that Emma's culpability and the prospect of her corrigibility serve as much to mask now as to focus.

We can begin with Knightley's misogyny, which is obliquely directed at the only absurd "woman of fortune" present, in this case Mrs. Elton, despite the fact that the most insensitive act by far at Box Hill—exceeding even Emma's insult—is Mr. Weston's preposterous anagram on Emma's "perfection," which he performs, with characteristic obtuseness, in the aftermath of her cutting riposte. Or we can proceed to the image of Miss Bates as a woman of distinction, whom Knightley, more than anyone, may have cause to remember as such and whose current degradation, though conveniently naturalized as an inevitable if regrettable course, also has a more specific and immediate etiology to which his concern bears remarkably suggestive witness. Or we can even pursue the matter, indeed the charge, of Emma's thoughtlessness here. Although true in the sense that Knightley means, the charge minimizes the genuine, if unconscious, threat that Miss Bates and her niece jointly figure in Emma's calculus—and to which her insult, particularly as an impulsive action, refers. But none of these perhaps is as important as the social stratification or class-based affiliation by which Miss Bates is deserving of sympathy according to Knightley. Here, in a remarkable revision of the self-regard in which Harriet and Emma are earlier conjoined on the basis of their sex, Miss Bates merits sympathy not only in light of her particular destiny, from which Emma—now as before—is in continuous flight, but, more important for Knightley's purposes, in light of who Miss Bates *was* and must forever be: a woman whose entitlements to sympathy and compassion are, no less than her former comforts, entitlements of birth. To be considerate of Miss Bates is to consider, first and foremost, the height from which she has sunk so that compassion is fundamentally—and more narrowly than the identity politics that earlier bind Emma to Harriet—an act of self-interest and self-promotion.[22]

The "resistance" that Emma conclusively abandons at Box Hill and against which her subsequent actions, from the consignment of Harriet to "nothing[ness]" (390) to her marriage to Knightley, remain a stay has a correlative in the relationship of Frank and Jane. The continued mystery of the latter relationship proves a resistance to the particular values that the narrative upholds in its strident subscription to the real and the representable. Although it is impossible to attach a specific value or valence either to Frank's machinations or to a relationship with Jane that is unique both in the dispersal of property it effects and in matching chronological peers, it is possible at the same time to idealize their relationship, along with Frank's other meliorative efforts, in the understanding that this idealization is entirely nostalgic and mitigated by "lived experience."

This is not, of course, how *Emma* is customarily interpreted or how Frank in particular is usually understood.[23] However, as Wayne Booth (*The Rhetoric of Fiction*) once again is nearly alone in inferring, the challenge posed by the mystery of Frank and Jane and by the narrator's failure to penetrate their relationship in any way spells trouble for the novel in its putative endorsement of Knightley and his probabilistic worldview.[24] The mystery proves troubling not necessarily because, like Miss Bates's dreaded tripartite utterance, it invokes a simultaneity that is out of control and a challenge thereby to the community's "imagined" sense of itself.[25] It is troubling because the stasis to which Highbury has reverted by the novel's close, and to which the narrator is as happily reconciled as are Knightley, Emma, and Emma's father, stands in problematic relation to several things. It stands opposed, first and foremost, to the dynamism of the novel's beginning and the initially exciting character on whom it focuses, whose temporal destiny is by the end a matter of narrative form as well as fact. And it stands opposed to the inferable future, where the dispensations of class reconstituted at the novel's close figure a more typical nostalgia that, far from a utopian dream, is at best a holding action shorn of anything approximating either mystery or idealization.

The Body in Persuasion *and* Sanditon

One of the great advantages to thinking about Jane Austen is the remarkable compression of her achievement and the sanction it confers on what I have been describing and also designating as Austen's "project." Although Austen's writing career can, like the contemporaneous romantic movement, be divided into early and late stages, or into works that belong to the late eighteenth century and the Regency period respectively, there is little doubt that all six novels were either conceived or revised (at least in part) over a period of no more than six years. This compression immediately poses problems to any critic committed (as I am) to tracing a trajectory of development where, under imperatives ranging from the aesthetic to the political, Austen's career is demonstrably one of steady transformation. But it is also felicitous to the critic for whom, as I hope the preceding chapters have made clear, the transformation of Austen's fiction is a consequence as well of the author's steady engagement with a host of problems, formal and cultural, by which her oeuvre is really a work in progress.

An example of this give-and-take may be found in *Mansfield Park*. The first novel by Austen to have been published at the time of its composition, *Mansfield Park*'s most remarkable and, to many readers, most disturbing feature— the narrator's allegiance to her dour and sanctimonious protagonist—recalls the narrative incompetence of Austen's early novels and their unease over the probabilistic worldview with which the novel's "rise" was coextensive. Narrative incompetence certainly works to different effect in a novel like *Northanger Abbey*, or to something apart from a wholesale endorsement of the ideology of domesticity, especially as a moral anchor for England's aspirations abroad.[1] Nevertheless, just as narrative bias provided Austen with the means to produce what in *Mansfield Park* is fundamentally a novel of the future, so the proximity of Austen's first three novels to *Mansfield Park*, even as works being readied for publication, had a reciprocal effect in making them the repositories of an ever growing awareness of what was at stake in Austen's fictional practice, particularly in its movement from epistolarity, and from the possibilities, social and hermeneutic, with which epistolary instability had been aligned.

We will never know the precise junctures at which *Sense and Sensibility* and, more speculatively, *Pride and Prejudice* were converted into direct narratives. Nor can we know with any certainty the point at which the novels' final constitution was also thematized or allegorized, reflecting an awareness of their status, and securing a space for the reader, that the regulatory work of direct narrative had also annexed. But despite the difficulty in pinpointing what Austen knew and when she knew it, there is reason to suspect that by the time of her novels' publication she recognized to a significant degree a homology between the novel's rise, in which she surely knew her instrumentality, and the particular version of social hegemony to which probabilistic—or again realistic—fiction was plainly suited. This is especially evident in the way that nostalgia, which in *Emma* looks longingly, even fatuously, to an interval when other prospects were abroad, remains—however consciously or prominently—an informing feature of all the novels, early and late.

Beginning with the eroticism of the first two published novels, operating first as a figure of plenitude, to which the imperatives of closure and comedy are inadequate, or, in the case of Lydia Bennet, as a disruptive force that casts the principal narrative of *Pride and Prejudice* and its regulatory disposition into dubious relief, the "desire for desire" is a factor in Austen's writing. Although increasingly instrumental in the striking detailism that Austen's contemporaries found more interesting than her plots, such desire is, in the early works especially, connected more broadly to the articulation of alternatives at variance with the particular *future* of which narrative closure remains an instance as well as a description.

Nostalgia is more noticeably an issue in *Northanger Abbey*, which, as the prefatory advertisement suggests, is a virtual study in belatedness. This is true not only with respect to the many material and cultural elements that (as Austen notes in the advertisement) are decades old, but with attention also to the "considerable changes" that take place over the course of the narrative itself. Notable among these changes is Catherine's development from a "strange" and "unaccountable" character into a sentimental heroine, whose marriageability (and serviceability to things as they are) derive from the recognition that her "real power"—and, by implication, woman's power—is "nothing."

Nor is nostalgia any less an issue in *Mansfield Park*. Here the representation of the future, or in *Mansfield Park*'s case the future of fictional representation, is a reaction formation to possibilities that are increasingly inconceivable, thanks to the now residual status of late-century domesticity. In this novel of the future a character such as Mary Crawford, to whom the prospects of the past are more cherishable than those of the present, becomes a negative and cautionary example, but in a way that underscores what has been *lost* in her transvaluation.

And then there is *Emma*. As we have just seen, the prospects for change in domestic life are narrowed over the course of *Emma*'s three volumes. This makes the act of reading the novel—or rereading it—indivisible from witnessing and reliving the temporal destiny of certain initiatives, and their projected goals, against which the emergent culture of middle-class domesticity *and* the older, land-based social hierarchy are provisionally allied.

In noting the prevalence of nostalgia as a reflexive element in the fictions prior to *Persuasion*, I am not minimizing the material and historical elements that, as my early chapters detail, contributed to Austen's awareness of her particular agency in the novel's rise and in the social work to which domestic fiction and realistic writing were already conscripted. From her abiding allegiance to epistolary instability, and the particular reading habits that epistolary "silence" cultivated and served, to her awareness of the naturalizing, indeed regulatory, bent of any art that spoke in the name of either probability or nature, to her recognition that the subordinate status of women, especially women of privilege, attested to the equally conscribed status of men, to her uncanny alignment with her romantic contemporaries in locating horizons of possibility in quotidian life, Austen—or the "historical Austen"—is far from seamlessly aligned with the major developments with which her achievement is usually deemed synonymous. It is not that such developments as the rise of the novel and the continued rise of bourgeois domesticity are alien or irrelevant to Austen's accomplishment. It is more that her growing, and at times inchoate, unease over the disposition of her achievement—on which a variety of recoverable influences and developments conceivably bear—became, in the six years during which all six novels were either composed or revised for publication, more acute and, as I hope my readings have illustrated, more knowing.

The question of knowingness, the reflexivity by which Austen anticipates and frequently matches the wisdom of posterity regarding the partialized, otherwise normative, version of gentry life that her novels allegedly propound, is hardly a simple one or one that can be introduced without considering again the method of interpretation here. Although I do not address this specifically in the introduction, a mode of reading that is fundamentally deconstructive, whether in identifying the various allegories of representation in the novels, or in stressing the metairony that supersedes narrative authority in these works, is the germ from which this book derives. Far from a point of origin, then, my recourse to historical method, no matter how discrete or of a piece with Austen's somewhat exceptional self-awareness, is the fortuitous result of an inquiry that ultimately found its bearing in the theories of de Certeau and others, where historical method and the prospect of historical agency are perforce linked.

Both a critique and an instance of historical method, my way with Austen takes seriously her function as an historian of her milieu, which takes seriously in turn both the milieu that her works attend to and the uncanny prospects to which that world, particularly in retrospect, had been surprisingly open. The "historical Austen," in other words, implicitly contests the assumption germane to historical method generally that the material and cultural circumstances of a given text, not to mention the novels at issue here, work somehow to divest the text of the awareness that has devolved most recently upon the historically minded reader. Critics may well have a point in arguing that Wordsworth's poems, to cite the most obvious contemporaneous example, are in a state of denial regarding both their motives and the history they put under erasure. Nevertheless, apart from the fact that such approaches merely recapitulate a way of reading Wordsworth practiced long before it was history or the French Revolution or the vagrant dwellers at Tintern Abbey that were an issue, it does not follow that every author is either disabled or sufficiently possessed of false consciousness to require the supplement of retrospective reading.[2]

Such circumspection is particularly relevant in the case of Jane Austen, who not only wrote at a moment of extraordinary transition in British life and letters but whose flailings in the welter of these changes, from developments in which she was instrumental to changes where she was merely powerless, were coordinated and given a second chance in the years that her novels achieved final form.[3] This interval, more than any other, remains the context par excellence where Austen is concerned. This is not because the years at Chawton supersede all other contexts and conditions to which her writing may be referred. It is because the extraordinary compression, under which twenty years of observation and struggle were suddenly available for reconsideration and revision, provided Austen with an aperture on her historicity as well as her grapplings with it that is fairly unique. We will never know at what point Colonel Brandon may have become a rigorously conceived figure for both narrative authority in *Sense and Sensibility* and the still larger cultural forces that governed it. But there is little doubt that by the time that *Sense and Sensibility* was forwarded to the printer Austen had come to know, better than she had initially, what she was in fact up to.

As the last of Austen's completed novels, not to mention one that followed in short order upon the two novels she had most recently published, *Persuasion* presents special problems along with special exegetical opportunities. While there is probably no novel by Austen to which the adjective *nostalgic* has been assigned with greater regularity, the version of nostalgia that we have been exploring here, involving the temporalized character of hope itself, makes the insubstantiality of change, or the displacement of the conditions under which substantive change was once fathomable or a possibility, the basis in *Persuasion* for a perplexity at once limiting and enabling. The central theme in *Persuasion*— as its posthumously bestowed title suggests—remains the coercive reach of culture, or what amounts, in Austen's reckoning, to the likely indivisibility of the individual's wants and what ideology, for want of a better term, has already mandated. Where previously, and as recently as *Emma*, there was a sense that the world is still pervious to otherness and variation, from the shadow narrative of Frank and Jane to the poultry pilferage that not even Mr. Woodhouse can control successfully, such alterity comes mostly at a price in the last completed novel.

Anne Elliot's refusal of Capt. Frederick Wentworth in the prehistory of the narrative and the mysterious physical transformation that she experiences in aftermath are factors unquestionably in Anne's exertion of responsible, even progressive, agency at the moment we first encounter her. But even as there is a palpable link between the mysterious loss of bloom and the still unravished Anne's ability to make a difference, whether in securing the Elliots' removal from Kellynch or in the numerous services she performs at Uppercross, where domesticity and her sister's debility bear a similar connection, it is difficult to rejoice in the particular autonomy that the narrative, in recognition of Anne's agency, confers upon her.[4] I am only the umpteenth reader to remark on the sense of isolation in *Persuasion*, and on the sympathetic identification that separates this most subjective of Austen's texts from the novel that precedes it, where the narrator and her protagonist are—until the very end—never on the same page.[5] What must be stressed about this development, specifically the movement from a "heroine whom no one . . . will much like"[6] to one whom everyone must like, is not just the abiding melancholy or sense of loss that the heroine's dilemma instills in *Persuasion*. Even more important is the improvement that such sympathetic alignment with the heroine holds for a narrative practice—specifically the practice of free indirect discourse—that, by its regulatory bent, had been as much an achievement as a liability.

Unlike *Mansfield Park*, where a similar alignment of narrator and protagonist abides, *Persuasion* demonstrates that sympathy and judgment no longer need be mutually exclusive any more than an understanding of Anne's limitations, particularly as someone who cannot finally prevent herself from "fall[ing] into a quotation" (83),[7] is reason to "like" her any less. It is more, in fact, that the otherness that had previously infiltrated Austen's novels in, for example, the practices of its less tractable or significant characters has been transferred willy-nilly to narrative practice itself, which tracks and even celebrates Anne's reunion with Wentworth while itemizing all that is lost in a trajectory where being in love also means being in language. Only by perplexity over the subject's fate, in other words, or by recognition that the body outside of quotation will be necessarily deformed in the same way that Anne's restored body is more nearly a simulacrum, is Austen in a position to liberate free indirect discourse from its directive or regulatory function. Although there may be a great deal left to lament in the world and in domestic life, it is the case in *Persuasion* that there is really nothing left, at least by way of opposition, to regulate and control.[8] After a relatively brief interval during which the Anne shorn of "bloom" enjoys success in resolving her family's fiscal difficulties and in helping to negotiate what, according to the novel's social allegory, involves a transfer of stewardship from the aristocracy to the professional classes, the novel's heroine undergoes a restoration that proves a precondition for her eventual marriage to a representative of the new order. Thus the rather bleak and dystopic future that *Mansfield Park* imagines and projects, moreover, under the nostalgic pressure of opportunities lost and possibilities foreclosed upon, is by *Persuasion* at any rate a done deal.

Something Like Anne Elliot

Much of the debate about *Persuasion* involves the novel's status as the last completed work by Austen, making it nearly impossible for most readers to ignore *Persuasion*'s relationship to the works that precede it. Whether it is *Persuasion*'s affinity with *Mansfield Park* as a "Cinderalla" story, or the novel's connection to *Sense and Sensibility* and the character of Marianne in the prestige it lavishes upon the heroine's longing, or simply the steady submersion in Anne's consciousness for which *Emma* is undoubtedly a precedent, *Persuasion* is as much a novel in its own right, as a work that, more than any other Austen novel, bears directly on a canon that appears suddenly to gain in coherence.[9] This tendency with *Persuasion* immediately puts one in mind of Derrida's notion of supplementarity. It does this because even as *Persuasion* may succeed in making Austen whole, its invariable function as an explanatory coda both exposes and opens the totality to which it has been added to a constitutive incompleteness.[10] Regardless of whether the heroine gets the man she has always wanted, or whether Wentworth represents a future to which Austen and Anne are happily reconciled, *Persuasion* reminds us that Austen's canon is fundamentally a work in progress: a body of writing informed by possibilities that, however disappointed or exiled to the realm of the nostalgic, are capable *as possibilities* of residing somewhere.

It is probably the case that *Persuasion* marks something of a change in

Austen's outlook in its increased focus on the individual subject and in its endorsement of the individualism of which military professionalism is a projection even as the novel reflects an abiding conservatism of which the heroine's stoicism is merely one aspect.[11] At the same time, such controversies regarding *Persuasion*—and the social and political valences of Austen's project overall— are from the perspective of this study beside the point. They are of little use because they fail to explain how a novel so plainly inured to things as they are—on which the aforementioned ideologies presumably bear—is also capable of marshaling that resignation to ends that are oppositional, or again nostalgic, in the way that Anne's progress, very much like Emma's, is readable as default, and as a falling away from the possibilities and practices that her restoration abruptly cancels.

I have already mentioned Anne's mysterious loss of bloom and the responsible, even progressive agency that she is capable of exerting in aftermath. What must be explored now is the novel's dilation on that connection. There is no question that Anne's father, Sir Walter Elliot, is among the most diminished and satirized of Austen's characters: a figure whose criteria of judgment—from birth to physiognomy—mark him as shallow and as representing a social order and its modes of discrimination that, beginning with Lady Catherine, have long been a point of contention in Austen. Nor is there any question that Anne's mysterious transformation in the years following her rejection of Captain Wentworth would seem to serve the antiaristocratic argument in showing the denaturing effects of her refusal, which we are given to believe was offered in deference to her family's values. Still, a closer look at the brief summary of Anne's past at the beginning of *Persuasion* suggests that, however much the refusal of Wentworth redounds on Anne's family in the unhappiness it provokes, Anne's recourse to her family's claims, and to the advice in particular of Lady Russell, in rejecting Wentworth is more a measure of her resourcefulness than the result of what Wentworth, in decrying her "feebleness of character," later terms "overpersuasion" (62).

In describing the early attachment that Anne is obliged to sever, the narrator offers a description of the relationship that, with the weight of information that has accumulated and will continue to accumulate, suggests that "overpersuasion" is far from the one-way street that Wentworth's condemnation implies. It is more that persuasion, or again "over-persuasion," is omnipresent and that even Anne's very personal recollections of Wentworth bear the marks of outside influence:

He was, at that time, a remarkably fine young man, with a great deal of intelligence, spirit and brilliancy; and Anne an extremely pretty girl, with gentleness, modesty, taste, and feeling.—Half the sum of attraction, on either side, might have been enough, for he had nothing to do, and she had hardly any body to love; but the encounter of such lavish recommendations could not fail. They were gradually acquainted, and when acquainted, rapidly and deeply in love. It would be difficult to say which had seen highest perfection in the other, or which had been the happiest; she, in receiving his declarations and proposals, or he in having them accepted. (29–30)

In the method of narration that we have come to associate with Austen, it is often difficult to distinguish a character's internal representation of her thoughts and feelings and the narrator's interpretation of them. Never is this difficulty more to the point than here. Although hardly rife with Austen's customary irony, the detachment essential to irony reasserts itself in a remembrance that teeters precariously on the brink of cliché of which Anne, as much as the narrator, is the presumable author.[12] The normative scenario, where Wentworth and Anne dissolve effortlessly into "he" and "she" roles, coupled with the rapid and by no means unorthodox acceleration of their mutual attraction into declarations of love has a certain girlish charm, particularly as a retrospection susceptible to idealization. But there lurks within this storybook scenario a more severe recognition of the flattening and depersonalizing effects of normative relations, not to mention the lop-sidedness of gender relations, that bears as much on the present—or on what, from the narrator's perspective, may be a gentle criticism of such arrangements—as it does on the past and on Anne's initial refusal.

That rejection, to which the narrative immediately and characteristically turns its attention, is understood in retrospect to have been the result of family pressure and of the influence of Lady Russell, who—whatever her lapses—is certainly a less toxic and ridiculous figure of traditionalism than Anne's father. Nevertheless the actual influences driving Anne's decision are represented, or again recollected, in a way that clearly complicates this interpretation of events, which is also Wentworth's interpretation:

She was persuaded to believe the engagement a wrong thing—indiscreet, improper, hardly capable of success, and not deserving it. But it was not a merely selfish caution, under which she acted, in putting an end to it. Had she not imagined herself consulting his good, even more than her own, she could hardly have given him up.—The belief of being prudent, and self-denying principally for *his* advantage, was her chief consolation, under the misery of a parting—a final parting; and every consolation was required, for she had to encounter all the additional pain of opinions, on his side, totally unconvinced and unbending, and of his feeling himself ill-used by so forced a relinquishment. (31)

Although the specter of "persuasion" is raised for the first time in the novel in describing Lady Russell's influence, it is not many sentences before the importance of that inaugural appearance (and the coercive force it designates) is compromised by other disclosures, notably the influence of Anne's altruism. While such self-denial is instrumental in marking Anne as an ethically informed subject, it is equally important in showing her resourcefulness. We see Anne's ability to marshal the coercive weight of class and family interests, along with the moral imperative to disinterestedness, in the service of *still other interests* that, while not strictly selfish, are directed toward an autonomy that Wentworth's obduracy (as revealed here) would likely stifle. It is unclear whether it is Anne herself or Anne according to the narrator who is protesting too much on the question of her selfishness. But the point to stress is that while it is presumably the narrator's purpose to introduce Anne's capacity for self-deception, if only to make her rejection of Wentworth vaguely tolerable, it is done less with the aim of criticizing Anne (in the manner, say, of *Emma*'s narrator) than with the object of showing Anne's remarkable ability to hold persuasion at bay *even by capitulation*. While autonomy and selfishness are not exactly one and the same, it is the case still that the *effect* of Anne's refusal, and of the persuasions she internalizes, is to escape persuasion along with the oppressive shape of life to come.[13]

What follows from here is the memorably cryptic account of Anne's physical transformation in the wake of her rejection, beginning with her sustained suffering and culminating in the "early loss of bloom" (31) that has not abated. And it remains an account, where Anne's demonstrable self pity is dutifully rendered by the narrator, making their apparent consensus on the cause of Anne's facial transformation a little suspect. In fact just as Anne is able to secure a space for herself amid the persuasions of family and moral authority, so it is the case here that, with the sudden agreement over its apparent cause, the "lasting effect" of Anne's early decision to remain single is readable in other ways. Anne's "loss of bloom," to put it bluntly, seems more a cause in its own right: an initiative that, as future events will shortly clarify, is remarkably on a continuum with the rejection that supposedly precipitated it.

The events to which I am referring involve the famous walk at Lyme later in volume 1, where Anne's miraculous restoration is as much an effect, or the result of persuasion, as it is apparently the cause of two men's admiration. But before we get to Lyme, and to the various persuasions that succeed in restoring Anne to desirability at the very moment they imbue Wentworth with a renewed desire for her, it must be emphasized that in the seven years that Anne has remained bloomless, she has also remained quietly autonomous and, in consequence, an effective agent. Readers are free to debate the extent of Anne's agency, including the political yield of getting her father and sister to lease their ancestral home and relocate to Bath. Yet despite the decidedly incremental nature of Anne's various interventions, which accords in any case with Austen's abiding fascination with the local as a site of possibility or difference, both the bricolage of Anne's overpersuasion and the loss of bloom that ensues follow her rejection of Wentworth in continuing to pave her egress from the heteronorma-tive economy and its strictures.

Much of Anne's resistance is in the past, and by the time we rejoin Anne in the present she is of a different mind regarding her previous decision. Not only is she "persuaded" now that "she should yet have been a happier woman in maintaining the engagement" (32–33); she is also convinced at this point that in breaking the engagement she was simply following Lady Russell's advice and adhering to her family's wishes. The memory of her former altruism or self-denial has apparently receded along with any sense of the complex of influ-ences that just two pages earlier had made it clear that however much Anne may have acceded to Lady Russell her decision to break the engagement was also linked to something that might be confused with selfishness. The narrator's ex-planation for the transformation in Anne's thinking is both simple and sugges-tive. Although Anne, she observes, "had been forced into prudence in her youth, she learned romance as she grew older—the natural sequence of an unnatural beginning" (33).

The narrator's point may seem obvious enough, but it is scarcely removed from perplexity. Beginning with the forces behind Anne's early prudence, which are notably opaque, the narrator's observation is additionally vexed by the con-tinued interchangeability of the "natural" and the "learned." Where Anne is sim-ply convinced that she made a mistake, even as she will expend a good deal of effort making the same mistake in continuing to resist Wentworth, the rather ironic notion of "learned romance" complicates the complexion of Anne's de-velopment. Is Anne's prudence less natural than her current discovery that ro-mance and love truly matter? Or is it a question of her having assimilated different lessons and discourses? In either case there is a problem in determin-ing the naturalness of Anne's early self-regard, where prudence is surely a factor, in conjunction with the concomitant, and presumably greater, naturalness of heterosexual desire. The particular difficulty in differentiating the natural from the discursive, which is registered in the oxymoron "learned romance" (not to mention the notion of "romance" itself), owes in no small measure, then, to Anne's earlier and continued imperative to self-preservation, where prudence—and the multiple forces that provoke it—is obviously a factor.

Much of what follows in *Persuasion* involves the competition between the impulses—or as the case may be, discourses—of romance and prudence. And while it may seem altogether churlish to reduce love and romance to a peda-gogical or disciplinary instrument, we are given, in Anne's continued resistance to Wentworth upon his reappearance in her life, some hint that her continued prudence—following her mysterious but equally innate loss of bloom—may well be the more "natural," or the more sustaining, of the two. It is not that the narrative is necessarily averse to erotic feeling, or that Anne is not plainly moved by desire, particularly when Wentworth comes to her assistance in relieving her of little Charles Musgrove or in "assist[ing] her into the carriage" (89). It is rather that such impulses are continually met by countervailing impulses, including the "pain" that immediately compounds Anne's "pleasure" in being helped into the carriage, that, however inflected by the past or by the still gloomy trajectory of heterosexual love into married life, are impulses nonetheless.

It is surely no accident that much of the circumstantial detail in *Persuasion*, particularly at the moment when Wentworth and Anne are brought into close proximity upon his return from the war, is taken up with issues of domesticity and marriage. These issues include the debility of Anne's sister, Mary, and the particular imbalance it demonstrates and serves, along with the marriage of Captain and Mrs. Harville, which is marked similarly by asymmetry. There is also, of course, Wentworth's sister and her husband, Admiral Croft. Their childless and companionate marriage is more than simply the exception that proves the rule here. It is a union, importantly, whose nearly cartoonish ecumenicism proves the backdrop for a rather heated debate over the appropriateness of having wives aboard ship where Wentworth typically takes the negative and customary position. Wentworth's position regarding women makes him, as Claudia Johnson has observed, the author of his own disappointment since the feebleness and fussiness that render women constitutionally unsuited for naval life in his view are the very aspects of femininity that make Anne culpable, as he sees it, in earlier rejecting him (*Jane Austen*, 149–57). Wentworth is wrong in accusing Anne of feebleness. But right or wrong, his endorsement of domestic ideology, and the imbalance it creates in its divisions of labor and ability, is sufficient to make desire and discourse coterminous in the same way that Anne's prudence remains—now as before—the comparatively natural response to an unnatural and regulated social world.

The impulsiveness peculiar to Anne's reticence regarding Wentworth, which is often construed as stoicism on her part, is evident from the moment of their reunion, where Anne's repeated observation to herself—"It is over! It is over. . . . The worst is over!"(60)—plainly oscillates between embarrassment at encountering Wentworth after so long a duration, where sexual desire no doubt figures prominently, and an equally spontaneous sense of relief over the termination of their attachment. And the tension continues in a variety of forms. In noticing, at one point, that Wentworth is looking at her, Anne speculates that he is "observing her altered features, perhaps, trying to trace in them the ruins of the face which had once charmed him" (71). The "perhaps" or caesura that intrudes upon Anne's fantasy undoubtedly looks toward erotic closure, but not without a certain apprehension over the prospect of Wentworth's picking up where he left off.

Several chapters later, in a conversation with the lovelorn, hopelessly romantic Captain Benwick, who is still pining for his recently departed fiancée, Anne is only too willing make her interlocutor privy to a future that, for her part, seems impossible. Recurring, once again, to the imbalance of gender relations against which her prudence has been arguably a defense, Anne reflects on her differences from Benwick: " 'And yet,' said Anne to herself, as they moved forward to meet the party, 'he has not, perhaps, a more sorrowing heart than I have. I cannot believe his prospects so blighted for ever. He is younger than I am; younger in feeling, if not in fact; younger as a man. He will rally again, and be happy with another' "(95). Apart from the recurrence of "perhaps," which again marks a nearly instinctive mitigation of the subject's normative yearning, the projection of the courtship plot onto some other figure looks in two directions simultaneously: to a desire for union whose projection is more properly a confession (much as Emma's matchmaking initiatives are often taken to signify her own desire to be married) as well as to another future, in this case to Anne's continued autonomy, for which the gender differences that she rehearses remain a powerful incentive.

Anne's resistance to imagining herself in a courtship narrative is also, of course, a means of steeling herself against Wentworth's suspiciously overt dalliances with the Musgrove sisters, Henrietta and Louisa. Nevertheless the substance of Anne's resistance—particularly as it stands distinct from mere denial—is given succinct if ultimately ironic confirmation in the scene that follows almost immediately upon the conversation with Benwick. This is Anne's memorable walk at Lyme, where she is "caught" in the triangulated—and reciprocally entrapped—gaze of two admiring men:

When they came to the steps, leading upwards from the beach, a gentleman at the same moment preparing to come down, politely drew back, and stopped to give them way. They ascended and passed him; and as they passed, Anne's face caught his eye, and he looked at her with a degree of earnest admiration, which she could not be insensible of. She was looking remarkably well; her very regular, very pretty features, having the bloom and freshness of youth restored by the fine wind which had been blowing on her complexion, and by the animation of eye, which it had also produced. It was evident that the gentleman, (completely a gentleman in manner) admired her exceedingly. Captain Wentworth looked round at her instantly in a way which shewed his noticing of it. He gave her a momentary glance,—a glance of brightness, which seemed to say, "That man is struck with you,—and even I, at this moment, see something like Anne Elliot again."(101)

Although Anne is necessarily mindful of the first admiring glance directed at her, it is not at all clear that the ventriloquism performed on Wentworth is anyone's doing but the narrator's. It makes sense that this is the case. Beyond the fact that Anne's fantasies of Wentworth are invariably fraught by some hesitation or impulse to self-preservation, the narrator's assumption of omniscience in surveying all three figures simultaneously is consistent with her perplexity throughout the novel over the constitution of sexual relations in general.

This perplexity, in which sexual desire and desirability are suspended somewhere between the natural and the discursive, or between the natural and the *naturalized*, is registered in the ambiguity of Anne's sudden restoration. Although we have only the narrator's word that Anne was aware of the gentleman's admiring look, it is significant that Anne's constitution as an object of desire is prior, in the narrator's accounting, to the otherwise natural explanation for her transformation. There is no reason to suppose that Anne was not already the beneficiary of the elements at the moment that her cousin William Walter Elliot (as it turns out) is disposed to take notice of her. Yet even as the narrator allows for this interpretation, it is an interpretation vexed by questions of causality or, again, issues of persuasion.

It is not enough for the narrator to observe that Anne was aware of the gentleman's glance for which the play of wind and physiognomy were chiefly responsible. The narrator makes a point of giving his glance an equal, if not greater, role in the *effect* of beauty, whose priority in turn, in this case as a discourse or desideratum, supersedes its immediate manifestation. If Anne is rendered beautiful by the animation of eye that she produces, it is because that "eye" (and the mind behind it) is already "caught" by an abstraction that Anne merely renders concrete. And were there any doubt of this "overpersuasion"— or of the interpellation, to be precise, that makes "internal persuasio[n]" (207) a register of coercion from without—there is the fortuitous addition here of Wentworth. Wentworth's renewed appreciation of Anne is more than the result of the triangulation that Mr. Elliot's admiration "instantly" adds to the scene. It is the effect as well of a mediation so pervasive that his designation of the object of beauty as "something like Anne Elliot" nearly beclouds the fact that, in becoming beautiful in the way that she has, Anne is more properly "like something" else here. Anne has become, thanks chiefly to a gaze that is *itself* an effect of discourse, the very simulacrum or type that her loss of bloom had earlier vitiated and on whose suppression her autonomy has depended.[14]

The perplexity on which the Lyme scene devolves entails more than the recognition that the natural or spontaneous is sufficiently adulterated that any opposition of the natural and the artificial, including the social artifice that the novel begins by excoriating, is already compromised. This perplexity also involves the alternative to persuasion, from the self-determination in which being Anne Elliot is a stay against being "something" desirable to other versions of autonomy or exteriority, where the body removed from quotation is reciprocally prone to abjection or degradation. The "autumnal" readings of *Persuasion*, that Claudia Johnson shrewdly cautions against, wherein the novel's tenderness on "romantic subjects" issues primarily from a "wistful and romantically unfulfilled" author "in the twilight of her life" (*Jane Austen*, 144), are perhaps are not so wide of the mark after all. This is not so because Austen, or her narrator, has finally relented amid her own debility and personal disappointment. It is that Anne's capitulation to desire or to what, in the above scene, is transparently the desire of the other, bifurcates in two directions that are basically dead ends. First, Anne's persuasion provides the occasion to reflect on what is lost by her capitulation and by the consignment to domesticity and married life that must follow. Second, Anne's metamorphosis at Lyme proves an occasion to parse the increasingly abstract or utopian comedy of Anne's opposition to normativity, and the actual ravages, beginning with her own defacement, that being out of quotation effectively mandates. All of this bespeaks a resignation quite different from the wish fulfillment borne of disappointment and terminal illness. For in the manner of virtually every other novel by Austen, *Persuasion* is affected still by the prospect of a different configuration among humans, or what amounts here to a tertium quid, to which the present dialectic of being in and out of discourse is simply inadequate.

This inadequacy becomes especially evident, along with the prospects that have been ruled out of bounds by the terms of the novel—and, by extension, the world—in the second key scene at Lyme. I am referring to Wentworth's remarkably unsuccessful attempt at catching Louisa Musgrove as she jumps down the steps, and his mortification upon dropping her. The episode is almost always viewed as a device through which Wentworth must acknowledge Anne's superiority of character in her ability to take control of the situation. Yet even with Anne's apparent vindication, the episode accords more directly with her sighting and consequent beautification in staging Wentworth's own interpellation. This cooptation is exposed and tried when, in watching Louisa fall, Wentworth experiences a wretchedness that instantly cancels the ease and self-possession that have been evident thus far in his flirtation with *both* Musgrove sisters. Wentworth's first words following Louisa's fall—"Is there no one to help me?"—are less an attempt, then, to take control through the issuance of orders than they figure a nearly infantile compulsion to resign responsibility. When help finally arrives and Wentworth is able with the aid of others to raise Louisa, his response accordingly is to abandon captaincy in "staggering against the wall for his support" and "exclaim[ing] in the bitterest agony, 'Oh God! her father and mother!' " (107).

At this point Anne intercedes, giving a series of orders that Wentworth echoes vacantly, which proves an instance, as well as an anatomy, of what it means *for him* to be in quotation and to be "something like" Captain Wentworth. For in his "horror," as Julia Kristeva might describe it, at having failed to support Louisa, Wentworth is put into a limbo that has always been relatively close by. He comes to "find" what Kristeva calls "the impossible within," which would be the alterity now, or internal difference, that necessarily opposes his fall into quotation or ideology; and he discovers, more importantly, that being self-possessed and in language as opposed to being merely "something like" Wentworth, on which internal difference suddenly weighs, paradoxically "constitutes [his] very being."[15] Suspended, in other words, between two impossibilities—the identity he assimilates unaware that it is a quotation and the abject alternative that he struggles against in that act of assimilation—Wentworth demonstrates how such resistance or confusion as he is currently experiencing is ultimately coextensive with the very selfhood, and with the particular persuasion, whose attenuation is perforce momentary.

Anne, who earlier resembles Wentworth in being similarly altered, is engaged in something quite different now. In her representation of the poise and self-control ordinarily characteristic of the captain, she moves quickly to mitigate the resistance posed by Wentworth's default. Reacting against Wentworth's inability to be himself or, again, to be "something like" Wentworth—either by catching Louisa or by responding promptly and rationally to her accident—Anne proves a cover for Wentworth's sudden abjection. And her motivation in helping him is clear. Observing Wentworth in a state of relief upon hearing of Louisa's excellent prospects for recovery, Anne is certain that neither his reaction to this news "nor the sight of him afterwards, as he sat near a table, leaning over it with folded arms, and face concealed, as if overpowered by the various feelings of his soul, and trying by prayer and reflection to calm them" could "[ever] be forgotten by her" (109).

There is little reason to dispute Anne's supposition that she will never forget this image. The question involves only what she will remember or, more precisely, what she *must* remember. As the deferral of the "sight" to the future (where it already assumes the status of memory) indicates, the spectacle of abjection currently before Anne—commensurate with her renewed visibility as "something like Anne Elliot"—is eminently transfigurable and, in effect, forgettable. Just as her earlier alteration beyond all recognition is increasingly a memory for Anne at this point, so the spectacle of Wentworth similarly altered is quickly relocated to a situation apart from its immediate actuality. But this is true only for Anne. For Austen, or the narrator, Wentworth stands, or in this case leans, in full view—so that despite the overall function of the narrative, which is to register perplexity over the ultimate "impossibility" of Anne's being anything apart from "something like Anne Elliot," *Persuasion* is also motivated by an ability to see that is no less an inability to forget.

One consequence of this nostalgia is a style and a hermeneutic unmistakably Austenian. Recording Anne's response to Wentworth's abjuration of his failure to have "done as he ought" with Louisa, the narrator makes the following observation:

Anne wondered whether it ever occurred to him now, to question the justness of his own previous opinion as to the universal felicity and advantage of firmness of character; and whether it might not strike him, that, like all other qualities of the mind, it should have its proportions and limits. She thought it could scarcely escape him to feel, that a persuadable temper might sometimes be as much in favour of happiness, as a very resolute character. (113)

The ostensible referent of these ruminations is Wentworth's earlier criticism of Anne's persuadability by which, as he believed, she was prevented by her family from marrying him. To Anne, then, "persuadability" is precisely a quality that Louisa, in refusing to heed Wentworth's injunction that she not jump the steps, has sadly lacked. Whether this thinking and the narrative's thinking are in any way commensurate is another matter. The referent or meaning of Anne's speculations would appear, in fact, to extend to a conception of persuasion that exceeds her meditations on the situation at hand. Although correct in drawing a distinction between her behavior and Louisa's, Anne is demonstrably unaware that the distinction as she conceives it is also quite negligible, in the same way that there is finally little distinction between the behavior of the two women and that of their male counterpart. In a world where compliance may issue as easily in a firm character as in an ostensibly persuadable one, it is impossible and merely self-congratulatory to limit persuasion to a particular version of obedience.

In the present example Louisa's presumed firmness of character reveals more than a simple lack of persuadability; it reveals, among other things, a persuasion in Wentworth's necessary "firmness." Louisa's conviction that there was no danger in jumping the steps despite Wentworth's advice against doing so is effectively met and recapitulated in Wentworth's self-recrimination: "Oh God! that I had not given way to her at the fatal moment! Had I done as I ought! But so eager and so resolute! Dear, sweet Louisa!" (113). The point here, which contradicts or sees beyond Anne's point, is twofold: first, that Wentworth and

Louisa are in agreement regarding Wentworth's obligation to act as "something like" Wentworth "ought," and second, that resoluteness is very much a function of persuadability. Whether it was Louisa's resolution to be caught, or Wentworth's persuasion to display firmness, or the way Wentworth's sense of giving way is suspended between a capitulation to Louisa according to the obligation to be firm and the physical act of having "given way" by *not* catching her (thereby showing the "persuadable temper" *of* "a very resolute character"), the particular happiness that Anne would deem a function of persuadability minimizes the insidious and extraordinary reach of persuasion in the many dispositions it governs. Such limitation is more than a function of Anne's wrongheadedness. It is a function ultimately of the narrator's canny collaboration with Anne, following which *other possibilities*, from the pervasion of persuasion on the occasion of Louisa's fall, to versions of happiness independent of those authorized by persuasion, are effectively broached.

Here the specters of the abject, unforgettable Wentworth and the previously abject Anne are central. Unlike Anne, whose defacement had previously been a stay against being "something like Anne Elliot," and against a version of felicity that in her current description issues largely from capitulation, the image of Wentworth shuttling in and out of quotation is a powerful if ultimately negative reminder that any other happiness, including the gratification of making a difference by being different, undoubtedly comes at too great a cost. Anne is surely right in questioning whether anything, much less something specific, could have occurred to Wentworth in his present and vacant state. For her curiosity, which tellingly wishes for a specific recognition on *his* part, is justified less by Wentworth than by the speculator herself, whose imaginary attempts at convincing Wentworth remain—in the context of both the narrative and the two critical scenes at Lyme—very real efforts at self-persuasion. The "inescapable" character of Anne's convictions, neatly transferred to someone who currently embodies what she was once, follows the equally inevitable narrative that Anne belongs to now in also remembering the "escape" *and* the particular "happiness" that "persuasion," no less than the novel so titled, glimpses by way of valediction.

Mrs. Smith's Plantation and the Two Endings

Anne's transformation at Lyme, which is both documented and deconstructed in the two critical scenes there, marks a turning point in the narrative that is irreversible. Despite some clumsy complications in volume 2 involving Mr. Elliot's interest in Anne and her family's efforts in persuading her to marry him, the end of *Persuasion*, no less than the resolution of *Pride and Prejudice* following Darcy's declarations in the second volume, is entirely a foregone conclusion. And like *Pride and Prejudice*, whose final volume assumes a nearly metafictional status in exposing (with an assist from Lydia) the cultural work that the Darcy-Elizabeth coupling otherwise mystifies, the second half of *Persuasion* follows upon the nodal scenes at Lyme in making Anne's inevitable fate as Mrs. Wentworth an object of sharply critical attention.

The only difference between the critical machinery in *Persuasion* and the critical machinery in Austen's other novels, including *Pride and Prejudice*, is that it no longer operates at the cost of narrative authority. With the scenes at Lyme as a model, in fact, the coincidence of sympathy and judgment, particularly as Anne is conscripted and rehabilitated within economy of the gaze, makes it clear that however much Anne is coopted or persuaded, this is not necessarily the narrator's wish. Rather, Anne's progress en route to becoming a captain's wife demarcates an inevitable course to which the narrator lends a critical eye simply by recounting. As a result the oppositional elements of Austen's previous novels, from the practices of seemingly marginal characters to the practices of those who are either directly derogated or, in the case of Catherine Morland, misunderstood, are incorporated to the narrator's perspective in *Persuasion* rather than becoming aspects of the novel against which narrative authority must be mobilized. It is not that Austen's narrator is without opinions in *Persuasion*, or that she fails to render judgments on, among other matters, Anne's family and their values. It is that with Anne as the focus here the narrator can engage in the business of criticism, which is also the business of disappointment, merely by attending to her subject.

We see this understanding quite clearly in the sequence of events at Lyme. Where the first scene demonstrates the persuasive effects of the male gaze and the persuasion in turn to which that gaze refers in always seizing, regardless of who is looking, on the object of beauty, the second scene explores the consequences of that demonstration. It is only after being transported back to the economy of normative relations by the gaze and by the discursive field it denotes that Anne can assist Wentworth in ways that, however called for by the situation at hand, have the additional, and readable, effect of papering over his default and failure to do as he "ought." This save is equally true of Anne's internal actions. Confronted with the decidedly specular and unforgettable image of the debased Wentworth, Anne mentally retrieves him from a position, which is the very one she had earlier occupied outside of quotation, by imagining a recognition on his part that is in fact a recent, and tentatively held, awareness of her own.

None of this is to suggest that Anne is not still an object of sympathetic identification, or that the narrative is somehow grudging in tracking her inevitable progress to matrimony. It is simply to emphasize that, even as the narrative follows and celebrates a reunion based on Wentworth's appreciation of Anne's competency as well as her beauty, it contains other elements that bear directly on the phenomenological sea change that Anne has undergone and from which she can scarcely remember her former self. The most notable of these changes, apart from Anne's remarkable pliancy where Mr. Elliot is concerned (which I am inclined, along with other readers, to regard as a badly executed sidebar to the narrative), involves her relationship with her former schoolmate Mrs. Smith. Despite the narrator's inscrutable blandness in this matter, it is virtually impossible to observe this relationship without puzzlement or the particular perplexity that *Persuasion* has ultimately substituted in place of nostalgia. Part of the problem is that Mrs. Smith, who is an invalid and a shut-in, focuses certain issues—from women's solidarity to the hidebound discriminations based on class or social status—by which Anne appears to acquit herself honorably. How, after all, are we to impugn Anne's good offices on behalf of a widow whose infirmity and lack of resources have consigned her to indigence and to living at certain buildings in Bath that Anne's father and her sister, Elizabeth, would never dream of visiting? The answer seems more or less self-explanatory, all the more in that Lady Russell, who is frequently a mediator between Anne and her father, supports such visits. But even more remarkable is the degree to which—with very few exceptions—Anne's support of Mrs. Smith is routinely interpreted according to the rather reductive protocols that the question, as I have framed it, supports.

To be sure, Mrs. Smith, like Miss Bates, is in one of those worsening predicaments to which women are constantly assigned in Austen's fiction. Nor is there any question that Anne's attention to her former friend, over and against her family's wishes, puts an ethical face not just upon the heroine herself but also upon an orientation that, in contesting the values attributed to rank and privilege, is progressive and individualistic in discovering merit in people regardless of whether they are named in the baronetage. Where questions arise is in the degree to which Anne's opposition to Sir Walter in this matter, and her subscription by implication to a standard of individual merit, of which Wentworth is also an exponent, is in any way vindicated by her actions here and by her judgment regarding her friend. For beyond the fact that Mrs. Smith is also a woman of rank and former "affluence," whose current predicament is the result of her past "dissipations" and those of her husband of whom "she had been very fond" (145), she is in the end a manipulative and mendacious person whose main goal is to regain her West Indian property, and the slaves that presumably go with it, even if that means encouraging Anne to marry someone—specifically Mr. Elliot—whom Mrs. Smith knows to be thoroughly ruthless.

The details of Mrs. Smith's caginess—from her ostentatious stoicism, to her penchant for gossip that is indistinguishable from surveillance, to her double-dealing in the matter of Mr. Elliot, who moves in her accounting from "a gentle-manlike, agreeable man" (184) to "a man without heart or conscience" (187)—are unnecessary to detail beyond this brief summary. What cannot be stressed enough is the pall that the episode involving her, which is prominent in the concluding volume, casts on the novel's drive to closure. Not only do Mrs. Smith's mendacity and greed pass without any reaction from Anne, who is unable or unwilling to connect the "manœuvres of selfishness and duplicity" that she finds "revolting" (195) in the account of Mr. Elliot to their immediate source. Mrs. Smith's principal object, which Wentworth will be instrumental in securing—the reacquisition of her plantation in the West Indies—has the additional effect of deconstructing any difference that might exist between the old order and the newer democratic order under whose auspices both slavery and the continued subjugation of women are also countenanced.

There may be some anachronism in making the West Indies, where Wentworth has been involved over the course of his career, the moral touchstone by which Anne's development or retrenchment is subject to evaluation. But there is a greater risk by far in assuming that Austen, who had read Thomas Clarkson's abolitionist tracts and claimed to "love" him as a result,[16] was not doing something significant simply in noting Anne's ready capitulation to her friend's sense of injury on the occasion of losing her property. Slavery in the Americas might not have been the abomination for Austen that it would become for Harriet Beecher Stowe. Nevertheless its irruption in *Persuasion* and, worse, its indivisibility from the narrative's comedic close, make the entire business of Mrs. Smith's West Indian property an important register of Anne's "fall" and, with it, the nondifference of the derogated world of Sir Walter and the "brave new world" that, for critics like Nina Auerbach, describes Austen's position here on the emergent England and its all-important navy.

Nowhere is this nondifference more crucial than in the treatment and condition of women, who, regardless of class, are magnets for a misogyny that is as rampant in *Persuasion* as it is anywhere in Austen. From Anne's two sisters to the conniving Mrs. Clay to the various sailors' wives beginning with Mrs. Harville and culminating in Louisa Musgrove, whose impending future as Mrs. Benwick provokes Wentworth to "surprise" that a "reading man" like Benwick could possibly choose Louisa as a wife (172–73), the women of *Persuasion* routinely oscillate between being deformed in a way that justifies their being subordinated and being subordinated so as to become deformed. This latter tendency, which we have encountered elsewhere in Austen, from the hysterical Mrs. Bennet to the kleptomaniacal Mrs. Norris, undoubtedly has some relevance to the character of

Mrs. Smith as well, who, like Mrs. Norris or Lady Bertram, is represented in all her odiousness as if this were inevitable or de rigueur.

But this tendency with women also has a more immediate import in *Persuasion*. Not only does it pass with Anne's consent even as she claims, as late as the penultimate chapter, to know better. It actually persists in the company of democratic developments, from the rise of professionalism to the tendency of couples to marry on the basis of mutual esteem rather than family edict, that bypass women at the same time that they depend on Anne for validation. Certain stark, declarative clauses regarding the novel's heroine in volume 2—that "Anne was caught" (163) or "She was lost" (165)—have a contextual basis that must be honored. However, like the altogether brilliant observation of Anne's "fall into a quotation," such statements maintain an indexical reach that bears attention. Even as Austen's narrator largely abandons her regulatory function of distributing praise and blame where the heroine is concerned, so the narrator remains, as the only locus of resistance left in the novel, a witness to certain developments that are routinely marked and defined without also being pressed in a specifically rhetorical, or again ideological, function.

Anne's dilemma, to be sure, or the statements bearing on it are scarcely immune to judgment or evaluation. However, these elements are informed by enough sympathy for Anne's powerlessness in the welter of discourse that any blame—and more important, praise—is largely nugatory. While Austen's narrator assuredly has an ideology, her values are sufficiently fragile in the face of persuasion that she comes to occupy a position whose virtual impossibility at once echoes and recapitulates the equally impossible positions of abject exteriority in which Anne first and then Wentworth temporarily find themselves. The difference is that where Anne and Wentworth are removed from their respective impossibilities by an interpellation, wherein each comes to resemble "something" suitable to the courtship plot, the narrator's consignment to an impossible position remains a relegation whose origin or root, despite its severance here, is the merely *possible*. It does not matter that the possible, or what has been the possible in Austen's fictions to this point, has been displaced in *Persuasion* to a degree that exceeds its displacement in either *Mansfield Park* or *Emma*. What matters finally is that the possibilistic positions and practices that have been variously undermined and ruled of bounds, here and elsewhere, have an afterlife in a *narrative practice* that is reciprocally removed from a regulatory or probabilistic function.

This particular development, which must be deemed a triumph for Austen, particularly in formal terms, is seen to advantage in the two endings of *Persuasion* that we are fortunate to have at our disposal. Significant, not least because the "original" ending of *Persuasion* is, as B. C. Southam reminds us, "the only [manuscript] fragment to have survived from the writing of the novels,"[17] the initial versions of chapters 10 and 11 in volume 2, which were distended into chapters 10, 11, and 12 in the published version, are especially important in their omission of certain details, notably the extended discussion on men and women that necessitated the addition of another chapter in the weeks following the novel's completion in July 1816. Austen also instituted a number of other changes in the final version that, as Southam notes, make that ending more satisfying on the grounds of verisimilitude. But the principal changes, which Southam's otherwise useful discussion overlooks, show by contrast that the original two-chapter ending of *Persuasion* was deficient less for its contrivances than for the narrator's relatively uncritical absorption in the lovers' reunion. Reifying the protagonists' wish-fulfilling fantasies, the narrator's almost breathless absorption in the original ending undoes much of the political and hermeneutic work, where in their rather obvious legitimation of middle-class dominance at home and abroad the lovers are necessarily diminished. The rapid and overheated closure of the original version, with its ampersands and other contractions, may very well prevent Anne and Wentworth from "com[ing] together with a full understanding of the past" (Southam, "Two Chapters," 94). But this version, contrary to Southam's sense of it, is not particularly demeaning to them. The problem with the original ending is that it is not critical enough, that it is too much a vehicle for the particular ideology that, as the final version shows by contrast, is not to be mounted so easily on the back of a woman's requital. The final version of *Persuasion* shows that, however much the narrative must yield to the terms of culture and society in securing Anne's marriage to Wentworth and in making them an exemplary couple, the narrative also follows its central character in being no more than a capitulation.

The final ending of *Persuasion* nicely justifies the novel's designation as the most subjective of Austen's texts in focusing on Anne's particular engagement with the world before her. Although this engagement no doubt characterizes the original ending as well, along with much of the narrative that precedes it, the final ending follows directly on the transformations at Lyme in effectively dissociating Anne from the narrator. If the focus on Anne's interiority at the novel's close necessarily accords with the ideology of individualism to which the narrative, or at least the courtship plot, would appear to subscribe, it is simultaneously a device by which, from the narrator's perspective, Anne is on her own and thereby set in relief. Thus while she does not hesitate to describe Anne's immediate milieu to the benefit of the heroine, the narrator is equally careful to mark the heroine's nondifference from that same order.

Beginning, as the first ending does, with Anne's disgust over the disclosures regarding Mr. Elliot that she has just received from Mrs. Smith, the published version of chapter 10 also differs from the original chapter in coordinating Anne's judgment on her cousin to a defense of her immediate family, whose vulnerability at the hands of this apparent schemer seems somewhat deserved. Mr. Elliot and Mrs. Clay may very well be as selfish as Anne worriedly opines. But they are certainly no more selfish than Elizabeth Elliot or Sir Walter, who make a notably appalling entrance here by initially mocking Lady Russell's physical appearance and by their usual attempts to avoid contact with people whom they deem inferior. Then, of course, there are the Musgrove sisters, whose impending marriages to Charles Hayter and Captain Benwick respectively are regarded by Anne with a condescension that jibes uneasily with her renewed interest in Wentworth (and in his hoped-for interest in herself) to which she and the narrative immediately turn their attention.

If, in comparison to these other couplings, not to mention the eventual union of Mr. Elliot and Mrs. Clay, Anne and Wentworth necessarily put an attractive face on the institution and ideal of a companionate marriage, their prestige is no less a matter of their *relative*—as opposed to pure—merit as individuals. The tedious conversation surrounding Henrietta's forthcoming marriage that commences chapter 11 may seem like so much ambient noise to Anne, who quietly endures it in the company of Wentworth at the White Hart hotel. Yet it is equally clear that the conversation's eventual and necessary "application" (217) to the heroine is plainly coextensive with the *entire* discussion— or what amounts really to the ambient field of discourse per se—that Anne fatuously finds irrelevant. Of particular relevance to Anne are Mrs. Croft's observations on the imprudence of marrying early and without means to which Anne suddenly attends with a "nervous" alacrity (217). The particular way this discourse reaches out to a reciprocally receptive Anne is significant. Not only does this recall Anne's "persuasion" at Lyme, which is tellingly reprised in the exchange of glances that she immediately shares with Wentworth, who is doubly "in language" now—both listening *and writing* a letter. It reveals, in necessarily simplifying the motives behind her initial rejection of him, Anne's thoroughgoing, and at this point literal, submersion in "quotation."

The bearing of the quotable on Anne's renewed love, which is really a new or "learned" love, is further reflected in the extended dialogue with Harville that ensues. This dialogue on the essential differences of men and women, which has no counterpart in the original ending, is important now for several reasons. In emphasizing the imbalance that currently characterizes gender relations, where women are neurotically "confined" and men are happily "forced on exertion"

(219), the dialogue both punctuates *and* punctures the marriage plot in *Persuasion* by exposing the false symmetry and the false democracy that sexual difference, and the marital ideal it serves, continues to uphold. More important, the dialogue also shows that even as Anne is sufficiently in quotation that she must confuse the material bases of a woman's disposition with what she and Harville repeatedly regard as natural and innate to women, she retains a sense, or more properly a memory, that something is not quite right or as it should be.

This recognition cum recollection figures most prominently in Anne's reminder to Harville that the many encomiums on male constancy over time owe to the fact that "the pen," as Anne nicely puts it, "has been in their hands" (221). It is manifest in other forms as well, from Anne's reprisal of the naturalized division of labor proscribed in the conduct manuals of Thomas Gisborne and others to her overdetermined insistence, in ostensible defense of women's loyalty, of "loving longest, when existence or when hope is gone" (222). While this concluding maxim confuses Anne's early love for Wentworth, which *was* resistible, with the "learned" and irresistible "romance" that currently governs her affections, the insistence on loving in the absence of *both* hope and existence has a curiously transhistorical reach. Although apposite to her revised sense of the past, in which she never stopped loving Wentworth, Anne's clinching claim on behalf of women's constancy bears powerfully and skeptically on her present and future condition, where marriage and the loss of existence—or such existence as Anne has known—maintain some relation.

None of this awareness, of course, is sufficient to prevent, or to delay beyond this point, the narrative's now inevitable movement to marital closure. But the dialogue on the sexes is sufficient to shadow this otherwise gratifying close and its attendant eclaircissement in ways that are palpable and evidently to the narrator's purpose. The letter to Anne, for example, that Wentworth has been composing during her debate with Harville, and which results immediately in their reunion as lovers, is not only filled with enough cliché and quotation to suggest that loving and learning are necessarily synonymous. Wentworth's letter reveals, more important—and by jointure of the hackneyed and coercive—that the "pen" is still in the hands of men. Thus while Anne's response to Wentworth's initiative is notably yielding, even as it is judged by the narrator to be something from which she must "recove[r]" (224), it is insufficient in dispelling a sense of the sacrifice or loss that marriage to Wentworth will entail.

Such loss emerges in *Persuasion*'s concluding sentences, where the "dread of a future war" and the "glor[y]" of "being a sailor's wife," are inextricably and pathetically yoked, never more perhaps than in the ironic designation of wifehood as a "profession" (237). But the real sense of loss, which is a reminder at the same time that the pen is not always in the hands of men, even if the prerogatives of professionalism are, comes in the two interrogatives that inaugurate the final chapter in both the original and published versions:

Who can be in doubt of what followed? When any two young people take it into their heads to marry, they are pretty sure by perseverance to carry their point, be they ever so poor, or ever so imprudent, or ever so little likely to be necessary to each other's ultimate comfort. This may be bad morality to conclude with, but I believe it to be truth; and if such parties succeed, how should a Captain Wentworth and an Anne Elliot, with the advantage of maturity of mind, consciousness of right, and one independent fortune between them, fail of bearing down every opposition? (233)

This is hardly the first time that Austen's narrator reverts to the first person in her fictions, or the first time that such reversion is an invitation to regard the narrator as a character with opinions of her own.

    Still, without exaggerating what might also have been a oversight or simply a shift that did not, in Austen's view, compromise the formal rigor of her achievement, the narrator's position seems largely descriptive of, even hostile to, its subject rather than supportive. The "bad morality," to which the narrator confesses yet assigns the mantle of "truth," may simply be the success with which young couples routinely meet at a time when "affective individualism" rather than "parental tyranny" increasingly governs relational decisions. But the "truth" of the narrator's convictions bears as much on this particular observation as it does on the horizon of disappointment to which marriage, in general, appears to give access. The two questions here, which are about resistance to marriage and about the sites from which either "opposition" or "doubt" may be registered, are not simply rhetorical. They are, like so many interrogatives in Austen, remarkably open-ended. They are questions, in other words, directed to a readership whose exposure to the prerogatives of the pen involves two things. It involves the ability to witness what the reader, no less than the writer, is also incapable of changing *and* the *inability* to resist what, for the reader no less than for Anne, is too imitable in the end to be opposed.

The Two Willingdens

One of the preoccupations of the critics who write on *Sanditon*, no less than of Austen's more uncritical enthusiasts, has been to speculate on the likely trajectory of the twelve-chapter fragment that Austen gave up writing several months before her death in 1817. Although the speculations on *Sanditon*'s eventual progress vary in certain particulars, they are nearly unanimous in discounting a striking prospect that is far from implausible given the information that *Sanditon* has already made available. I am referring to the possible recruitment of Miss Lambe, the wealthy "half Mullato" from the West Indies who arrives at Sanditon in the final pages, to a courtship plot involving the impoverished and comically rakish Sir Edward Denham. This specter of miscegenation and its projected adulteration of aristocratic bloodlines is undoubtedly deflected by Miss Lambe's ambiguous constitution as someone "chilly and tender" (373)[18] and by the likelihood that Clara Brereton, the protegée of Sir Edward's wealthy and selfish stepmother, Lady Denham, will presumably serve his expectations as felicitously as she will Austen's purposes as a comedienne of manners.[19] Nevertheless the radical otherness to which the West Indian refers us and onto which the plot of *Sanditon* might well have opened, cannot be underestimated. I say this not because I am convinced that this is how things would have developed had Austen lived to finish *Sanditon*. Rather I emphasize its possibility as a line of development largely to discountenance the speculations that proceed from the assumption that *Sanditon* is a novel that, however eccentric, is characteristically Austenian in some conventional way.

While readers are quick to observe that *Sanditon* differs from Austen's previous productions in making the heroine, Charlotte Heywood, a reliable observer whose judgments on the outlandish aspects of the culture of invalidism are immune to any further ironization or criticism, most readers are equally determined to coordinate *Sanditon* to aspects of Austen's writings on which her role in the genesis of realism, particularly as a regulatory apparatus, is based. According to Marvin Mudrick, the irony that pervades Austen's oeuvre as a defensive apparatus against the blameworthy is extended in *Sanditon* in what is virtually a panirony wherein everything—from "the society of appearances [Austen] lives in" to "*all* the personal impulses conniving with or at war against it"—is exposed in its "intrinsic equivocalness" (257). Although such equivocalness undoubtedly hearkens in directions apart from the fundamentally conservative disaffection that Mudrick and readers after him plausibly regard as having inspired this archly satiric work, almost no one will take seriously the reversion in *Sanditon* to a mode of characterization that, however indebted to certain eighteenth-century precedents, is even more remarkable in the mode of fictional representation from which it is a departure. There exists, of course, a long and venerable link between satiric convention and a largely conservative ideology. At the same time, the prevalence in *Sanditon* of characters at once flat and hyperbolic has the more immediate effect of undoing the somewhat sinister work of naturalization that fictions of probability routinely performed in the service of conservative political goals.

There is little doubt that Austen's various achievements prior to *Sanditon* did more in the end for fictions of probability and for the institution of realism they helped spawn than the productions of any other contemporary novelist. Still it would be both wrong and anachronistic to take her instrumentality in the institution of the novel as evidence of Austen's political or, for that matter, aesthetic affiliations. Even if Austen was the most important and influential novelist of her period, especially in retrospect, she was, as recently as *Persuasion*, demonstrably at odds with the social and political work in which both her fictions and their deployment of free indirect discourse were paradoxically quite central. Such self-contestation may not have been sufficiently obvious or detrimental to impress subsequent generations with Austen's ambivalence regarding certain representational conventions and their aims. Yet it is one of the larger claims of this book that at the moment of their inception, when protocols of reading and writing were less firmly entrenched, Austen's works were both readable and writeable to other effects, many of which stand in uneasy relation to the development of the novel as an increasingly mimetic genre.

In raising the specter of the antireal, particularly as a contestional mode where realism is concerned, I am not suggesting that probabilistic fiction maintains a referentiality independent of either contrivance or of the many complications that language, as an arbitrary and figurative apparatus, brings to any verbal act. I am suggesting only that the origins of fiction in *the fictive*, the fabulous, or in this case the allegorical were relatively close by at the juncture that the novel had presumably risen and that they were a palpable resource for a writer whose project, as we have seen, was taken up with disentangling the quotidian and the probable. This point, or one akin to it, is touched on comically in *Sanditon* when Sir Edward, who fashions himself a latter-day Lovelace, speaks approvingly of novels that display "Human Nature with Grandeur" and "in the Sublimities of intense Feeling" in contrast to novels concerned only with the "vapid tissues of ordinary Occurrences" (*Sanditon*, 357). Sir Edward's comments work undoubtedly to satirize contemporary literary criticism, including the debate over the "progress of romance." But the larger point, to which his dissection of the current fictional scene refers us, is that the novel, if only by the narrative currently before us, is a genre with a past as well as a future.

Austen's recourse, then, to a representational mode whose characters are flat and thematic, as opposed to round and complex, should not surprise us in *Sanditon* any more than this recursion to the exaggerated or the allegorical represents a departure from her achievement to date.[20] Just as Austen's characteristic mode invariably involves the situation of a central and complex consciousness within a field of types and sketches, many of whom—including Colonel Brandon—work to allegorical or thematic purposes, so her project overall is virtually suspended between certain generic imperatives, the majority clustering around free indirect discourse as an armature of the realistic imagination, and a generic memory (for want of a better term) where, in modes ranging from allegory to epistolarity, reading and interpretation may ultimately supersede narrative authority. Sir Edward, as Tony Tanner remarks, is clearly misreading Richardson's *Clarissa* in adopting Lovelace as a role model. Yet as Tanner is also quick to observe, the epistolary form that Richardson deployed as a vehicle for instruction gave rise in the end to an "ineradicable ambiguity" to which the "portrait of Sir Edward" clearly refers us (278–80).

The deployment in *Sanditon* of a fictive mode that is chiefly allegorical rather than either probable or realistic is important for two reasons. It is important for the reading practices that it necessarily encourages *and* for its radical subjection of Austen's world to an alterity or defamiliarity that, in the manner of the miscegenation plot, is at crosspurposes with domestic fiction, particularly as a vehicle of regulation. Over and against the ostensible purpose of this satire, which apparently is to lament the shifting sands on which the "new" as such has been erected, allegory's inevitable recursion to the thematic and the abstract manages in a single stroke to do two things. It upends the naturalizing work of probabilistic fiction in its conservative manifestation; and it underscores, in this particular instance, the culture of sickness to which the status quo—as both represented and advocated by fictions of probability—is figuratively tantamount.

The initial sense that "there is something wrong here" (*Sanditon,* 321), which the entrepreneurial Mr. Parker observes on the occasion of injuring his ankle in the inaugural episode, follows nicely on the heels of Austen's fictions to date. But *Sanditon* also proves an elaboration on *Persuasion*'s sense that its heroine, for example, is somehow "lost" or "caught" in Mr. Parker's immediate assurance to his wife that a "cure" (322) for what is wrong is presumably close by. In the very way that, in allegorical terms at least, Mr. Parker's confidence fixates on a horizon of melioration, it manages, according to these same terms, both to meet and miss its mark in the erroneous assumption that a surgeon is within a very short distance from them.

Mr. Parker's actual mistake is that the town of Willingden, where his carriage has overturned and where he had hoped to find a surgeon to employ at his resort in Sanditon, is not the same Willingden where there *is* a surgeon "wishing to form a separate Establishment" (323). Parker's misrecognition, then, neatly juxtaposes the panacea of professionalism and another type of cure to which medicine, or more properly the medical "Establishment," is altogether inimical. It is by no means clear that the Willingden without a surgeon is demonstrably a better place than the Willingden unvisited, where there are currently at least two doctors. Still, in the context of Austen's *allegory*, the two Willingdens are not, strictly speaking, different places. Rather they represent or figure *different prospects* for "Willingden" in the same way that the plot of *Sanditon* may conceivably extend either to miscegenation or to a more conventional, less disruptive resolution.

Most commentary on *Sanditon* has focused justifiably on the culture of invalidism to which the new in Austen's reckoning is pretty much equivalent. From the speculative ventures of the entrepreneurial Mr. Parker to the already decaying resort that he is in the process of developing to the numerous affectations of Regency society, ranging from ostentatious philanthropy to excessive hypochondria and self-absorption, the world depicted in this fragment would appear to justify Alistair Duckworth's sense of its being so "removed from traditional grounds of moral action that its retrieval through former fictional means is no longer possible" (221).[21] There is something ingenious in Duckworth's interpretation, particularly its ability to marshal a fictional mode that is the very antithesis of regulatory writing—or such writing as Austen would have produced were she inclined—in the service of a fundamentally conservative action. If *Sanditon* appears to be a work by anyone but the author of *Mansfield Park*, it is not because the author is changed utterly. It is because the adoption of "an unswervingly moral stance would," as Duckworth speculates, have necessarily "condemn[ed]" both Austen and *Sanditon* "to a continually melancholic recognition of the disparity between moral ideal and social fact" (221).

Such melancholy also accounts for Marvin Mudrick's conception of *Sanditon* as opposed to virtually everything in life. What such claims for Austen's sudden or eventual disenchantment do not address, however, is the melancholy or disappointment that has long informed her writing and to which the perplexity of *Persuasion*, no less than the allegory at hand, may be referred. If *Sanditon* assumes a fictional form where there is evidently no room or prospect for the moral alternative that abides in a character such as *Mansfield Park*'s Fanny Price, it is not because these alternatives are no longer available. It is because such alternatives are, along with the institution of domestic fiction, sufficiently part of the problem to warrant a different approach.

One way of getting at this new approach, which is as consistent with *Sanditon*'s peculiar detachment as it is with the works that precede it, is to follow Austen's invitation to read *Sanditon* allegorically, particularly regarding the "something" that "is wrong here." In this we are presented with three modes of engagement in the form of three types of characters. There are characters, like Mr. Parker, who know "something is wrong" and engage it through the offices of either doctors or other institutions of healing. There are also characters, like the selfish and autocratic Lady Denham, who are plainly part of what is wrong "here" even as they regard themselves and the hierarchical world they live in as apogees of health. Last but not least there are the hypochondriacs, specifically Arthur, Diana, and Susan Parker. Although obsessively aware of their bodily infirmities and functions, these characters are plainly intent on healing themselves rather than relying on the institutions of what their brother suggestively terms "civilization."

Tony Tanner offers a similar assessment of *Sanditon* in observing that the main characters are best understood "from the point of view of the various discourses which they employ—or which employ them: namely, the discourses of advertising, hypochondria and quack medicine, money, and literary criticism" (264). Where such "discourse-imbrication," as Tanner terms it, leads to a "group glossolalia" in which the prospects for genuine communication and social health are essentially nil, it is the argument here that not all of these discourses work in the all-consuming way that he outlines. Where the discourses of advertising and money, for example, are indivisible from those characters who, as Tanner suggests, are fundamentally employees, the discourse of hypochondria, whose adherents are self-sufficient rather than "helpless Invalides" (363), bears additional scrutiny. It warrants this attention thanks largely to the novel that precedes *Sanditon*, where the abject body in pain and the body in quotation bear a similar disaffiliation. Very much like *Sanditon*'s valetudinarians, the heroine of *Persuasion* not only appropriates a number of discourses or persuasions on behalf of her continued autonomy. She also maintains her autonomy under the sign of pallor rather than at the disposal of ideology, which is responsible, in turn, for her ambiguous restoration.

Without minimizing the extraordinary lengths that the hypochondriacs of *Sanditon* sometimes go to heal themselves, or the satiric yield of their efforts, it is interesting that in addition to being the most vital and dynamic characters here, the hypochondriacs are, in their peculiar bodily absorption, the characters *least affected* by outside influence, notably the discourses of professionalization and medicine. Nor is it any coincidence that in same way the body in endless complaint remains, like the ravaged Anne of *Persuasion*, a body outside or apart from "quotation," it is reciprocally the case that such bodies, from the gluttonous Arthur to the anorexic Susan to the frenzied Diana, remain, in Austen's culminating allegorical stroke, exceptionally healthy.[22]

There is undoubtedly something melancholy (to borrow Duckworth's notion) about a world whose only escape or opposition is available in the form of pathological abjection. But there is also something bracing about a possibility that, however consigned to the realm of the ridiculous, marks an alternative to the "group glossolalia" where, to follow Mr. Parker's own logic, "civilization" remains a homeopathic entity whose afflictions and remedies are virtually undifferentiable. Regardless of whether the trajectory of Jane Austen's achievement is, as *Sanditon* makes clear, a progress toward an ever greater melancholia or disenchantment with all that is "wrong here," it remains a project consistently inflected by the prospect of a significantly different and more equitable configuration among humans, to which disappointment, however prevalent, is always answerable.

Notes

Abbreviations

ELH   *English Literary History*
MLQ   *Modern Language Quarterly*
PQ   *Philological Quarterly*
RES   *Review of English Studies*
SiR   *Studies in Romanticism*
TSLL *Texas Studies in Literature and Language*

Introduction

1. See, for example, Marilyn Butler, *Jane Austen and the War of Ideas* (Oxford: Clarendon Press, 1975), and Alistair Duckworth, *The Improvement of the Estate* (Baltimore: Johns Hopkins University Press, 1971). See also Nancy Armstrong, *Desire and Domestic Fiction: A Political History of the Novel* (New York: Oxford University Press, 1987), 3–160; Gary Kelly, *English Fiction of the Romantic Period, 1798-1830* (London: Longman, 1989), 111–38; and Deborah Kaplan, *Jane Austen among Women* (Baltimore: Johns Hopkins University Press, 1992). Among the feminist approaches to Austen that are historical in focus, see especially Mary Poovey, *The Proper Lady and the Woman Writer* (Chicago: University of Chicago Press, 1984), 172–246; Margaret Kirkham, *Jane Austen, Feminism, and Fiction* (Totowa: Barnes and Noble, 1983); Claudia Johnson, *Jane Austen: Women, Politics, and the Novel* (Chicago: University of Chicago Press, 1988); and Alison G. Sulloway, *Jane Austen and the Province of Womanhood* (Philadelphia: University of Pennsylvania Press, 1989).

2. I am indebted here to the call for a denser history that Michel de Certeau urges as a corrective to the "realistic" or historical practice, whose status as an "objective discourse" is marked by a fidelity to the "thinkable" rather than to what may have in fact happened. See especially *Heterologies: Discourse on the Other*, trans. Brian Massumi (Minneapolis: University of Minnesota Press, 1986), and *The Writing of History*, trans. Tom Conley (New York: Columbia University Press, 1988).

3. *The Country and the City* (New York: Oxford University Press, 1973), 115–16.

4. References to Scott's review are to the text in *Jane Austen: The Critical Heritage*, ed. B. C. Southam (London: Routledge and Kegan Paul, 1968), 59–69. For a quite different interpretation, both of Austen's impact on her immediate readership and of Scott's assessment of Austen's newness in this regard, see Clifford Siskin, "Jane Austen and the Engendering of Disciplinarity," in *Jane Austen and the Discourses of Feminism*, ed. Devoney Looser (New York: St. Martin's, 1995), 51–67. According to Siskin, Austen's writings were "received not only as pleasurable but as *comfortable*" and this "comfort," he argues, was instrumental in the "privileged position" that her fictions rather quickly achieved (58–61). Although Siskin enlists "history" to justify his claim, it is the view here that Austen's immediate (and historicizable) reception was at the very least, and with Scott as perhaps the prime example, remarkably overdetermined and a good deal more dynamic and unsettling.

5. *The Order of Mimesis: Balzac, Stendhal, Nerval, Flaubert* (Cambridge: Cambridge University Press, 1986).

6. "L'Effet de réel," *Communications* 11 (1968): 84–89.

7. See Clara Reeve, *The Progress of Romance* (Colchester, 1785). See also Richard Payne Knight, *An Analytical Inquiry into the Principles of Taste* (London, 1805).

8. "The Rhetoric of Temporality," in *Blindness and Insight: Essays in the Rhetoric of Contemporary Criticism*, 2d ed. (Minneapolis: University of Minnesota Press, 1983), 206.

9. *The Rise of the Novel* (Berkeley: University of California Press), 193.

10. Marilyn Butler, *Maria Edgeworth: A Literary Biography* (Oxford: Clarendon Press, 1972), 445.

11. *The Romantic Ideology: A Critical Investigation* (Chicago: University of Chicago Press, 1983), 18–19.

Chapter 1. History, Silence, and "The Trial of Jane Leigh Perrot"

1. I am indebted, for historical and biographical particulars regarding both Austen and her family, to three recent biographies: John Halperin's *The Life of Jane Austen* (Baltimore: Johns Hopkins University Press, 1984); Park Honan's *Jane Austen: Her Life* (London: Weidenfeld and Nicolson, 1987); and David Nokes's *Jane Austen: A Life* (Berkeley: University of California Press, 1998). For Austen's relationship to the wars with France, see Warren Roberts, *Jane Austen and the French Revolution* (London: Macmillan, 1979). In addition to her brothers Francis and Charles, who served in the British navy against France, Austen's first cousin Eliza, Countess de Feuillide, was initially married to a French nobleman who died during the Revolution. Eliza subsequently married Austen's older brother Henry.

2. For readings of Austen that recur to history as a way of positioning her writings ideologically, see Marilyn Butler, *Jane Austen and the War of Ideas* (Oxford: Clarendon Press, 1975); Alistair Duckworth, *The Improvement of the Estate* (Baltimore: Johns Hopkins University Press, 1971); Claudia Johnson, *Jane Austen: Women, Politics, and the Novel* (Chicago: University of Chicago Press, 1988); Margaret Kirkham, *Jane Austen: Feminism and Fiction* (Totowa: Barnes and Noble, 1983); and Alison G. Sulloway, *Jane Austen and the Province of Womanhood* (Philadelphia: University of Pennsylvania Press, 1989).

3. *Jane Austen among Women* (Baltimore: Johns Hopkins University Press, 1992).

4. For the "subversive" Austen, see Johnson, *Jane Austen: Women, Politics, and the Novel*. See also Sandra Gilbert and Susan Gubar, *The Madwoman in the Attic: The Woman Writer and the Nineteenth-Century Literary Imagination* (New Haven, Conn.: Yale University Press, 1979), 107–83. For the more constrained Austen, see Sulloway, *Jane Austen and the Province of Womanhood*, and especially Mary Poovey, *The Proper Lady and the Woman Writer* (Chicago: University of Chicago Press, 1984), 172–246.

5. *Desire and Domestic Fiction: A Political History of the Novel* (New York: Oxford University Press, 1987), 136–38.

6. A similar view of Austen's function in both addressing and facilitating the transformation of English culture from a largely patriarchal order to an order, whose focus on the individual was a consequence, in turn, of the increasingly alienating effects of capitalism and related consumerism, is advanced by James Thompson in *Between Self and World: The Novels of Jane Austen* (University Park: Pennsylvania State University Press, 1988).

7. *English Fiction of the Romantic Period, 1789–1830* (London: Longman, 1989), 19.

8. The most comprehensive treatment of Austen in conjunction with nineteenth-century realism is George Levine's *The Realistic Imagination* (Chicago: University of Chicago Press, 1981), which regards Austen's coordination of the imperatives of self to those of society as a foundational moment in realistic practice. I take up Levine more directly in Chapter 5 of this book.

9. Ann Bermingham remarks, with an assist from Roland Barthes, on the efforts to naturalize enclosural practices through landscape gardening in *Landscape and Ideology: The English Rustic Tradition, 1740–1860* (Berkeley: University of California Press, 1986), 1–54.

10. Although, as Bermingham notes in *Landscape and Ideology*, "picturesque nature" (particularly "as defined by Price and Knight") "embodied the values and worldview of the wealthy landowning class" (83), she notes, too, that "at a deeper level the picturesque endorsed the results of agricultural industrialization" and, by implication, the "industrial employer-employee relationship, bounded only by a cash nexus," that was gradually supplanting the "paternalistic, quasi-feudal system of reciprocal rights and duties" that the picturesque, with its "emphasis on age," simultaneously upheld (74–75). Through its various affiliations, then, the picturesque ultimately served a larger, if still specific, hegemony that included, all complaints to the contrary, the new industrial class.

11. Jean-François Lyotard, "Answering the Question: What Is Postmodernism?," in *The Postmodern Condition: A Report on Knowledge*, trans. Geoff Bennington and Brian Massumi (Minneapolis: University of Minnesota Press, 1984), 79.

12. For a treatment of classic realism that interrogates the degree of political unconsciousness on the part of its nineteenth-century practitioners (including Austen), see Levine, *The Realistic Imagination*. See also, of course, Ian Watt, *The Rise of the Novel* (Berkeley: University of California Press), 290–301.

13. B. C. Southam, "*Lady Susan* and the Lost Originals, 1795–1800," in *Jane Austen's Literary Manuscripts* (London: Oxford University Press, 1964), 45–62. According to Southam, both *Pride and Prejudice* and *Sense and Sensibility* were originally novels-in-letters (like *Lady Susan*) whereas *Northanger Abbey*, the first novel that Austen tried to have published, was likely never an epistolary novel.

14. For the linguistic implications of free indirect discourse, see especially Ann Banfield, *Unspeakable Sentences: Narration and the Representation of Language in Fiction*

(London: Routledge and Kegan Paul, 1982). Among the most important features of free indirect discourse or what Banfield calls "represented speech and action" is its sheer impossibility in linguistic terms, since in narrative, according to Banfield, "language emerges free of communication and confronts its other in the form of a sentence empty of all subjectivity" (10). As arguably the first truly effective practitioner of such discourse, Austen, I believe, either intuited or recognized these implications, particularly to the degree that narrative technique is largely a device in her hands rather than the expression of an actual human subject.

15. "Realism and the Cinema: Notes on Some Brechtian Theses," in *Tracking the Signifier* (Minneapolis: University of Minnesota Press, 1985), 35. See also Dorrit Cohn, *Transparent Minds: Narrative Modes for Presenting Consciousness in Fiction* (Princeton, N.J.: Princeton University Press, 1978).

16. My conception of silence in Austen differs significantly from Susan Lanser's sense of "reticence" in Austen's fiction, which she construes as something of a reaction formation to the initial rejection of *Northanger Abbey* and, in particular, of its authorial voice. ("Sense and Reticence: Jane Austen's 'Indirections,' " in *Fictions of Authority: Women Writers and Narrative Voice* [Ithaca: Cornell University Press, 1992], 61–80.) Austen's "mov[e] . . . from epistolarity" (as Lanser terms it) may well reflect a "certain impatience with the (now waning) letter novel" (67–68). But it also retains the extra-fictional apparatus that merely organizes the discourse of an epistolary fiction (Lanser, *The Narrative Act: Point of View in Fiction* [Princeton, N.J.: Princeton University Press, 1981], 147) without also making that organizational imperative either tantamount or prelusive to the authority of a vocal and more public narrative voice. Consequently, unlike the "hierarchical interrelationships" that, as Lanser shows, inform the textual voice in realistic or free indirect discourse (*The Narrative Act*, 108–48), the peculiar leveling attendant upon epistolarity (where a character has at least as much authority as the extrafictional collater), and upon the residue of epistolary silence in Austen's more "realistic" and seemingly authoritative fictions, is directed, among other things, toward an undermining of the very authority to which (as Lanser contends) Austen otherwise aspires.

17. See, for example, Elizabeth Deeds Ermath, *Realism and Consensus in the English Novel* (Princeton, N.J.: Princeton University Press, 1983).

18. *The Constitution of Society: Outline of the Theory of Structuration* (Berkeley: University of California Press, 1984).

19. Michel Foucault, *The Order of Things: An Archaeology of the Human Sciences* (New York: Vintage, 1970), xxiii; Williams, *The Country and the City* (New York: Oxford University Press), 115.

20. Malcolm Elwin, *Lord Byron's Wife* (New York: Harcourt, Brace, 1962), 159.

21. *The Journal of Mary Frampton*, ed. Harriot Georgiana Mundy (London: Sampson Low, 1885), 226.

22. *The Origins of the English Novel, 1600–1740* (Baltimore: Johns Hopkins University Press, 1987), 212–70.

23. The radical nature of Austen's "historical" practice, as I detail in the next chapter, was not lost on her contemporaries, who regularly credited her with having initiated a practice of social history or a history of ordinary life in contradistinction to history so-called, which was a genre akin to romance in dealing exclusively with great people and extraordinary events.

24. Randolph Trumbach, *The Rise of the Egalitarian Family: Aristocratic Kinship and Domestic Relations in Eighteenth-Century England* (New York: Academic Press, 1978); Lawrence Stone, *The Family, Sex, and Marriage in England, 1500–1800* (New York: Harper and Row, 1979). See also Leonore Davidoff and Catherine Hall, *Family Fortunes: Men and Women of the English Middle Class, 1780–1850* (Chicago: University of Chicago Press, 1987).

25. See especially Davidoff and Hall, *Family Fortunes*, who track the gradual and systematic containment of middle-class women in the nineteenth century.

26. For a discussion of the Austen family's finances and the financial realities of gentry women in general, see Edward Copeland, *Women Writing About Money: Women's Fiction in England, 1790–1820* (Cambridge: Cambridge University Press, 1995), 1–115.

27. *The Country and the City*, 115.

28. *The Practice of Everyday Life*, trans. Steven Rendall (Berkeley: University of California Press, 1984), 25.

29. "Panopticism," in *Discipline and Punish: The Birth of the Prison*, trans. Alan Sheridan (New York: Vintage, 1979), 195–228.

30. See both *The Writing of History*, trans. Tom Conley (New York: Columbia University Press, 1988), and *Heterologies: Discourse on the Other*, trans. Brian Massumi (Minneapolis: University of Minnesota Press, 1986).

31. In this sense Austen addresses a problem that, as Jim Reilly has recently observed, has significant bearing on representational practice in nineteenth-century fiction: namely, the sense (which Reilly derives variously from Nietzsche, Benjamin, and Adorno) that the writing of history succeeds in doing nothing more than dissolving history "into voluminous discourse" (*Shadowtime: History and Representation in Hardy, Conrad, and George Eliot* [London: Routledge, 1993], 37). Such dissolution, then, creates a "blind spot" (23) that Bentham, for his part, underscores in privileging fiction as a better form of history writing. Yet, as Bentham also suggests (and Austen shows), it is a blind spot whose illumination is impossible without first acknowledging the fundamental opacity and incomprehensibility of events—past, passing, and to come.

32. *Room for Maneuver: Reading (the) Oppositional (in) Narrative* (Chicago: University of Chicago Press, 1991).

33. *Authoritarian Fictions: The Ideological Novel as a Literary Genre* (New York: Columbia University Press, 1983).

34. S. H. Romilly, *Letters to "Ivy" from the First Earl of Dudley* (London: Longmans, 1905), 194.

35. References to Austen's correspondence are to the texts of her letters in *Jane Austen's Letters to Her Sister Cassandra and Others*, 2d ed., ed. R. W. Chapman (London: Oxford University Press, 1959). As Chapman indicates in his introduction, Austen's sister Cassandra apparently destroyed the greater part of their correspondence several years before her own death. This correspondence may well have included more specific (and indeed candid) references to Perrot's trial. Nevertheless the references to Aunt Perrot that have survived seem candid enough, suggesting another motivation behind the absence of any reference to her legal difficulties.

36. *Grand Larceny: Being the Trial of Jane Leigh Perrot, Aunt of Jane Austen* (London: Oxford University Press, 1937).

37. David Gilson, *A Bibliography of Jane Austen* (Oxford: Clarendon Press, 1982), 454.

38. Dyce's marginalia appears in the editions of Austen's novels that formerly belonged to him and are now in the library of the Victoria and Albert Museum, London.

39. The most widely circulated transcript of the Perrot trial, the Taunton edition, is reprinted in facsimile as an appendix to MacKinnon's book. The Bath edition, a copy of which is in the British Library, was published by one of Perrot's alleged blackmailers, William Gye, whose interest in the millinery shop and involvement in the case overall is typically downplayed in this less detailed account. Still another transcript of the trial was published in London of which there is only one known copy extant. The account of the trial in the *Lady's Magazine* (Apr. 1800), which included an engraving of Mrs. Perrot, is a composite of the Bath and Taunton transcripts whereas the lengthy account in the *Bath Herald* (5 Apr. 1800) derives almost exclusively from the transcript taken for eventual publication in Taunton. The only other known newspaper accounts, those in the *Bath Journal* (31 Mar. 1800) and the *Bath Chronicle* (5 Apr. 1800), were the result of independent reportage.

40. The parts of the letters to the Perrots that I cite are from my transcriptions of the actual letters, which I examined in the presence of their current holder, Mrs. Evelyn Fowle of Hampshire, England.

41. The transcript of Perrot's courtroom speech is the text of that speech in a letter to her cousin Mountague Cholmeley that Perrot wrote several days after her acquittal. All references to this speech (207–12) and to the other letters that passed between Perrot and her friends and family at the time of her incarceration and trial are to the texts of the letters in *Austen Papers, 1704–1856*, ed. R. A. Austen-Leigh (London: Spottiswoode, Ballantyne, 1942).

42. Given the fundamentally secretive nature of kleptomania—as distinct from, say, juvenile shoplifting—it is perhaps not surprising that the psychoanalytic literature on this problem, which requires that subjects admit to such behavior, is remarkably meager. *The Concordance to the Standard Edition of the Complete Psychological Works of Sigmund Freud,* 2d ed., 6 vols., ed. Samuel A. Guttman, with the collaboration of Stephen M. Parrish and Randall L. Jones (New York: International Universities Press, 1984) lists only three allusions to "stealing" of this kind (696), and I have been able to locate no more than a dozen or so individual psychoanalytic papers on the problem. Nevertheless, among those who have investigated stealing or kleptomania (a word which, according to the *Oxford English Dictionary,* came to use in English only in 1830 or about the time that Britain had evolved into a commodity-consuming culture), there is general consensus on a number of matters relevant to Perrot's case. To begin with, the overwhelming majority of these cases involve women for whom stealing is "restitutive" or a means to "regaining something . . . previously possessed" (Pietro Castelnuovo-Tedesco, "Stealing, Revenge, and the Monte Cristo Complex," *International Journal of Psychoanalysis* 55 [1974]: 174). Moreover, this "something previously possessed," or otherwise taken from the female subject, may have never been actually possessed, save in the form of "narcissistic omnipotence" (174). Thus, Karl Abraham theorizes that the kleptomaniac's acts— which typically involve the stealing of fetish objects like lace—are tantamount to stealing (and thereby regaining) the penis or phallus ("The Female Castration Complex," in *The Selected Papers* [London: Hogarth, 1948], 338–68). This point is also made by Charles W. Socarides ("Pathological Stealing As a Reparative Move of the Ego," *Psychoanalytic Review* 41 [1954]: 246–52) and by George Zavitzianos ("Fetishism and Exhibitionism in the Female and Their Relationship to Psychopathy and Kleptomania," *International Journal*

of Psychoanalysis 52 [1971]: 297–305), whose kleptomaniacal subject either "demonstrated the wish to forcibly remove the penis, acquire it for herself, or to become actually transformed into a man" (Socarides, 248) or actually became "in fantasy phallic" whereby "her feelings of inferiority [were] replaced by feelings of self-confidence and of well-being" (Zavitzianos, 300). While these investigations proceed along fairly specific lines, there is little doubt that "feelings of inferiority," particularly as they relate to women, have a social basis as well. Thus, while historian Elaine Abelson is rightfully wary of the medicalization of female shoplifting of which modern psychoanalysis is arguably an extension, she nevertheless concurs with many psychoanalytic findings—at least regarding motivation—in noting that the medicalization of female shoplifters in mid-century (by which they were variously considered sick or biologically challenged) was still another constraint placed on women. For once discovered, the female shoplifter bore the onus for the "calculated arousal of desire in an environment [the department store] dedicated to sensory stimulation and unfettered abundance" (*When Ladies Go A-Thieving: Middle-Class Shoplifters in the Victorian Department Store* [New York: Oxford University Press, 1989], 11). It is probably worth noting, then, that with her particular wealth and status, Jane Leigh Perrot was clearly at the vanguard of the consumerist culture that middle-class women would shortly enter in large numbers, giving rise to the department store, where theft—especially by bourgeois women who could afford what they stole—became a regular occurrence and was, by late century, "widely considered an 'epidemic' " (Patricia O'Brien, "The Kleptomania Diagnosis: Bourgeois Women and Theft in Late Nineteenth-Century France," *Journal of Social History* 17 [1983–84]: 66).

43. Adela Pinch offers a related, if variant, reading of the Perrot story and its fictional appropriation by Thomas De Quincey in his narrative "The Household Wreck" in "Stealing Happiness: Shoplifting in Early Nineteenth-Century England," in *Border Fetishisms: Material Objects in Unstable Places* (New York: Routledge, 1998), 122–49. Pinch argues that shoplifting, particularly by genteel ladies in the early nineteenth century, is a register of resentment, albeit one "that expresses an uneasiness that dogs modern consumer society—an uneasiness that finds its home in the concept of fetishism—that happiness might in fact be found in the material thing" (133).

Chapter 2. The Picturesque, the Real, and the Consumption of Jane Austen

1. References to *Emma* are to the novel edited by James Kinsley (Oxford: Oxford University Press, 1971).

2. Katie Trumpener, "The Time of the Gypsies: A 'People without History' in the Narratives of the West," *Critical Inquiry* 18 (1992): 843–84. For a view of the function of gossip in *Emma*, particularly as a means of regulation and surveillance apparently endorsed in the narration, see Casey Finch and Peter Bowen, " 'The Tittle-Tattle of High-bury': Gossip and the Free Indirect Style in *Emma*," *Representations* 31 (1990): 1–18.

3. Unless otherwise cited, references to the picturesque theorists are to William Giplin, *Three Essays: On Picturesque Beauty; on Picturesque Travel; and on Sketching Landscape* (London, 1792); Uvedale Price, *An Essay on the Picturesque As Compared with the Sublime and the Beautiful; and on the Use of Studying Pictures for the Purpose of Improving Real Landscape* (London, 1796); and Richard Payne Knight, *An Analytical Inquiry*

into the Principles of Taste (London, 1805). I also refer to an earlier work by Gilpin, *Observations on the River Wye and Several Parts of South Wales, etc. Relative Chiefly to Picturesque Beauty; Made in the Summer of the Year 1770* (London, 1782); and to a poem by Knight (addressed to Price), *The Landscape: A Didactic Poem in Three Books* (London, 1794).

4. Rosalind Krauss, *The Originality of the Avant-Garde* (Cambridge, Mass.: MIT Press, 1985), 151–70. See also Kim Ian Michasiw, "Nine Revisionist Theses on the Picturesque," *Representations* 38 (1992): 76–100.

5. For an altogether different reading of Austen's relationship to and use of the picturesque, see Jill Heydt-Stevenson, "Liberty, Connection, and Tyranny: The Novels of Jane Austen and the Aesthetic Movement of the Picturesque," in *The Lessons of Romanticism,* ed. Thomas Pfau and Robert F. Gleckner (Durham, N.C.: Duke University Press, 1998), 261–79. According to Heydt-Stevenson, the picturesque provided Austen with a template on which she modeled a somewhat moderated ideal of female agency and autonomy that stood midway between the masculinist sublime and the ideal of womanhood for which the beautiful was (in Burke's theory at least) something of a placeholder.

6. See Krauss, *The Originality of the Avant-Garde.* See also Martin Price, "The Picturesque Moment," in *From Sensibility to Romanticism,* ed. Frederick W. Hilles and Harold Bloom (New York: Oxford University Press, 1965), 259–92; and, more recently, Ann Bermingham, "The Picturesque and Ready-to-Wear Femininity," in *The Politics of the Picturesque,* ed. Stephen Copley and Peter Garside (Cambridge: Cambridge University Press, 1994), 81–119; Vivien Jones, " 'The Coquetry of Nature': Politics and the Picturesque in Women's Fiction," in *The Politics of the Picturesque,* 120–44; and David Worrall, "Agrarians Against the Picturesque: Ultra-radicalism and the Revolutionary Politics of Land," in *The Politics of the Picturesque,* 240–60.

7. Although it is arguable that the picturesque is taken seriously in *Mansfield Park,* insofar as it is plainly endorsed by the female protagonist, Fanny Price, the various allusions to picturesque theory in other Austen novels—specifically *Northanger Abbey, Sense and Sensibility,* and *Pride and Prejudice*—tend generally to ridicule picturesque strictures.

8. See, most recently, Nancy Armstrong, *Desire and Domestic Fiction: A Political History of the Novel* (New York: Oxford University Press, 1987), 134–60, and Gary Kelly, *English Fiction of the Romantic Period, 1789–1830* (London: Longman, 1989), 111–38.

9. See, for example, Susan Gilbert and Sandra Gubar, *The Madwoman in the Attic: The Woman Writer and the Nineteenth-Century Literary Imagination* (New Haven, Conn.: Yale University Press, 1979), 105–83; Johnson, *Jane Austen: Women, Politics, and the Novel;* and Margaret Kirkham, *Jane Austen: Feminism and Fiction* (Totowa, N.J.: Barnes and Noble, 1983).

10. As indicated in previous chapters, my conceptions here of agency and oppositionality are indebted to the post-Foucauldian investigations of Michel de Certeau, Pierre Bourdieu, and Anthony Giddens. I am also indebted to Ross Chambers's application of de Certeau to various writing and reading practices in *Room for Maneuver: Reading (the) Oppositional (in) Narrative* (Chicago: Univeristy of Chicago Press, 1991).

11. For the relationship between picturesque theory and the practice of enclosure, see Ann Bermingham, *Landscape and Ideology: The English Rustic Tradition, 1740–1860* (Berkeley: University of California Press, 1986), 9–85.

12. Knight was not the only contemporary reader to lament "character inconsis-

tency" in Richardson or the "status inconsistency" that, as Michael McKeon notes, some of Richardson's contemporaries saw at the heart of a "linguistic incompetence of an author who clownishly confounds the language of servants with that of their masters" (*The Origins of the English Novel: 1600–1740* [Baltimore: Johns Hopkins University Press, 1987], 411–12).

13. Although various English gardening practices in the late seventeenth and early eighteenth centuries were scarcely naive about the impositions on or idealizations of the landscape that these various practices represented, "landscape gardens in their turn," as John Dixon Hunt remarks, "came to be revised in the light of the growing taste for 'natural' scenery." Thus, while a given garden "could not" necessarily "accommodate a landscape imagery comparable to that of Scotland or the Lake District," it "could adapt itself to be less artificially contrived." And "the man largely responsible for such changes in design, perhaps the most radical of all landscape gardeners, was 'Capability' Brown" (*The Figure in the Landscape: Poetry, Painting, and Gardening During the Eighteenth Century* [Baltimore: Johns Hopkins University Press, 1976], 187). All the same, for theorists of the picturesque the more "natural" scenery developed by Brown and by his follower Humphry Repton was—like the almost probable fictions that Knight and Gilpin similarly criticize—sufficiently artificial to call attention to its naturalizing work, but insufficiently natural to obscure its artificiality to begin with, or the fact that its "nature," as it were, was no less an idea, no less a fiction, than the nature of earlier gardening practices. Or, put another way, the premonitions of postmodernism that Rosalind Krauss detects in the writings of Giplin are more readable in the work of Brown and his followers, whose "nature" is more natural by being artificial rather than by approximating a more mystified, more essentialist, nature such as picturesque theory advocates.

14. See Raymond Williams, *Problems in Materialism and Culture* (New York: Verso, 1980), 31–49.

15. For the political valences of picturesque theory, especially regarding contemporary politics in Britain, see Jones, " 'The Coquetry of Nature'. "

16. John Barrell, *The Birth of Pandora and the Division of Knowledge* (Philadelphia: University of Pennyslvania Press, 1992), 41–62.

17. For a discussion of consumption as production, particularly regarding the practice of reading, see Michel de Certeau, *The Practice of Everyday Life*, trans. Steven Rendall (Berkeley: University of California Press, 1984), 165–76.

18. Unless otherwise indicated, page references to the published reviews of Austen are to the texts of those reviews reprinted in *Jane Austen: The Critical Heritage*, ed. B. C. Southam (London: Routledge and Kegan Paul, 1968). My recovery of additional contemporary response to Austen, both public and private, is indebted to information contained in David Gilson's comprehensive *A Bibliography of Jane Austen* (Oxford: Clarendon Press, 1982). For an earlier survey of some of these materials, which argues against the once-prevailing notion that Austen was largely unknown to her contemporaries, see Charles Beecher Hogan, "Jane Austen and Her Early Public," *RES* 1 (1950): 39–54.

19. *Lord Granville Leveson Gower: Private Correspondence, 1781–1821*, ed. Castalia Countess Granville (London: John Murray, 1917), 2: 418.

20. Nicholas A. Joukovsky, "Another Unnoted Contemporary Review of Jane Austen," *Nineteenth-Century Fiction* 29 (1974–75): 336–38.

21. Malcolm Elwin, *Lord Byron's Wife* (New York: Harcourt Brace, 1962), 159.

22. S. H. Romilly, *Letters to "Ivy" from the First Earl of Dudley* (London: Longmans, 1905), 194.

23. Maria Edgeworth, *Letters from England, 1813–1844*, ed. Christina Colvin (Oxford: Clarendon Press, 1971), 46.

24. *The Hamwood Papers of the Ladies of Llangollen and Caroline Hamilton*, ed. G. H. Bell (London: Macmillan, 1931), 351.

25. References to the opinions of both *Mansfield Park* and *Emma* solicited by Austen herself (which she in turn transcribed) are to the text in *Plan of a Novel According to Hints from Various Quarters by Jane Austen with Opinions on "Mansfield Park" and "Emma" Collected and Transcribed by Her and Other Documents* (Oxford: Clarendon Press, 1926). For an extended treatment of the "opinions" as an alternative to the "masculine literary culture" represented in the reviews of Austen's novels and as a precursor, accordingly, to a way of reading Austen that is recognizably "Janeite" in its communitarian aspects, particularly regarding the intimacy that readers feel with respect to certain characters, see Laura Fairchild Brodie, "Austen and the Common Reader: 'Opinions of *Mansfield Park*,' 'Opinions of *Emma*,' and the Janeite Phenomenon," *TSLL* 37 (1995): 54–71. While Brodie has some interesting things to say about Austen's rather novelistic transcription of her friends' opinions, the binarism of male and female protocols of reading seems exaggerated and in fact contradicted in any number of published reviews as well as in comments by writers such as Edgeworth.

26. *The Journal of Mary Frampton, from the Year 1779, until the Year 1846*, ed. Harriot Mundy (London: Sampson Low, 1885), 226.

27. *Romilly-Edgeworth Letters, 1813–1818*, ed. Samuel Henry Romilly (London: John Murray, 1936), 92.

28. The implication that Frank's engagement is at least known to the narrator (if not to other characters as well) comes in the sequence of Scott's summary in which the "concealed affair" is among the earliest details he discloses. "While Emma is thus vainly engaged in forging wedlock-fetters for others, her friends have views of the same kind upon her, in favour of a son of Mr. Weston by a former marriage, who bears the name, lives under the patronage, and is to inherit the fortune of a rich uncle. Unfortunately Mr. Frank Churchill had already settled his affections on Miss Jane Fairfax, a young lady of reduced fortune; but as this was a concealed affair, Emma, when Mr. Churchill first appears on stage, has some thoughts of being in love with him herself" (66).

29. William S. Ward, "Three Hitherto Unnoted Contemporary Reviews of Jane Austen," *Nineteenth-Century Fiction* 26 (1971–72): 469–77.

30. Marilyn Butler, *Maria Edgeworth: A Literary Biography* (Oxford: Clarendon Press, 1972), 445.

31. *Memoir and Correspondence of Susan Ferrier, 1782–1854*, ed. John A. Doyle (London: John Murray, 1898), 128.

32. *The Letters of Thomas Moore*, ed. Wilfred S. Dowden (Oxford: Clarendon Press, 1964), 1:396.

33. For other reviews of *Emma*, see Southam, ed., *Jane Austen: The Critical Heritage*, 70–77, and Ward, "Three Hitherto Unnoted Contemporary Reviews," 474–77. Among the more opinionated contemporary comments that I do not treat are those of Mary Russell Mitford, whose letters to Sir William Elford, written in her mid-twenties, use the occasion of Austen's most recent production (which she, unlike many others, knew to be

written by "Miss Austen") to display her own wit and erudition. Thus, *Emma*, which Mitford deems the "best . . . of all her charming works," provokes comments on the pleasures of "reading and re-reading Bacon," whom Mitford compares to Shakespeare and prefers ultimately to both Addison and Johnson. There may well be a connection between the pleasure of Austen's text (as Mitford has experienced it) and the "liveliness of illustration" in Bacon "which brings everything before our eyes." But there is, more important, a fascination here with a certain authoritative viewpoint evident in Bacon and apparently lacking in Austen, who provides only "amusement," which in turn reflects Mitford's unresponsiveness to Austen's antithetical achievement. (A. G. L'Estrange, *The Life of Mary Russell Mitford* [London: Bentley, 1870], 1:331.)

34. Southam, ed., *Jane Austen: The Critical Heritage*, 77.

35. J. G. Lockhart, *Memoirs of Sir Walter Scott* (London: Macmillan, 1900), 4:476.

36. *The Journal of Sir Walter Scott*, ed. W. E. K. Anderson (Oxford: Clarendon Press, 1972), 121.

37. For a discussion of the sense of "actual infinity"—as opposed to a sense of "infinite progressivity"—characteristic of Schlegelian romanticism, see Philipe Lacoue-Labarthe and Jan-Luc Nancy, *The Literary Absolute: The Theory of Literature in German Romanticism*, trans. Philip Barnard and Cheryl Lester (Albany: State University of New York Press, 1988).

38. "The Divine Miss Jane: Jane Austen, Janeites, and the Discipline of Novel Studies," *Boundary 2* 23 (1996): 143–63. References to Kipling's "The Janeites" are to the text in his *Debits and Credits* (London: Macmillan, 1926), 147–76.

Chapter 3. Why Jane Austen Is Not Frances Burney

1. References to *Northanger Abbey* are to the novel in *Northanger Abbey, Lady Susan, The Watsons, and Sanditon*, ed. John Davie (Oxford: Oxford University Press, 1980).

2. For the tradition of "refinement" as a basis for modernity, with particular emphasis on the Romantics' self-legitimating claims, see Robert J. Griffin, *Wordsworth's Pope: A Study in Literary Historiography* (Cambridge: Cambridge University Press, 1995), 64–87. See also Barbara M. Benedict, *Making the Modern Reader: Cultural Mediation in Early Modern Literary Anthologies* (Princeton, N.J.: Princeton University Press, 1996), 214–15, who stresses Austen's disapproval here of anthologizing practices that were (in contrast to earlier anthologies) pedagogical and disciplinary in scope and function.

3. The notion of counterhegemony as a fundamentally resistant coalition of seemingly disparate groups derives obviously from Antonio Gramsci's notion of hegemony and, more recently, from the extensions of Gramsci's thought on hegemony in collections such as *Gramsci and Marxist Theory*, ed. Chantal Mouffe (London: Routledge and Kegan Paul, 1979). For Gramsci's own speculations on these issues as culled from his diaries, see Gramsci, *Selections from Cultural Writings*, ed. David Forgacs and Geoffrey Nowell-Smith, trans. William Boelhower (Cambridge, Mass.: Harvard University Press, 1985).

4. For a treatment of *Northanger Abbey* as embracing (rather than critiquing) "gothic feminism" in its attention to "the potential for evil in life" chiefly in the way women are routinely "innocent victim[s] of the patriarchy," see Diane Hoeveler, "Vindicating *Northanger Abbey*: Mary Wollstonecraft, Jane Austen, and Gothic Feminism," in

Jane Austen and Discourses of Feminism, ed. Devoney Looser (New York: St. Martin's, 1995), 117–35. Two other studies take up this theme as well: Paul Morrison, "Enclosed in Openness: *Northanger Abbey* and Domestic Carceral," *TSLL* 33 (1991): 1–23; and Judith Wilt, "Jane Austen: The Anxieties of Common Life," in *Ghosts of the Gothic: Austen, Eliot, and Lawrence* (Princeton, N.J.: Princeton University Press, 1980), 121–72.

5. *Biographia Literaria*, ed. James Engell and W. Jackson Bate (Princeton, N.J.: Princeton University Press, 1983), 2:6–7.

6. See, most recently, Michael Gamer, *Romanticism and the Gothic: Genre, Reception, and Canon Formation* (Cambridge: Cambridge University Press, 2000). Although Gamer does not speculate much on what the gothic may or may not have achieved as a genre in its own right, he rightly emphasizes the degree to which the Romantics' aversion to the gothic also masked their indebtedness to the genre and their willingness to appropriate certain of its elements in the interest of gaining a readership. See also Karen Swann, " 'Christabel': The Wandering Mother and the Enigma of Form," *SiR* 23 (1984): 533–53; James Averill, *Wordsworth and the Poetry of Human Suffering* (Ithaca, N.Y.: Cornell University Press, 1980); and Stephen M. Parrish, *The Art of the "Lyrical Ballads"* (Cambridge, Mass.: Harvard University Press, 1973).

7. Paul de Man, "Literary History and Literary Modernity," *Blindness and Insight* (New York: Oxford University Press, 1971), 142–65.

8. My view of Austen's "romanticism" differs dramatically, then, from Nina Auerbach's comparatively undialectical conception of romantic writing and Austen's relationship to it. According to Auerbach, fiction of the romantic period is "the laughing denial of Romantic hopes for illumination" and transcendence in the poetry so that "the prisons that pervade romantic fiction" and, by extension, the world of Austen's heroines are in the end "a mockery of life's promises and life's ultimate reality" (11) as opposed to a world that, regardless of its constraints, is simultaneously a site of possibility and a reminder therefore that change, like politics, is irreducibly local. For Auerbach's treatment of both Austen and romanticism, see *Romantic Imprisonment: Women and Other Glorified Outcasts* (New York: Columbia University Press, 1985).

9. See again Deborah Kaplan, *Jane Austen Among Women* (Baltimore: Johns Hopkins University Press, 1992).

10. See again Gary Kelly, *English Fiction of the Romantic Period 1798–1830* (London: Longanan, 1989), 111–38; and Nancy Armstrong, *Desire and Domestic Fiction: A Political History of the Novel* (New York: Oxford University Press, 1987), 96–160.

11. See, most recently, Catherine Gallagher, *Nobody's Story: The Vanishing Acts of Women Writers in the Marketplace 1670–1820* (Berkeley: University of California Press, 1994), 203–56.

12. *Evelina or the History of a Young Lady's Entrance into the World*, ed. Edward A. Bloom (Oxford: Oxford University Press, 1968), 7–8. All further references are to this edition of the novel.

13. *The Progress of Romance and the History of Charoba, Queen of Aegypt* (Colchester, 1785), 111.

14. See again Roland Barthes, "L'effet de réel," *Communications* 11 (1968): 84–89.

15. See, for example, Julia Epstein, *The Iron Pen: Frances Burney and the Politics of Women's Writing* (Madison: University of Wisconsin Press, 1989), 93–122, who stresses Evelina's tactical manipulation of Villars in her "carefully edited" letters to him by which

she maintains the "selective privilege of the creative artist" (99–100). See also Kristina Straub, *Divided Fictions: Fanny Burney and Feminine Strategy* (Lexington: University of Kentucky Press, 1987), 23–108, who details the novel's ambivalence regarding Evelina's destiny in marriage and its adumbration of an alternative society. Other relevant readings of the novel include Margaret Anne Doody, *Frances Burney: The Life in the Works* (New Brunswick, N.J.: Rutgers University Press, 1988), 35–65, and William C. Dowling, "*Evelina* and the Genealogy of Literary Shame," *Eighteenth-Century Life* 16, 3 (1992): 208–20.

16. For a discussion of narrative form and its ideological implications, see McKeon, *The Origins of the English Novel, 1600–1740* (Baltimore: Johns Hopkins University Press, 1987), 212–70.

17. What all of this means, again, is that the probable, while ostensibly a representational end for Burney and her colleagues, is also a *means* by which her fiction is easily diverted from the ends that probability is alleged to serve: specifically, the dampening of great expectations. Thus the deployment of probability in the service of expectations at once reasonable and patently fantastic not only exerts considerable pressure on the peculiar hierarchy sustained by the novel's constitution as "a dialectical unity of opposed parts": a constitution in which "progressive ideology subverts aristocratic ideology, and is in turn subverted by conservative ideology" (McKeon, 267). Also occluded by the novel's ultimately conservative appearance is the degree to which the probable—by its constitution as a regulatory apparatus—is necessarily an unstable or, at the very least, an overtaxed category in *Evelina*, referring to a number of ends and *possibilities*, not all of them embraced by the heroine's narrative or amenable to its apparent purpose.

18. Douglas Lane Patey, *Probability and Literary Form: Philosophic Theory and Literary Practice in the Augustan Age* (Cambridge: Cambridge University Press, 1984), 214.

19. I am alluding to the title of Smith's 1787 novel, *The Romance of Real Life*.

20. Patey, *Probability and Literary Form*, 196–97.

21. See Barbara J. Shapiro, "*Beyond Reasonable Doubt*" and "*Probable Cause*": Historical Perspectives on the Anglo-American Law of Evidence (Berkeley: University of California Press, 1991).

22. Lorraine Daston, *Classical Probability in the Enlightenment* (Princeton, N.J.: Princeton University Press, 1988), 183.

23. For a different view of Austen's relationship to the discourses of both probability and romance, see Deborah Ross, *The Excellence of Falsehood: Romance, Realism, and Women's Contribution to the Novel* (Lexington: University of Kentucky Press, 1991), 166–207. Noting that probability and absolute order were by no means coterminal by the end of the eighteenth century, Ross argues that the aspects of Austen's fiction that can be associated with romance or with romanticism (in contradistinction to realism) manage—in a single stroke—both to contest or criticize the order that currently abides (the erstwhile probable world) and to work as an armature of regulation in accordance with a fundamentally Christian notion of providence. In other words the aspects of Austen's fiction that contravene the discourse of probability, most notably her endings, do so less in the service of a possibility that is close at hand than on behalf of altogether mystified and metaphysical *improbable*, of some possibility at the end of time, whose function in turn is containment rather than the encouragement or representation of meaningful and necessary change.

24. See, for example, Warwick Wroth, *The London Pleasure Gardens of the Eighteenth Century* (London: Macmillan, 1896). See also A. S. Turberville, *Johnson's England: An Account of the Life and Manners of His Age* (Oxford: Clarendon Press, 1933), 1:188–93, 2:196–98. My account of the pleasure gardens is indebted primarily to Wroth.

25. *A Sunday Ramble; Or, Modern Sabbath-Day Journey; In and About the Cities of London and Westminster* (London, 1776).

26. John Trusler, *The London Adviser and Guide* (London, 1786), 164.

27. For discussion of the politically ambivalent character of Burney's fictions, see Straub, *Divided Fictions,* and Claudia Johnson, *Equivocal Beings: Politics, Gender, and Sentimentality in the 1790s* (Chicago: University of Chicago Press, 1995), 141–88. For a reading of Burney as a more focused feminist, see Epstein, *The Iron Pen.*

Chapter 4. Lady Susan *and the Failure of Austen's Early Published Novels*

1. "Achieving Authority: Jane Austen's First Published Novel," *Nineteenth-Century Fiction* 37 (1983): 531–51.

2. There is a difference, obviously, between female eroticism or desire, with its implicitly utopian investment in a world elsewhere, and male eroticism, which in the example of someone like the lecherous Sir John Middleton, on whose good offices the Dashwood women are dependent, works in consort with the established order in Austen's novel and with the peculiar insensibility characteristic of male-female relationships in the world as it is.

3. References to *Sense and Sensibility* are to the text of the novel edited by James Kinsley (Oxford: Oxford University Press, 1970).

4. *Narrative and Its Discontents: Problems of Closure in the Traditional Novel* (Princeton, N.J.: Princeton University Press, 1981), 68.

5. Barbara M. Benedict also notes the interchange between the positions nominally represented by the two sisters, in particular the sentimentality or emotion that routinely invades Elinor's more disinterested position ("Jane Austen's *Sense and Sensibility*: The Politics of Point of View," *PQ* 69 [1990]: 453–70). She observes too that this represents something of a challenge to the disinterested narrative viewpoint and moral authority, which are figured by Elinor. But her argument is hampered by a too easy conflation of epistolarity and emotionalism—as well as by the assumption that is Elinor rather than, say, Brandon, who most accurately represents narrative authority. Benedict is also reluctant to regard Austen's reflections on novelistic authority (such as they are) in a larger political light, which requires among other things a more expansive view of what epistolarity would have meant to Austen.

6. See again Benedict, "Jane Austen's *Sense and Sensibility*," 455–58.

7. Colin MacCabe, "Realism and the Cinema: Notes on Some Brechtian Theses," in *Tracking the Signifier* (Minneapolis: University of Minnesota Press, 1985), 35, 39.

8. "*Lady Susan* and the Lost Originals, 1795–1800," in *Jane Austen's Literary Manuscripts* (London: Oxford University Press, 1964), 45–62.

9. Here my reading of both *Lady Susan* and epistolarity in Austen differs significantly from Mary Favret's extended discussion of these same issues in *Romantic Correspondence: Women, Politics, and the Fiction of Letters* (Cambridge: Cambridge University

Press, 1992), 133–75. According to Favret, "epistolary art is [in *Lady Susan*] in league with social consensus and parental authority. Rather than managing the letter into a parody of anarchy, Austen begins to see it in a more threatening aspect, as a paradigm of law" (14–45). In my view the situation is, if anything, completely reversed, with the "law" clearly coming with the irruption of narrative or omniscient authority at the novella's close. My view of *Lady Susan* may be similarly distinguished from that of A. Walton Litz, who although concurring that the "epistolary form precluded any significant authorial comment," contends at the same time that this omission was a consequence of Austen's relative immaturity as a writer. According to Litz, Austen's "irony had not evolved to a point where she could establish a presiding moral vision" and "make" what in this instance are "badly needed social and moral discriminations" (*Jane Austen: A Study of Her Artistic Development* [London: Chatto and Windus, 1965] 44).

10. References to *Lady Susan* are to the novel in *Northanger Abbey, Lady Susan, The Watsons, and Sanditon*, ed. John Davie (Oxford: Oxford University Press, 1980), 208–72.

11. The centrality of *Lady Susan*, as I construe it, differs decidedly from the seemingly similar claim by Marvin Mudrick that *Lady Susan* is Austen's "first completed masterpiece" and a "quintessence of [her] most characteristic qualities and interests" (*Jane Austen: Irony As Defense and Discovery* [Princeton, N.J.: Princeton University Press, 1952], 138). In Mudrick's view, the novella's centrality resides entirely in its detached and ironic stance to the world rather than in the more active and activist engagement with the reader that the epistolary form provided.

12. References to *Pride and Prejudice* are to the text edited by James Kinsley (Oxford: Oxford University Press, 1970).

13. See Anthony Giddens, *The Constitution of Society: Outline of the Theory of Structuration* (Berkeley: University of California Press, 1984).

14. See John Rajchman, "Foucault's Art of Seeing," *October* 44 (1988): 89–117.

15. See especially Richard Payne Knight, *An Analytical Inquiry into the Principles of Taste* (London, 1805).

16. For a discussion of the problem of visual pleasure and the male gaze, as it entails an appropriative fixation on the woman's body through the mechanisms of voyeurism and fetishism, see especially Laura Mulvey, "Visual Pleasure and Narrative Cinema," *Screen* 16 (1973): 6–18. Several critics have subsequently explored the bearing of Mulvey's argument on the female beholder, whose position—fostered by the conventions of the cinema—is generally regarded as more ambiguous and less stable than that of the male. These critics include Theresa de Lauretis, "Desire in Narrative," in *Alice Doesn't: Feminism, Semiotics, Cinema* (Bloomington: Indiana University Press, 1984), 103–57; Mary Ann Doane, *The Desire to Desire: The Woman's Film of the 1940s* (Bloomington: Indiana University Press, 1987); and E. Ann Kaplan, *Women and Film: Both Sides of the Camera* (London: Methuen, 1983). Miriam Hansen has subsequently challenged the parochial nature of these assertions in arguing for the subversive potential of the cult of Valentino in "Pleasure, Ambivalence, Identification: Valentino and Female Spectatorship," *Cinema Journal* 25 (1986): 6–32. A useful postscript to these discussions (and aligned more with my position) is Edward Snow's "Theorizing the Male Gaze: Some Problems," *Representations* 25 (1989): 30–41. Snow argues that recent feminist analyses of the "viewing situation," particularly their critique of "its hegemony and controlling power," would "grant to [the male gaze] exactly the reality it lacks," endangering thereby "a way of seeing" that "beyond ironizing and deconstructing desire, transfigure[s] and reabsorb[s] it" (40).

17. *The Proper Lady and the Woman Writer* (Chicago: University of Chicago Press, 1984), 203.

18. Wayne Booth, for example, is surely correct in observing of Collins's "wonderfully self-betraying speech of proposal [to Elizabeth]" that "this precise self-portrait of a grasping foolish clergyman is just right, at *this* spot, in *this* novel" (*A Rhetoric of Irony* [Chicago: University of Chicago Press, 1971], 198). For throughout much of the novel, as Brower notes in bemoaning the relative absence of irony in the novel's third volume (*The Fields of Light* [New York: Oxford University Press, 1951], 180–81), there is little doubt where the narrator stands or, more immediately, to where, in the author's estimation, Darcy stands relative to his male counterparts.

Chapter 5. Narrative Incompetence in Northanger Abbey

1. "*Lady Susan* and the Lost Originals, 1795–1800," in *Jane Austen's Literary Manuscripts* (London: Oxford University Press, 1964), 60–61.

2. *Jane Austen: A Study of Her Artistic Development* (London: Chatto and Windus), 68.

3. Nor, it must be emphasized, do these alignments, either individually or dialectically, conflict in any real way with Austen's apparent and concomitant subscription to domestic ideology, save perhaps in the degree to which domesticity, in effectively identifying and thereby fixing the woman's place within the context of marriage and the nuclear family, is generally continuous with certain emergent social formations, notably the "affective individualism" that, as historians Lawrence Stone and Randolph Trumbach have shown, both accompanied and abetted family's atomization into smaller and more modern units.

4. *The Realistic Imagination* (Chicago: University of Chicago Press, 1981), 61–80. For a related reading that seeks also to recuperate the satiric drift of the novel "as a good-natured comic *exposé* of the overly sympathetic imagination which *makes* [Gothic] novels a substitute for life" (522), see Frank J. Kearful, "Satire and the Form of the Novel: The Problem of Aesthetic Unity in *Northanger Abbey,*" ELH 22 (1965): 511–27.

5. References to *Northanger Abbey* are to the novel in *Northanger Abbey, Lady Susan, The Watsons, and Sanditon,* ed. John Davie (Oxford: Oxford University Press, 1980).

6. *The Progress of Romance* (Colchester, 1785).

7. For a treatment of the homoerotic bond uniting Mary and Fanny in *Mansfield Park*, which "emerges as a protest against a narrative mandate of heterosexual closure as well as a social and political act countering the tyranny of the culturally prescribed ending of marriage" (169), see Misty G. Anderson, " 'The Different Sorts of Friendship': Desire in *Mansfield Park,*" in *Jane Austen and the Discourses of Feminism,* ed. Devoney Looser (New York: St. Martin's, 1995), 167–83. For a more wide-ranging treatment of same-sex desire, with particular attention to the "sapphic" dimension to romantic friendship among women as it is variously addressed and endorsed by Austen and her pre-Victorian contemporaries, see Lisa L. Moore, *Dangerous Intimacies: Toward a Sapphic History of the British Novel* (Durham, N.C.: Duke University Press, 1997).

8. For a more conventional view of Catherine's development, see, for example, Avrom Fleishman, "The Socialization of Catherine Morland," ELH 41 (1974): 649–67.

9. A number of studies regard the gothic elements in *Northanger Abbey* as more

than merely parodic and as bearing either on the vulnerability of women or on certain dangerous proclivities to feeling, whose purpose in turn may not always be to regulate or control. They are Daniel Cottom, *The Civilized Imagination: A Study of Ann Radcliffe, Jane Austen, and Sir Walter Scott* (Cambridge: Cambridge University Press, 1985), 71–87; Diane Hoeveler, "Vindicating *Northanger Abbey*: Mary Wollstonecraft, Jane Austen, and Gothic Feminism," in *Jane Austen and the Discourses of Feminism*, 117–35; Coral Ann Howells, *Love, Mystery, and Misery: Feeling in Gothic Fiction* (London: Athlone, 1978), 114–30; Maria Jerinic, "In Defense of the Gothic: Rereading *Northanger Abbey*," in *Jane Austen and the Discourses of Feminism*, 137–49; Paul Morrison, "Enclosed in Openness" *Northanger Abbey* and Domestic Carceral," TSLL 33 (1991) 1–23; and Judith Wilt, *Ghosts of the Gothic: Austen, Eliot, and Lawrence* (Princeton, N.J.: Princeton University Press, 1980), 121–72.

10. *Jane Austen: Women, Politics, and the Novel* (Chicago: University of Chicago Press, 1988), 28–48. See also Margaret Kirkham, *Jane Austen, Feminism and Fiction* (Totowa: Barnes and Noble, 1983), 87–90. Although stressing Austen's recuperation of Radcliffe, Kirkham is more interested in identifying General Tilney as a representative patriarchal tyrant than she is convinced that Austen's heroine is "sufficiently aware of [society's] real defects" (90) such as they are construed.

11. See again Moore's *Dangerous Intimacies*, which is concerned with precisely this distinction, as both a cultural and literary phenomenon, in the late eighteenth century.

12. Julia Kristeva, *Powers of Horror: An Essay on Abjection*, trans. Leon S. Roudiez (New York: Columbia University Press, 1982), 202.

Chapter 6. Jane Austen's Future Shock

1. For Mudrick's critique of the novel as both unironic and severely moral, see *Jane Austen: Irony As Defense and Discovery* (Princeton, N.J.: Princeton University Press, 1952), 155–80. See also Amis, "What Became of Jane Austen?," *Spectator* (4 Oct. 1957): 33–40. Trilling's defense of the novel and its heroine in particular as a stay against modernity and against the secular tide of much twentieth-century discourse appears in *The Opposing Self* (New York: Viking, 1955), 206–30. Thomas R. Edwards Jr. argues similarly and powerfully for the novel's stand against self-culture in "The Difficult Beauty of *Mansfield Park*," *Nineteenth-Century Fiction* 20 (1965): 51–67.

2. For the anti-Jacobin or Burkean reading of *Mansfield Park*, in which the novel's opposition to excessive individualism is justified by recourse to a variety of then-contemporary discourses, including the so-called paper wars of the 1790s regarding the proper improvement of the landscape, see Duckworth, *The Improvement of the Estate* (Baltimore: Johns Hopkins University Press, 1971), 35–80. See also Butler, *Jane Austen and the War of Ideas* (Oxford: Clarendon Press, 1975), 219–49. More recently Said has drawn a direct line linking British imperialism, with particular emphasis on the West Indies where the Bertram family owns both land and (by implication) slaves, and the conditions of domestic tranquillity such as Austen's novel necessarily endorses (*Culture and Imperialism* [New York: Knopf, 1993], 80–97). Said is certainly right in underscoring the connection between the novel and the imperialistic project. But he clearly fails to take sufficient stock of Austen's quite similar awareness regarding the futures of both

England and the novel, all of which make *Mansfield Park* much less politically unconscious. Moreover, as a number of other critics have already noted, the implication here
that Austen was of necessity either oblivious to or tacitly supportive of either slavery or
the need for slaves abroad is far from clear-cut or even derivable from the novel. They
include Moira Ferguson, "*Mansfield Park*: Slavery, Colonialism and Gender," *Oxford Literary Review* 13 (1991): 118–39 (an essay that predates Said's argument and to which he
makes no reference); and Susan Fraiman, "Jane Austen and Edward Said," *Critical Inquiry* 21 (1995): 805–21.

    3. *A Reading of Mansfield Park: An Essay in Critical Synthesis* (Minneapolis: Univer-
sity of Minnesota Press, 1967).

    4. Although I have quoted her selectively here, Romilly's complete statement to
Maria Edgeworth makes it plain (as does her grammar) that she credits the novel's
verisimilitude as something distinct from its moral dimension. "Have you read *Mansfield Park*—It has been pretty generally admired here—and I think all novels must be
that are true to life, which this is, with a good story vein of principle running thro the
whole. It lacks that elevation of virtue, something *beyond* nature, that gives the greatest
charm to a novel but still it is real natural everyday life and will amuse an idle hour well
in spite of its faults" (*Romilly-Edgeworth Letters 1813–1818*, ed. Samuel Henry Romilly
[London: John Murray, 1936], 92). Mrs. Pole's statement is from *Plan of a Novel According to Hints from Various Quarters by Jane Austen with Opinions on "Mansfield Park" and
"Emma" Collected and Translated by Her and Other Documents* (Oxford: Clarendon
Press, 1926), 17.

    5. The conception of Fanny Price as a "heroine [with] nothing to learn" is a com-
monplace in Austen criticism. Nevertheless I am grateful to David Nokes for this particular reiteration in *Jane Austen: A Life* (Berkeley: University of California Press, 1998),
413. In a view of Fanny that differs sharply from mine, Allen Dunn maintains that Fanny
"embraces what a modern reader might call an ethic of fairness and restraint," which not
only "authorizes her own self-mastery" but, in enabling her "to judge herself objectively,"
also gives Fanny the "right of judging Mary" ("The Ethics of *Mansfield Park*: MacIntyre,
Said, and Social Context," *Soundings* 78 [1995]: 496). An openly anachronistic appropriation of the novel, which takes its lead from Alasdair MacIntyre's similar use of *Mansfield Park* in *After Virtue: A Study in Moral Theory* (Notre Dame, Ind.: University of
Notre Dame Press, 1981), Dunn's reading is additionally limited by a failure to take sufficient stock of the formal elements of the text, in particular the narrator's bias, which
is routinely confused with Austen's position, as Dunn argues for the complexity and
heterogeneity of Fanny's "ethical commitments" (484). If complexity and heterogeneity
characterize any practices or positions in the novel, it would be those of the other characters, most notably the Crawfords, whom Fanny and the narrator do not scruple to
judge and condemn. While Dunn is right in providing a corrective to Said's too facile coordination of the novel with imperialism, he would be better served by returning the
novel to the various social and historical contexts, including Austen's other fictions, on
which an understanding of her practice, particularly in social and political matters, ultimately depends.

    6. Joel C. Weinsheimer verges on this point in observing that the "ideal" in *Mans-
field Park* "seems imposed on a group of characters incapable of supporting it." Here,
Weinsheimer is speaking chiefly of Fanny and Edmund, whose moral authority, he feels,
is intentionally compromised by Austen rather than made equivalent to the novel's pur-

pose. As a result "the real world appears resolutely intransigent and unwilling or unable to achieve the completeness of which it seemed capable" (*"Mansfield Park*: Three Problems," *Nineteenth-Century Fiction* 29 [1974]: 204). I agree with Weinsheimer's sense that the repositories of value are somehow wanting in this text, but not for the reasons he ascribes. For Weinsheimer the novel's "difficulties" are in the end "excellences," or privileged ambiguities, in which "the novelist raises metaphysical and moral complexities that she seems either unable or unwilling to clarify completely" (205). Such may be the case, but the supplement of historical inquiry, as I hope to demonstrate, goes some way in resolving the problem surrounding the apparent lack or urgency of the novel's moral center.

7. These and related details are recounted in the following biographies, to which I am indebted throughout: John Halperin, *The Life of Jane Austen* (Baltimore: Johns Hopkins University Press, 1984); Park Honan, *Jane Austen: Her Life* (London: Weidenfeld and Nicolson, 1987); and David Nokes, *Jane Austen: A Life* (Berkeley: University of California Press, 1998).

8. For the resistance of Austen and her contemporaries to more astringent forms of social codification, see Lisa L. Moore, *Dangerous Intimacies: Toward a Sapphic History of the British Novel* (Durham, N.C.: Duke University Press, 1997); and Roger Sales, *Jane Austen and Representations of Regency England* (London: Routledge, 1994). See also Amanda Vickery, *The Gentleman's Daughter: Women's Lives in Georgian England* (New Haven, Conn.: Yale University Press, 1998).

9. *Jane Austen: A Critical Heritage*, ed. B. C. Southam (London: Routledge and Kegan Paul, 1968), 164.

10. Ruth Bernard Yeazell, "The Boundaries of Mansfield Park," *Representations* 7 (1984): 133–52; Julia Prewitt Brown, *Jane Austen's Novels: Social Change and Literary Form* (Cambridge, Mass.: Harvard University Press, 1975), 80–100.

11. For the affinities of Fanny's character and romantic versions of selfhood, see Nina Auerbach, "Jane Austen's Dangerous Charm: Feeling As One Ought About Fanny Price," in *Romantic Imprisonment: Women and Other Glorified Outcasts* (New York: Columbia University Press, 1985), 21–37.

12. For alternative views of the novel's difficulty, see again Trilling, *The Opposing Self*; Edwards, "The Difficult Beauty of Mansfield Park"; and Weinsheimer, "*Mansfield Park*: Three Problems."

13. See Misty G. Anderson, " 'The Different Sorts of Friendship': Desire in *Mansfield Park*," in *Jane Austen and the Discourses of Feminism*, ed. Devoney Looser (New York: St. Martin's 1995).

14. Claudia Johnson makes a related claim, arguing (against Duckworth and Butler) that the novel's "enterprise is to turn conservative myth sour" (*Jane Austen: Women, Politics, and the Novel* [Chicago: University of Chicago Press, 1988], 97). This souring, as she views it, is "animated by the preoccupations of the 1790s" (96) rather than by an impending future in which a "sour" or "miserable" conservatism will unfortunately hold sway, particularly in representational and novelistic matters.

15. C. W. Pasley, *Essay on the Military Policy and Institutions of the British Empire* (London, 1810), 465.

16. For an anatomy of freedom as it was understood by Austen's radical contemporaries, see Thomas McFarland, *Paradoxes of Freedom: The Romantic Mystique of Transcendence* (Oxford: Clarendon Press, 1996).

17. Thomas Clarkson to whose *Abolition of the African Slave Trade* (1808) Austen is presumably referring here also deserves comment, particularly in light of her stated, if somewhat ambiguous, affection for him. Although it was clearly possible at this time to be both an abolitionist and a social conservative in the manner of, among others, Thomas Gisborne, who in addition to his conduct manuals authored a well-known anti-slavery tract in response to Parliament's halfhearted initiatives on that front (*Remarks on the Late Decision of the House of Commons Respecting the Abolition of the Slave Trade* [1798]), Austen's endorsement of Clarkson, particularly in the company of these others, is of a piece ultimately with the progressive tenor of her despair over the future prospects of England to which slavery, imperialism, and domestic ideology are all immaculately fitted.

18. *Christian Researches in Asia with Notices on the Translation of the Scriptures into the Oriental Languages* (New York, 1812).

19. Austen was also reading John Carr's *Descriptive Travels in the Southern and Eastern Parts of Spain and the Balaeric Isles, in the Year 1809* (London, 1811) at the same time she was reading both Pasley and Buchanan. Although credited only as a source of information about Gibraltar (*Letters*, 292) to which Austen had referred in the novel she was currently composing, Carr's travelogue of Spain during the Peninsular War also unites the piquancy and luridness of description that Buchanan marshals on behalf of British enlightenment and superiority, with Pasley's pragmatic focus on British military aims, present and future. Like Pasley, Carr does not entirely dismiss the potentiality of an enslaved Europe (366). But like both Pasley and Buchanan, he is confident that British leadership is Europe's and the world's only hope (365).

20. *An Enquiry into the Duties of the Female Sex* (London, 1797).

21. There is some debate among critics and scholars about the degree of Austen's subscription to Gisborne's conduct manual. Yeazell, for example, regards *Mansfield Park*'s stance toward private theatricals as signifying Austen's endorsement of Gisborne's strictures against such activities ("*Boundaries*," 137) whereas David Nokes, with a nearly preternatural sensitivity to the tonal nuances of Austen's letters, regards Austen's gratitude to her sister for recommending that she read Gisborne ("I am pleased with it, and I had quite determined not to read it" [*Letters*, 169]) as entirely "mischievou[s]" (286). Obviously I concur with Nokes's view, which only a longer view of Austen can confirm, even as the bearing of Gisborne on *Mansfield Park* is, as Yeazell suggests, quite real. Austen's disaffection with books of this ilk is inferable from both her letters and novels, but it is made especially clear in *Pride and Prejudice* when Collins chooses Fordyce's *Sermons to Young Women* (1766) to read aloud to the Bennet sisters only to be interrupted by Lydia after a "monotonous" recitation of three pages (60). Joseph Litvak also takes up Gisborne in his reading of *Mansfield Park*, but his point, in addition to tracking the antitheatrical strictures of both texts, is that both Gisborne and Austen are bedeviled by a prohibition that applies just as much to good conduct or role playing as to bad (*Caught in the Act: Theatricality in the Nineteenth-Century English Novel* [Berkeley: University of California Press, 1992], 1–26).

22. In inveighing against the propensity "to push fashions in dress, which is also very frequent in country towns" (341), despite the fact that the country is generally more conducive to the "time," "calmness," and "deliberation" necessary to the proper performance of wifely duties (314), Gisborne instructs women to obscure their distinction (high or low) whenever possible, which amounts, in turn, to a leveling according to a

generalized middle-class standard. "Wives of clergy," for example, are instructed to be "shining models of unaffected humility and moderation" (347) in the same way that "wives of officers in the military" who are "at war" are advised to "guard against every symptom of levity" and "every trace of inadvertence" (352). Similarly the "wife" of a "manufacturer" or "entrepreneur" should "resist displays of extravagance" as should the wife of a "tradesman" (356).

23. I am referring here to Stewart's notion of a "new antique," which she regards as the hallmark of such "distressed" genres as the archaic ballad, the fairy tale, or romance that proliferated at the time Austen was drafting her initial novels. Such distress, according to Stewart, is an aspect of modernity by which an author seeks to "bypass the contingencies of time" and, with these, the historical context of the literary work. (*Crimes of Writing: Problems in the Containment of Representation* [New York: Oxford University Press, 1991], 67–74.) In many ways *Mansfield Park* is also a symptom of distress, but in this case the distress is registered in a thoroughgoing adherence to both genre and context even as they are also or only inferable at this point and in a developmental stage.

24. References to *Mansfield Park* are to the text of the novel edited by James Kinsley (Oxford: Oxford University Press, 1990).

25. There are numerous instances where Fanny's thoughts and those of the free indirect stylist converge to the point where it is impossible to differentiate between them. The following description of Fanny's "reflections" on Mary will suffice as an example: "Miss Crawford was very unlike her. She had none of Fanny's delicacy of taste, of mind, of feeling; she saw nature, inanimate nature, with little observation; her attention was all for men and women, her talents for the light and lively" (73).

26. References to Inchbald's translation are to the text of *Lovers' Vows* in *The British Theatre; or, A Collection of Plays* (London: Longman, 1808), 23:1–72.

27. *The Works of Charles and Mary Lamb*, ed. E. V. Lucas (London: Dent and Methuen, 1903), 1:99.

28. For a similarly antiessentialist reading of Fanny's role playing, which uses the theatricals episode to focus the impossibility of true feeling, or a feeling not also mitigated and controlled by some theatrical apparatus or role, see David Marshall, "True Acting and the Language of Real Feeling: *Mansfield Park*," *Yale Journal of Criticism* 3 (1989): 87–106. Marshall, however, makes no attempt to contextualize this aspect of the novel, or to account for it by means of contextualization, and is content, more or less, to admire its proleptic reach as a prototheoretical instance. Joseph Litvak argues similarly that the novel bears witness to a "subtler and more comprehensive form of theatricality" (*Caught in the Act*, 16) despite its biases. And while his argument is indeed contexualized by recourse to both Hazlitt and Gisborne, it is for the purpose of pointing up an aporia in which theoretical retrospection, rather historical recovery, reigns supreme. Or as Litvak puts it with deconstructive brio: "Theatricality is not a single, unitary phenomenon but an already self-divided set of practices capable of serving both reactionary and subversive causes" (28). I agree entirely with the political ambivalence of the novel such as Litvak describes it. However, I disagree with his sense that this remains an inevitable contradiction to which the novel and its author are rendered vulnerable by their respective essentialisms and ideologies. The ambivalence of *Mansfield Park* is there, but rather consciously so and in recognition of certain developments and prospects to which it is barely reconciled.

29. See E. M. Butler, " 'Mansfield Park' and Kotzebue's 'Lovers' Vows,' " *Modern*

Language Review 28 (1933): 326–37, who notes the parallels and, more important, the inversions whereby "the moral standard subverted by Kotzebue [is] neatly re-inverted" (326). More recently Dvora Zelicovici has argued, on the contrary, that the play "shares the same moral premises and poses the same moral problems as [the] book" and that it is the "actors [who] are blind to the moral lessons of the play" ("The Inefficacy of *Lovers' Vows*," *ELH* 50 [1983]: 532–33).

Chapter 7. Nostalgia *in* Emma

1. *Jane Austen: The Critical Heritage, 1870–1940*, vol. 2, ed. B. C. Southam (London: Routledge and Kegan Paul, 1987), 265.
2. G. Armour Craig raises the issue of Highbury's belatedness in reminding us that Highbury, "like The Crown, its principal inn, . . . is just a little seedy. . . . Highbury, in short, is no longer an eighteenth century country town nor is it yet a fashionable suburb like Richmond" ("Jane Austen's *Emma*: The Truths and Disguises of Human Disclosure," in *In Defense of Reading*, ed. Reuben Brower and Richard Poirier [New York: Dutton, 1962], 235–55).
3. See, for example, Alistair Duckworth, *The Improvement of the Estate* (Baltimore: Johns Hopkins University Press, 1971), and, most influentially, Wayne C. Booth, *The Rhetoric of Fiction*, 2d ed. (Chicago: University of Chicago Press, 1983), 242–66. See also George Levine, *The Realistic Imagination* (Chicago: University of Chicago Press, 1981), 208. For an especially nuanced treatment of this dynamic, with particular attention to the "communal" aspects of both Emma's development and of the narrative technique by which her progress is variously monitored and understood, see Frances Ferguson, "*Emma* and the Impact of Form," *MLQ* 61 (2000): 157–80.
4. For a nice discussion and overview of the issues surrounding the question of narrative authority in both *Emma* and other Austen novels, see Tara Ghoshal Wallace, *Jane Austen and Narrative Authority* (New York: St. Martin's, 1995). As Wallace rightly observes—although not to the degree or conclusion that I do—"*Emma* sometimes privileges narrative authority, asking readers to trust what they are told, and sometimes urges readers to resist, to read against the grain, to challenge *any* voice that claims to be authoritative" (78).
5. References are to *Emma*, ed. James Kinsley (Oxford: Oxford University Press, 1980).
6. *Jane Austen: The Critical Heritage, 1870–1940*, vol. 2, ed. Southam, 245–72.
7. "The Plot of *Emma*," in *Emma*, ed. Stephen M. Parrish (New York: W. W. Norton, 1972), 456.
8. For Brontë's critique of Austen as being concerned exclusively with "genteel society," see Southam, ed., *Jane Austen: The Critical Heritage*, vol. 2, 126–28. For Williams's assessment, see *The Country and the City*, (New York: Oxford University Press, 1973), 108–19.
9. I am indebted in this and in many other matters relating to *Emma* to Susan Wolfson, with whom I have been discussing the novel for over a decade. For a distillation of Wolfson's position on *Emma* and its relation to the conventional wisdom on the novel, which she impressively summarizes as a point of departure, see "Boxing Emma; or

the Reader's Dilemma at the Box Hill Games," in *Re-reading Box Hill: The Practice of Reading the Practice of Everyday Life*, ed. William Galperin, Romantic Praxis Series/Romantic Circles (University of Maryland, 2000), http://www.rc.umd.edu/praxis/boxhill. Wolfson notes, for example, that "[e]ven as Miss Bates provokes ridicule, this is never separate from a horrific identification" and that her power as such is "her resistance to exorcism from this tangled web" (8).

10. "On Narcissism," in *General Psychological Theory: Papers on Metapsychology*, ed. Philip Rieff (New York: Macmillan, 1963), 56–82.

11. The now-classic political reading of *Emma*, which nevertheless confuses Knightley's bias with Austen's apparently "unquestioning acceptance of class society," is Arnold Kettle's in *An Introduction to the English Novel* (London: Hutchinson, 1951), 1:90–104.

12. *A Rhetoric of Irony* (Chicago: University of Chicago Press, 1971), 42–44.

13. The most sustained treatment of Miss Bates's impoverishment and its implications for the novel overall is Mary-Elisabeth Fowkes Tobin's "Aiding Impoverished Gentlewomen: Power and Class in *Emma*," *Criticism* 30 (1998): 413–30. Although Tobin argues, to my mind incorrectly, that the effect of the novel overall is to "brus[h] away most of the concerns that might arise in the reader's mind concerning the way women are treated in this society," she rightly emphasizes the degree to which Miss Bates is used to focus "women's lack of power and legal authority" (425). More contrarian readings of Miss Bates include Wolfson, "Boxing Emma," and D. A. Miller, who sees the "expansionist" tendencies of her endless chatter as opposing the "closural system" of "novelistic form" (*Narrative and Its Discontents: Problems of Closure in the Traditional Novel* [Princeton, N.J.: Princeton University Press, 1981], 37–41).

14. On the question of misogyny in the novel, particularly as it impacts on the usual response to Emma herself, see Claudia Johnson, *Jane Austen: Women, Politics, and the Novel* (Chicago: University of Chicago Press, 1988), 121–43.

15. "Wordsworth," in *Complete Prose Works*, ed. R. H. Super (Ann Arbor: University of Michigan, 1973), 9:42.

16. *Our Village: Sketches of Rural Character and Scenery* (London, 1824), 2.

17. *On Longing: Narratives of the Miniature, the Gigantic, the Souvenir, the Collection* (Durham, N.C.: Duke University Press, 1993), 23.

18. On this point see especially Amanda Vickery, *The Gentleman's Daughter: Women's Lives in Georgian England* (London: Routledge, 1994). Although it is the purpose of Vickery's study to revise the histories that regard domesticity in the nineteenth century, with its doctrine of separate spheres, as delimiting to women, it is by no means accidental that her recuperation of domestic life, chiefly "the possibilities of lives lived within the bounds of propriety" (12), focuses on an interval, chiefly the late eighteenth and early nineteenth century, which predates the moment when the various ossifications and codifications that Leonore Davidoff and Catherine Hall detail (*Family Fortunes: Men and Women of the English Middle Class, 1780–1850* [Chicago: University of Chicago Press, 1987]) took full shape.

19. In a recent essay that takes up the issue of nostalgia in Austen, Nicholas Dames stresses that nostalgia in Austen's writing, which he deems a "newer," less pathological nostalgia, "idealizes not only what cannot be returned to but also what is not of any more consequence—not only a *lost* time (as opposed to a still-real place) but also a time that is felt to be causally *unrelated* to the present" ("Austen's Nostalgics," *Representations* 73 [2001]: 130). From my perspective, needless to say, this is something of a misrepresentation.

For just as the "real" of Austen's earlier novels is alternately a residual "place" *and* an emergent one, or a real "over time" in which past and present are perforce linked, so *Emma* literally witnesses the waning of certain liberatory initiatives wherein the heroine's development is alternately a retrenchment and, for the reader no less than for Mrs. Elton, a reminder, by increasingly negative example, of the "good old days."

20. "Misreading *Emma*: The Powers and Perfidies of Interpretive History," *ELH* 51(1984): 338.

21. A sense of the range and complexity of the Box Hill episode, on both ideological and interpretive grounds, is amply available in the six essays included in *Re-reading Box Hill*. In addition to Wolfson's essay the collection includes George Levine, "Box Hill and the Limits of Realism"; Michael Gamer, "Unanswerable Gallantry and Thick-headed Nonsense: Rereading Box Hill"; Deidre Lynch, "Social Theory at Box Hill: Acts of Union"; Adam Potkay, "Leaving Box Hill: Emma and Theatricality"; and William Walling, "Saying What One Thinks: Emma—*Emma*—at Box Hill."

22. For an especially severe reading of Knightley here as someone who does not always practice what he preaches to Emma and whose practices are in general, self-legitimating, see again Wolfson, "Boxing Emma."

23. Among the typically severe readings of Frank, the more important and influential, in addition to those by Booth (*The Rhetoric of Fiction*) and Duckworth, are Marilyn Butler, *Jane Austen and the War of Ideas* (Oxford: Clarendon Press, 1975), 250–74; and Richard Poirier, *A World Elsewhere* (New York: Oxford University Press, 1966), 144–207.

24. This point is touched on by Levine, who stresses the countervailing forces of indeterminacy that Knightley's always superior understanding of how things are only partly mitigates ("Box Hill and the Limits of Realism").

25. I am referring to the notion of simultaneity or "temporal coincidence" and its attendant bearing on nationalism that Benedict Anderson (with an assist from Walter Benjamin) explores in *Imagined Communities: Reflections on the Origin and Spread of Nationalism* (London: Verso, 1983), 9–36. According to Anderson the instrumentality of simultaneity in the "birth of the imagined community of the nation can best be seen" through "two forms of imagining which first flowered in Europe in the eighteenth century: the novel and the newspaper." These "forms," he argues, "provided the technical means of 're-presenting' the *kind* of imagined community that is the nation" (24–25). There are, needless to say, many aspects of *Emma* that are at crosspurposes with this unificatory function. Still, for an excellent reading of the Box Hill episode (and by implication the entire novel) as reflecting the coincidences from which a national identity emerges, see Lynch, "Social Theory at Box Hill".

Chapter 8. The Body in Persuasion *and* Sanditon

1. B. C. Southam suggests that the 1816 revisions to *Northanger Abbey*, which followed the publication of *Mansfield Park* in 1814, were "very thorough indeed" and apparently responsible for a "comic tone" that is "remarkably assured" ("*Sanditon*: The Seventh Novel," in *Jane Austen's Achievement*, ed. Juliet McMaster [London: Macmillan, 1976], 3–4).Yet insofar as the narrator's tone in *Northanger Abbey* is also unduly authoritative and ultimately too assured, it is not clear that a novel that, as Southam maintains

elsewhere ("*Lady Susan and* the Lost Originals," in *Jane Austen's Literary Manuscripts* [London: Oxford University Press, 1964]), was arguably the first of Austen's novels to have been originally drafted as a direct narrative, was as affected by the 1816 revisions, particularly in matters of narrative authority, as it was by certain decisions that may date to the moment of its inception.

2. For the "New Historical" approach to Wordsworth see especially Marjorie Levinson, *Wordsworth's Great Period Poems: Four Essays* (Cambridge: Cambridge University Press, 1986), and Alan Liu, *Wordsworth: The Sense of History* (Stanford, Calif.: Stanford University Press, 1989).

3. The question of change during the interval in which Austen was writing has come under scrutiny by David Spring who maintains that the "rural elite was neither going bankrupt in the early nineteenth century nor disintegrating spiritually and socially" and that there were "no winners or losers" in the ostensible rise of the "bourgeoise in which the landed class was equally involved and instrumental" ("Interpreters of Jane Austen's Social World: Literary Critics and Historians," in *Jane Austen: New Pespectives*, ed. Janet Todd [New York: Holmes and Meier, 1983], 53–72). This is not, however, what many other readers, including Southam ("*Sanditon*: The Seventh Novel") believe, nor does it take into account the considerable changes in domestic life and in the lives of educated women that Austen effectively oversaw and documented.

4. Stuart Tave, in particular, stresses Anne's "usefulness to others" and the "self-command and sense of duty that make [her] actions possible" (*Some Words of Jane Austen* [Chicago: University of Chicago Press, 1973], 286). In his view Anne is a paragon of agency, whose autonomy and judgment are never violated, not even in conjunction with Mrs. Smith, whom Tave regards as a merely clumsy addition.

5. On Anne's sense of isolation and the narrative's sympathetic identification with her, see especially A. Walton Litz, *Jane Austen: A Study of Her Artistic Development* (London: Chatto and Windus, 1965), 150–60.

6. James Edward Austen-Leigh, *Memoir of Jane Austen* (Oxford: Clarendon Press, 1926), 157.

7. References to *Persuasion* are to the text of the novel in *Persuasion*, ed. John Davie (Oxford: Oxford University Press, 1990).

8. Although Tara Ghoshal Wallace rightly emphasizes Anne's fallibility as a heroine, she construes the narrator's sympathy with Anne as a means by "which Austen deliberately compromises her own narrative authority and indeed questions the sources of any narrator's authority" (*Jane Austen and Narrative Authority*, [New York: St. Martin's, 1995], 115). While the interrogation of narrative authority is a major element in Austen's writings, *Persuasion* is arguably the last place where it occurs, largely because the narrator is capable here of representing her heroine both sympathetically and judgmentally, which is continuous in turn with the narrator's perplexity over the constitution of human relations in general.

9. Nina Auerbach stresses *Persuasion*'s link to both *Sense and Sensibility* and *Mansfield Park* in "O Brave New World: Evolution and Revolution in *Persuasion*," in *Romantic Imprisonment: Women and Other Glorified Outcasts* (New York: Columbia University Press, 1985), 38–54; and Alistair Duckworth notes the similarity with *Emma* as well as with *Sense and Sensibility* (*The Improvement of the Estate* [Baltimore: Johns Hopkins University Press, 1971], 179–208), where *Persuasion* also provides a retrospection on the major themes and developments in the Austen canon. *Persuasion* is marshaled also to

retrospective purposes in Claudia Johnson's treatment in *Jane Austen: Women, Politics, and the Novel* (Chicago: University of Chicago Press, 1988), 144–66.

10. Jacques Derrida, *Of Grammatology*, trans. Gayatri Chakravorty Spivak (Baltimore: Johns Hopkins University Press, 1976), 141–64.

11. For readings of the novel as a progressive statement in support of the developing culture of individualism or as a meditation on the dissolution of the old order, see especially Auerbach, "O Brave New World"; Julia Prewitt Brown, *Jane Austen's Novels: Social Change and Literary Form* (Cambridge, Mass.: Harvard University Press, 1975), 128–50; Marvin Mudrick, *Jane Austen: Irony as Defense and Discovery* (Princeton, N.J.: Princeton University Press, 1952), 207–40; Tony Tanner, *Jane Austen* (Cambridge, Mass.: Harvard University Press, 1986), 208–49; and despite his conservative reading, Duckworth, *The Improvement of the Estate*. Those who regard *Persuasion* as supporting tradition and the landed order as part of England's future as well as its past include David Spring, "Interpreters of Jane Austen's Social World," and John Wiltshire, *Jane Austen and the Body* (Cambridge: Cambridge University Press, 1992), 155–96. David Monaghan, by contrast, sees the novel as "fractured into two contradictory halves" that support the old and new orders respectively (*Jane Austen: Structure and Social Vision* [London: Macmillan, 1980], 162).

12. Tara Ghoshal Wallace also stresses the "prosaic," hence ironic, nature of Anne's remembrance of the courtship (*Jane Austen and Narrative Authority*, 101).

13. In a related reading that deals similarly—that is, dialectically—with the dynamic of persuasion here, Adela Pinch argues that *Persuasion* "present[s] us with a heroine who seems to resist knowing what she doesn't already know, and who experiences knowledge of others' wishes and desires as a form of oppressive persuasion" (*Strange Fits of Passion: Epistemologies of Emotion, Hume to Austen* [Stanford, Calif.: Stanford University Press, 1996], 44–45). Although my reading credits Anne with knowing, at least intuitively, what Pinch claims "she doesn't already know," so much so that much of the novel is about "disowning knowledge" (to borrow Stanley Cavell's term), my approach is also proximate to Pinch's in weighing the tension "between pressures from without and internal desires." We differ primarily in our conceptions of how that "conflict" is resolved. For Pinch the resolution is poised between a subscription to "outside influence" *and* by "a kind of consciousness that is constituted as resistance to outside influence" (154) whereas I argue that such resistance dissipates in the welter of outside influence.

14. In a variant reading of this scene that also focuses on questions of spectation and the so-called male gaze, Robyn R. Warhol seeks to differentiate the male way of looking and the narratological practice it figures from Anne's, and by implication Austen's, way of both seeing and narrating, which looks beyond the object to the interior of the subject ("The Look, the Body, and the Heroine: A Feminist-Narratological Reading of *Persuasion*," *Novel* 26 (1992): 5–19.

15. *Powers of Horror: An Essay on Abjection*, trans. Leon S. Roudiez (New York: Columbia University Press, 1982), 5.

16. *Jane Austen's Letters*, ed. R. W. Chapman, 2d ed. (London: Oxford University Press, 1959), 292.

17. "The Two Chapters of Persuasion," in *Jane Austen's Literary Manuscripts* (London: Oxford University Press, 1964), 86. Litz also examines the two endings in *Jane Austen: A Study of Her Artistic Development*, 156–60.

18. References to *Sanditon* are to the text of the novel in *Northanger Abbey, Lady Susan, The Watsons, and Sanditon*, ed. John Davie (Oxford: Oxford University Press, 1980).

19. For an overview of the various attempts to complete *Sanditon* see Roger Sales, *Jane Austen and Representations of Regency England* (London: Routledge, 1994), 214–26. Southam and Duckworth speculate on the possible deliberation of the narrative in *Jane Austen's Literary Manuscripts*, 109–29, and *The Improvement of the Estate*, 222–29, respectively.

20. For Austen's instrumentality in the creation of round and complex characters, see especially Deidre Lynch, *The Economy of Character* (Chicago: University of Chicago Press, 1998).

21. Approaches similar to Duckworth's include Southam's two studies in *Jane Austen's Literary Manuscripts*, 101–35, and his "*Sanditon*: The Seventh Novel;" Wiltshire, *Jane Austen and the Body*, 197–221; and Sales, *Jane Austen and Representations of Regency England*, 200–221. For a more autobiographical interpretation in which *Sanditon* is seen as a means of coping with its author's final illness, see Litz, *Jane Austen: A Study of Her Artistic Development*, 160–69.

22. Although John Wiltshire views the hypochondriacs as reflecting Austen's disenchantment with the growing culture of imagination and self-absorption, he is notable in observing that the hypochondriacs' "bodies have become the grounds of inventiveness and energy, preoccupying their imaginations and becoming the source of sufficient activity to direct the conduct of every hour of the day" (*Jane Austen and the Body*, 199).

Index

Abelson, Elaine, 250 n.42

Abraham, Karl, 250 n.42

aesthetic theory, 2, 8. *See also* picturesque; realism

affective individualism, 26–27, 139, 148, 238, 260 n.3

Amis, Kingsley, 154, 261 n.1

Analytical Inquiry into the Principles of Taste (Knight), 56–58, 246 n.7, 251 n.3

Anderson, Benedict, 268 n.25

Anderson, Misty G., 260 n.7, 263 n.13

anti-Jacobinism, 1, 17, 103–4, 155

aristocratic narratives, 24–26, 92

Armstrong, Nancy, 18, 28, 168, 201, 245 n.1, 247 n.5, 252 n.8, 256 n.10

Arnold, Matthew, 200, 267 n.15

Atlas (journal), 4, 77–78

audience, Austen's contemporary: and affective individualism, 26–27; and Austen's conception of history, 157–58; and Austen's realistic detail, 3–4, 6, 24, 25, 67–69, 71–72, 74–76; and Bentley's edition, 75–78; and challenges to picturesque theory, 2–3, 8–9, 53, 60, 61–81; conservative conceptions of Austen's motives, 77; critical reviews, 68–71, 72–78, 180, 182; and didactic aspects of novels, 62, 64–65; and domestic fiction, 77–78, 157–58; earliest readers, 61–66; *Emma*, 2–3, 9, 38–39, 53, 60, 66–75, 76, 180–84, 190–91, 201, 254 n.33; and historical aspects of novels, 24, 25, 75–77, 248 n.23; and insularity of early novels, 157; interest and amusement of novels, 62, 63–65, 68, 77; *Lady Susan*'s women readers, 123–24; *Mansfield Park*, 23–24, 39, 64–65, 72, 154, 155–61, 168–69, 254 n.25, 262 n.4; *Northanger Abbey*, 38–39, 72–73, 83–86, 163; and nostal-

gia, 201; *Persuasion*, 72; and plots and characters, 3, 62–63, 65, 78–80; and posthumously published novels, 72–75; *Pride and Prejudice*, 23–24, 25, 62–65; reading practices, 6–7, 65–66, 77–78; *Sense and Sensibility*, 62; Victorian readers and the Janeites, 78–81, 254 n.25, 255 n.38. *See also* Scott, Walter

Auerbach, Nina, 233, 256 n.8, 263 n.11, 269 n.9, 270 n.11

Austen, Cassandra, 27, 34, 36, 249 n.35

Austen, Edward, 27, 157

Austen, Frank, 64, 72, 157, 165

Austen, Henry, 38, 72, 73, 246 n.1

Austen, James Edward, 38

Austen family, 17, 27

Austen Leigh, Rev. James, 38, 269 n.6

Austen-Leigh, Richard, 38

Averill, James, 256 n.6

Bacon, Francis, 254 n.33

Banfield, Ann, 115, 247 n.14

Barbauld, Anna, 61

Barrell, John, 59, 253 n.16

Barthes, Roland, 4, 90, 246 n.6, 247 nn. 9, 10, 256 n.14

Bath Chronicle, 40, 250 n.39

Bath Journal, 40, 250 n.39

Belinda (Edgeworth), 152, 156

Benedict, Barbara M., 119, 255 n.2, 258 nn. 5, 6

Benjamin, Walter, 268 n.25

Bentham, Jeremy, 31, 249 n.31

Bentley, Richard, and *The Standard Novels*, 75–78

Bermingham, Ann, 247 nn. 9, 10, 252 nn. 6, 11

Bessborough, Lady, 62

nostalgia, 5–6, 267 n.19; and disappearing British society, 200–203, 216; domestic ideology and women's roles, 202–3, 216, 267 nn. 18, 19; and *Emma*, 196, 200–203, 204–6, 209, 210–13, 215, 216, 267 nn. 18, 19; and fictions prior to *Persuasion*, 5–6, 215–17; and hegemonic social order, 114–15, 215; and lived experience, 202, 213; and *Mansfield Park*, 11, 171, 178, 202, 215, 219; and new style of novel, 6; and *Northanger Abbey*, 215; and *Persuasion*, 209, 217–19, 229; and possibility, 205–6; and *Pride and Prejudice*, 215; and probabilistic fiction and hegemony, 215; and *Sense and Sensibility*, 114–15; simultaneity and community identity, 213, 268 n.25; and utopia, 201–3, 213

novels and literary culture: and aristocratic narratives, 24–26, 92; defense of the novel in *Evelina*, 89–90; domestic fiction, 69–70, 77–78, 87, 157–58; and "fictitious biography," 69–70; fictive or fabulous as resource for writers, 240; and the gothic, 84, 86–87, 256 n.6; and hegemonic social order, 139, 158–59, 215, 260 n.3; and historical interpretations of Austen, 18–19; and historical work of novels, 24–26; *Northanger Abbey*'s digression on the novel, 9–10, 82–87, 88, 89, 144–45; nostalgia and new style of novel, 6; picturesque and narrative fiction, 8, 48–50, 52–59, 60–61, 68, 75, 92–93, 128, 253 n.13; probability and realistic fiction, 42, 73–74, 89–96, 239–40; progressive linear narratives, 24–26, 92; reading and domestic fiction, 77–78, 157–58; reading and oppositionality, 65, 152; and realism in fiction, 42, 66–70, 73–74, 78–81, 89–96, 139–40, 239–40; rise of the novel and epistolarity, 120–21; rise of the novel and free indirect discourse, 5, 20–21; rise of the novel and social history, 1–2; and romance genre, 90; and romanticism, 84, 85, 86–87, 256 n.8; and Scott's response to *Emma*, 3–4, 66–69, 73; and tautology of fear, 94–95; Victorian readers and Janeites, 78–81, 254 n.25, 255 n.38; women writers and women readers, 18, 83–85, 89–90, 158; and writing of history, 25, 30–31, 69–70, 73–74, 90, 248 n.23, 249 n.31. *See also* audience, Austen's contemporary; epistolarity; free indirect discourse

O'Brien, Patricia, 250 n.42
omniscience. *See* free indirect discourse

On Longing (Stewart), 201–2, 267 n.17
oppositionality, 29–36; and Austen's critique of patriarchy and hegemony, 53; Austen's fiction and hegemonic ends of realistic writing, 77–78; and de Certeau, 29–30, 31, 33, 65; and *Emma*, 12, 59–61, 70, 210; and epistolarity in *Lady Susan*, 120–21, 258 n.9; and free indirect discourse, 33, 77–78, 151–52; and irony, 32–36; and "irresistible *vraisemblance*," 4–5, 78; and narrative functions and textual functions, 33, 34; and *Northanger Abbey*, 143–44, 152; and picturesque, 59–61; and possibility, 30–31, 43; and *Pride and Prejudice*, 65; and probabilistic agenda, 143–44; and reading practices, 65, 77–78, 152; and realism, 4–5, 29–31, 33–34, 77–78; and silence, 29–31, 33–34; and the writing of history, 30–31
Origins of the English Novel (McKeon), 24–25, 248 n.22, 252 n.12, 257 nn. 16, 17
Our Village: Sketches of Rural Character and Scenery (Mitford), 201, 267 n.16

parody, 139–40, 141, 143. *See also* irony
Parrish, Stephen M., 256 n.6
Pasley, Charles W., 161–66, 172, 263 n.15, 264 n.19
Patey, Douglas Lane, 94, 257 nn. 18, 20
Peninsular Wars, 163, 264 n.19
Perrot, Jane Leigh, 32, 34–43; accounts of trial, 39, 40, 250 nn. 39, 41; and Austen's fiction, 37, 38; and Austen's silence, 7–8, 34–36, 38, 40, 41–42, 43; class and entitlement of, 42, 43; and Dyce, 38–39; kleptomania of, 8, 38, 42–43, 250 n.42, 251 n.43; and letters, 34–35, 39–41, 249 n.35, 250 n.41; narrative trajectory of story, 36–38, 41–42
Persuasion, 12–13, 217–38; Anne's agency/ autonomy, 218, 220, 222–23, 225, 226, 228–29, 230, 231, 243, 269 n.4; Anne's altruism and self-denial, 222, 223, 270 n.13; Anne's physical transformation, "loss of bloom," 222–23, 226, 230; Anne's rejection of Wentworth, 220–22; Anne's relationship with Mrs. Smith, 232; Anne's reunion with Wentworth, 224–25; Anne's transformation in thinking, 223–24, 232; Anne's walk at Lyme, 222, 225–27, 231; and Aunt Perrot's story, 37; and the canon, 219, 269 n.9; contemporary readers of, 72; and courtship/marriage plots, 221, 225, 235, 237; dialogue on the sexes, 236–37; and *Emma*, 219, 269 n.9; and focus

Acknowledgments

Portions of this study appeared initially, and in different form, in the following places: *Co(n)texts: Implicazioni testuali, Criticism, Eighteenth-Century Life, European Romantic Review, Janeites: Austen's Disciples and Audiences, The Lessons of Romanticism: A Critical Companion,* and *The Wordsworth Circle.* I thank the editors of these volumes and their publishers for permission to reprint these materials. Parts of the study were also delivered as talks at the following conferences: American Conference on Romanticism (1994), NASSR Conference (1994, 1995), Radical London Conference (1995), Narrative Society Conference (1996), Interdisciplinary Nineteenth-Century Studies Conference (2001), and the Wordsworth Summer Conference (1996). Sections of the study were also given as lectures at a number of academic institutions, including the College of William and Mary, the Columbia University Seminar, New York University, Oregon State University, Reed College, SUNY-Buffalo, Temple University, the University of Alberta, Lancaster University, the University of London, the University of Maryland, and the University of Trento. I am grateful to the sponsors of these forums and to the various audiences for their encouragement and support as well as for many thoughtful and helpful responses. In addition, I want to thank my students at Rutgers University, both undergraduate and graduate, whose responses and queries forced me continually to rethink and (I hope) to refine many of my assumptions and claims regarding Jane Austen's writings. I am also grateful to Rutgers for providing me with a research stipend and with leave time, both of which proved necessary to the completion of this study.

In the decade or so that I have been at work on Jane Austen, I have accumulated many debts intellectual and otherwise. For favors, large and small (but mostly large), I want to thank Bryan Cheyette, Jay Clayton, Timothy Corrigan, Rosemary Cullen, William Dowling, Sandy Flitterman-Lewis, Evelyn Fowle, Neil Fraistat, Marilyn Gaull, Keith Hanley, Jerrold Hogle, Anne Janowitz,

Deborah Kaplan, George Landow, George Levine, Helen Lefroy, Herbert Lindenberger, Carla Locatelli, Anne Mellor, David Miall, Raimonda Modiano, Alan Nadel, Thomas Pfau, Roger Porter, Barry Qualls, Tilottama Rajan, William Ray, David Robinson, Larry Scanlon, Robert Schwartz, Lisa Steinman, Garrett Stewart, Henry Sussman, Cheryl Wall, Orrin Wang, and Carolyn Williams. I also want to thank the libraries of Rutgers University and the University of Pennsylvania as well as the Bath Library, the British Library, the Hampshire Record Office in Winchester, the Library Company of Philadelphia, and the library of the Victoria and Albert Museum.

Marianne DeKoven, Elin Diamond, and Adam Potkay read parts of the book and gave me timely and much-needed encouragement. Other colleagues—Thomas Edwards, Colin Jager, Michael McKeon, Adela Pinch, William Walling, and Susan Wolfson—read the entire manuscript with attention and generosity. The book is much improved for their efforts. I am also grateful to Eric Halpern, director of the University of Pennsylvania Press, for his continued support and to Deidre Lynch, whose report to the Press did everything a reading should do and much, much more.

Finally, I want to thank my parents, Rose and Gabriel Galperin, for their love and support and my wife, Tina Zwarg, who has endured this study in more forms and permutations than she or I would probably care to recall. Our conversation, suffice it to say, is the sustenance of my life as both a person and a scholar. The book is dedicated to someone whose generosity and curiosity have been exemplary to me since I can remember.